Edited by Hywel Coleman

Dreams and Realities:
Developing Countries and the English Language

KU-114-933

ISBN 978-086355-659-3

© **British Council 2011**/Design Department/B027
10 Spring Gardens
London SW1A 2BN
UK

www.britishcouncil.org

The United Kingdom's international organisation
for cultural relations and education opportunities.

A registered charity: 209131 (England and Wales), SC037733 (Scotland)

Contents

Foreword

Michael Carrier

I am delighted to introduce Dreams and Realities: Developing Countries and the English Language. The publication brings together work from contributors with a wide range of backgrounds and origins, covering differing contexts and tackling the topic from a variety of angles.

The British Council has worked to promote and to encourage debate on the role, teaching and learning of English worldwide since its foundation in 1934. We remain equally committed to this today, as reflected in this publication.

English is continuing to grow as the world's de facto lingua franca, and as an important communication tool that brings people together. We believe that English opens doors, creates opportunities for mobility and education, supports economic growth through international trade and helps to create new international communities – allowing people from diverse backgrounds to build a more positive intercultural dialogue.

Governments recognise the importance of English to their economies and societies and to the fulfilment of the personal aspirations of their citizens, understanding its capacity to empower and support development. They want to make the learning and teaching of English in their education systems as effective as possible, responding to demand from their citizens who wish to have access to the information, education and economic opportunities of a globalised world.

There are many complex issues associated with these aspirations and challenges that need to be addressed. The chapters in this book investigate a stimulating range of topics and issues: the perceptions of individuals and communities of the status, role and benefits of English; issues of language policy, such as when and how to introduce English into the school system; issues around the relationship between the use of the mother tongue or English as a medium of education; the challenges of introducing effective change in education systems to achieve the best balance for learners; issues of the role and position of 'local Englishes' and how they are used alongside global standard English; issues of equity: the widening of access to English; the contribution of English to national and international development; and the role and particular challenges of English in 'fragile' situations.

Individual papers will be available on the British Council's website **www.teachingenglish.org.uk**, which will provide further links and a wider selection of papers and research from around the world, including case studies and resources for those working in this field. I hope that the papers provide helpful background and stimulus for further research in this area. I would welcome suggestions for new research projects to deepen our collective knowledge.

Finally, I would like to express our thanks to all of the researchers who have written chapters for this publication and to our editor, Hywel Coleman, not only for lending us his considerable professional expertise, but also for accepting and meeting the challenge of producing a publication of high quality in a very short space of time.

Michael Carrier
Head of English Language Innovation, British Council

Acknowledgements

I would like to express my thanks to the British Council for inviting me to edit this volume and, in particular, to Adrian Odell for his constant support and patience throughout the editing process.

From my first contact with the contributors until the submission of the final manuscript, the preparation of this book was completed in just over seven months. This was achieved through a lot of nagging on my part and a great deal of hard work on the part of the 18 contributors. I am extremely grateful to them all, not only for their very varied and thought-provoking contributions but also for the patience with which they responded to my endless requests and reminders.

Four people – Martin Lamb, Adrian Odell, Danny Whitehead and Eddie Williams – provided very useful feedback on some of the chapters. Thank you for this.

I am responsible for any remaining deficiencies.

Hywel Coleman
Jakarta, March 2011

Developing countries and the English language: Rhetoric, risks, roles and recommendations

Hywel Coleman

Introduction

The purpose of this book is to examine the claims that have been made for the importance of English in development, to point out where these claims do not appear to be justified, to consider whether the pursuit of English in the name of development carries with it any dangers, to identify those areas in which English really does appear to have a useful role to play and to formulate recommendations.

Some of the 15 chapters which follow this introductory chapter take a broad geographical sweep while others focus on particular countries. Fifteen countries are selected for detailed discussion, six in Asia (Bangladesh, China, India, Indonesia, Pakistan and Sri Lanka) and nine in Africa (Cameroon, Democratic Republic of Congo, Eritrea, Ethiopia, Kenya, Malawi, Rwanda, Uganda and Zambia). According to the United Nations Human Development Programme (UNDP 2010), four of these 15 countries (China, Indonesia, India, Pakistan) are categorised as having Medium Human Development, one (Eritrea) cannot be classified because of insufficient data, while the remaining ten are all categorised as having Low Medium Human Development. Meanwhile, four of these countries are classified by the United Nations as being among the world's 'least developed' nations; these are DR Congo, Eritrea, Ethiopia and Malawi. (There is some overlap between the UNDP's 'Low Human Development' category and the UN's 'least developed' category).

The 18 contributors to this book all originate from and/or are currently working in and/or have extensive previous experience in the contexts which they discuss. The contributors include among their number English teachers, development project leaders, teacher trainers, international agency personnel and researchers.

Thematic groupings

The 15 chapters are organised into five thematic groupings, which deal with policy planning and implementation; perceptions of English; social and geographic mobility; developing English in development contexts; and English in fragile contexts. Inevitably, there is overlap between the interests of the five groupings; the categories are not watertight.

Policy planning and implementation

In Chapter 2, 'Challenges for language policy, language and development', Chris Kennedy's wide-ranging contribution explores the relationships between language policy, language and development. He identifies nine challenges that emerge. These include, for example, the challenge of recognising that language may play only a subsidiary role in certain types of development projects.

Chapter 3, 'Language policy, politics and development in Africa' by Eddie Williams, is also broad in scope, looking at evidence from almost every country in Sub-Saharan Africa, but focusing in particular on Malawi, Rwanda and Zambia. Williams proposes that the failure of education to have an impact on development indicators in many African countries is due not to the lack of availability of education but, rather, to the ineffectiveness of the education which is available. The ineffectiveness of education, in turn, can be partly attributed to language policy.

Ramanujam Meganathan, in Chapter 4, 'Language policy in education and the role of English in India: From library language to language of empowerment', uses documentary evidence to create an extraordinarily complex picture of language policy in the 35 states and Union Territories in India. India's three-language policy in education is well known, but it is not until one sees the details laid out state by state as is done here – with no two states offering the same range of languages – that the complexity of the arrangement becomes apparent. Using longitudinal data, Meganathan is also able to identify the rapidly expanding role of English in education in India.

Chapter 5, the fourth contribution to the debate on language policy, is Hywel Coleman's analysis of the financial resources made available to the so-called 'international-standard schools' in Indonesia. These schools are, for the most part, state institutions and at least nominally are English medium. They constitute an elite sub-system within Indonesia's overall state education system; they are allocated very substantial block grants and are also permitted to charge fees. Coleman attempts to understand the rationale for this subsidising of English medium education.

Perceptions of English

Stakeholders' perceptions of English are an important element of several chapters in the book. Three chapters in which perceptions are a core issue – all from Africa – are gathered together in this thematic grouping.

Juliet Tembe and Bonny Norton, in Chapter 6, 'English education, local languages and community perspectives in Uganda', trace the perceptions of urban and rural communities in Uganda towards their own local languages, regional languages and English. It transpires that rural communities are generally more inclined to accept the use of mother tongues in schools than are urban communities, while urban parents are generally more insistent that their children should be involved.

Gladys Ngwi Focho, in Chapter 7, 'Student perceptions of English as a developmental tool in Cameroon', describes a very unusual situation. Unlike most of the other contexts discussed in this book, in Francophone Cameroon the secondary school students appear to have little interest in English; French provides them with the access they need to the outside world. Focho herself, however, believes that 'the case for English for development is a compelling one' and she therefore endeavours to convince her students of this.

While Tembe and Norton in Chapter 6 and Focho in Chapter 7 focus on individual countries in Africa, Nigussie Negash, in Chapter 8, 'English in Africa: An impediment or a contributor to development?', undertakes a broad survey across the continent, though at the same time he draws substantially on evidence from Ethiopia. Negash contrasts the opinions of 'experts', who argue for caution in, for instance, adopting English as a medium of instruction in school, with the views of many of his survey interviewees and other informants, who appear to perceive English in a very positive light.

Social and geographical mobility

This thematic grouping begins with Martin Lamb's study, in Chapter 9, 'A "Matthew Effect" in English language education in a developing country context'. Lamb demonstrates, with longitudinal evidence from schools in Indonesia, that children's socio-economic background has a massive impact on their response to the learning of English. This explains why children in the same class may respond very differently to the English lessons that the school offers to them. Those from aspirational middle class families consistently improve their English language competence throughout the time they spend in school, although their success depends to a considerable extent on non-school factors, including the individual child's view of him- or herself as a future user of English. Their peers from more modest backgrounds, however, fail to make much progress in English, despite having to study it for a total of six years in secondary school. As the successful children improve their English so they increase their chances of gaining access to the best universities and future employment. Meanwhile, as their peers fail to improve their English so they gradually lose the possibility of pursuing higher education.

The second chapter in this thematic grouping, Chapter 10, 'Language and migration: The social and economic benefits of learning English in Pakistan' by Tony Capstick, addresses a very different sort of mobility. Capstick looks at the phenomenon of marriage migration between Mirpur in Azad Jammu and Kashmir (AJK) in Pakistan and several cities in the UK. This form of migration has been taking place for several decades and has led to the creation of very strong social, cultural and economic links between AJK and the cities of the North of England. Capstick looks at this phenomenon from a language perspective and in particular he considers the implications of UK legislation in 2010, which requires migrants to provide evidence of their English language competence.

The situation described by Chefera Hailemariam, Sarah Ogbay and Goodith White in Chapter 11, 'English and development in Eritrea', has some similarities with that described by Capstick in Chapter 10 in that a considerable proportion of Eritrea's population are eager to leave their country or have already done so. Eritrea, although a small nation of just over five million people (see Appendix 2), has one of the world's largest proportions of its population living abroad. More than one million Eritreans live in other parts of the world but, for the most part, they maintain strong contacts with their homeland. As second and third generation Eritreans are born and grow up abroad, English takes on an increasingly important role as the language of communication between the diaspora and their families still in Eritrea.

Migration also features in Chapter 5, although as a subsidiary issue. Coleman notes that the huge numbers of migrant workers from Indonesia who go to Saudi Arabia, Kuwait, Hong Kong and elsewhere and who frequently experience great difficulty while they are abroad generally have no language training before leaving their country. Negash, Chapter 8, also discusses migration from Africa, but he pays particular attention to professional migration and the negative impact this can have on, for example, health services in migrants' home countries.

From this thematic grouping a picture emerges of the complex nature of migration. It may take place for marriage between branches of the same community which are settled in different parts of the world (Pakistan and the UK), for temporary employment (Indonesians in the Middle East), for long-term professional employment (African doctors in North America) or for political reasons. English plays a role in each of these different types of migration.

Developing English in development contexts
This thematic grouping focuses on English language teaching projects in developing countries. Philip Seargeant and Elizabeth Erling in Chapter 12, 'The discourse of "English as a language for international development": Policy assumptions and practical challenges', focus their attention on a very large project to improve the teaching of English in schools in Bangladesh. The project is funded by the UK Department for International Development (DFID) and involves the UK Open University and the BBC, in addition to the Bangladeshi authorities. Seargeant and Erling use this opportunity to critique the project's rationale and they express concerns about the claims the project makes for the impact that it will have on the development of Bangladesh.

Martin Wedell in Chapter 13, 'More than just "technology": English language teaching initiatives as complex educational changes', expresses very similar doubts about whether the objectives of two large-scale English language teaching projects, one in Africa and one in Asia, are achievable. He then proceeds to analyse in detail why projects like this frequently fail and makes a series of recommendations for rescuing them.

In Chapter 14, 'English as the language for development in Pakistan: Issues, challenges and possible solutions', Fauzia Shamim considers a number of different aspects of the history and role of English in Pakistan. She then looks at an English language teaching project, now concluded, and considers why it achieved no long-term sustainability even though it was initially successful. Shamim concludes that there was a failure from the beginning to plan for 'maintenance strategies' in addition to the core 'development strategies' of the project.

It is instructive to note that all three of the contributions to this thematic grouping express doubts and concerns. Despite substantial financial investment and, doubtless, the hard work of the many well intentioned individuals involved in these projects, there is no sense of celebration in these accounts of English language teaching projects. This contrasts vividly with many of the English language teaching project accounts which were produced in the early years of what we might call the 'Language and Development' movement. For example, many of the English language project accounts presented at the 1st Language and Development conference in Bangkok in 1993 (eventually published as Kenny and Savage 1997) were highly optimistic in outlook and confident that progress was being made. This suggests that Language and Development has now reached a stage of maturity where it can be more analytical and self-critical.

English in fragile contexts
The last two chapters in this book form a small thematic grouping which looks at the role of English and the scope for English language teaching in 'fragile contexts', countries which are emerging from long periods of civil strife.

Psyche Kennett, in Chapter 15, 'English as a tool for conflict transformation', describes the role that English plays in Sri Lanka after the ending of the war in the north and east of the country: government troops do not speak Tamil, refugees do not speak Sinhala, aid workers speak neither language and so they all speak English with each other. Kennett is involved in the STEPS (Skills through English for Public Servants), a project which aims to encourage communication between civil servants at the local level with the public, NGOs, international humanitarian workers and central government. Her project does not merely teach English but integrates this with the development of skills needed for negotiation and consensus seeking.

Finally, Danny Whitehead, in Chapter 16, 'English language teaching in fragile states: Justifying action, promoting success and combating hegemony', examines the role of English in the Democratic Republic of Congo. Adopting a Gramscian approach, he concludes that there is a case for English language teaching in this context as one component in a broader mother tongue-based education system.

Analysis
Cutting across the five thematic groupings are three major issues to which the contributors return repeatedly and which match the objectives of this book. These are the rhetoric regarding English in development contexts, the risks that, in some circumstances, are associated with English and the roles which English is actually able to play. We can add recommendations to this list.

Rhetoric
Here is a shocking statistic from the most recent Human Development Report (UNDP 2010; see also Appendix 2 at the end of this volume). In the 42 countries of the world which UNDP considers to be 'very highly developed', eight mothers die in childbirth for every 100,000 live births. Meanwhile, in the 23 'least developed' countries, 786 mothers die for every 100,000 live births. These two simple numbers – 8 and 786 – illustrate starkly the vast differences in opportunities and risks faced by people in the most privileged and the least privileged countries in the world. Giving birth in one of the least developed countries is one hundred times more dangerous than it is in one of the most developed.

Juxtapose this fact with the statement by a former Minister of Education of Pakistan quoted by Shamim in Chapter 14. The minister argues that the economic future of his country requires the comprehension and use of English to be as widespread as possible: 'This is now an urgent public requirement.' Shamim points out, however, that the perceived need for English in Pakistan is driven, to some extent at least, by 'folklore' and by parents' dreams about the wonderful future which their children will experience if they learn English.

So, going back to the UNDP data concerning the risks involved in childbirth, what has English got to do with this? Clearly, not very much, or at least not directly. However, language more broadly does have a very important role to play. One way in which the dreadful maternal mortality rate in the least developed countries could be reduced would be by providing far more practical training for nurses, midwives and traditional childbirth helpers in language which they understand and in language which they themselves can then use with mothers (Wariyar 2010). Very often, this will mean using a local language rather than an official language – and quite possibly a language which has never been written down, a language which has no recognised standing and which is held in low esteem. Foreign languages, however prestigious, are of no value at all in such circumstances. In many circumstances, therefore, using a local language may be a far more 'urgent public requirement' than using English.

Government pronouncements regarding the developmental importance of English – such as that quoted by Shamim – are made throughout the developing world and they are repeated frequently. Conversely, we rarely find cases of government pronouncements regarding the necessity of using local languages in order to increase the impact of public health, education and other development activities.

In Chapter 12, Seargeant and Erling use documentary evidence associated with the large English language teaching project in Bangladesh to identify an 'emergent ideology' of English for international development. This ideology takes as self-evident the idea that competence in English can be equated with economic or social development, even though the precise nature of that relationship is often unclear. Seargeant and Erling conclude that policies which are based on the assumptions inherent in this ideology are unlikely to generate positive outcomes because they fail to take into account the realities of the context in which they are to be applied.

The same ideology is identified by Williams, in Chapter 3. In many countries in Africa, he suggests, 'access to a global language such as English is a political imperative'. It is so powerful that no politician will dare to recommend that their citizens should be denied such access, however inadequate the available English language provision may be in reality.

The same phenomenon is described by Tembe and Norton, in Chapter 6. The authors note that in rural and urban schools in Uganda parents hold somewhat ambiguous attitudes towards English and local languages. Both groups are concerned that their children should be exposed to an international language – in particular English – in order to 'catch up in this fast-moving world'. At the same time, parents recognise the value of local languages but do not necessarily feel that they should be taught and used in school.

The rhetoric of English and development is also discussed by Wedell in Chapter 13. He notes the worldwide perception that teaching English to all learners in state schools is an important way of 'increasing the human capital on which future national economic development and political power depends'. Wedell also finds little hard evidence that providing universal English language teaching brings any benefits or is cost effective.

Coleman, in Chapter 5, also identifies an ill-defined concern with 'globalisation' and 'international competition' as being the motivating force for the establishment of an English medium school system within the state education sector in Indonesia. The terms 'globalisation' and 'international competition' are repeated, mantra like, in official documents and constitute the rationale for an educational innovation which appears to give greatest benefit to an already privileged sector of society.

In India, too, the rhetoric of English for development is pervasive. In Chapter 4, Meganathan quotes a government report from 2006 which describes the English language in India as being 'a symbol of people's aspirations for quality in education and fuller participation in national and international life.' Meganathan also refers to the establishment of a temple to the 'English Goddess' which has been built by Dalit (formerly 'untouchable') villagers in Uttar Pradesh. Pandey (2011) reports on this temple in more detail, quoting a Dalit leader in the village where the temple is located:

> English is the milk of a lioness ... only those who drink it will roar. ... With the blessings of Goddess English, Dalit children will not grow to serve landlords or skin dead animals or clean drains or raise pigs and buffaloes. They will grow into adjudicators and become employers and benefactors. Then the roar of the Dalits ... will be heard by one and all.

The Dalit dream is a beautiful one, yet full of pathos. When the Dalits of Uttar Pradesh are all fluent in English, who then will clean the drains and raise the livestock? Another marginalised group that has not yet learnt English? Or will the cleaning and livestock raising be carried out by people who are well rewarded and appreciated for what they do? And, before that happens, what new obstacles will have been put in the paths of the Dalit to resist their development? The plight experienced by the Dalits is caused not by their inability to speak English but by the way that Indian society is constructed.

The claims made for English and for increased use of English in education, then, are ubiquitous. But, as Grin suggests, when making claims about the social and economic value of specific languages:

> It is important ... to be absolutely unambiguous about what claims are actually being made – that is, what causal relationships are invoked and what hard facts are supposed to illustrate (if not prove) the relationship. (Grin 2009:7)

Risks

What, next, are the risks associated with English which the contributors to this volume identify? Let us look first at another statistic from UNDP's 2010 Human Development Report. In the 42 'very highly developed' countries, the average adult has spent 11.3 years in full-time education. In the 23 'least developed' countries, on the other hand, the average adult has spent only 3.7 years in full-time education. Members of society in the least developed countries, then, are unlikely to be able to make optimum contributions to their communities if they have been educated for only one third of the duration that adults in the most developed nations have experienced (even assuming that there is no difference in the quality of the education available in the most and least developed countries – an assumption that seems unlikely to be accurate).

So once again we need to ask what role English has, if any, in reducing this huge differential. The answer appears to be that in some circumstances English may actually be contributing to the problem. It has been demonstrated that in many developing countries children are more likely to drop out of school if the school language is not the home language (Pinnock 2009), yet there is a growing trend in some countries for English to be used as the medium of instruction even in the earliest years of primary education (Coleman 2010b). In other words, in certain contexts if English is used as the medium of instruction children are less likely to complete their primary education.

Five contributors to this collection identify risks associated with the use of English in education and one looks at a case of English being used to discourage and prevent immigration into the UK.

Williams, in Chapter 3, argues that in those Sub-Saharan African countries where English is the medium of instruction and where children do not use English at home, a largely teacher-centred approach is likely to 'disadvantage children ... who do not understand the teacher or the textbooks'. In the short term, children may drop out of school or may fail examinations; this has been known for a long time. But in the longer term, Williams suggests, even those who manage to satisfy all the requirements and complete primary education may still have benefited little from their education because they understood so little of it. Part of the evidence for this argument is that the death rate of children whose mothers have completed (English medium) primary education in several Sub-Saharan African countries is not very different from that of children whose mothers have no education. Williams concludes that policy makers often fail to understand how difficult it is to conduct state education 'in a language that few learners, and not all teachers, have mastered'. Similarly, policymakers 'do not appreciate the risk to national development, nor the threat to national stability' which arise from their policies.

Shamim argues, in Chapter 14, that successive governments in Pakistan have announced policies of increasing access to English with the stated aim of achieving equality of opportunity. But implementation always falls short of what is required. In consequence, English in Pakistan continues to play a gate-keeping role and effectively excludes the majority of the population from higher education and all but the most menial of jobs in the civil service. Shamim describes the situation that has been created as one of 'linguistic apartheid'. Tariq Rahman, Pakistan's leading linguist, analyses the linguistic apartheid phenomenon in the following way:

> The ruling elite finds it in its interest to teach a few in English, most others in Urdu and not to use the people's smaller languages at all for teaching. If this is changed the power equation of this country will change also. That is why such an unjust medium of instruction policy will not change. **(Rahman 2010)**

In Chapter 4, Meganathan suggests that the rapid spread in the use of English in education in India's states and Union Territories 'further intensifies the already existing divide between English language-rich children and English language-poor children'.

Coleman, in Chapter 5, also worries that the Indonesian International School System is creating – or consolidating – a social divide between those who can afford to send their children to these English medium schools and the rest of the population.

Still in Indonesia, Lamb's research, reported in Chapter 9, suggests that the social, economic and cultural capital provided by middle class children's home background and their early experiences in school can lead to a 'massive competitive gain' over children from more modest backgrounds. In turn, this can lead to a 'widening economic and cultural class divide' over the long term.

In Chapter 10, Capstick takes an innovative approach to migration by examining in detail the expectations of four young people in Mirpur, Azad Jammu and Kashmir, who are hoping to move to the UK as the spouses (or future spouses) of British citizens of Pakistani origin. Capstick demonstrates that, as a consequence of UK immigration legislation introduced in late 2010, English is being used as a mechanism for controlling immigration. The UK government's argument that the new English language requirement will enable migrants to become actively engaged in their communities seems to be harking back to a mythical ideal of small villages in rural England in which everybody is involved in the local boy scouts and girl guides groups, the Women's Institute, the Young Farmers' Club and so on – an ideal which is reproduced every evening in the radio soap *The Archers*. The reality in urban Britain, where most of the population live, is quite different. Yet Capstick quotes research which suggests that South Asian migrants in the UK do indeed develop 'strong bonds and links' within their own communities and provide active support to each other, possibly to a greater extent than is commonly practised among the majority community. Capstick concludes that English is being given a gate-keeping role, a mechanism for discrimination which contravenes human rights, most glaringly so if it prevents families from living together.

Roles

As we have seen, some of the claims made for English do not seem to be well founded and in certain contexts there may be risks associated with the use of English. So what benefits can English actually bring? Coleman (2010) attempted to identify some of the roles that English has been asked to play in development contexts. He identified four broad areas where there is evidence that English makes a contribution:

- increasing employability

- facilitating international mobility (migration, tourism, studying abroad)

- unlocking development opportunities and accessing crucial information

- acting as an impartial language in contexts where other available languages would be unacceptable.

Unfortunately we cannot always be sure that English will succeed in playing the roles it is given!

Some of the contributors to this volume have confirmed this categorisation. For example, Kennett in Chapter 15, describes the work of the STEPS (Skills through English for Public Servants) project in Sri Lanka, which aims to encourage communication between civil servants at the local level with the public, NGOs, international humanitarian workers and central government. Her project does not merely teach English but integrates this with training in the development of skills needed for negotiation and consensus seeking. Previous projects in Sri Lanka have also endeavoured to encourage the use of English as a means of communication between the two main ethnic groups in the country; examples are the Primary English Language Project or PELP (Hayes 2002) and the Training for ELT Communities Project (Lunt and Hamlyn 2007). Research is needed to establish the extent to which these three projects have managed to achieve long lasting effects, but Kennett has already noted that many of her course participants who originate from different ethnic groups keep in touch with each other after the training has ended.

A second example of English being asked to play an impartial or link language role is given by Tembe and Norton, in Chapter 6. They show that parents in Uganda believe that in a country with multiple languages but no national language, like theirs, English plays a crucially important integrative role.

Negash, in Chapter 8, adopts a muscular position in support of English – as a lingua franca within Africa, in entertainment and the media, in international diplomacy, for commerce and tourism, in migration and in education. Some of these roles are covered in the categorisation proposed by Coleman (2010) but others are additional.

Focho's attempt, described in Chapter 7, to raise the awareness of her students in Francophone Cameroon regarding the benefits of English had only mixed results. By the end of the experiment the students were persuaded that English has value within the education system in Cameroon (for promotion to a higher class and for studying at university) and they also recognised that English is valuable for communicating with native speakers. In other respects, however, the students remain largely unpersuaded.

We have seen already that the Eritrean migrants, described by Hailemariam et al. in Chapter 11, apparently require English in order to maintain contact with their families in Eritrea. For those still in Eritrea, however, English also functions as a means of accessing what the authors term the 'imagined community' of Eritreans abroad. For those left behind in Eritrea, then, English is part of the dream of life elsewhere.

Recommendations

Kennedy, in Chapter 2, recommends that those working in the area of language and development need to do more 'to understand the complexity of LP [language planning] and development issues' so that they can find ways of managing the complexity.

Seargeant and Erling in Chapter 12 suggest that the discourse of English for international development needs to be challenged. What is needed is detailed research into 'the affordances that actual English use can achieve in specific contexts.'

In Chapter 13, Wedell recognises that – despite the lack of evidence that universal English teaching brings the benefits expected from it – it is important to take steps to ensure that these English programmes are made as effective as possible. For this to happen, he proposes, three issues need to be recognised and taken into account: educational change takes time and effort; schools and classrooms are not uniform in nature; and many different stakeholders are affected by and, in turn, can have an impact on educational change.

Shamim, in Chapter 14, makes three recommendations for the Pakistani context: that children's proficiency in both English and Urdu, the national language, should be improved; that there should be a balance between 'felt needs' and the provision of facilities for learning English; and that there should be wide-ranging debate concerning the relationship between language and development, leading eventually to a practicable policy.

Williams in Chapter 3 suggests that 'effective teaching of English as a subject' is needed in Sub-Saharan Africa, although he seems sceptical as to the likelihood of this happening. Meganathan makes an identical recommendation for India in Chapter 4.

In Chapter 9, Lamb makes three important recommendations aimed at minimising inequality in the provision of English language education in Indonesia. These include using classroom time to encourage all pupils – and especially the more disadvantaged – to critically engage with the English which is already in their environment.

Finally, Whitehead, in Chapter 16, recommends that English language teaching (ELT) in development should be recognised as a specialised branch of ELT. This will require a high level of professionalisation among its practitioners, he suggests. ELT in development should also be characterised by rigorous monitoring and evaluation. Whitehead also makes recommendations for the role of English in fragile states: English must be empowering for those who are learning it and it must not be allowed to replace mother tongues.

Conclusions

The study of Language and Development has a history going back less than 20 years. During that time considerable progress has been made.

■ There has been a clear movement away from simple descriptions of English language teaching projects in development contexts which tended to characterise some of the early Language and Development conferences (see the Language and Development conferences website at **www.langdevconferences. org**). As the contributions to this book demonstrate, people working in the field are now much more likely to adopt a critical perspective towards their work.

■ There is now a greater understanding that English is not the only language that plays a role in the development process. Other international languages, national languages and local languages all have important and complementary roles to play.

■ There is increased awareness that 'development' does not necessarily mean just economic development at a national level. Development has a much broader meaning (see the Millennium Development Goals, Appendix 3).

■ There is increased willingness to question some of the claims that have been made for English as a means to development.

But we still need to learn much more about how development economists, human rights lawyers, educationists other than language teachers and other development specialists look at language and work with language. We need to venture out from the cosy and comfortable world of English language teaching and continue to ask ourselves challenging questions about the value of what we are doing.

References

Coleman, Hywel. 2010a. *English in Development.* London: British Council. Available online at *www.teachingenglish.org.uk/transform/books/english-language-development*

Coleman, Hywel. 2010b. *Teaching and Learning in Pakistan: The Role of Language in Education.* Islamabad: British Council. Available online at *www.britishcouncil.org/pakistan-ette-role-of-language-in-education.htm*

Grin, F. 2009. *Promoting language through the economy: Competing paradigms*. In J.M.Kirk and D. Ó Baoill (eds), *Language and Economic Development: Northern Ireland, the Republic of Ireland and Scotland*, 1-12. Belfast: Cló Ollscoil na Banríona.

Hayes, D. (ed.). 2002. *Making a Difference: The Experience of the Primary English Language Project,* Sri Lanka. Colombo: British Council.

Kenny, B. and Savage, W. 1997. *Setting the scene*. In B.Kenny and W.Savage (eds), *Language and Development: Teachers in a Changing World*, 1-12. Harlow: Longman.

Lunt, R. and Hamlyn, A. 2007. *Lessons from a training project in war-affected areas of Sri Lanka*. In H.Coleman (ed.), *Language and Development: Africa and Beyond*, 139-152. Addis Ababa: British Council.

Pandey, G. 2011. *An 'English goddess' for India's down-trodden*. *BBC News South Asia* 15 February 2011. Available online at *www.bbc.co.uk/news/world-south-asia-12355740*

Pinnock, Helen. 2009. *Language and Education: The Missing Link*. Reading: CfBT Education Trust and Save the Children.

Rahman, T. 2010. *Medium of instruction debate*. *The News on Sunday* (Pakistan) 28 November 2010.

UNDP (United Nations Development Programme). 2010. *The Real Wealth of Nations: Pathways to Human Development*. *(Human Development Report 2010.)* Basingstoke and New York: Palgrave Macmillan for UNDP. Available online at *http://hdr.undp.org/en/media/HDR_2010_EN_Complete_reprint.pdf*

Wariyar, Unni. 2010. Mbarara University Hospital, South Western Uganda: Project Report. London: VSO.

Policy planning and implementation

2

Challenges for language policy, language and development[1]

Chris Kennedy

What I want to do in this chapter is to explore some of the connections between language policy, language and development and signal a number of challenges that arise from the inter-connections.

Language policy

Language policy (LP) is the deliberate attempt to change an individual's or community's use of a language or languages or a variety or varieties. Communities exist at local, regional, national, international or, increasingly, cross-border (Omoniyi 2004) levels and agents of LP may try to influence the language behaviour of such different groups (or users). LP decision-takers are also found operating at different levels from macro to meso to micro, and they can be groups or individuals acting within local, regional, national and international contexts. The levels, both those pertaining to those creating policy and those affected by policy, are imprecise and not always easily defined; where on the cline you put different language policies can be subjective. Traditionally, LP has been seen as operating at macro-levels; for example, national initiatives by governments. The recognition of other levels, however, is important since we then become aware that LP is carried out not only by governments but also by groups and individuals. Policy initiatives may be targeted not only at national groups but also at group and individual users in regional and local contexts. The levels of policy makers and of users (those affected by policies) indicate the potential complexity of LP and its implementation in development.

The complexity becomes more apparent once you look at the notion of context. A growth metaphor with reference to plants and horticulture helps here. Plants are 'programmed' to grow and they will grow assuming that the conditions match their particular characteristics, though they will also modify themselves and adjust to conditions for which they were not originally suited. Plants' rate of growth and their survival depend on the context, on soil and climate. They are part of an ecological system. The same can be said for humankind in the context of socio-economic development. People wish to improve themselves (it seems a natural human inclination for people to wish to have better lives, however defined) but their development will be made more or less difficult depending on whether local contexts enable or prevent their wish to develop. One challenge is to implement policy to create a match between people's aspirations and the context in which they live and work, even if that means that the policy may have to change the context in some way. This manipulation of context is something which agents of innovation are well aware of and an integration of innovation studies, development and language policy is well overdue.

Language and development

A useful definition of both language and development is given by Markee (2002:266) who rephrases language as 'communicative competence', and explains development 'as a reduction in participants' vulnerability to things they do not control'. We might wish to add that development implies greater far-reaching participant benefits including an equitable sharing of resources and a distribution of socio-political and economic power and influence.

The field of language and development is complex, with numerous inter-connections and links. This is a further challenge: to recognise complexity and to avoid simplistic solutions to problems, but also to try to manage solutions out of the chaos that lead in some way towards a positive beneficial outcome for participants (Larsen-Freeman and Cameron 2008).

Let me tease out a little of what I mean by language and development. A useful categorisation is provided by Appleby et al. (2002) who distinguish between language **in, as, for** and **of** development. Language **in** development refers to the role of languages in national socio-economic development and raises questions of the place of English and other languages in contributing to that development; language **as** development refers to the provision of language teaching and language projects where language provision is an end in itself; language **for** development is language used as an essential tool for the development of different domains such as business, science, media and law. (The) language **of** development category is somewhat different from the preceding three since it refers to actual language used, in terms of its lexico-grammatical and discourse properties, whereas the other three refer more to the roles and functions of language. The language **of** development is the discourse which attaches itself to development issues and is used by various stakeholders in development projects. The approach and its aims are closely allied to critical discourse analysis.

These are useful distinctions when talking about language and development since identifying which aspects (**in, as, for** and **of**) are involved can clarify the issues. At times the distinctions are not clear-cut and there will be occasions when more than one category is applicable, but the categories are especially useful in LP situations where they help to identify the ideology of a particular language policy, whether a policy is explicit in its objectives, or whether there are policy confusions. In cases of governmental, top-down LP, the distinctions (**in, as, for**) may occur at different levels as the policy is implemented with the language **of** development providing an over-arching discourse. Thus the decision by the Malaysian government (subsequently reversed) to teach school Maths and Science subjects through the medium of English (Hashim 2009) was a language in development decision (English was regarded as being important in the nation's socio-economic life) while its use in the domains of science and technology was particularly important (language **for** development). These language and development decisions (language in and language for) were then implemented as English language programmes in schools and at that point, as so often in top-down innovations, the resources provided (especially materials and training) proved to be inadequate to enable the ideological ends to be met.

LP, language and development

The example of Malaysia provides a useful way of looking at the different categorisations (in, as, for) with reference to language policy, especially where that policy involves English. There are few countries where governments (correctly or incorrectly) do not espouse the belief that English is essential in socio-economic development and adopt language policies accordingly which either require English as a major subject on the curriculum or indeed have opted for English-medium education (language **as** a tool for development), or require English **for** development in particular domains, though the latter category is often part of language policies adopted by the private sector, especially in business domains. The danger arises where the emphasis on English is misplaced and where other priorities such as poverty alleviation or mother tongue literacy would be more appropriate. This seems to be the view taken by aid development agencies at present. The British and Swedish development aid organisations, for example, have as their overall aims the alleviation of poverty. DfID, the British aid agency, says that its main aims are 'to get rid of extreme poverty' and 'to reach the Millennium Development Goals (MDGs)' (DfID 2011; on the MDGs, see Appendix 3 at the end of this volume). SIDA, the Swedish development agency, states that it works 'to reduce poverty in the world' with an overall goal of 'making it possible for poor people to improve their living conditions' (SIDA 2011). Meanwhile, the German aid organisation GIZ (formerly GTZ) has 'sustainable development' as its aim (GIZ 2011).

There are few aid projects that deal directly with language and development. In most cases, language – frequently English – is used in education or agricultural projects, for example, as a means of communication, as a 'service' or 'carrier' language. The days when international aid agencies funded large English language projects as development activities have largely passed. An exception to this general trend is the major nine-year GBP50 million (USD77 million) English language project in Bangladesh. This project, known as 'English in Action' (EIA), is being funded by DfID; according to Seargeant and Erling (2011, Chapter 12 this volume), the project's prima facie objective is to develop English language skills 'which will allow for participation in the financial, political and knowledge economies' which are 'conducted at a global level'. Seargeant and Erling, however, fear that this objective is influenced by 'abstract assumptions and received wisdom about the role that English plays in globalised societies' rather than a careful analysis of actual needs. An alternative explanation as to why such a large project was implemented against what appears to be present aid policy is that the decision was driven more by political than linguistic motivations. Since Bangladesh is at present relatively politically stable – compared, for example, to Pakistan – the British government possibly decided that such a project would help to preserve that stability.

The only other UK-based organisation that appears to be highlighting English language in its projects is the British Council, which uses English as one of its carriers of cultural relations. Otherwise, the general lack of enthusiasm for English language aid projects is understandable given a shortage of financial aid resources, the emphasis on the alleviation of poverty, the fact that governments themselves are responding to their own educational and English language needs and the widespread availability of private sector provision for English language (although arguably private sector provision benefits only the relatively well-off). (Kennedy 2010).

This cautious attitude towards English language in development aid projects is supported by academic researchers. Tupas (2009) thinks, for example, that LP is a form of social development planning and that rather than immediately defining language problems that need solving through LP, we should look at local social needs first and only then see where language policy might or might not assist in achieving social objectives. A similar case is made by Djité (2008) who, while not denying the importance of language in development, is clear that we must first identify what the needs and wants of local communities are in, for example, the domains of health and education. Only then should we examine whether language should play a role in answering those needs; we should not assume that the language chosen should be English as other languages may well be a more appropriate and relevant choice.

LP and applied linguists

This brings us to the division between those who take LP decisions (practitioners) and those who advise or comment on those decisions (often applied linguists). Politicians and planners do not pay much attention to applied linguists working in the LP field. Kaplan and Baldauf (2007) believe applied linguists do not have the same impact on language policy practice as, for example, medical advisers have on health policy. They over-rate the influence of advisers in other fields but they make a valid point. There are many reasons for this lack of influence. They believe that health issues are more tangible, results more visible and returns more immediate. This is the case where more mechanistic solutions to problems can be successful and measured (for example, in the case of inoculation) though there will also be other public health issues, where solutions are not as simple, which may be nearer to the sort of problems arising from language policy, especially those areas that, like language, intersect with attitudes and beliefs and behavioural change; for example, smoking and diet campaigns.

There is also the problem (in this context) that language is used by all and we are all competent (or believe we are competent) in language use. Advice therefore may not be welcome if users are not aware of language issues. Srikant Sarangi (Sarangi 2009) met resistance advising doctors on doctor–patient communications. The doctors denied communication problems and said they knew what they were doing. Sarangi explained to the doctors that if he cut himself he would see blood but he would need doctors to tell him the composition of the blood and explain to him the process of clotting and healing. The study of language, he explained, was somewhat similar: an apparently simple surface phenomenon requires expertise for deeper analysis.

That language is not regarded as important as, for example, health is shown by the fact that I know of no Ministry of Language though governments generally have a Ministry of Health. Organisations do exist that advise governments and advocate policy on language. I am thinking particularly of national language academies, often attached to Ministries; for example, the Académie française, the Pusat Bahasa in Indonesia and in Malaysia and the Icelandic Language Institute (Hilmarsson-Dunn 2006). However, these organisations have a restricted role in that they advise on corpus issues (generally of a lexical nature), not those related to status planning, and are concerned with linguistic cultivation and purification. The general (unsuccessful) track record of language academies also indicates the potential problems of centralised control over language. It is better to regard language as part of culture belonging to other domains, especially the domain of education, where language may still play a major role in development without however being allocated a specific 'Ministry of Language'.

Applied linguists should be prepared to engage with language and development problems but also be aware of the attitudes that underlie them. We need theories that can be applied to social problems to produce evidence-based research but we also need to be able to communicate research findings to users in intelligible ways without either alienating or confusing them. We need in particular, according to Kaplan and Baldauf (2007), to realise that LP is essentially a political process so that we can find ways of engaging with the politicians rather than commenting from the sidelines. Applied linguists have to accept that other issues may assume an importance politically (for example, the provision of fresh water or food supplies) and that language might at best be a component of aid projects (language for development) rather than be part of separate language projects (language as development).

Language policy and social development

As we have seen, Tupas (2009) believes that LP is a part of social development and that we should look at the social needs of communities and only then see whether there is a role for language in helping to satisfy those needs. It is useful then to have access to a model of social development against which we could measure the appropriacy of LP interventions.

Table 1 shows three stages or classifications of society: (A) Traditional, (B) Contemporary and (C) Emergent. The terms I have used are not crucial. The important thing is to understand the idea of three stages of social development over time, corresponding very roughly to the first half of the 20th century (A), the latter half of the 20th century (B) and the beginning of the 21st century (C). The concept of a tripartite division and the categories within it are selected and adapted from Kalantzis and Cope (2008).

Table 1: Three stages of social development		
(A) Traditional	**(B) Contemporary**	**(C) Emergent**
rationalist economics	behavioural economics	knowledge society
rational	romantic	criticality
highly structured	neo-liberalism	distributed knowledge
top down	soft power	collaboration
centralisation	decentralisation	micro-agency
nationism/nationalism	globalisation	diversity
state power	localisation	public/private partnership
predictability	uncertainty	fuzziness/complexity
mass production 'Fordism'	choice/market-driven	mobility/flexibility
stratified society	less stratified society	multiple identities
collectivist cultures	individualism	participation

I do not have room here to gloss the categories in each of the three stages but I hope they are self-explanatory. From an historical viewpoint, the social development expressed from left to right of the table (i.e. from Stage A to B to C) is one from simplicity to complexity; from mono- to multi-dimensions; from structure to fluidity; from macro to micro.

We can illustrate such changes in society by looking at their everyday realisations. Thus working spaces have moved from the concept of individual offices (Stage A of the table) to open plan (Stage B) to spaces with multiple and changing purposes (Stage C). Readers may have experienced such space changes also in education, with children at one school sitting in rows at desks attached to the floor; another school might have children working in groups around moveable tables; another might not have classrooms at all as we know them but modular spaces that change according to the needs of the children. These differences in use of space reflect the three stages of social development (A, B and C): they are indicative of the way a society thinks about education, which, in turn, is related to social development.

As a further example, architectural styles can illustrate social changes more dramatically. The Willis (formerly the Sears Building) in Chicago, built in 1973, reflects a 'Traditional' style, the Petronas Towers in Kuala Lumpur are an example of 'Contemporary' style, while the proposed Dubai Opera House illustrates 'Emergent' design.[2] The Dubai building shows a design fluidity in marked contrast to the angular and structured lines of the Chicago building, and the individualistic ornamental spires of the Petronas Towers. Such visual symbols demonstrate how social developments permeate all areas of our lives and can indicate a stage or stages of a society's development. I am arguing that language planners and development agents must be aware of these stages if they are to design appropriate language and development interventions which will be successfully implemented.

Classifying societies in this way is crude in that a particular society will not be totally at one stage or another since different domains within societies may be at different stages. The categories represent generalisations and there will be hybridity (Pennycook 2007) and considerable seepage between them. Nor will there necessarily be linear development since economic or political crises may cause a society or domains within it to move from one classification to another. We should also be aware of the dangers of imposing a top-down a priori classification on a society (with dangers of stereotyping) and allowing this to determine development policy. It is better to work bottom-up, analysing a situation and arriving at the categories after local post hoc investigation of processes and practices (Holliday 2005). I am not suggesting that one classification (whether A, B or C) is necessarily better than another, but something like Table 1 could be a useful device when planning language policies that fit development needs. You could describe a society and either match policies to categories, or decide that a policy will assist in moving a domain from one category to another, or be forewarned of mismatches between an existing social stage and future development plans.

Table 2: Three types of education system
(terms and categories from Kalantzis and Cope 2008)

Didactic	Authentic	Transformative
structural approaches	communicative approaches	task-based approaches
skills for the many, education for the few	transferable skills	variety of learning
Institutions	institutions/off-site	new technologies
teacher control	learner autonomy	collaborative learners
Transmission	interpretation	enquiry
book culture	book plus IT	greater variety of media
knowing that	knowing how	knowing why
defined role for teachers	greater teacher roles	teachers as educators, catalysts, agents
uniform learners	individuality	learner differences

We can see the implications for the domain of education and development. Table 2 illustrates the different stages of education deriving from the tripartite social classification in Table 1. Problems arise when policy initiatives, whether guided by local governments or development agencies, are designed to change an education system from, for example, a Didactic to a Transformative stage (Honna and Takeshita 2005). This is not to say that attempts should not be made to move an education system or part of it from one stage to another, but development agents should be made fully aware of what they are attempting to do and should justify their decision, since an existing system may already be achieving good results; alternatively, improvements could be added to the system without creating an entirely different one. Care should be taken not to attempt too extreme a shift from one system to another, nor too rapid a shift, as otherwise the development may fail. We need adaptive rather than mechanistic language and development policies (Swanson and Bhadwal 2009) that make changes while taking into account the local context.

Changes in LP

We can see also use the classifications in Table 1 – (A) Traditional, (B) Contemporary, (C) Emergent – to look at developments in language policy and planning that have impacted on development issues.

There have been criticisms of the 1970s view of LP (for example, Ricento 2006a). LP at that time reflected the socio-political conditions of the period and was concerned with top-down centralised policies and a rationalist technocratic view of planning, especially in connection with the problems of newly independent states in a post-colonial period. LP at the time was reflecting characteristics of the 'Traditional' classification in Table 1.

These criticisms are to some extent true (any activity will be influenced by the dominant ideologies of the time) but it must be said that the criticism should be levelled more at the actual political practice of LP, which was and still is in many situations top-down, with little reference to the language ecologies and contextual realities surrounding the political processes and the decisions taken (Samuelson and Freedman 2010).

Those who were actually writing about LP at the time were closer to current concerns in LP than some present-day writers admit, although the location of their case studies naturally reflected a post-colonial world of newly-independent states. If we take one of the series of seminal publications that was produced in the late 1960s and 1970s and compare a number of the issues raised at the time with current preoccupations it is clear that there are similarities. *Can Language be Planned?* (Rubin and Jernudd 1971), a collection of papers resulting from a seminar in Hawaii in 1968-69, tackles a number of concerns which pre-date those current today. The question 'Can language be planned?' is not answered with a triumphant yes, but with a degree of circumspection and hedging. The papers in the collection represent a number of different disciplines and attempt to look at LP from a multi-disciplinary point of view; the limitations of LP are explicitly mentioned. The notion of levels of language planning and concerns for what would now be called micro-planning (see below) are described. LP is regarded very much as part of a socio-economic political context.

It is true that there was a period during the 1980s and early 1990s when LP fell out of the academic mainstream (although clearly it continued as a political process). Quite why that occurred is a complex issue partly to do with attitude changes towards concepts of social planning and partly because of political changes in funding (for example, the Ford Foundation – which had earlier supported several LP surveys – lost interest and withdrew its support). What we are witnessing today is evidence of a cycle or spiral of change which has renewed interest in LP but which now reflects the concerns of a view of social development described in columns B and C of Table 1.

Present and future of LP and development

LP as a discipline is no different from other disciplines such as social planning, economics and linguistics itself, all of which have changed through the late 20th and early 21st centuries as the cultures from which they are derived have changed (reflected in a move from column A to columns B and C in Table 1).

The earlier LP case studies and investigations built up a descriptive database from which we were able to produce models of language planning based on the questions of 'what actors attempt to influence what behaviours of which people for what ends under what conditions by what means through which decision-making processes with what effect?' (Cooper 1989:98). Now, although descriptive studies continue to be made, there is a much broader concern for a deeper more critical interpretation of the processes of LP and for looking at it from several viewpoints. Such a variety of approaches can be found in Ricento (2006b), a collection which has contributions reflecting political, economic and cultural viewpoints (a broader aspect which was apparent as early as the 1970s), methodologies ranging from historical investigation to linguistics (via ethnography and psycho-sociology) and topics ranging from identity to human rights and linguistic imperialism.

The challenge given these different approaches is to create a unifying theory. However, given that LP is a part of social and development planning, it is unlikely that this will be achieved. Any such unifying theory would be unable to distil the complexity in any form other than the most simplistic. We are better to remain looking at LP and development from a number of angles and drawing conclusions from them, what has been called a process of 'imaginisation' (Morgan 2006), using metaphors to look at processes from several viewpoints in order to produce rich descriptions of them.

We can situate present LP (or at least academic commentaries on its practice) in an 'Emergent' paradigm (see Table 1) which includes critical LP. Just as linguistics, politics and sociology have developed 'critical' schools of thought where the criticality refers to an ideology of social change and of exposing deep structural inequalities beneath surface processes, so LP has developed a critical aspect. This began with Tollefson's criticism of what he calls the neoclassical approach and his suggestion to replace such an approach with the historical-structural approach, placing politics at the centre of the LP enterprise and regarding LP as a process of different levels from macro to micro, from governmental levels to – for example – classrooms (Tollefson 1991).

Macro and micro issues in LP and development

The macro-micro distinction is one which has been gaining more ground recently (e.g. Omoniyi 2007) and it has several interpretations. There is also a meso level but I shall not go into detail here; establishing a meso-level is somewhat subjective but it lies between the macro (supranational or national) and the micro (individual, group or institution).

One example of the macro-micro distinction is that which looks at levels of educational policy and implementation from government to classroom and how agents at the different levels implement the policy which is handed down to them. This approach describes micro implementation of a macro policy and is concerned with linkages between the levels and issues such as decentralisation and centralisation (Kennedy 2001).

A second view takes a more overtly political stance and is influenced by Foucault's notion of governmentality (Foucault 1991). This approach examines the actions and strategies of agents of planning and development – whether politicians, advisers or educators – and in particular the discourses they adopt to implement micro aspects of macro-policy. It deconstructs their actions by examining their language. We need to examine not so much laws and regulations but how people behave in certain situations and talk about issues (Curdt-Christiansen 2009). This approach has much in common therefore with the category of the language of development described above.

Linked to these concerns of the micro is the question of agency. The switch from the macro to the micro has brought an already existing concern with agents into an LP and development focus. I say 'already existing' since in educational development there has always been considerable interest in learners and teachers and their role in the curriculum, though their language and how they express their views has not until now been a major concern. Within an 'Emergent' LP framework, however, we are now more interested in how these agents at micro levels implement a policy but especially how they use language while implementing.

The third element of micro-policy is the concern with individuals, groups or institutions who create their own LP without being directly linked to a macro-policy handed down to them for implementation. An institution might in fact produce local counter-language policies from those proposed at macro (e.g. national) levels. It is an interesting question to what extent any institution or group while developing a micro-policy is linked in some way to macro-policy, since the group is part of a society and is therefore not operating in a socio-cultural vacuum. This is one way an agenda of development issues can be pursued by micro-agencies pushing upward towards the macro and presenting counter-policies.

One example of an LP and development micro-policy implemented in accord with a larger government macro-policy is the decision by AKTEL (a major Bangladeshi telecommunications company, now rebranded ROBI) and the Daily Star (a national newspaper chain) to provide free newspapers regularly to Bangladeshi schools. These newspapers contain specially-written sections on English language to improve students' linguistic and reading skills (Daily Star 2009). A critical language policy and development approach would want to discuss the motives of a telecommunications company and a national newspaper in collaborating on such a development project but here I shall just provide it as an example of micro-planning.

A further instance, also from Bangladesh though not as directly concerned with language, is an example of micro-development related to social, economic and political planning. It is the establishment of the Grameen Bank (***www.grameen-info.org/***) founded by Professor Muhammad Junus. This is a bank that supports rural development by giving small loans to the poor without demanding financial guarantees. It is not without its critics and has now grown into a number of inter-related businesses, but it started by recognising the needs and wants of poor people in a local context and devising simple appropriate solutions to their problems, bypassing the traditional macro-processes of banking. The micro-credit scheme in many ways is a return to the notion of appropriate technology espoused many years ago by Schumacher (Schumacher 1973), who formulated his seminal ideas in a 'Traditional' society but which now seem as relevant in 'Emergent' times (to use the terms in Table 1).

The macro-micro distinction has also been discussed by Spolsky (2009) who suggests we should consider a new term to describe LP activities, namely language management. This re-definition of LP may be part of a need to fit LP more clearly into a neo-liberal approach where ideas are marketed and branded and newness is regarded as important, though I suspect those proposing such a new term would object to the idea of language management being part of a neo-liberal discourse. Spolsky (2009) regards LP as consisting of three inter-related aspects: practices, beliefs and management. In his description, LP is the superordinate term but it is more appropriate, if we wish to adopt the term at all, to regard language management as the superordinate from which language policy and practice derive. Considering LP as a form of language management might have the effect of bringing LP and development management closer together.

Conclusion

At the beginning of this chapter I said that I would describe some of the inter-relationships between LP, language and development and indicate the challenges that face those of us working in these areas.

Here is a summary of some of those challenges arising from the discussion. The challenges are to:

- understand the complexity of LP and development issues and find ways of managing the complexity

- use, but with circumspection, social models of development to evaluate the appropriacy and relevance of LP and development plans

- realise that local context and local issues are crucial to LP and development

- accept development priorities (such as health and education) and realise that language may play a subsidiary role in such projects

- promote language in, as and for development only when there is a clear language need assessed at local levels

- consider the appropriate and relevant roles of all languages in development, not solely English

- examine LP and development problems from a multi-disciplinary and critical perspective and try to combine macro and micro approaches

- examine the role of agents in LP and development

- engage with political practitioners in LP and development and present research that is accessible and relevant to them.

Notes

1. This is a revised version of a plenary paper presented at the eighth Language and Development Conference in Dhaka, Bangladesh, 23-25 June 2009.

2. Further details of the three buildings discussed are as follows: The 1973 Willis Tower (Sears Building), Chicago, can be seen at *www.chicagoarchitecture. info/Building/375/The-Willis-Tower.php*. The architect was Bruce Graham from Skidmore, Owings and Merrill and the structural engineer was Fazlur Khan. The 1998 Petronas Towers, Kuala Lumpur, can be seen at *www.fotolibra.com/ gallery/339356/klcc-petronas-twin-tower-malaysia/*. The architects were César Pelli and Djay Cerico. The futuristic design of the proposed Dubai Opera House and Cultural Centre can be seen at *www.designboom.com/weblog/cat/9/view/3045/dubai-opera-house-by-zaha-hadid.html*. The architects are Zaha Hadid and Patrik Schumacher.

References

Appleby, R., Copley, K., Sithirajvongsa, S. and Pennycook, A. 2002. *Language in development constrained: Three contexts. TESOL Quarterly* 36(3), 323-346.

Hashim, A. 2009. *Not plain sailing: Malaysia's language choice in policy and education*. In L.Lim and E.Low (eds), *Multilingual, Globalising Asia*, 36-51. (AILA Review 22.) Amsterdam: Benjamins.

Cooper, R. 1989. *Language Planning and Social Change. Cambridge: Cambridge University Press.*

Curdt-Christiansen, X.L. 2009. *Invisible and visible language planning: Ideological factors in the family language policy of Chinese immigrant families in Quebec. Language Policy* 8(4), 351-375.

Daily Star. 2009. *Star-Aktel initiative for school-goers launched. Daily Star* 5th February 2009. Available online at *www.thedailystar.net/newDesign/news-details. php?nid=74493*.

DfID (Department for International Development). 2011. *Who we are and what we do: Structure and staff. London: DfID*. Available online at *www.dfid.gov.uk/About-DFID/Quick-guide-to-DFID/Who-we-are-and-what-we-do/*

Djité, P. 2008. *The Sociolinguistics of Development in Africa. Clevedon: Multilingual Matters.*

Foucault, M. 1991. *Governmentality*. In G.Burchell, C.Gordon and P.Miller (eds), *The Foucault Effect: Studies in Governmentality*, 87-104. *Chicago: University of Chicago Press.*

GIZ (Deutsche Gesellschaft für Internationale Zusammenarbeit). 2011. *Services: We work for sustainable development. Eschborn: GIZ*. Available online at *www.gtz.de/en/692.htm*.

Hilmarsson-Dunn, A.M. 2006. *Protectionist language policies in the face of the forces of English: The case of Iceland. Language Policy* 5(3), 295-314.

Holliday, A. 2005. *The Struggle to Teach English as an International Language. Oxford: Oxford University Press.*

Honna, N. and Takeshita, Y. 2005. *ELT in Japan: Policy plans and their implementations. RELC Journal* 36(3), 363-83.

Kalantzis, M. and Cope, B. 2008. *New Learning. Cambridge: Cambridge University Press.*

Kaplan, R. and Baldauf, R. 2007. *Language policy spread. Language Problems and Language Planning* 31(2), 107-129.

Kennedy, C. 2001. *Language use, language planning and ESP.* In J.Flowerdew and M.Peacock (eds), *Research Perspectives on EAP*, 25-41. *Cambridge: Cambridge University Press.*

Kennedy, C. 2010. *Learning English in a global context.* In S.Hunston and D.Oakey (eds), *Introducing Applied Linguistics,* 84-93. London: Routledge.

Larsen-Freeman, D. and Cameron, L. 2008. *Complex Systems and Applied Linguistics. Oxford: Oxford University Press.*

Markee, N. 2002. *Language in development. TESOL Quarterly* 36(3), 265-274.

Morgan, G. 2006. *Images of Organisation. Updated ed. London: Sage.*

Omoniyi, T. 2004. *The Sociolinguistics of Borderlands: Two Nations, One Community. Trenton, NJ: Africa World Press.*

Omoniyi, T. 2007. *Alternative contexts of language policy and planning in Sub-Saharan Africa. TESOL Quarterly* 41(3), 533-549.

Pennycook, A. 2007. *Global Englishes and Transcultural Flows. London: Routledge.*

Ricento, T. 2006a. *Language policy: Theory and practice. In T.Ricento (ed.), An Introduction to Language Policy,* 10-23. *Oxford: Blackwell.*

Ricento, T. (ed.). 2006b. *An Introduction to Language Policy. Oxford: Blackwell.*

Rubin, J. and Jernudd, B. (eds). 1971. *Can Language be Planned? Honolulu: Hawai'i University Press.*

Samuelson, B.L. and Freedman, S.W. 2010. *Language policy, multilingual education and power in Rwanda. Language Policy* 9(3), 191-215.

Sarangi, S. 2009. *Bringing together communities of interest. Paper presented at Connecting Discourses conference, Centre for Applied Linguistics, University of Warwick*, May 2009.

Schumacher, E.F. 1973. *Small is Beautiful: A Study of Economics as if People Mattered. London: Blond and Briggs.*

Seargeant, P. and Erling, E.J. 2011. *The discourse of 'English as a language for international development': Policy assumptions and practical challenges.* Chapter 12, this volume.

SIDA (Swedish International Development Co-operation Agency. 2011. *Organisation. Stockholm: SIDA.* Available online at *www.sida.se/English/About-us/Organization/*.

Spolsky, B. 2009. *Language Management. Cambridge: Cambridge University Press.*

Swanson, D. and Bhadwal, S. 2009. *Creating Adaptive Policies. London: Sage.*

Tollefson, J. 1991. *Planning Language, Planning Inequality. Harlow: Longman.*

Tupas, T.R.E. 2009. *Language as a problem of development*. In L.Lim and E.Low (eds), *Multilingual, Globalising Asia*, 23-35. *(AILA Review 22.) Amsterdam: Benjamins.*

Language policy, politics and development in Africa

Eddie Williams

Introduction

'Africa is the only continent where the majority of children start school using a foreign language,' observes a recent UNESCO report (Ouane and Glanz 2010). This chapter will argue that this language policy is a significant contributory factor to the lack of development in the continent. The Western media have made many optimistic predictions for Africa in the last two decades: 2005 was declared the 'Year of Africa' (Wickstead 2005:37), while following the fall of apartheid in South Africa, the 'African Renaissance' envisioned by Nelson Mandela was much heralded in the closing years of the 20th century by Bill Clinton and Thabo Mbeki among others (Tikly 2003). On the heels of the 2010 football World Cup in South Africa there are optimistic forecasts for that country, and for a halo effect over the entire continent[1]. However, the renaissance has not yet materialised, and the pessimistic comment from Tabatabai (1995:31), that there was 'an unmistakable trend towards the Africanisation of poverty', is confirmed in the UN Human Development Report for 2010, with African countries occupying 28 of the bottom 30 countries (UNDP 2010). In addition, widespread violence has been witnessed across the continent: recent years have seen massacres in Darfur, election riots in Kenya, religious killings in Nigeria, with ongoing conflict in Sudan and the eastern provinces of the Democratic Republic of Congo, while the rule of law seems febrile in much of the remainder of the continent. One remedy to this widespread lack of stability is held to be development, and an adequately educated population is claimed to be one of the necessary conditions for this, whether it be human development (focused on human needs in terms of health, democratic participation, freedom from abuse, etc.), or economic development (measured in terms of increased prosperity of the state).

However, the link between education and development is contested (Rogers 1990, Street 1984), while the notion that education alone can cause development is palpably mistaken. Thus, although Anderson (1966:347) estimated that 'about 40 per cent of adult literacy ... is a threshold for economic development' (a claim ironically dubbed the 'magical figure of 40 per cent' by Rogers 1990:3; see also

Street 1984:2, Rassool 1999:81), he is at pains to point out that 'that level of education would not be a sufficient condition in societies lacking other support systems' (Anderson 1966:347). Indeed, a great deal of research over the past half century supports the view that adequate education is a necessary, but not sufficient, condition for both human and national economic development (Knight and Sabot 1990, Lockheed et al. 1980, Moock and Addou 1994). Furthermore, research has also demonstrated that education can be a cause of economic development, as opposed to simply correlating with it (Hicks 1980, Wheeler 1980). In a particularly wide-ranging review, Azariadis and Drazen (1990) examined the development history of 32 countries from 1940 to 1980, and concluded that, while there was variation from country to country, a threshold level for a number of factors, including the educational quality of the labour force, was a necessary, but not sufficient[2], condition for rapid economic growth. What they see as particularly significant is that not one of the countries where the threshold level of labour force educational quality was not met managed to achieve rapid growth.

A worrying observation, however, is that the effects of education seem weaker in Sub-Saharan Africa than in other areas of the world. Fotso (2006:10) reports that the infant mortality rate of children up to the age of one year, per 1,000 live births for children born to women in Malawi with no education is 98.6 compared to 104.0 for children born to women with eight years of primary education. Fotso's explanation is 'that the mortality pattern whereby children from mothers with some primary education stand greater risk to die than those whose mother have no formal education, reflect, at least in part, the differentials in under-reporting of deaths by education (sic)'. This explanation is, as he admits, speculation. Earlier research had, however, come to similar conclusions: Hobcraft (1993), who reviews a number of major studies, notes that the length of mothers' education has far less effect on child survival for African countries than for countries elsewhere. Hobcraft's method was to calculate the odds ratio for the 'maternal education contrast' (an odds ratio of 0.5 means that the child of a mother with seven or more years of education has a 50 per cent probability of dying before age two, compared with the child of a mother with no education). In all nine Latin American countries studied the ratio was below 0.5. On the other hand, ratios in Mali, Zimbabwe, Botswana and Uganda were 0.75 to 0.8, and in Ghana, 0.95. In short, seven years of mothers' education in Ghana made little difference to a child's survival chances. Hobcraft could find no convincing explanation for his findings. The work of Cochrane and Farid (1989) had also concluded that in Sub-Saharan Africa there are smaller differentials in birth rates between the rural uneducated and the urban educated than in other regions (particularly Latin America).

We explore below the reasons for this failure of much African primary education to ameliorate infant mortality. For the moment, we may note that one reason for the lack of positive impact of education in Sub-Saharan Africa is that what contributes to development is not simply 'education' in the sense of providing schools, teachers and materials for learners, but effective education, and that a crucial feature of much formal African education is precisely that it is lacks effectiveness.

Language and education

By far the greater part of formal education in Africa takes place in the primary school classroom; primary to secondary transition rates are, with a few exceptions (e.g. Botswana, South Africa), low. As a prime site of communication, it is clear that the language of the primary classroom is crucial, whether the class operates through child-centred activities, where knowledge is created through negotiation and where pair or group discussion is a frequent feature, or is run along teacher-dominated lines, where knowledge is transmitted from teacher to learners. It might be suggested, however, that if students do not understand the language that the teacher is using (with the same language also serving as the language of the textbooks) then learners in a teacher-dominated class are at more of a disadvantage than those in a learner-centred class, where there is at least the option of communicating with each other in a familiar language. Although in rich countries, especially the English-speaking ones, child-centred education is assumed to be the norm in state systems, there is ample research to suggest that in much of Sub-Saharan Africa the teaching is largely teacher dominated. It is not the purpose of this chapter to judge between the merits of child-centred versus teacher-dominated classrooms, but merely to point out the singular disadvantage of children in a teacher-dominated class who do not understand the teacher or the textbooks.

By way of example there follows an extract from a third-year reading class in Zambia (Williams 1996:199). It is typical of teaching in most 'Anglophone' Sub-Saharan African countries:

Teacher: We are going to read the story that is Chuma and the Rhino. That is paragraph three and four, which has been written on the board. Who can read the first sentence in paragraph three? Yes?

Pupil: Look at that hippo's mouth father.

Teacher: Read aloud.

Pupil: Look at that hippo's mouth father.

Teacher: Once more.

Pupil: Look at that hippo's mouth father.

Teacher: Yes. The sentence is 'Look at that hippo's mouth father'.

Class: Look at that hippo's mouth father.

Teacher: Look at that hippo's mouth father.

Class: Look at that hippo's mouth father.

The lesson continues in this vein, with no attention to the presentation or checking of meaning. Such rote-repetition of written text without comprehension is a 'reading-like' activity, but not reading in the sense of cognitive engagement with text (although it qualifies as a 'literacy practice'). Likewise, copying from the blackboard without comprehension is 'writing-like' but not 'true' writing, and has a similar implication for effective education.

It should come as no surprise that children subjected to this type of teaching fail to achieve command of English adequate for academic purposes. Their weak command of English (which, let us not forget, was the language of instruction in all subjects for the class above) is amply evidenced by test results from many quarters of Africa. In Zambia and Malawi, Williams (1996) administered modified cloze tests of 30 items in English and in ChiChewa (an important language spoken in both countries) to Year 5 students in six primary schools in each country. In Malawi 203 students out of 290 (70 per cent) were judged to have 'inadequate reading comprehension' in English, and in Zambia 150 out of 227 (66.1 per cent). This conclusion is roughly in line with other findings. Williams (1998) estimated that 74 per cent of Zambian students and 78 per cent of Malawian students at Year 6 had 'inadequate reading comprehension' in English, while the SACMEQ studies[3] (Nkamba and Kanyika 1998, Milner et al. 2001) concluded that 74.2 per cent of Zambian students and 78.4 per cent of Malawian pupils at also at Year 6 did not reach a minimum 'level of mastery' in reading English. Similar low levels of reading have been documented by SACMEQ for other countries in southern Africa: for Zimbabwe, Machingaidze et al. (1998:71) conclude that at Grade 6 between 60 per cent and 66 per cent of pupils did not reach 'the desirable levels' of reading in English. Comparable findings are reported for Zanzibar (Nassor and Mohammed 1998), Mauritius (Kulpoo 1998), and Namibia (Voigts 1998), and suggest that about two thirds of the students in each country are highly likely to have difficulties in understanding their English school texts in other subjects, and that very few of the remaining third have fluent comprehension. The situation in Rwanda is more drastic: results of a study by Williams et al. (2004), who tested 251 Year 6 students in five primary schools indicated that only two (0.77 per cent) could read adequately for their studies in English at primary level. These findings suggest that the Rwandan government's current policy – that English should be the sole medium of instruction from Year 3 of primary schooling – is likely to face difficulties (although fewer than those arising from the policy in force from 2009 until 2011, which decreed that English should be the sole medium of instruction from Year 1).

Conversely, in educational contexts where African languages are taught and employed as media of instruction, students display considerable proficiency, as might be expected. Test findings in African languages from the same primary school students in Malawi, Zambia and Rwanda as reported in the previous paragraph (Williams 1996 for Malawi and Zambia, Williams et al. 2004 for Rwanda,) tell a very different story. In Rwanda, testing in KinyaRwanda of the same 251 Year 6 students concluded that the vast majority of students (over 90 per cent) could read independently in that language. These were students who, at the time of testing (2003), had experienced KinyaRwanda as a medium of instruction. Likewise, the 290 Malawian students who scored poorly in English achieved a median score of over 65 per cent on ChiChewa tests, and the conclusion was that the overwhelming majority of Malawian students were adequate readers in ChiChewa. On the other hand, in Zambia, on a near-identical ChiNyanja test (ChiChewa and ChiNyanja being effectively two labels for one language), but where the local languages are largely neglected as subjects, and not used as media of instruction, the median score was ten per cent with only five students out of 227 scoring over 50 per cent.

If children in developing countries have little exposure to the language of instruction (be it English, French, Portuguese, etc.) outside the school, and if teaching the language of instruction is ineffective inside the school, then low quality education is inevitable. There is a considerable risk in such cases that the school experience may be a stultifying, rather than an enlightening one. Indeed, it is entirely likely that the above-mentioned findings by Cochrane and Farid (1989), Hobcraft (1993) and Fotso (2006), of the relatively weak effects of education on child survival in Sub-Saharan Africa, are simply the result of education in Africa being less effective, and the fact that the learners lack proficiency in the language of instruction must be a contributory factor.

The cognitive gains from investment in inadequate education are, as one would expect, negligible (Knight and Sabot 1990). Crucially then, it is effective education that enables individuals to acquire knowledge and skills, which in turn can contribute to development. The overwhelming case for educating children in a familiar language has been echoed, in the case of Africa, by repeated calls from educationists over the last hundred years (from the United Missionary Conference in Kenya in 1909, to the African Conference on Integration of African Languages and Cultures into Education, Burkina Faso, 2010) advocating a central role for African languages in primary education. Despite such views being widespread, governments have shown little will to change their policies, and their favouring of exoglossic languages such as English is generally supported by local communities for whom 'English equals education'. Families see English as a 'strong' language, and primary school English as the first step towards the coveted white-collar job. Although simple conversational skills (exemplified by responses to banal questions such as 'What is your name?' 'How old are you?' posed by one-off visitors to African classrooms) may be acquired within a year or two, what governments and families appear not to appreciate is the considerable amount of time, effort and resource that is needed to learn a language to a point where learners are capable of using it for academic purposes – widely agreed to take five to seven years (cf. Cummins 2000).

Political motivations in language policy

Why is the solution advocated by so many, namely to use a known language (probably, but not necessarily the child's mother tongue) not implemented in primary schools? One important answer is that the political will is lacking. The reasons for this lack of political will are various, some being relatively obvious and explicit, others more subtle. African governments invariably cite the need for national unification and development as reasons for eschewing African languages. John Mwanakatwe, Minister of Education in post-independence Zambia, a country with some 20 different languages (Kashoki 1990), spelled out the motivation clearly:

Even the most ardent nationalists of our time have accepted the inevitable fact that English – ironically a foreign language and also the language of our former colonial master – has definitely a unifying role in Zambia. (Mwanakatwe 1968)

Furthermore, the role of schools was crucial in promoting this unity through English:

> For the sake of communication between Zambians whose mother tongues differ and in order to promote the unity of the nation, it is necessary for all Zambian children to learn the national language [i.e. English] as early as possible, and to use it confidently. **(Ministry of Education Zambia 1976, para. 47)**

A similar situation obtained in Malawi, which has around 14 indigenous languages (Lewis 2009); although English was not regarded as the sole linguistic means of fostering national unity (ChiChewa was, from 1969, the medium of instruction in the first four years of primary education), it was an official language, and it is clear that within the 'upper levels' of state institutions English was intended to play a unifying role. It was made compulsory in parliament, and under the regime of President Banda all Members of Parliament were 'required to pass a stringent test' in it (Schmied 1991:24). While opting for English may have succeeded in preventing conflict in the educational arena between competing language groups, and while its dominance in the same arena is largely welcomed by the public, the language has, however, created division between, on the one hand, those who have good access to it, typically members of the reasonably well-off urban groups, and, on the other hand, those who do not, typically the members of poor urban and especially rural groups.

There is, however, a small but increasing proportion of pupils throughout Africa who gain access to high-quality English teaching through attending private fee-paying primary schools. Referring to this effect of English in Malawi, Kayambazinthu (1999:52) says that:

> The dominance and limited access to English ... has created an élite group, [whose] proficiency in English is near-native ... these élites maintain and regularly use their knowledge of English in their professional environments, where they typically occupy the middle ranks of the political, administrative and academic institutions.

Far from being a source of unity, the use of English in education in Africa has become a factor in national division, while the distribution of English proficiency in society is an indicator of the extent of this division. As Heugh (1999:306) puts it:

> ... the role of superimposed international languages has been hugely overestimated in their capacity to serve the interests of the majority on the continent [...] these languages serve only the interests of the élites.

'Élite closure' is the term Myers-Scotton (1990) has coined for the process whereby a small dominant establishment in African countries ensures that they and their families have access to high standards of English while inadequate education systems mean that this is largely denied to the majority. Perhaps the most extreme current example occurred in Rwanda where, following the massacres of 1994 and the intervention of the 'Anglophone' RPF (Rwandan Patriotic Front), political and economic power has tended to be concentrated in the hands of a relatively small English-speaking group, mainly educated in Uganda, who in 2009 introduced legislation to 'anglicise' Rwanda, with a 'straight for English' policy in primary education, accompanied by Rwanda joining the (ex-British) Commonwealth. This policy was modified in February 2011 such that KinyaRwanda became the medium of instruction for the first three years, with English as a subject. Nonetheless, since Rwanda is one of the few African countries where almost all inhabitants already share a common language (KinyaRwanda), this language policy does not seem to be focused on unification. It is therefore almost certain that Rwanda will generate a small English-proficient élite.

Likewise, as far as development is concerned, many governments look upon English as a vital tool. Yisa Claver (Director, Policy Planning at the Ministry of Education in Rwanda) commenting on Rwanda's 2009 decision to go 'straight for English' as a medium of instruction was clear on the role of the language in development:

> Really it is not choosing English for its own sake ... This is a way to make Rwanda to be equal, to use English ... English is now a world language, especially in trade and commerce. Rwanda is trying to attract foreign investors – most of these people are speaking English ... It's choosing English as a medium of instruction so we Rwandans of today, and tomorrow, will benefit. **(Quoted in McGreal 2009)**

To date, however, there is no doubt that in other countries in Africa, the dominant role of English in primary schools (the only level of education for the vast majority of people in poor countries) has proved to be a barrier to education, and hence to development, for the majority, since most students fail to acquire adequate academic competence in the language. It is no surprise then, that, whether one looks at development in terms of economic progress or of human needs, poor countries such as Malawi, Zambia and Rwanda that use English or French as a means of 'accessing development' have not hitherto made great strides, as Table 1 suggests.

Table 1: Indicators of development for Malawi, Zambia and Rwanda (UNICEF 2010)			
Indicator	Malawi	Zambia	Rwanda
Population below USD1.25 (GBP0.81) per day poverty line (%) (1992–2007)	74	64	77
GDP per capita average annual growth rate (%) (1990–2008)	0.6	0	1.5
Life expectancy in years (2008)	53	45	50
HIV/AIDS : 15–49 year old population (%) (2007)	11.9	15.2	2.8

In short, there is no evidence to suggest that the use of exoglossic languages such as French and English have contributed to development in proportion to their excessive dominance in educational and other official domains[4]. Nothing leads one to doubt Djité's opinion of nearly two decades ago (Djité 1993:149) that exoglossic languages have led neither to unity nor to development:

> Reliance and dependency on superimposed international languages to achieve development in Africa over the last three decades has proven to be a failure. Instead of leading to national unity, this attitude has significantly contributed to the socio-economic and political instability of most African countries.

Governments, however, are not entirely to blame: they have strong support from the majority of parents, for whom 'education equals English'. In South Africa, for example, local communities determine the medium of education for any given primary school, and although there is theoretically a choice of any of the 11 'official' South African languages as media of education, in practice the choice is overwhelmingly for English, which is regarded as a 'strong' language (Heugh 1999, Webb 1999). And of course, parents are not entirely misguided on that point – many white-collar jobs require English; however, to mystify millions of children over several generations in order for the few survivors (often taught at private schools or élite state schools) to obtain relatively well-remunerated employment is a questionable policy.

Zambia provides clear evidence of this 'education equals English' attitude: in 1996, the year when the Zambian policy document *Educating our Future* was being drafted, and also a general election year in the country, politicians were worried that to promote Zambian languages as media of instruction at the expense of English would be a potential vote-loser. 'It proved not possible, for political reasons, to go as far as changing the medium of instruction to a local language' (Linehan 2004:7). Ruling politicians 'made clear to senior education officials that unless a non-contentious formula [for including local languages] could be found, the political preference would be for maintenance of the status quo, with English remaining in the same position as it had done from 1965' (Linehan 2004:7). The compromise position was, that initial literacy in year one should be in one of the seven 'educationally approved' Zambian languages, while English continued officially to be the medium of instruction. Even so, some Zambian Members of Parliament protested that the 'new language policy ... forces children to learn in a foreign language' (Linehan 2004:8). Rather unexpectedly, 'a foreign language' here refers to a Zambian language, rather than to English.

The obverse of this over-estimation of English is the under-estimation of African languages, and the negative impact of English on national self-esteem. An early expression of this came in 1969 from Kapepwe, at the time Vice President of Zambia, who said:

> We should stop teaching children through English right from the start because it is the surest way of imparting inferiority complex in the children and the society. It is poisonous. It is the surest way of killing African personality and African culture. **(Cited in Serpell 1978:432)**

Factors in development

One should not, of course, overstate the case for local languages in education; likewise, one should not overstate the case for education as a factor in development. Appropriate language policies are not the entire answer to poor quality education, and effective education is not the entire answer to human and economic development. Hawes et al. (1986:13) point out that 'it would be foolish to make exaggerated claims for the power of education to solve [Africa's] profound problems'. For many African countries, there are a host of inhibiting domestic factors, including corruption, administrative inefficiency and armed conflict within or between countries. Likewise, climatic disasters frequently blight agricultural production, while the high incidence of HIV/AIDS is particularly debilitating at every level of society; the extent to which an effective state education system can operate within a malfunctioning state is debatable.

However, although there is no grand theory for sustainable development (see Kaul 1996, whose UN Committee concluded 'We simply do not know' how to achieve this aim), what is not disputed is that if poor countries are to provide better lives for their people in the modern world, then they need to acquire economic capital, social capital and human capital. By way of conclusion, we shall examine these three types of capital in the general African context:

Economic capital

In Africa, the framework of global economic structures within which countries have to operate renders economic growth problematic. Internationally, the industrialised countries have built up a technical advantage in manufacture which, without protectionism or massive technology transfer, is not likely to be bridged. With the failure of economic growth through structural adjustment programmes of the early 1990s in poor African countries (*The Economist* 1995:48), the developed world has since been seeking answers to development in policies oriented more to human needs (DfID 1997:1.7), while the World Bank 'is defining a new role for itself as a global welfare agency and is placing education firmly at the centre of its strategy' (Ilon 1997:414).

Although the 21st century has seen partial debt relief for a number of African countries, whether this is sufficient to turn around African economies is open to question. Likewise, adverse conditions of trade (e.g. rich countries imposing tariffs on imports from developing countries, while subsidising their own exports), although showing signs of ameliorating (UN 2005:38-39), are not likely to undergo the kind of changes that will bring about significant benefits in Africa. In short, as far as economic capital is concerned, outside agency, largely Western, has hitherto lacked the will to help Africa, while African agency lacks the resource. For most children in Africa, the 'level playing field' will continue to look decidedly uphill: poor quality education is both a cause and an outcome of poverty, at household and national levels (cf. Kadzamira and Rose 2003, Colclough et al. 2000). It remains to be seen to what extent the considerable and ongoing Chinese activity in Africa, in terms of investments, loans and a growing Chinese diaspora in Africa (see Addis Fortune 2010, Foster et al. 2008) affects this economic scene, and indeed, the linguistic landscape in Africa.

Social capital

While Bill Clinton's famous message 'It's the economy, stupid!' helped to secure victory for him in the US Presidential Election of 1992, development in Africa is not a matter of simply attending to economics. A number of observers of the African scene (e.g. Edwards 1999, Pakenham 1991, Reader 1997) claim that African countries will develop not through achieving a level economic playing field, but through transforming themselves into 'polities' – a 'polity' being a cohesive and functioning state (Edwards 1999:68). What polities need to function successfully is 'social capital', which is defined as a critical mass of trust, reciprocity and a sense of obligation between members of the polity at all levels, with governments and individuals committed to the welfare of all their fellow citizens.

Africa's crisis in this analysis is largely, although not entirely, brought about through a lack of social capital. Edwards (1999:66) claims that 'development needs stability, stability requires a legitimate state, and legitimacy rests on ... a level of political participation that is meaningful in local terms'. Many development specialists claim that it is 'the polity' that distinguishes the East Asian experience from that of most of Africa (e.g. Sachs 1996, cited in Edwards 1999:68) while Robinson (1996:170-171) stresses the importance of the social and political elements in development:

> [There is a] growing appreciation in development circles that development is certainly not only about economics, and may not even be primarily about economics ... [S]ocial and political development are seen as the underpinnings of economic development at least as much as the other way around (and probably more).

Likewise, over three decades ago President Kaunda of Zambia was wont to draw attention to the lack of 'civic responsibility' in his country, while Bamgbose (1991:44) claims that 'the primary causes of poverty are deficiencies in education, organisation and discipline'. In such analyses, the lack of social capital is seen as brought about by corrupt individual performances, which can be remedied when honest individuals take over.

Bayart (1993), however, has a different take on the nature of political power in the African state – that of 'the politics of the belly', where the expectation is that 'big men' generally, and state leaders in particular, will amass and redistribute wealth. Bayart is at pains to point out that this is not 'similar to a more or less erratic, 'political culture' for which it might be possible to substitute 'good governance'; rather it is a system of historic action whose origins must if possible be sought in the Braudelian longue durée.' (Bayart 1993:ix). And again:

> Anyone seeking to dismiss this form of politics as no more than a symptom of corruption or of the decadence of the state is making a grave mistake. These representations can be institutional. The authors of Nigeria's draft constitution in 1976, for example, defined political power as 'the opportunity to acquire riches and prestige, to be in a position to hand out benefits in the form of jobs, contracts, gifts of money, etc. to relations and political allies.' **(Bayart 1993:xvii)**

If Bayart's disquieting analysis of the exercise of power in Africa is correct, then the accumulation within African countries of social capital is problematic, since it suggests that leaders at all social levels will continue to amass wealth at the expense of the population generally, but will redistribute it to a group of 'relations and political allies'. True, individual leaders may be deposed by violence or the ballot box, but the system will continue. Thus Finlayson (2005:48) notes that although Bakili Muluzi, who took over democratically as President of Malawi from Kamuzu Banda, claimed to be a reformer, in due course 'Bad habits cultivated under the dictatorship of Kamuzu Banda started to reassert themselves ... [T]he slide into autocracy and corruption became inexorable'.

If Bayart's analysis is wrong, and the many cases of autocracy and corruption by African leaders are a matter of one-off deviancies which may in principle be halted, then the accumulation of social capital may be a more feasible eventuality. In either case, it is not clear that this mode of exercising political power, whether it is rooted in 'tradition' (for want of a better term), or simply the result of a sequence of rapacious leaders, can itself generate the agency for its own demise.

Human capital

What is crucial in human capital is effective education. Although there is no simple causal connection from the language through which education is conducted to the well-being of the state, the weight of evidence suggests that literacy skills are more easily acquired in a language with which learners are familiar, leading to more effective education; in turn, effective education can contribute to poverty alleviation and development. It is abundantly clear that education in a language that few learners, and not all teachers, have mastery of, detracts from quality and compounds the other problems arising from economically impoverished contexts. Robinson (2005:186) concludes from his review of Ouane (2003) that such 'patterns of language use in education systems continue to contribute to failure, alienation and waste', while Kelly (1995:6) delivers a harsher judgment on the compounding effect of the Zambian language policy:

> The colossal neglect of education during the years of economic collapse, droughts and sickness are among other adverse factors. But ... were it not for the language policy, we would have had better educated people who would have known better how to cope with the economic problem, and even with those arising from drought, AIDS and other extrinsic factors. **(my emphasis)**

While it is all very well to advocate that children be taught through their mother tongue, or at least a language with which they are familiar, an issue that cannot be avoided in this context is the choice of language of instruction. Sub-Saharan African countries are multilingual, some intensely so: even identifying the languages in a country can be problematic. Thus the 1990 Census of Zambia (CSO 1995:34) says, 'it has been estimated that the country has 72 tribes, each with its own unique language or dialect'. On the other hand, the Zambian linguist Kashoki (1990:109) claims that Zambia has 'approximately 80 Bantu dialects' which are grouped into slightly over 20 more or less mutually unintelligible clusters or 'languages', while Lewis (2009) lists 40 indigenous languages for Zambia. While this indeterminacy arises from political versus linguistic criteria for defining 'a language', it nonetheless suggests there will be difficulties in even arriving at the number of 'mother tongues' eligible as media of instruction (and Zambia is of course not the only country to feature such indeterminacy). Nonetheless, whatever method may be used to arrive at a total, the number of languages in Zambia, and in most African countries, remains considerable. Africa has between 1,000 and 2,500 depending on definitions, according to Ouane and Glanz (2010:8), who go on to say 'It is assumed that managing so many speech communities is problematic and costly'.

While practical solutions to this reality do not readily present themselves, one answer is to employ a language which is closely related to those spoken by all the learners, provided of course that they share related languages – thus the use of ChiChewa in Malawi does not seem to pose problems for speakers of other African languages in the country, according to research by Williams (2006:125-26). Where circumstances allow, this strategy offers a reasonable solution. Similarly, in urban contact areas where there is particularly intensive multilingualism, the most appropriate solution would seem to be to employ the language in which the learners communicate with each other outside the classroom. Such solutions require careful research and preparation, and are unlikely to be cost-free. Nevertheless, they arguably offer better value than using an ex-colonial language, where the learners' lack of proficiency in the medium of instruction means that there is massive wastage in the attempt to build human capital.

Conclusion

It is difficult to disagree with the above indictment by Kelly of the Zambian language policy. And of course, not only Zambia but the majority of African countries are affected by their educational language policy's failure to contribute to human capital. The crucial issue is how to take account of language diversity and at the same time deploy an educational language policy that is effective in empowering learners. African languages must play a part here, and at the same time access to a global language such as English is a political imperative: no African politicians are prepared to deny their citizens such access, inadequate though it may be in reality.

Effective teaching of English (or other ex-colonial language) as a subject in Africa, which is what occurs in much of the rest of the world, is the most obvious answer, rather than employing it as a medium of instruction. As to addressing the apparent lack of political will in this matter, there is no simple answer: African politicians seem convinced that the best way to teach English is to use it as a medium of instruction. However, they do not seem to have fully understood the difficulties of conducting state education in a language that few learners, and not all teachers, have mastered, nor have they understood the advantages of educating learners in their own languages. Likewise, it would appear that these politicians do not appreciate the risk to national development, nor the threat to national stability, posed by 'élite closure' which arises from their current educational language policies. There is also a less generous answer: that African politicians have indeed understood the issues, but that, in the final analysis, they have more pressing concerns than attempting to improve the welfare of their people through appropriate educational language policies.

Notes

1. 'A great 2010 World Cup can open doors for all of Africa, bringing much needed infrastructure, tourism and money to a continent that needs it more than any other.' (Burtner 2009)

2. Azariadis and Drazen offer no precise explanation for the failure of economic growth in countries where the threshold level of education obtained but they speculate on the effects of 'wasteful economic policies, wars and other political upheavals, natural disasters' (1990:519), together with flaws in the working of credit markets.

3. Large-scale pieces of research carried out on behalf of UNESCO by the Southern Africa Consortium for Monitoring Educational Quality.

4. In UNDP's Human Development Index for 2010, Malawi is ranked 153 out of 169 countries, Zambia 150 and Rwanda 153 (UNDP 2010; see also Appendix 1 below).

References

Addis Fortune. 2010. *Africa: China's complex view of Africa. All Africa.com*, 8 June 2010. Available online at *http://allafrica.com/stories/201006100397.html*

Anderson, C.A. 1966). *Literacy and schooling on the development threshold: Some historical cases*. In C.A.Anderson and M.J.Bowman (eds.), *Education and Economic Development*, 347-362. London: Frank Cass.

Azariadis, C. and Drazen, A. 1990. *Threshold externalities in economic development. The Quarterly Journal of Economics*, 501-526.

Bamgbose, A. 1991. *Language and the Nation. Edinburgh: Edinburgh University Press for the International African Institute.*

Bayart, J.-F. 1993. *The state in Africa: The Politics of the Belly. London: Longman.*

Burtner, K. 2009. *World Cup 2010 in South Africa: World event helps South Africa's economy. Suite 101.com* 11 May 2009. Available online at *http://south-africa.suite101.com/article.cfm/world_cup2010_in_south_africa*

Cochrane, S.H. and Farid S.M. 1989. *Fertility in Sub-Saharan Africa: Analysis and Explanation. World Bank Discussion Paper 43. Washington DC: World Bank.*

Colclough, C., Rose, P., and Tembon, M. 2000. *Gender inequalities in primary schooling: The roles of poverty and adverse cultural practice. International Journal of Educational Development* 20(1), 5-29.

CSO (Central Statistical Office), Zambia. 1995. *Census of Population, Housing and Agriculture, Volume 10. Lusaka: Central Statistical Office.*

Cummins, J. 2000. *Language, Power and Pedagogy: Bilingual Children in the Crossfire. Clevedon: Multilingual Matters.*

DfID (Department for International Development). 1997. *Eliminating World Poverty: A Challenge for the 21st Century. UK Government White Paper*, November, 1997. London: DfID.

Djité, P.G. 1993. *Language and development in Africa. International Journal of the Sociology of Language* 100/101, 149-166.

(The) Economist. 1995. *Biting the hand that squeezed them. Anonymous article*, 21 October 1995.

Edwards, M. 1999. *Future Positive: International Cooperation in the Twenty-first Century. London: Earthscan/Kogan Page.*

Finlayson, G. 2005. *Malawi: A suitable case for treatment? NORRAG News* 36, 48-49.

Foster, V., Butterfield, W., Chen, C. and Pushak, N. 2008 **Building Bridges: China's Growing Role as Infrastructure Financier for Sub-Saharan Africa**. Washington, World Bank. Available online at *www.globalclearinghouse.org/infradev/assets%5C10/ documents/Building%20Bridges.%20China%27s%20Growing%20Role%20as%20 Infrastructure%20Financier%20for%20Sub-Saharan%20Africa%20-%20Foster%20 %282009%29.pdf*

Fotso, J.-C. 2006. *Malawi's Future Human Capital: Is the Country on Track to Meeting the MDGs in Education? Laxenburg, Austria: International Institute for Applied Systems Analysis. www.iiasa.ac.at/Admin/PUB/Documents/IR-06-020.pdf*

Hawes, H., Coombe, T., Coombe, C. and Lillis, K. (eds). 1986. *Education Priorities and Aid Responses in Sub-Saharan Africa. London: ODA/University of London Institute of Education.*

Heugh, K. 1999). *Languages, development and reconstructing education in South Africa. International Journal of Educational Development* 19, 301-313.

Hicks, N.L. 1980. *Is there a trade-off between growth and basic needs? Finance and Development* 17(2), 17-20.

Hobcraft, J. 1993. *Women's education, child welfare and child survival: A review of the evidence. Health Transition Review* 3(2), 159-75.

Ilon, L. 1997. *The changing role of the World Bank: Education policy as global welfare. Policy and Politics* 24(4), 413- 424.

Kadzamira, E. and Rose, P. 2003. *Can free primary education meet the needs of the poor? Evidence from Malawi. International Journal of Educational Development*, 23, 501-516.

Kashoki, M.E. 1990. *The Factor of Language in Zambia. Lusaka: Kenneth Kaunda Foundation.*

Kaul, I. 1996. *Globalisation and human development*. Paper presented at EADI Annual Conference, Vienna, September 1996.

Kayambazinthu, E. 1999. *The language planning situation in Malawi. In R.B.Kaplan and R.B.Baldauf (eds), Language Planning in Malawi, Mozambique and the Philippines, 15-85. Clevedon: Multilingual Matters.*

Kelly, M. 1995. *Language policy in education in Zambia.* Paper presented at the Zambia National Reading Forum, Lusaka.

Knight, J.B. and Sabot, R.H. 1990. *Education, Productivity and Inequality: The East African Natural Experiment. Oxford: Oxford University Press for the World Bank.*

Kulpoo, D. 1998. *The Quality of Education: Some Policy Suggestions Based on a Survey of Schools: Mauritius.* (Southern Africa Consortium for Monitoring of Educational Quality, Policy Research Report 1.) *Paris: International Institute for Educational Planning, UNESCO.*

Lewis, M.P. (ed.). 2009. **Ethnologue: Languages of the World**. 16th edition. Dallas, Tex: SIL International. Available online at *www.ethnologue.com/*

Linehan, S. 2004. *Language of instruction and the quality of basic education in Zambia.* Paper prepared for UNESCO.

Lockheed, M.E., Jamison, D.T. and Lau, L.J. 1980. *Farmer education and farm efficiency: A survey. Economic Development and Cultural Change* 29, 37-76.

Machingaidze, T., Pfukani, P. and Shumba, S. 1998. *The Quality of Education: Some Policy Suggestions Based on a Survey of Schools: Zimbabwe.* (Southern Africa Consortium for Monitoring of Educational Quality, Policy Research Report 3.) *Paris: International Institute for Educational Planning, UNESCO.*

McGreal, C. 2009. *Why Rwanda said adieu to French. Guardian Weekly* 16 January 2009. Available online at *www.guardian.co.uk/education/2009/jan/16/rwanda-english-genocide*

Milner, G., Chimombo, J., Banda, T. and Mchikoma, C. 2001. *The Quality of Primary Education in Malawi: An Interim Report.* (Southern Africa Consortium for Monitoring of Educational Quality Working Document.) *Paris: International Institute for Educational Planning, UNESCO.*

Ministry of Education, Zambia. 1976. *Education for Development: Draft Statement on Educational Reform. Mimeo. Lusaka: Ministry of Education, Zambia.*

Moock, P.R. and Addou, H. 1994. *Agricultural productivity and education. In International Encyclopedia of Education, Volume I*, 244-54. Oxford: Pergamon Press.

Mwanakatwe, J.M. 1968. *The Growth of Education in Zambia since Independence. Lusaka: Oxford University Press.*

Myers-Scotton, C. 1990. *Élite closure as boundary maintenance: The evidence from Africa. In B.Weinstein (ed.), Language Policy and Political Development*, 25-41. Norwood, NJ: Ablex.

Nassor, S. and Mohammed, K.A. 1998. *The Quality of Education: Some Policy Suggestions Based on a Survey of Schools: Zanzibar.* (Southern Africa Consortium for Monitoring of Educational Quality, Policy Research Report 4.) *Paris: International Institute for Educational Planning, UNESCO.*

Nkamba, M. and Kanyika, J. 1998. *The Quality of Education: Some Policy Suggestions Based on a Survey of Schools: Zambia.* (Southern Africa Consortium for Monitoring of Educational Quality, Policy Research Report 5.) *Paris: International Institute for Educational Planning, UNESCO.*

Ouane, A. (ed.). 2003. *Towards a Multilingual Culture of Education. Hamburg: UNESCO Institute for Lifelong Learning.*

Ouane, A. and Glanz, C. 2010. *Why and How Africa Should Invest in African Languages and Multilingual Education. Hamburg: UNESCO Institute for Lifelong Learning.*

Pakenham, T. 1991. *The Scramble for Africa. London: George Weidenfield and Nicolson.*

Rassool, N. 1999. *Literacy for Sustainable Development in the Age of Information. Clevedon: Multilingual Matters.*

Reader, J. 1997. *Africa: A Biography of the Continent. Harmondsworth: Penguin.*

Robinson, C.D.W. 1996. *Language Use in Rural Development: An African Perspective. The Hague: Mouton de Gruyter.*

Robinson, C.D.W. 2005. *Review of Ouane, A. (ed.) 2003. International Journal of Educational Development* 25, 183-186.

Rogers, A. 1990. *Background to the seminar. In B.Street (ed.), Literacy in Development, 2-4. London: Education for Development and the Commonwealth Institute.*

Sachs, J. 1996. *Growth in Africa. The Economist* 29 June 1996, 19-21.

Schmied, J. 1991. *English in Africa. London: Longman.*

Serpell, R. 1978. *Some developments in Zambia since 1971. In S.Ohannessian and M.Kashoki (eds), Language in Zambia, 424-447. London: International African Institute.*

Street, B.V. 1984. *Literacy in Theory and Practice. Cambridge: Cambridge University Press.*

Tabatabai, H. 1995. *Poverty and inequality in developing countries: A review of evidence. In G.Rodgers and R. van der Hoeven (eds), New Approaches to Poverty Analysis and Poverty, Volume 3*, 13-35. *Geneva: International Labour Office.*

Tikly, L. 2003. *The African Renaissance, NEPAD and skills formation: An identification of key policy tensions. International Journal of Education Development* 25(3), 543-564.

UN (United Nations). 2005. *The Millennium Development Goals. New York: United Nations.*

UNDP (United Nations Development Programme). 2010. *The Real Wealth of Nations: Pathways to Human Development. (Human Development Report 2010, 20th Anniversary Edition.) Basingstoke and New York: Palgrave Macmillan for UNDP.* Available online at *http://hdr.undp.org/en/*

UNICEF (United Nations Children's Fund). 2010. *Info by Country: Eastern and Southern Africa. New York: UNICEF*. Available online at *www.unicef.org/infobycountry/esaro.html*

Voigts, F. 1998. *The Quality of Education: Some Policy Suggestions Based on a Survey of Schools: Namibia. (Southern Africa Consortium for Monitoring of Educational Quality, Policy Research Report 2.) Paris: International Institute for Educational Planning, UNESCO.*

Webb, V. 1999). *Multilingualism in democratic South Africa: The overestimation of language policy. International Journal of Educational Development 19*, 351-366.

Wheeler, D. 1980. *Human Resources Development and Economic Growth in Developing Countries: A Simultaneous Model.* World Bank Staff Working Paper 407. Washington DC: World Bank.

Wickstead, M. 2005. *Has 2005 been the year of Africa? NORRAG News* 36, 37-38.

Williams, E. 1996. *Reading in two languages at Year 5 in African primary schools. Applied Linguistics* 17(2), 182-209.

Williams, E. 1998. *Investigating Bilingual Literacy: Evidence from Malawi and Zambia. London: DfID Education Research.*

Williams, E. 2006. *Bridges and Barriers: Language in African Education and Development. Encounters Series. Manchester: St.Jerome.*

Williams, E., de Montfort-Nayimfashe, L., Ntakirutimana, E. and O'Sullivan, B. 2004. *Proficiency in French, English and KinyaRwanda in the Primary and Secondary Sectors of the Rwandan Education System. Unpublished report commissioned by CfBT Education Trust for the Department for International Development.*

4

Language policy in education and the role of English in India: From library language to language of empowerment

Ramanujam Meganathan

Introduction

Throughout India, there is an extraordinary belief, among almost all castes and classes, in both rural and urban areas, in the transformative power of English. English is seen not just as a useful skill, but as a symbol of a better life, a pathway out of poverty and oppression. Aspiration of such magnitude is a heavy burden for any language, and for those who have responsibility for teaching it, to bear. The challenges of providing universal access to English are significant, and many are bound to feel frustrated at the speed of progress. But we cannot ignore the way that the English language has emerged as a powerful agent for change in India. (Graddol 2010:120)

This chapter explores language policy-making processes in the Indian context, implementation issues and the place and role of English in school education. Language in education policy derives from the Indian Constitution which guarantees linguistic rights to all citizens; most importantly, members of minority groups (both religious and linguistic) are granted a special right to be educated in their mother tongue. Despite this consensus, there have been numerous political and educational controversies regarding implementation of these constitutional provisions.

The national language policy (or strategy) for school education, the three-language formula recommended by the National Commission on Education 1964–1966, was incorporated into the national education policies of 1968 and 1986. Accommodating at least three-languages in school education has been seen as a convenient strategy, but concerns have also been expressed from various quarters about its 'unsatisfactory' implementation.

India's pluralism is reflected in its linguistic diversity. According to the 1971 census, the country has 1,652 languages belonging to five different language families: Indo-

Aryan, Dravidian, Austro-Asiatic, Tibeto-Burmese and Semito-Hamitic (GOI 1971). The Indian constitution identifies 22 'recognised languages'. About 87 languages are used in print media, 71 languages are used on radio and the administration of the country is conducted in 15 languages. According to Rao (2008), two decades ago the number of languages used as media of instruction was about 60 but by the time Rao's study was carried out the number had dropped to 47. (As we will see below, it appears that this number has now fallen further still.) English – formerly perceived as a library language and the language of higher education – is now in demand by every quarter as a means of progress and the key to a better life. As Graddol points out, the language which was a 'key part of the mechanism of exclusion because of its very unequal distribution in society' is now seen 'as a means of inclusion' (Graddol 2010:120). The English language in India today is both an admired and a hated phenomenon. On the one hand, there is an increasing demand for the language which is associated with progress and development, while on the other the language is perceived as a killer of native or indigenous languages.

The demand for English emerges from many factors, as recognised by the position paper on the teaching of English produced by the National Council of Educational Research and Training (NCERT 2006) in connection with the National Curriculum Framework 2005 (NCERT 2005):

> *English in India today is a symbol of people's aspirations for quality in education and fuller participation in national and international life ... The level of introduction of English has now become a matter of political response to people's aspirations, rendering almost irrelevant an academic debate on the merits of a very early introduction.* **(NCERT 2006:1)**

However, the disparity in the quality of English language education experienced by children further intensifies the already existing divide between English language-rich and English language-poor children. The present condition of English language teaching in the varied contexts of India is summed up in the following manner:

1. ↑↑TP ↑↑EE (e.g. English medium private/government aided elite schools): Proficient teachers; varying degrees of English in the environment, including as a home or first language.

2. ↑TP ↑EE (e.g. New English medium; private schools, many of which use both English and other Indian languages): Teachers with limited proficiency; children with little or no background in English; parents aspire to upward mobility through English.

3. ↓TP ↓EE (e.g. Government-aided regional medium schools): Schools with a tradition of English education along with regional languages, established by educational societies, with children from a variety of backgrounds.

4. ↓↓TP ↓↓EE (e.g. Government regional medium schools run by district and municipal education authorities): They enrol the largest number of elementary school children in rural India. They are also the only choice for the urban poor (who, however, have some options of access to English in the environment). Their teacher may be the least proficient in English in these four types of school.

TP = Teachers' English language proficiency; EE = English language environment
(Kurrien 2005 quoted in NCERT 2006:9)

The rest of this chapter consists of seven sections, beginning with a brief historical overview of the three-language policy. The next section discusses the number of languages taught in Indian schools. This is followed by details of languages taught as first, second and third languages. The following section looks at the languages used as media of instruction. There is then a section focusing on the introduction of the second and third languages. The penultimate section then summarises all the findings reported here which relate to English and the chapter ends with a conclusion.

Language policy in school education: The three-language formula

Language planning for school education in India can be seen more as a question of status planning rather than corpus or acquisition planning. The language policy which emerged as a political consensus in the formative years of independence is also an illustration of democratic processes in the Asian context. The three-language formula emerged as a policy or a strategy after a quarter of a century of debate and deliberations from political and academic perspectives by educational advisory bodies and politicians representing national and regional interests.

The Central Advisory Board on Education (CABE), the oldest statutory body on education in India, initiated the discussion on languages in school education in the 1940s and this continued to be a major concern in their discussions until 1960. CABE identified five major issues which required attention:

1. The number of languages to be taught at various levels of school education

2. The introduction of second and third languages

3. The place and role of English

4. The place and role of Hindi

5. The teaching of Sanskrit and minor language(s) in school.

The Board devised the 'three-language formula' in its 23rd meeting held in 1956 with a view to removing inequalities among the languages of India. It recommended that three-languages should be taught in the Hindi as well as non-Hindi-speaking areas of the country at the middle and high school stages and suggested the following two possible formulae:

1. (a) i. Mother tongue or
         ii. Regional language or
         iii. A composite course of mother tongue and a regional language or
         iv. A composite course of mother tongue and a classical language or
         v. A composite course of regional language or a classical language,
    (b) Hindi or English
    (c) A modern Indian language or a modern European language provided it has not already been taken under (a) and (b) above.

2. (a) As above

(b) English or a modern European language

(c) Hindi (for non-Hindi-speaking areas) or another modern Indian language (for Hindi-speaking areas)

(MOE 1957, quoted in Agarwal 1993:79)

The three-language formula was simplified and approved by the Conference of Chief Ministers held in 1961 as follows:

1. The regional language or the mother tongue when the latter is different from the regional language

2. Hindi or any other Indian language in Hindi speaking areas; and

3. English or any other modern European language.

(GOI 1962:67)

CABE also deliberated in detail on the study of English as a compulsory subject as recommended by the education ministers' conference held in 1957:

1. English should be taught as a compulsory language both at the secondary and the university stages, students acquire adequate knowledge of English so as to be able to receive education through this language at the university level.

2. English should not be introduced earlier than class V. The precise point at which English should be started at the middle stage was left to each individual state to decide.

(MOE 1957, quoted in Agarwal 1993:98)

A comprehensive view of the study of languages at school was undertaken and concrete recommendations were made by the Education Commission between 1964 and 1966 (MOE 1966). The Commission, having taken account of the diversity of the Indian context, recommended a modified or graduated three-language formula:

1. The mother tongue or the regional language

2. The official language of the Union or the associate official language of the Union so long as it exists; and

3. A modern Indian or foreign language not covered under (1) and (2) and other than that used as the medium of instruction.

(MOE 1966:192)

The Commission's observation on the status and role of English is of importance from the point of view of language planning and the way the language was perceived by policy planners. The Commission said:

*English will continue to enjoy a high status so long as it remains the principal
medium of education at the university stage, and the language of administration
at the Central Government and in many of the states. Even after the regional
languages become media of higher education in the universities, a working
knowledge of English will be a valuable asset for all students and a reasonable
proficiency in the language will be necessary for those who proceed to the
university. (MOE 1966:192)*

This brief historical scan of the evolution of the language policy in India tells us how
the apprehension about the dominance of English (as a colonial language which
signifies the master's language) has been naturally alleviated by the role which
the language has attained. This is in spite of the efforts (political and systemic) to
contain its spread. Today, every child and parent wants the language.

Number of languages available and taught

The Sixth All India School Education Survey in 1993 explored the number of
languages actually taught and the number of languages actually used as media
of instruction at different stages of schooling throughout India. It also found the
number and percentage of schools teaching particular languages and using
specific languages as media of instruction (NCERT 1993). The Seventh All India
Survey replicated this research in 2002 and its report was published in 2007
(NCERT 2007).

According to the 2002 Survey, the number of schools in the country having
primary, upper primary, secondary and higher secondary stages are 850,421,
337,980, 130,675 and 43,869 respectively (NCERT 2007).

Some of the findings of the two surveys are summarised in Table 1.

Table 1: School language policies in India (per cent)

Policies	Primary		Upper primary		Secondary	
	1993	2002	1993	2002	1993	2002
'Three-Language Formula' offered	*	*	82.16	90.61	79.54	84.86
Two or more languages offered	34.85	91.95	95.56	90.61	96.65	84.86
Hindi taught as first language	40.49	59.70	38.25	39.92	30.85	33.08
Hindi taught as second language	11.97	-	29.81	-	31.99	-
English taught as first language**	2.09	-	4.52	9.89	6.57	13.26
English taught as second language	60.33	-	55.05	-	54.12	-

*The Three-language Formula comes into effect from Class 6.
**Although it is very difficult to define English as a first language in India, some schools and school
systems mentioned it as a first language.

Table 1 shows that in 2002 nearly 91 per cent of schools followed the three-language formula at the upper primary stage and almost 85 per cent did so at the secondary stage. An increase in the percentage of schools following the formula can be seen because in 1993 the corresponding figures were 82 per cent and almost 80 per cent respectively.

Table 1 also reveals that in 2002 almost 40 per cent of schools at the upper primary stage and 33 per cent at the secondary stage were teaching Hindi as a first language. These figures show a slight increase compared to 1993 when the comparable figures were 38 per cent and 31 per cent respectively.

Meanwhile, in 2002 almost ten per cent of schools at the upper primary stage and 13 per cent of schools at the secondary stage claimed to be teaching English as a first language. Although these figures are still relatively modest they indicate that the percentage of schools teaching English as a first language had more or less doubled over a period of ten years, from five per cent and seven per cent respectively. (It has to be remembered that the term 'first language' is used here in the context of India's three-language policy. In other words, it is the first language which the child encounters at school and not necessarily the child's own first language or mother tongue.)

Box 1 lists all the languages taught in each state and Union Territory. The information shown here was collected from curricular documents, syllabi and statements by officials in the states and UTs. The information covers all stages of schooling from Primary to Higher Secondary, from Classes I to XII. The languages listed here are taught as first, second, third, classical and elective languages.

Box 1: Languages taught in the school curriculum			
No.	**State/Union Territory**	**Languages available/offered**	**Total languages available**
1.	Andhra Pradesh	Telugu, Urdu, Hindi, Tamil, Kannada, Oriya, Marathi, Sanskrit, Persian, Arabic, English	11
2.	Arunachal Pradesh	English, Hindi, Sanskrit, Assamese, Butia, Bhoti	6
3.	Assam	Assamese, Bengali, Bodo, Garo, Hindi, Khasi, Manipuri, Mizo, Nepali, Urdu, Hmar, Sanskrit, Persian, Arabic, English	15
4.	Bihar	Hindi, Urdu, Bengali, English, Bhojpuri, Arabic, Maithili, Persian, Magahi, Sanskrit	10
5.	Chhattisgarh	Hindi, English, Marathi, Bengali, Gujarati, Tamil, Punjabi, Urdu, Sindhi, Telugu, Malayalam, Sanskrit, Kannada, Oriya	14
6.	Goa	Konkani, Marathi, Hindi, English, Urdu, French, Portuguese, Sanskrit, Arabic	9
7.	Gujarat	Gujarati, Hindi, Marathi, English, Urdu, Sindhi, Tamil, Sanskrit	8
8.	Haryana	Hindi, English, Punjabi, Sanskrit, other MILs	4

9.	Himachal Pradesh	Hindi, English, Sanskrit, other MILs	3
10.	Jammu and Kashmir	Urdu, Kashmiri, English, Dogri, Punjabi, Arabic, Sanskrit, Persian, Gojri, Pahari, Hindi	11
11.	Jharkhand	Bengali, English, Hindi, Urdu, others	4
12.	Karnataka	Kannada, English, Hindi, Marathi, Urdu, Telugu, Tamil, Sanskrit, Arabic, Konkani, Persian	11
13.	Kerala	Malayalam, Tamil, Kannada, Sanskrit, Hindi, English, Urdu, Arabic, French, Latin, Syriac, Russian	12
14.	Madhya Pradesh	Hindi, English, Urdu, Marathi, Sanskrit, Punjabi, Sindhi, Malayalam, Persian, Arabic, French, Russian	12
15.	Maharashtra	Data could not be collected	-
16.	Manipur	Manipuri, Hindi, English, Bengali, Paite, Hmar, Thadou-Kuki, Mizo, Tangkhul, Zou, Nepali, Kom, Vaiphei, Mao	14
17.	Meghalaya	Data could not be collected	-
18.	Mizoram	Mizo, English, Hindi, Bengali, Nepali, Manipuri	6
19.	Nagaland	English, Jenyidie, Sumi, Ao, Lotha, Hindi, Bengali	7
20.	Orissa	Oriya, Urdu, Bengali, Hindi, Telugu, English, Sanskrit, Persian	8
21.	Punjab	Punjabi, Hindi, Urdu, English, Sanskrit, Persian, Arabic, Nepalese, Tibetan, French, German, Portuguese, Russian, Bengali, Gujarati, Marathi, Telugu, Tamil, Malayalam, Oriya, Kannada	23
22.	Rajasthan	Hindi, English, Sanskrit, Urdu, Sindhi, Gujarati, Punjabi, Malayalam, Tamil, Rajasthani, Prakrit, Persian	12
23.	Sikkim	English, Nepali, Bhutia, Lepeha, Limboo, Newari, Tamang, Sharpa, Gurung, Rai, Manger, Sunuwar, Hindi	13
24.	Tamil Nadu	Tamil, Malayalam, Telugu, Urdu, English, Hindi, Kannada	7
25.	Tripura	Bengali, Kokbarok, English, Bishnupriya, Chokma, Manipuri, Holam, Kuki, Lakshai, Hindi	10
26.	Uttar Pradesh	Hindi, English, Sanskrit, Urdu, Pali, Arabic, Persian, Latin, Gujarati, Punjabi, Bengali, Marathi, Assamese, Kannada, Kashmiri, Sindhi, Tamil, Telugu, Malayalam, Nepali, French, German, Tibetan, Chinese, Russian	25
27.	Uttaranchal	Hindi, Sanskrit, English, Urdu, Bengali, Punjabi, Nepali,	7
28.	West Bengal	Bengali, English, Hindi, Urdu, Oriya, Tamil, Telugu, Gujarati, Tibetan, Nepali, Santhali as first language with Alchiki script	11
29.	Andaman and Nicobar Islands	English, Hindi, Tamil, Telugu, Bengali	5
30.	Chandigarh	Punjabi, Hindi, Urdu, English, Sanskrit, Persian, Arabic, Nepalese, Tibetan, French, German, Portuguese, Russian, Bengali, Gujarati, Marathi, Telugu, Tamil, Malayalam, Oriya, Kannada	21

31.	Dadra Naagar Haveli	English, Gujarati, Hindi, Marathi, Sanskrit, others	5
32.	Daman and Diu	Gujarati, Hindi, English	3
33.	Delhi	Hindi, Urdu, Punjabi, English, Sanskrit; also any modern Indian language as students wish	5
34.	Lakshadweep	Data could not be collected	-
35.	Puducherry	Tamil, Malayalam, Telugu, Urdu, English, Hindi, French, Kannada	8

Box 1 shows that three states/UTs did not provide data. Among the remaining 32 states/UTs, Daman and Diu offers the smallest number of languages – just three – while at the other extreme 21 languages are taught as subjects in Chandigarh, 23 in Punjab and 25 in Uttar Pradesh.

Table 2: Most frequently mentioned languages offered by states/UTs		
No.	**Language**	**Number of states/UTs offering this language N=32**
1=	Hindi	32
1=	English	32
3=	Urdu	21
3=	Sanskrit	21
5	Bengali	15
6	Tamil	13
7	Telugu	12
8=	Arabic	11
8=	Persian	11
10=	Punjabi	10
10=	Marathi	10
12=	Malayalam	9
12=	Kannada	9
12=	Gujarati	9
15	French	7
Sub-total		222
60 other languages		98
Total		320

Table 2 summarises the data in Box 1. The total number of language choices available is 320, an average of ten language choices per state/UT, with, as we saw, a range from three to 25. The two most frequently offered languages are Hindi and English, both of which are taught in all 32 states which made data available.

Another 13 languages are frequently offered by between seven and 21 different states. These 15 most frequently taught languages, therefore, account for 222 (69 per cent) of the 320 language choices available. A further 60 different languages are offered, accounting for just 98 language choices (1.6 states/UTs per language). Thus, in total, 75 different languages are taught in Indian schools (excluding the three states for which information is not available), but Hindi and English between them account for 20 per cent of all the language choices available.

Languages taught as first, second and third language

Languages are taught or available to learners as first, second and third language.

Regarding the number of languages available and offered to students in 2002, the numbers are:

Upper primary
96.32 per cent of schools offered just one language as the first language 3.68 per cent of schools offered a choice of two or more languages as the first language

Secondary
93.62 per cent of schools offered only one language as the first language 6.38 per cent of schools offered a choice of two or more languages as the first language

Full details of the languages taught as first, second and third language in each state/UT are given in Box 2.

Box 2: First, second and third languages					
No.	State/Union Territory	Stage of schooling	Languages available/offered		
			1st language	2nd language	3rd language
1.	Andhra Pradesh	Primary	Mother tongue/ regional language, Telugu, Urdu, Hindi, Tamil, Kannada, Oriya, Marathi, Sanskrit, Persian, Arabic	-	English from Class III
		Upper Primary	Telugu, Urdu, Hindi, Tamil, Kannada, Oriya, Marathi, Sanskrit, Persian, Arabic	Hindi, English	English, Hindi
		Secondary	Mother tongue, Telugu, Urdu, Hindi, Tamil, Kannada, Oriya, Marathi, Sanskrit, Persian, Arabic	Hindi	English

2.	Arunachal Pradesh	Primary	English	Hindi	-
		Upper Primary	English	Hindi	Sanskrit, Assamese, Butia, Bhoti
		Secondary	English	Hindi	-
		Higher Secondary	English	-	-
3.	Assam	Primary	Assamese, Bengali, English	English	-
		Upper Primary	Assamese, Bengali, English	English	Arabic, Assamese, Hindi, Sanskrit
		Secondary	Assamese, Bengali, English	English	-
4.	Bihar	Primary	Hindi, Urdu, Bengali	English	-
		Upper Primary	Hindi, Urdu, Bengali	English	Sanskrit
		Secondary	Hindi, Urdu, Bengali	English	
5.	Chhattisgarh	Primary	Hindi, English	Hindi, English	-
		Upper Primary	Hindi, English	Hindi, English	Sanskrit
		Secondary	Hindi, English	Hindi, English	Sanskrit
6.	Goa	Primary	Konkani, Marathi	English	-
		Upper Primary	English	Hindi	Konkani, Marathi
		Secondary	English	Hindi	Konkani, Marathi, French, Portuguese
		Higher Secondary	English	Konkani, Hindi, Marathi, Urdu, French	Modern Indian language (MIL)
7.	Gujarat	Primary	Gujarati, English	Gujarati, Hindi	-
		Upper Primary	Gujarati, English	Gujarati, Hindi	Hindi, English
		Secondary	Gujarati, English	Gujarati, Hindi	Hindi, English
8.	Haryana	Primary	English, Hindi, MIL	-	-
		Upper Primary	English, Hindi, MIL	English, Hindi	Punjabi, Sanskrit, MIL
		Secondary	English, Hindi, MIL	English, Hindi	-
9.	Himachal Pradesh	Primary	Hindi, English	-	-
		Upper Primary	English, Hindi	English, Hindi	Sanskrit
		Secondary	English, Hindi	English, Hindi	Sanskrit

10.	Jammu and Kashmir	Primary	Hindi, Urdu	English	Kashmiri
		Upper Primary	Hindi, Urdu	English	Kashmiri
		Secondary	Hindi, Urdu	English	Dogri, Punjabi, Arabic, Sanskrit, Persian
		Higher Secondary	English	Hindi, Urdu	Dogri, Punjabi, Arabic, Sanskrit, Persian
11.	Jharkhand	Primary	Bengali, English, Hindi, Sanskrit, others	-	-
		Upper Primary	Bengali, English, Hindi, Urdu, others	English, Hindi, Sanskrit, others	English, Hindi, Sanskrit, others
		Secondary	Bengali, English, Hindi, Urdu, others	English, Hindi, Sanskrit, others	English, Hindi, Sanskrit, others
12.	Karnataka	Primary	Kannada, English, Hindi, Marathi, Urdu, Telugu, Tamil	-	-
		Upper Primary	Kannada, English, Hindi, Marathi, Urdu, Telugu, Tamil	Kannada, English	Kannada, English, Sanskrit, Hindi, Arabic, Persian, Konkani
		Secondary	Kannada, English, Hindi, Marathi, Urdu, Telugu, Tamil	-	Kannada, English, Sanskrit, Hindi, Arabic, Persian, Konkani
13.	Kerala	Primary	Malayalam, Tamil, Kannada	English	-
		Upper Primary	Malayalam, Tamil, Kannada; Option: Sanskrit/ Arabic/Urdu	English	Hindi
		Secondary	English	Malayalam/ Tamil, Kannada, Sanskrit, Arabic, Urdu, Hindi, Syriac, French	-

14.	Madhya Pradesh	Primary	Mother tongue	General English or General Hindi	Urdu, Sanskrit, Marathi or any other MIL
		Upper Primary	Mother tongue	General English or General Hindi	Urdu, Sanskrit, Marathi or any other MIL
		Secondary	Hindi, English, Urdu Sanskrit	Hindi, English	Any other MIL other than languages studied as Language L1 and L2
15.	Maharashtra	Primary	Hindi, Marathi	English	-
		Upper Primary	Marathi, English	Hindi, Marathi, others	English, Hindi, others
		Secondary	Marathi, English	Hindi, Marathi, others	English, Hindi, others
16.	Manipur	Primary (two languages)	Manipuri, Hindi, one of ten recognised tribal languages/MIL	English	-
		Upper Primary (three languages)	Manipuri, Hindi, one of ten recognised tribal languages/MIL	English	Manipuri, Hindi, one of ten recognised tribal languages/MIL
		Secondary (two languages)	Manipuri, Hindi, Assamese, Bengali, Mizo, Paite, Hmar, Tangkhul, Nepali, Zou, Thadou-Kuki, Vaiphei, Korm, Mao	English	-
17.	Meghalaya	Primary	English, Garo, Khasi, others	English, Garo, Khasi, others	-
		Upper Primary	English, Garo, Khasi, others	English, Garo, Khasi, Hindi, others	Hindi, others
		Secondary	English, Garo, Khasi, others	English, Garo, Khasi, Hindi, others	Hindi, others
18.	Mizoram	Primary	Mizo	English	Hindi
		Upper Primary	Mizo	English	Hindi
		Secondary	English	Mizo	Hindi up to Class VIII
		Higher Secondary	English	Mizo	-

19.	Nagaland	Primary	English	MIL, alternative English	Hindi
		Upper Primary	English	MIL, alternative English	Hindi
		Secondary	English	MIL, alternative English	-
		Higher Secondary	English	MIL, alternative English	-
20.	Orissa	Primary	Oriya	English	-
		Upper Primary	Oriya, Hindi, Sanskrit, others	English	Hindi, Sanskrit
		Secondary	Oriya, Hindi, Sanskrit, others	English	Hindi, Sanskrit
21.	Punjab	Primary Class I–III	Punjabi, Hindi and Urdu as first language	English as compulsory language	-
		Primary Class IV–V as 2nd language	Punjabi, Hindi, Urdu	English as compulsory language	Punjabi, Hindi, Urdu (if not studied as L1)
		Upper Primary	Punjabi, Hindi, Urdu	English	Punjabi, Hindi, Urdu and many more MIL (not studied as L2)
		Secondary	Punjabi (pass in Punjabi is compulsory)	English	Hindi; one of following languages can be taken as elective subject: Sanskrit, Urdu, Persian, Arabic, Nepalese, Tibetan, French, German, Portuguese, Russian, Bengali, Gujarati, Marathi, Telugu, Tamil, Malayalam, Oriya, Kannada

22.	Rajasthan	Primary	Hindi	English	-
		Upper Primary	Hindi	English	Sanskrit, Urdu, Sindhi, Gujarati, Punjabi
		Secondary	Hindi	English	Sanskrit, Urdu, Sindhi, Gujarati, Punjabi
23.	Sikkim	Primary	English	MIL/local/tribal languages	Hindi (from Class IV-V)
		Upper Primary	English	MIL/local/tribal languages	Hindi
		Secondary	Data could not be collected		
24.	Tamil Nadu	Primary	Tamil, Telugu, Kannada, Urdu, Malayalam, Hindi	English	-
		Upper Primary	Tamil, Telugu, Kannada, Urdu, Malayalam, Hindi	English	-
		Secondary	Tamil, Telugu, Kannada, Urdu, Malayalam, Hindi	English	-
25.	Tripura	Primary	Bengali, Kokborok, English, Bishnupriya, Manipuri, Chokma, Holam, Kuki	English	-
		Upper Primary	Bengali, English	English, Bengali	Sanskrit, Hindi
		Secondary	Bengali, English	English, Bengali	-
26.	Uttar Pradesh	Primary	Data could not be collected		
		Upper Primary	Data could not be collected		
		Secondary	Hindi, Urdu	English	Sanskrit, Urdu
27.	Uttaranchal	Primary	Hindi, Urdu, Sanskrit	English	-
		Upper Primary	Hindi, Urdu, English	English, Hindi, Sanskrit, others	English, Sanskrit, Urdu
		Secondary	Hindi, Urdu, English	English, Hindi. Sanskrit, others	English, Sanskrit, Urdu

28.	West Bengal	Primary	Bengali, Hindi, Nepali, Santhali, Telugu, Oriya	English	-
		Upper Primary	Bengali, Hindi, Santhali, Tamil, Telugu, Oriya, Urdu, Nepali, Gujarati, Tibetan	English	Hindi, Sanskrit, others
29.	Andaman and Nicobar Islands	Primary	Hindi, Tamil, Telugu, Bengali	English	-
		Upper Primary	Hindi, Tamil, Telugu, Bengali	English	-
		Secondary	Hindi, Tamil, Telugu, Bengali	English	-
30.	Chandigarh	Primary	Punjabi, Hindi, Urdu	English as compulsory language	Punjabi, Hindi Urdu (not studied as L1)
		Upper Primary	Punjabi, Hindi, Urdu	English	Punjabi, Hindi, Urdu and many more MIL (not studied as L1)
		Secondary	Punjabi (pass in Punjabi is compulsory)	English	Hindi; one of following can be taken as elective subject: Sanskrit, Urdu, Persian, Arabic, Nepalese, Tibetan, French, German, Portuguese, Russian, Bengali, Gujarati, Marathi, Telugu, Tamil, Malayalam, Oriya, Kannada
31.	Dadra Nahar Haveli	Primary	Gujarati, Hindi, Marathi	English	Sanskrit
		Upper Primary	English, Gujarati, Marathi	Hindi	English, Gujarati, Hindi, Sanskrit, others
		Secondary	English, Gujarati, Marathi	Hindi	English, Gujarati, Hindi, Sanskrit, others

32.	Daman and Diu	Primary	Gujarati	Hindi	-
		Upper Primary	Gujarati	Hindi	English
		Secondary	Gujarati	Hindi	English
33.	Delhi	Primary	Hindi	English, Urdu, Punjabi	-
		Upper Primary	Hindi	English	Sanskrit, Urdu, Punjabi, any other MIL
		Secondary	Hindi	English	Sanskrit, Urdu, Punjabi, any other MIL
34.	Lakshadweep	Primary	Data could not be collected		
		Upper Primary	Arabic, English, Malayalam	English, Hindi, English	Hindi, Malayalam
		Secondary	Arabic, English, Malayalam	English, Hindi, English	Hindi, Malayalam
35.	Puducherry	Primary	Tamil	English	-
		Upper Primary	Tamil	English	Hindi
		Secondary	Tamil	English	Hindi

As shown in Box 2, the 'first language' offered at the primary stage is usually – but not always – the language of the region or the language of neighbouring states; this is in line with the requirement that the 'first language' provided at the primary-level school should be the child's mother tongue or home language. At the secondary stage it is also usually the mother tongue or home language, the language of the region or the state or the language of a neighbouring state which is offered. English is also available as a first language in some states.

Various patterns emerge in different regions of the country. In the primarily Hindi-speaking states the languages offered are generally Hindi, Urdu, English, Sanskrit and the language of the neighbouring state. For example, Bengali is available in the state of Bihar (which borders West Bengal) and Marathi is available in the state of Madhya Pradesh (which borders Maharashtra, the home of Marathi).

The states of the southern part of India tend to offer all four major languages of the region – Tamil, Telugu, Kannada and Malayalam – as well as Urdu, Hindi and Sanskrit and the languages of neighbouring states. The state of Karnataka has Konkani as a language in addition to the languages mentioned above. These states also offer Persian and Arabic.

The states of Punjab, Gujarat, Maharashtra, Orissa and West Bengali fall into a different category. At the primary stage they tend to offer the state's majority language, Hindi, Urdu and another modern Indian language as first language and then English as second language. At the upper primary stage the scene is a bit different. For example, Maharashtra has Marathi and Hindi as first languages and English as second language at the primary stage; however, at the upper primary stage Marathi and English become first languages and Hindi becomes the second language. It is clear, then, that Marathi, Hindi, English and other modern Indian languages (MIL) are studied as first, second and third languages in the state. Similarly, Punjab offers Punjabi, Hindi and Urdu as first language and English as a compulsory second language. Meanwhile, Orissa provides Oriya and English as first and second language respectively at the primary stage while Oriya, Hindi, Sanskrit or another MIL are studied as first language at the upper primary stage with English as second language and Hindi or Sanskrit as third language.

The states of the North East region offer some of the tribal languages of that region together with English, Hindi, Sanskrit and Bengali. Some of the North East states teach English as a first language.

The state of Jammu and Kashmir stands alone on many counts. It is the only state which introduces the third language as late as Class IX; consequently, the duration of study of the third language is reduced to only two years.

Tables 3 and 4 summarise the data of Box 2. Data was provided by all 35 states/UTs, but with some gaps. Table 3 shows the number of first, second and third language choices offered by the states at each school level as well as the total number of individual languages made available by the states at each school level. It can be seen that collectively the 33 states for which data is available, provide 83 choices of first language at primary level (an average of 2.5 languages per state); these choices involve 25 different languages. The richest choice is available for first languages at the upper primary level (an average of 2.8 language choices per state) while the least choice is offered for third languages at the primary level (an average of only 0.4 languages per state; in other words, many states do not offer any third language at the primary level). In terms of individual languages, the richest choice is for first languages at the secondary level where, across India, 27 different languages are available. The least choice occurs at the primary level where for both second and third languages only seven different languages are offered.

Table 3: Numbers of first, second and third language choices and number of individual languages offered by states/UTs (N=35)

School Level	Language choices offered by states/UTs						Individual languages available		
	L1		L2		L3		L1	L2	L3
	N	$\bar{x}$	N	$\bar{x}$	N	$\bar{x}$			
Primary N=33*	83	2.5	33	1.0	12	0.4	25	7	7
Upper primary N=34**	95	2.8	48	1.4	69	2.0	23	8	19
Secondary N=34***	93	2.7	51	1.5	88	2.6	27	15	25
Sub-total	271		132		169		31	16	30
Total	572						75		

* Data for primary level missing from two states
** Data for upper primary level missing from one state
*** Data for secondary level missing from one state

Table 4: Languages most frequently offered by states/UTs as L1, L2 and L3 (N=35)					
School level	L1/L2/L3	English	Hindi	Urdu	Sanskrit
Primary N=33*	L1	10	18	7	2
	L2	23	5	1	0
	L3	1	4	2	2
Upper primary N=34**	L1	16	16	11	3
	L2	27	14	0	2
	L3	8	18	6	15
Secondary N=34***	L1	17	18	10	3
	L2	21	14	1	3
	L3	8	12	6	12
Total		131	119	44	42

* Data for primary level missing from two states
** Data for upper primary level missing from one state
*** Data for secondary level missing from one state

Table 4 shows the frequency with which the four most popular languages – Hindi, English, Urdu and Sanskrit – are offered as first, second and third languages at each of the three school levels. It can be seen from this analysis that English is the most frequently offered second language (offered by 27 of 34 states at the upper primary level, 23 of 33 states at the primary level and 21 of 34 states at the secondary level). However, Hindi is the most frequently offered first language and third language at almost all educational levels.

Media of instruction

The three-language formula envisaged that children in primary school would study through their mother tongue and that this would lead to harmonious personal development and contribute to a pedagogically sound high quality education. This vision was proposed by the Education Commission in 1964–1966 and was reflected again in the national curricular frameworks from 1975, the National Education Policy (GOI 1986) and the Programme of Action (GOI 1992). In this section we discuss the extent of mother tongue schooling in 2002 (NCERT 2007) in comparison with the situation ten years earlier (NCERT 1993).

Table 5 summarises the proportion of primary and upper primary schools which taught using the mother tongue in 1993 and 2002.

Table 5: Schools teaching through mother tongue in India (per cent)				
Policies	Primary		Upper primary	
	1993	2002	1993	2002
Rural schools	91.70	92.39	89.49	92.71
Urban schools	91.32	90.39	86.07	87.37
All schools	91.65	92.07	88.64	91.34

The Seventh Survey found that in 2002 just over 92 per cent of primary schools were teaching through the mother tongue; ten years earlier the figure was almost identical, just below 92 per cent. Rural schools showed an increase of less than one per cent in their tendency to use the mother tongue while urban schools showed a decline of less than one per cent over the ten-year period.

As far as the upper primary stage is concerned, more than 91 per cent of schools were using the mother tongue in 2002, an increase of just over two percentage points compared to 1993. In 1993 rural upper primary schools were about three per cent more likely to use the mother tongue compared to urban schools. By 2002 the proportion of both rural and urban schools using the mother tongue had increased, but the rate of increase was slightly higher in the rural schools.

Overall, then, more than 90 per cent of schools at the primary and upper primary stages teach through the children's mother tongue; there was a slight overall increase in the number of schools teaching through the mother tongue between 1993 and 2002.

The Seventh Survey also found that 12.14 per cent of primary schools, 14.47 per cent of upper primary schools and 8.53 per cent of secondary schools were offering two or more media of instruction. The sixth Survey, a decade earlier, showed that the equivalent figures were 7.21 per cent, 12.49 per cent and 13.34 per cent respectively. In other words, the proportion of primary and upper primary schools offering multiple media of instruction had increased while the proportion of secondary schools making such an offer had declined quite sharply.

The sixth and seventh surveys also reported how many schools were teaching through the media of Hindi and English. The findings are summarised in Table 6. In 1993 Hindi was used as a medium of instruction in 42 per cent of primary schools, 41 per cent of upper primary schools and 34 per cent of secondary schools. By 2002 the figures had become almost 47 per cent at primary level, just over 47 per cent at upper primary and 41 per cent at secondary. That is to say, there had been an increase in schools offering Hindi medium education at each educational level over the decade, but secondary schools continued to be rather less likely than primary and upper primary schools to do this.

Table 6: Schools with Hindi and English medium policies in India (per cent)

Policies	Primary		Upper primary		Secondary	
	1993	2002	1993	2002	1993	2002
Hindi as medium	42.26	46.79	40.93	47.41	33.94	41.32
English as medium	4.99	12.98	15.91	18.25	18.37	25.84

The pattern regarding the use of English as a medium of instruction is rather different. In 1993 English was used in five per cent, 16 per cent and 18 per cent of primary, upper primary and secondary schools respectively. But in 2002 the equivalent figures were 13 per cent, 18 per cent and 26 per cent. In other words, the tendency for schools to offer English as a medium of instruction had increased at every level over the decade, with the most rapid increases occurring in primary and secondary schools.

It is particularly striking that over a quarter of all secondary schools in India now claim to offer English as a medium of instruction.

It is also interesting to note that the number of states/UTs offering education at primary and upper primary levels through the medium of languages other than the majority language increased from 30 to 32, indicating an increasing awareness of the need to cater to the needs of linguistic minorities.

Box 3 shows, state by state, the languages offered as media of instruction at each educational level.

No.	State/Union Territory	Media of instruction		
		Primary	**Upper Primary**	**Secondary**
1.	Andhra Pradesh	Telugu, Urdu, Oriya, English, Hindi, Marathi, Kannada, Tamil	Telugu, Urdu, Oriya, English, Hindi, Marathi, Kannada, Tamil	Telugu, Urdu, Oriya, English, Hindi, Marathi, Kannada, Tamil
2.	Arunachal Pradesh	English, Hindi	English	English
3.	Assam	Assamese, Bengali, Bodo, English	Assamese, Bengali, Bodo, English, Hindi, others	Assamese, Bengali, Bodo, English. Hindi, others
4.	Bihar	Hindi, Urdu, Sanskrit, English	English, Hindi, Sanskrit, Urdu	English, Hindi, Sanskrit, Urdu, others
5.	Chhattisgarh	Hindi, others	Hindi, others	English, Hindi, others
6.	Goa	English, Konkani, Marathi, Urdu, Kannada (dual medium)	English, Marathi	English, Marathi
7.	Gujarat	Gujarati, others	English, Gujarati, Hindi, others	English, Gujarati, Hindi, others
8.	Haryana	English, Hindi, others	English, Hindi, Sanskrit, others	English, Hindi, Sanskrit, others
9.	Himachal Pradesh	English, Hindi, others	English, Hindi, others	English, Hindi, others
10.	Jammu and Kashmir	Dogri, English, Hindi, Kashmiri, Urdu, others	Dogri, English, Hindi, Kashmiri, Urdu, others	Dogri, English, Hindi, Kashmiri, Urdu, others
11.	Jharkand	English, Hindi, Sanskrit, others	Bengali, English, Hindi, Sanskrit, others	Bengali, English, Hindi, Sanskrit, others
12.	Karnataka	Kannada, English, Hindi, Marathi, Tamil, Telugu, Urdu, Malayalam, Sanskrit, Arabic	Kannada, English, Hindi, Marathi, Tamil, Telugu, Urdu, Malayalam, Sanskrit, Arabic	Kannada, English, Hindi, Marathi, Tamil, Telugu, Urdu, Malayalam, Sanskrit, Arabic
13.	Kerala	Malayalam, English, Tamil, Kannada (dual medium)	Malayalam, English, Tamil, Kannada (dual medium)	Malayalam, English, Tamil, Kannada (dual medium)
14.	Madhya Pradesh	Hindi, English, Urdu, Marathi	English, Hindi, Urdu, Marathi, others	English, Hindi, Urdu

15.	Maharashtra	Marathi, Hindi	English, Marathi, Hindi, others	English, Marathi, Hindi, others
16.	Manipur	English, Hindi, Manipuri, others	English, Hindi, Manipuri, others	English, Hindi, Manipuri, others
17.	Meghalaya	English, Garo, Khasi, others	English	English
18.	Mizoram	English, Mizo	English, Mizo, others	English, Mizo, others
19.	Nagaland	Angami, Ao, English, Hindi, Konyak, Lotha, Sema, others	Angami, Ao, English, Hindi, Konyak, Sema, others	Angami, English, Hindi, others
20.	Orissa	English, Oriya	English, Hindi, Oriya, others	English, Hindi, Oriya, Sanskrit, others
21.	Punjab	English, Hindi, Punjabi	English, Hindi, Punjabi, others	English, Hindi, Punjabi, others
22.	Rajasthan	Hindi, others	Hindi, others	Hindi, others
23.	Sikkim	English, others	English, others	English, others
24.	Tamil Nadu	English, Tamil (dual medium)	Tamil, Telugu, Malayalam, Urdu, Kannada	Tamil, Telugu, Malayalam, Urdu, Kannada
25.	Tripura	Bengali, Kokborok, English, others	Bengali, English, others	Bengali, English, others
26.	Uttar Pradesh	Hindi, others	English, Hindi, Sanskrit, others	English, Hindi, Sanskrit, others
27.	Uttaranchal	Hindi, others	English, Hindi, Urdu, others	English, Hindi, Urdu, others
28.	West Bengal	Bengali, others	Bengali, Hindi, English, Urdu, Oriya, Tamil, Telugu, Gujarati, Tibetan, Nepali	Bengali, Hindi, English, Urdu, Oriya, Tamil, Telugu, Gujarati, Tibetan, Nepali
29.	Andaman and Nicobar Islands	Bengali, English, Hindi, Tamil, Telugu	Bengali, English, Hindi, Tamil, Telugu	Bengali, English, Hindi, Tamil, Telugu
30.	Chandigarh	English, Hindi, Punjabi, others	English, Hindi, Punjabi, others	English, Hindi, Punjabi, others
31.	Dadra Nagar Haveli	English, Gujarati, Hindi, Marathi	English, Gujarati, Hindi, Marathi, Sanskrit	English, Gujarati, Hindi, Marathi, Sanskrit
32.	Daman and Diu	English, Gujarati	English, Gujarati	English, Gujarati
33.	Delhi	English, Hindi, Urdu, others	English, Hindi, Urdu, others	English, Hindi, Urdu, others
34.	Lakshadweep	Malayalam, others	English, Malayalam, others	English, Malayalam
35.	Puducherry	English, Tamil, others	English, Tamil, others	English, Tamil, others

From Box 3 we can see that at least two languages are available as the media of instruction in each state/UT, while two states (Karnataka and West Bengal) offer as many as ten. The state with the largest number of media of instruction at the primary level is Nagaland, with at least seven languages on offer.

There is a general tendency for a wider range of languages to be made available as media of instruction in upper primary and secondary schools compared to primary schools. An example is Orissa, which offers just Oriya and English as media of instruction at the primary level but in addition provides Hindi, Sanskrit and other MILs at the secondary stage.

Other states and UTs, however, offer the same number of media of instruction at all levels. These include Daman and Diu, which provides only Gujarati and English in primary, upper primary and secondary schools.

Yet other states have a policy of offering a wider range of languages of instruction in primary schools compared to higher levels. Goa provides an illustration here, where five languages – Konkani, Marathi, Kannada, Hindi and English – are used at the primary level but only two – Marathi and English – are available at the upper primary and secondary levels.

Unlike the rest of the country, three states (Goa, Kerala and Tamil Nadu) have a 'dual medium' policy, which means that two different media of instruction are available in the same school.

Tables 7 and 8 summarise the data recorded in Box 3. From Table 7 we can see that the 35 states/UTs offer a total of 355 language choices for medium of instruction, with somewhat greater choice at the upper primary and secondary levels (124 choices each) compared to the primary level (107 choices). The total number of individual languages offered as medium of instruction is 31. As we noted in the Introduction above, according to Rao (2008), approximately 60 languages were used as media of instruction in the 1980s and 47 were used as media at the time of Rao's own survey.

Table 7: Number of language choices and number of individual languages offered as medium of instruction by states/UTs (N=35)

School level	Language choices offered by states/UTs	Individual languages available
Primary	107	31
Upper primary	124	25
Secondary	124	24
Total	355	31

Meanwhile, Table 8 summarises information concerning the five most frequently reported languages used as media of instruction. It is interesting to note that higher proportions of states and UTs claim to make English available as a medium of instruction than do those offering Hindi as a medium; this pattern applies at all three educational levels. For example, 33 of 35 states say that they offer English as a medium of instruction at the secondary level, while only 24 states offer Hindi as a medium at this level.

Table 8: Languages most frequently offered by states/UTs as medium of instruction (N=35)

School level	English	Hindi	Urdu	Tamil	Sanskrit
Primary	27	21	7	6	3
Upper primary	32	24	9	7	6
Secondary	33	24	9	7	7

However, a word of caution is required here. The fact that a state allows English to be offered as a medium of instruction does not mean that every school in the state will be able to implement this policy, nor that every child in each school will choose English. In fact, as we saw from Table 5, 91 per cent of schools teach through the mother tongue, while from Table 6 it was observed that only 26 per cent of schools offer English as a medium of instruction compared to 41 per cent offering Hindi as medium.

Introduction of second and third languages

This section considers the points in a child's education when the second and third languages are introduced and the number of years which are allocated for studying these languages.

Introduction of second language

Table 9 summarises policies regarding when the second language should be used. In all states and UTs the second language is introduced within the first five years of schooling.

Table 9: Introduction of second language (N=35)

Class at which L2 is introduced	Duration of study (years)	States/Union Territories
Class I	10	Andhra Pradesh (English), Arunachal Pradesh (Hindi), Bihar (Urdu, Bengali), Chhattisgarh (English/MIL), Goa (English), Gujarat (English), Himachal Pradesh (English), Jammu and Kashmir (English), Madhya Pradesh (General English/General Hindi), Manipur (Hindi/one of the recognised languages/MIL), Mizoram (English), Nagaland (MIL/Alternative English), Punjab (Hindi, Punjabi, Urdu), Rajasthan (English), Sikkim (MIL), Tamil Nadu (English), Tripura (English), Uttaranchal (English), Andaman and Nicobar Islands (Hindi/English), Chandigarh (Hindi/English), Delhi (English, Urdu, Punjabi), Puducherry (English)
Class III	8	Assam (Hindi/Bengali), Kerala (English), Orissa (English, Hindi, Sanskrit), Daman and Diu (Hindi), Dadra Nahar Haveli (Hindi)
Class V	5	Karnataka (English), West Bengal (English)

From Table 9 it can be seen that 22 out of the 35 states/UTs introduce the second language from the first year of schooling; in the other states teaching of the second language starts either in Class III (for example, Assam) or in Class V (Karnataka and West Bengal).

In 21 cases the second language is English while Hindi is offered as a second language in eleven states. Urdu, Bengali and Punjabi are also offered as second languages in states where these languages are spoken or which have neighbour states where they are spoken. Out of the 21 states offering English as the second language, 17 introduce it from Class I, two from Class III and two from Class V.

Assuming children stay in school until they complete Class X, those in the majority of states will be able to study their second language for ten years. However, those who begin studying the second language in Class III will be able to study it for a maximum of eight years and children in Karnataka and West Bengal will be able to study English as their second language for just five years.

Introduction of third language

Only 26 states reported offering a third language, but there is considerable variation in policy, as Table 10 indicates. Fourteen states introduce the third language from Class VI, meaning that children who stay in school until the end of Class X will be able to study that language for five years. Four states start the third language in Class V, so allowing children six years of study. Three states offer a third language from Class III and two make third language provision from Class IV. Just one state begins third language teaching in Class VII, another in Class VIII and yet another in Class IX.

Table 10: Introduction of third language (N=26)

Class at which L2 is introduced	Duration of study (years)	States/Union Territories
Class III	8	Manipur, Mizoram (Hindi), Nagaland (Hindi), Uttaranchal (English, Sanskrit, MIL])
Class IV	7	Punjab (Hindi, Punjabi, Urdu, any MIL), Sikkim (Hindi)
Class V	6	Dada Nagar Haveli, Goa (Marathi, Konkani, French, Portuguese), Kerala (Hindi)
Class VI	5	Andhra Pradesh (Hindi), Arunachal Pradesh (Sanskrit, Assamese, Butia), Assam, Bihar, Chhattisgarh, Gujarat, Karnataka, Madhya Pradesh (Urdu, Sanskrit, Marathi or any MIL), Rajasthan (Sanskrit, Urdu, Sindhi, Gujarati, Punjabi, any MIL), Uttar Pradesh (Sanskrit, Urdu, any MIL), West Bengal (Sanskrit, Hindi), Andaman and Nicobar Islands, Daman and Diu (English), Delhi (Sanskrit, Urdu, Punjabi, any MIL).
Class VII	4	Tripura (Sanskrit, Hindi)
Class VIII	3	Orissa (Hindi, Bengali, Sanskrit, Telugu, MIL)
Class IX	2	Jammu and Kashmir (Dogri, Boding, Punjabi, Arabic, Sanskrit, Persian)

The third language in most non-Hindi-speaking states is Hindi if it has not already been introduced as a second language, while in Hindi-speaking states it is Urdu, Sanskrit, Punjabi, Persian or the language of a neighbouring state.

English is mentioned as a third language by only two states (Uttaranchal from Class III and Daman and Diu from Class VI).

The role and place of English

English was perceived as a library language during the formative years of India's independence; indeed at one point there was a proposal that Hindi should be given fully fledged official language status and that English should be abolished from public use. However, having been granted 'associate official language' status (though it is still not a language listed in the eighth schedule of the Indian constitution), English continued to dominate higher education. Increasingly, it has been spreading its wings and is moving into school education.

This study has found that:

- 75 different languages are used in India's education system.

- 31 different languages are used as media of instruction; this is approximately half the number of languages that were being used for this purpose in the 1980s.

- English is taught somewhere in the curriculum of all the 32 states and Union Territories which provided data for the survey reported here. Only Hindi is taught in as many states.

- The percentage of schools teaching English as a 'first language' doubled between 1993 and 2002 from five per cent to ten per cent in primary schools and from seven per cent to 13 per cent in upper primary schools.

- English is offered as a second language by more states than any other language.

- 33 of 35 states claim to offer English as a medium of instruction; this is more than any other language.

- Between 1993 and 2002 there was an increase in the proportion of schools offering English as a medium of instruction; the sharpest increase (from five per cent to 13 per cent) occurred in primary schools.

- By 2002, more than a quarter of all secondary schools were offering English as a medium of instruction.

- English is offered as a second language in 19 states, of which 16 introduce it in Class I, one in Class III and two as late as Class V.

There has been a shift in perception as the demand for English is now felt in every quarter, even though there are pedagogically sound arguments against the early introduction of the language. As mentioned in the introduction to this chapter, the recent curricular revision at the national level – which culminated in the framework for the National Curriculum 2005 – records half a century of development in attitudes towards English. English is now an institutionalised subject in the school curriculum.

However, English is still simultaneously sought after and suspected (Tickoo 1996). The motives, generally, are not only social-political but academic too. While the demand increases on the one hand, the quality of English language education in our state-run schools, more particularly in rural schools, presents an abysmal picture. The divide between urban and rural is further exacerbated by the increasing tendency to use English as a medium of instruction. This paradox of demand and suspicion is reflected through the paradox of access depicted by the report of the National Knowledge Commission (NKC):

> There is an irony in the situation. English has been part of our education system for more than a century. Yet English is beyond the reach of most of our young people, which makes for highly unequal access. Indeed, even now, barely more than one percent of our people use it as a second language, let alone a first language ... But NKC believes that the time has come for us to teach our people, ordinary people, English as a language in schools. Early action in this sphere would help us build an inclusive society and transform India into a knowledge society. *(GOI 2007)*

The National Focus Group on Teaching of English has adopted a strong position in addressing the 'English language question':

> English is in India today a symbol of people's aspiration for quality in education and a fuller participation in national and international life. Its colonial origins now forgotten or irrelevant, its initial role in independence India, tailored to high education now felt to be insufficiently inclusive socially and linguistically, the current state of English stems from its overwhelming presence on the world stage and the reflection of this in the national arena. *(NCERT 2006:1)*

Stating that 'English does not stand alone', the National Focus Group's position paper argues that:

> (English) needs to find its place. (i) Along with other Indian Languages (a) in regional medium schools, how can children's other languages strengthen English learning? (b) in English medium schools, how can other Indian languages be valorised, reducing the perceived hegemony of English? (ii) In relation to other subjects, a language across the curriculum perspective is perhaps of particular relevance to primary education. Language is best acquired through different meaning-making contexts and hence all teaching in a sense is language teaching. This perspective also captures the centrality of language in abstract thought in secondary education. *(NCERT 2006:4)*

As stated above, English language education has to find its place in the holistic and broader plan of language education where it plays a complementary and supplementary role in the creation of multilinguals/bilinguals. The National Curriculum Framework 2005 stresses the need for a multilingual education from the beginning of schooling and English has its place in this scheme. However, the Framework also cautions about the danger of introducing English (or, for that matter, any language) without ensuring that the basic provisions and infrastructure for its study are already in place. Language teachers with a satisfactory level of proficiency and quality materials to support the teaching-learning process are among the essentials for language learning in any context and are even more important in the case of second or third languages.

Conclusions

Language policy in India has adapted itself to the changing demands and aspirations of people over the period of time from 1947 to the present. Change has occurred on many counts. Firstly, the question of a national language – which was wisely addressed during the formative years of independence by not declaring any language as the national language – has now been permanently settled. The existence of English in India means that it is no longer necessary to consider the issue of a national language. In other words, India does not need a national language since there are no functions which a national language might play that are not already fulfilled in some other way. The beneficiaries of this de facto policy are the indigenous Indian languages in the regions where they prevail; if any additional function were to be required then it could be satisfied by bringing in English.

In a way an associate official language, English knowingly or unknowingly has played an instrumental role in maintaining the diversity of India's language scene because the existence of English has meant that it has not been necessary to select any one Indian languages as a national language. In fact, the states which used to rally to slogans such as angriji hatao (remove English) are now eagerly introducing English in the first year of schooling.

English today is almost a compulsory second language. Once deprived sections of the society now perceive the language as an instrument for progress. The recent news of a temple for English language in a village in the Hindi heartland (Pandey 2011) tells the thing.

However, the public's demands are not being met meaningfully. Most schools in the country do not have the facilities and proficient teachers needed to cater to the demand. As mentioned above, meaningful language education requires teachers who are skilled and knowledgeable as well as contextualised materials (print and others). But an enabling English language environment in the school also needs to be ensured. The most important of these three prerequisites is the English teacher, but the English language proficiency of English language teachers in quite a number of schools is questionable. Consequently, teacher education is one major area which needs drastic changes if quality teachers are to become available. Materials development (particularly textbooks) for the teaching and learning of English has not yet been professionalised. On the contrary, materials development has been commercialised to the extent that India now has thousands of publishers who publish English language textbooks. An enabling English language environment also cannot be created overnight. Learners need to experience appropriate input so that they can become engaged with the language, but a language teacher who himself or herself does not possess the required proficiency cannot create such an environment. Children need to feel the language in the air in school because, for the vast majority of children, English is not available outside school. The creation of such an enabling environment has to be encouraged through curricular and other activities in and outside school.

It is better to have English taught as a subject rather than impose a bad English medium education. Equipping English language education with the essentials in the native medium schools would benefit learning in general and language learning in particular. But converting schools to become English medium without proper support would be detrimental and counterproductive. Schools can be developed as multimedia schools where both the content subjects and the language are taught and learnt well in a complementary and supplementary manner. A 'language across the curriculum' perspective and a strategy of multilingualism (NCERT 2005) would be of benefit on many counts. The centrality of language in learning needs to be recognised. English, then, can play a vital role as a language of mutual benefit – benefiting Indian languages as well as itself – and so enriching education as a whole.

References

Agarwal, S.P. (ed.). 1993. *Commissions and Committees in India, Volume 5. New Delhi: Concept Publishing Company.*

GOI (Government of India). 1962. *Annual Report 1961-1962. New Delhi: Ministry of Education.*

GOI (Government of India). 1971. *Census of India 1971. New Delhi: Office of the Registrar General and Census Commissioner, India.*

GOI (Government of India). 1986. *National Policy on Education (NPE). New Delhi: GOI.*

GOI (Government of India). 1992. *Programme of Action (POA) NPE. New Delhi: GOI.*

GOI (Government of India). 2007. *Report of the National Knowledge Commission. New Delhi: GOI.* Available online at *www.knowledgecommission.gov.in*

Graddol, D. 2010. *English Next India. New Delhi: British Council.*

Kurrien, J. 2005. *Notes for the Meeting of the National Focus Group on Teaching of English and Notes on Introduction of English at the Primary Stage.* Unpublished document.

MOE (Ministry of Education). 1957. *Annual Report. New Delhi: GOI.*

MOE (Ministry of Education). 1966. *Report of the Education Commission 1964-1966. New Delhi: GOI.*

NCERT (National Council of Educational Research and Training). 1993. *Sixth All India School Education Survey. New Delhi: NCERT.*

NCERT (National Council of Educational Research and Training). 2005. *National Curriculum Framework 2005. New Delhi: NCERT.*

NCERT (National Council of Educational Research and Training). 2006. *National Focus Group Position Paper on Teaching of English. New Delhi: NCERT.*

NCERT (National Council of Educational Research and Training). 2007. *Seventh All India School Education Survey: Media of Instruction and Languages Taught. New Delhi: NCERT.*

Pandey, G. 2011. *An 'English goddess' for India's down-trodden. BBC News South Asia* 15 February 2011. Available online at *www.bbc.co.uk/news/world-south-asia-12355740*

Rao, S. 2008. *India's language debates and education of linguistic minorities. Economic and Political Weekly* 6 September 2008.

Tickoo, M.L. 1996. *English in Asian bilingual education: From hatred to harmony. Journal of Multilingual and Multicultural Development* 17, 2-4.

5

Allocating resources for English: The case of Indonesia's English medium International Standard Schools[1]

Hywel Coleman

Introduction

This chapter examines a recent innovation in Indonesia's education system: the establishment of English medium 'International Standard Schools' (ISS). Although the ISS programme has its supporters (e.g. Bax 2010), it has been subject to considerable criticism in Indonesia for threatening national unity and contravening the national constitution, for exacerbating social divisions and for demanding too much of teachers who have to teach their subjects through English (Darmaningtyas 2010, Kompas 2010a, 2010b).

This chapter, however, focuses specifically on the issue of the allocation of resources for the ISS programme. The objectives are to identify anomalies associated with resource allocation, to highlight the differential access which different socio-economic groups have to this programme and to ask a question about the difficulty which governments seem to have in planning language education (especially English) in such a way that a balance is achieved between national development objectives and the empowerment of citizens at the individual level.

The chapter falls into six sections. The first provides a brief overview of Indonesia and its current development context. The second section describes the ISS programme in Indonesia; from this description it emerges that the use of English as the medium of instruction is one of the most prominent features of these schools. The third section examines in detail the ways in which ISSs are financed. Next, the chapter looks at how the concept of 'globalisation' is used as a rationale for the establishment of ISSs. The fifth section identifies a constituency in Indonesian society which faces the challenges of 'globalisation' in a direct way but which does not have access to the ISS system. The sixth and final section summarises the findings and discusses their implications.

The chapter makes extensive use of financial data concerning per capita income, routine funding allocations for schools, funding of the ISS programme and migrant workers' remittances back to Indonesia. These figures are all, to a certain degree, tentative. Nevertheless, regardless of the precise degree of accuracy of these figures, the author believes that the trends and patterns which emerge are valid.

The development context of Indonesia

This section looks briefly at Indonesia's overall human development situation, at per capita income and at a number of education indicators. Further key development indicators can be seen in Appendix 2 at the end of this volume.

With a population of over 230 million, Indonesia is the fourth most populous country in the world. UNDP places Indonesia at 108th position in its Human Development Index (UNDP 2010; see also Appendix 1). This puts it at the mid-point of countries categorised as having 'medium human development', coming just below Namibia, Honduras and Maldives and slightly above Kyrgyzstan, South Africa and Syria.

According to UNDP, Indonesia's gross national income per person is almost USD4,000 (IDR35 million, GBP2,500) per year (UNDP 2010; see also Table 1 below and Appendix 2). Indonesian government figures, however, are more modest; in December 2010 the Co-ordinating Minister for Economic Affairs was reported to have predicted that per capita income for 2010 would be USD3,000 (IDR26.5 million, GBP1,900; Antara 2010).

Table 1: Per capita income, Indonesia[2]

Category	Period	USD ($)	IDR (Rp000)	GBP (£)
National, per capita (UNDP 2010)	Annual	4,000	35,682	2,591
	Monthly	333	2,974	216
	Daily	11	98	7
National, per capita (Antara 2010)	Annual	3,000	26,762	1,943
	Monthly	250	2,230	162
	Daily	8	73	5
Industrial labourer (per capita), Jakarta (BPS 2009)	Annual	1,809	16,133	1,172
	Monthly	151	1,344	98
	Daily	5	45	3
Batik dyer (female, range), East Java (Ratna 2010)	Annual	164–984	1,500–9,000	107–636
	Monthly	14–82	125–750	9–53
	Daily	0.47–2.73	4–25	0.30–1.77
Poverty line (UNDP 2010)	Annual	456	4,070	296
	Monthly	38	335	24
	Daily	1.25	11	0.81

However, even these average figures may be misleading. For example, government statistics show that the average monthly income of an industrial labourer in Jakarta in the third quarter of 2009 was only IDR1.34 million (BPS 2009), equivalent to GBP98 or USD151. Meanwhile, female batik dyers on the island of Madura, East Java, are reported to earn between IDR125,000 and IDR750,000 per month (between GBP9 and GBP53, between USD14 and USD82), depending on their productivity (Ratna 2010). Poverty is widespread; UNDP (2010) records that 30 per cent of the Indonesian population survive below the poverty line of USD1.25 (GBP0.80, IDR11,000) per day.

In contrast, there is also extreme wealth. The Forbes list of the world's billionaires (Kroll and Miller 2010) identifies seven Indonesians who individually are worth between USD1 billion and USD3.5 billion (between GBP0.6 billion and GBP2.2 billion, between IDR9 trillion and IDR31 trillion).

With regard to education, Indonesian legislation requires that all children should attend nine years of compulsory schooling (six years in primary school and three years in junior secondary school). The medium of instruction in schools is Bahasa Indonesia, the national language. English is a compulsory subject throughout junior secondary and senior secondary schools, although many primary schools also teach English as an additional subject.

The nine years of education in primary and junior secondary school are (nominally) free of charge. Central government provides a grant known as BOS (bantuan operasional sekolah, school operational support), which is calculated according to the formula shown in Table 2 and paid quarterly via district education offices.

Table 2: Annual BOS grant from central government to schools, per pupil, 2011[3]

Location	Level	USD ($)	IDR (Rp000)	GBP (£)
Rural district	Primary	43.51	397	28.19
	Junior secondary	62.47	570	40.47
Urban district	Primary	43.84	400	28.40
	Junior secondary	63.02	575	40.83

According to this formula a rural primary school, for example, will receive a BOS grant of IDR397,000 (GBP28 or USD44) per year for every enrolled pupil. This central government grant is expected to cover 70 per cent of school costs (excluding teacher salaries); the remaining 30 per cent is supposed to be covered by a matching school operational support grant from the district government.

Actual participation in primary schools is reasonably high, with a net enrolment ratio in 2008 of 96 per cent. In junior secondary schools, the gross enrolment ratio in 2008 was 89 per cent while the net enrolment ratio for all secondary schools was 68 per cent (UNESCO 2010). However, the push to achieve universal participation in nine years of primary and junior secondary education is a relatively recent phenomenon. Consequently, the average Indonesian adult has spent only 5.7 years in school (UNDP 2010; see also Appendix 2).

The overall achievements of the Indonesian education system are rather disappointing. The findings of the 2009 Programme for International Student Assessment (PISA) survey of what 15-year-olds who are still in school know and can do (OECD 2010) show that, in reading ability, Indonesia comes at 56th place out of 64 countries. In mathematics, Indonesian 15-year-olds come in 59th place (jointly with Tunisia) while in science, too, Indonesia is in 59th place. (See Table 3.)

Table 3: What 15-year-olds in school in five Asian countries know and can do (OECD 2010)

Country	Reading		Mathematics		Science	
	Score	Rank/64	Score	Rank/64	Score	Rank/64
Korea	539	1	546	3	538	5
Hong Kong	533	3	555	2	549	2
Singapore	526	4	562	1	542	3
Thailand	421	49	419	50=	425	48
Indonesia	402	56	371	59=	383	59

To summarise:

■ Indonesia – with its very large population – falls in the middle of the range of countries with medium human development.

■ National per capita income figures are uncertain and may be misleading, but it is clear that rural craftspeople can expect to earn at most IDR750,000 per month (GBP53, USD82) – and possibly much less than that – whereas urban factory labourers can take home about IDR1.3 million (just under GBP100, USD150) per month on average.

■ Three people in every ten exist below the poverty line, making do with IDR11,000 (GBP0.80, USD1.25) per day or less.

■ Compulsory education lasts for nine years and about 96 per cent of children attend primary school, but the participation rate for junior secondary school is lower.

■ Schools receive annual grants from central government, which are worth about IDR400,000 (GBP28, USD44) per pupil for primary schools and IDR575,000 (GBP41, USD63) per pupil for junior secondary schools.

■ On an international measure of educational outcomes, Indonesia performs poorly compared to neighbouring countries in East and Southeast Asia.

The International Standard Schools programme

Indonesia's ISS programme is described here in terms of the background and objectives of the scheme, the number of schools participating in the scheme, the socio-economic background of pupils, the role of English and actual practice in participating schools.

Background and objectives

The Soeharto-era government of Indonesia (1966–1998) required that all Indonesian nationals should attend Indonesian schools. Access to international schools operating in the country was strictly restricted to the children of expatriates. Following the collapse of the Soeharto government and the liberalisation of Indonesian society, demands were made by the aspirant upper middle class that their children should also be allowed to study in international schools. The true international schools, however, were – and still are – unwilling to open their doors too widely.

In the face of this reluctance of international schools to admit the children of Indonesian nationals and in response to market demand, some very expensive fully Indonesian private 'international' schools were established. These cater for the extremely wealthy and are beyond the reach even of the average middle class family. There was still, then, an unfulfilled demand from the middle classes for 'international-like' education.

In a development which surprised many observers, Law No 20 of 2003 on the National Education System (Republik Indonesia 2003) introduced the concept of 'International Standard Schools' (SBI, sekolah bertaraf internasional). The law required that central government and/or local governments should work to establish 'one International Standard School at every educational level' (Republik Indonesia 2003, Article 50, Clause 3).[4]

This was followed in 2005 by Government Decree No 19 on National Standards for Education, which specified that central government should co-operate with local government to provide at least one school per district at the primary level and at least one at the secondary level which could be 'developed to become an International Standard School' (Republik Indonesia 2005, Article 61, Clause 1).[5]

In the same year, the Ministry of National Education's Strategic Plan for 2005–2009 stated:

> In order to improve the nation's ability to compete ... central government and the relevant rural district government [kabupaten] or urban district government [kota] [need to] develop 112 international standard primary, junior secondary, senior secondary and vocational secondary schools throughout Indonesia.
> **(Depdiknas 2005)[6]**

This was followed in 2007 by the appearance of government guidelines, which for the first time defined what is meant by 'International Standard School' and which laid down criteria for quality assurance. The definition states that an ISS is:

> A school ... which fulfils all the National Standards for Education and which is further enriched by taking into consideration the education standards of one member nation of the Organisation for Economic Co-operation and Development (OECD) and/or another advanced nation which has particular strengths in education such that it achieves competitive advantage in the international forum.
> **(Depdiknas 2007:7)[7]**

The same document identifies nine areas in which the quality of ISSs is to be guaranteed, with indicators for each area (Depdiknas 2007:v–vii). The nine areas and some examples of their respective indicators are summarised in Table 4. (The complete document is very lengthy; Table 4 simply provides one or two sample indicators for each of the nine areas.)

The publication of the 2007 ISS guidelines was followed in 2008 by the appearance of very detailed handbooks for the implementation of education of an international standard in primary schools (Depdiknas 2008a) and in junior secondary schools (Depdiknas 2008b).

Table 4: Nine areas for quality assurance in Indonesia's International Standard Schools (extracted from Depdiknas 2007)

Areas for quality assurance	Examples of quality indicators
1. Accreditation	... school is also accredited by a school accreditation body in an OECD member nation
2. Curriculum	... lesson content equivalent to or higher than that taught in an OECD member country
3. Learning-teaching process	Science, mathematics and core vocational subjects are taught using English ... In primary schools, teaching science and mathematics through English begins in Year 4.
4. Evaluation	... 'enriched' with modes of evaluation employed in an OECD member country
5. Teachers	Teachers of science, mathematics and core vocational subjects are able to deliver lessons through English
6. Headteachers	Headteacher has active mastery of English ... possesses international vision, capable of developing international links
7. Facilities and resources	Internet access
8. Management	School is multicultural
9. Financing	Achieves Indonesian National Education Standard for school financing.

More recent legislation (for example, Republik Indonesia 2010) has emphasised that there are to be two categories of school: 'fledgling' International Standard Schools (RSBI, Rintisan Sekolah Bertaraf Internasional) and definitive International Standard Schools (SBI, Sekolah Bertaraf Internasional).[8] The assumption is that not every school will be able to satisfy the ISS criteria immediately. The 'fledgling' or 'candidate' ISSs will therefore be given support over a number of years to enable them to develop to the point where they will be able to achieve full ISS status. The most recent legislation states that primary schools will be supported for seven years while junior secondary, senior secondary and vocational secondary schools will be supported for six years (Republik Indonesia 2010, Article 144 Clause 5 and Article 146 Clause 5). However, a speech by the Minister of Education in April 2010 indicated that the maximum duration for which junior secondary schools can expect to be supported is four years while senior secondary schools will be supported for five years; the duration of support for primary schools was not stated (Kompas 2010c).

The Minister added that if, by the end of the period of support, a school has still not succeeded in achieving the required standard then its status will return to being a 'national standard school'.

Number of participating schools

Interviews with senior officials in the Ministry of National Education on 06 April 2009 indicated that by the end of 2009 there would be approximately 190 ISSs at the primary level, as summarised in Table 5. Nevertheless, a speech by the Minister of National Education in April 2010 indicated that in fact only 136 primary ISSs had been established (Kompas 2010c).

Table 5: Primary level (SD) International Standard Schools in Indonesia, 2007–2010 (interview data and Ministerial speech)

Category	Interview data				Ministerial speech (Kompas 2010c)
	2007	2008	2009 (planned)	Total	
Newly established	22	-	-	22	?
Converted	38	66	66	170	?
Total	60	66	66	192	136

Meanwhile, Table 6 shows that approximately 200 ISSs at the junior secondary level had been established by the end of 2008, together with 192 schools at the senior secondary level and 158 at the vocational secondary level. By April 2010, according to the Minister of National Education, 738 ISSs had been established at these levels (Kompas 2010c).

Table 6: International Standard Schools other than primary in Indonesia, 2007–2010 (extracted from Ministerial publication, interview data and Ministerial speech)

Category	Depdiknas (2009:24) and interview data				Ministerial speech (Kompas 2010c)
	2007	2008	2009 (planned)	Total	
SMP (junior secondary school)	99	100	?	199 + ?	300
SMA (senior secondary school)	101	91	?	192 + ?	320
SMK (vocational secondary school)	59	99	?	158 + ?	118
Total	259	290	150	699	738

By 2010, therefore, the total number of ISSs at all levels was 874; this constituted just 0.46 per cent of the 190,000 schools in Indonesia (Kemdiknas 2009).[9]

It appears that by early 2011 the number of schools had increased further. There are also indications in the draft Five Year Development Plan for Education in Indonesia for the period 2010–2014 that the number of ISSs is likely to be increased further still. The Plan states that:

The Ministry plans that by 2014 at least one primary school and one junior secondary school in each rural and urban district will have been prepared to become International Standard Schools. ... The [programme for the] development of outstanding schools ... has a target that at least one senior secondary school/ vocational secondary school in each rural district/urban district will have become an outstanding local school or an International Standard School by 2014. (Depdiknas 2008c:64, 66)[10]

As there are approximately 500 rural and urban districts in Indonesia (Depdagri 2010), this implies that by 2014 there should be approximately 2,000 ISSs throughout the country (one primary, one junior secondary, one senior secondary and one vocational secondary school per district). Thus the number of ISSs will have to more than double between 2010 and 2014 if this target is to be met.

Socio-economic background of pupils

The schools which have been encouraged to apply for international standard status are schools which are already outstanding. As one senior official in the Ministry of National Education expressed it, 'The schools selected are the "cream of the cream"' *(Interview, 06 April 09).*

Headteachers of ISSs are keen to emphasise that their pupils come from wealthy professional families, as the following interview extracts illustrate:

Our parents are busy. Children are brought to school by their drivers and nursemaids. (State primary school, Jakarta, 07 April 2009)

Parents are middle to upper class. (Private primary school, Tangerang, 08 April 09)

The pupils have no problems with English – they are the children of rich parents and we select them rigorously as well.
(State junior secondary school, Jakarta, 07 April 09)

Some headteachers expressed frustration that they were expected to provide opportunities for children from less prosperous backgrounds:

Our parents are middle class and above, mostly from this housing complex. We are supposed to accept pupils with good results from neighbouring sub-districts but we're reluctant to do that because this will be a financial burden on the school. We'd have to arrange transport to collect the children and take them home. (Private primary school, Makassar, 20 April 2009)

Only half jokingly this headteacher added, 'Our motto is berTARAF internasional dan berTARIF internasional [international STANDARD and international FEES]!'

Role of English

The role which English is given in Table 4 is notable. English is to be used as the medium of instruction for science, mathematics and core vocational subjects from Year 4 of primary school and throughout junior secondary school, senior secondary school and vocational secondary school. Meanwhile, teachers must possess the competence required to teach their subjects through English while headteachers are required to have 'active' mastery of the language.

Regarding the use of English, the primary school handbook says only that pupils must leave school 'possessing the competence to communicate ideas and information to others in Indonesian and foreign languages (primarily English)' (Depdiknas 2008a:29).[11] Furthermore, the professionalism of 'teachers and other educational staff [i.e. the headteacher] will be demonstrated by their mastery of English' while staff development will include 'improving the competence of teachers in foreign languages, primarily English' (Depdiknas 2008a:30).[12] Nothing is said regarding the use of English as the medium of instruction – not even from Year 4.

On the other hand, the junior secondary school handbook – a massively detailed document almost 300 pages in length – makes it clear that English has an important role in the teaching-learning process:

> ... science and mathematics lessons use English, whilst other subjects apart from foreign languages must use Indonesian ... during the teaching-learning process, apart from using Indonesian and English, other languages which are frequently employed in international meetings may also be used, such as French, Spanish, Japanese, Arabic and Chinese. **(Depdiknas 2008b:37)**[13]

Actual practice

Actual practice in ISSs is very varied. In 2009 some schools claimed that they were still thinking about the meaning of becoming 'international' and had so far introduced very few changes:

> We've been having internal discussions within the school about what being an SBI means – whether it concerns the learning process, the way we evaluate the pupils, and whether all competencies should be developed, not only the academic ones; for example, dancing, sports. **(Interview with teacher in charge of SBI programme in a state primary school, Jakarta, 07 April 2009)**

Other schools have provided specially equipped classrooms for their SBI classes as well as other privileges which the regular classes do not enjoy:

> Each SBI class is air conditioned and is fitted with an LCD projector and computers. There are individual chairs for the pupils [i.e. not benches] and lockers where pupils can keep their things ... We employ some foreign teachers who come once or twice a month; we want to increase our SBI pupils' exposure to native speakers of English ... We have outdoor activities to supplement routine lessons and links with companies such as PERURI [National Mint] ... I put the young energetic teachers who are on short term contracts in the SBI classes, not the old civil servant [i.e. tenured] teachers; the young ones have TOEFL scores of at least 500 ... I know that some schools even have a special uniform for the pupils in their SBI classes, but we don't do that here. **(Interview with headteacher of state junior secondary school, Jakarta, 07 April 2009)**

Practice in schools regarding the use of English also varies. As we noted above, the government's handbook for ISS primary schools does not require the use of English as a medium of instruction, even from Year 4. In practice, however, many primary schools do use English to some extent or other. Some schools just 'slip some English words' into subject lessons whereas others are enthusiastically using English as the medium of instruction for maths and science from Year 1.

As we have seen, junior and senior secondary schools are required to use English as the medium of instruction at least for mathematics and science, but here again practice varies a great deal, with some lessons being taught exclusively in English and others in which English is used merely to open and close lessons while the content is delivered using Bahasa Indonesia.

Anecdotal evidence suggests that the offer to use English as the medium of instruction is very attractive to aspirational middle class parents. It is this aspect of the ISS scheme which members of the public are most likely to mention if asked what characterises ISSs.

Summary

- Legislation passed in 2003 required ISSs to be established at each educational level in each district of Indonesia. A succession of official documents and announcements between 2005 and 2010 then clarified the scheme in increasing detail.

- There is continuing uncertainty concerning several aspects of the ISS scheme, including the duration of support, the number of schools to be supported and the point at which English is supposed to be introduced as the medium of instruction. This suggests that policy has been developed in an ongoing manner since the scheme was first announced in 2003.

- By 2010 there were 874 ISSs. This means that fewer than one in every 200 schools has joined the scheme. Some targets suggest that the number of schools in the scheme should more than double by 2014, but it is unclear how realistic this ambition is.

- ISSs appeal to the prosperous middle class. Headteachers appear to relish this fact.

- The most prominent selling point of the ISS scheme is the requirement to use English as the medium of instruction for certain subjects. However, it appears that this requirement has been quietly modified for primary schools since no mention of English appears in later documentation.

- Actual practice in ISSs is extremely varied. Some provide special facilities and privileges for their ISS classes to which pupils in mainstream classes are denied access. Some schools use English as the medium of instruction (including some primary schools, despite the disappearance of the requirement to use English at the primary level). Other schools appear to pay lip service to the use of English.

Financing of International Standard Schools

In this section we look in detail at the roles of central government, district government and parents in the financing of the ISS scheme. In addition to the school operational support (BOS) funds which all primary and junior secondary schools receive – already discussed – ISSs receive a substantial subsidy from central government.

Sources of funding

The funding system for ISSs as it had been implemented during 2007 and 2008 was explained by a senior official in the Ministry of National Education (Interview 06 April 2009) in the following way:

■ In 2007, IDR350 million was allocated to each ISS for infrastructure improvement

■ In 2007, IDR100 million was allocated to each junior and senior secondary school for headteacher and teacher improvement

■ In 2008, IDR50 million was allocated to each ISS for unspecified purposes.

Thus, as Table 7 shows, each ISS at junior and senior secondary levels could expect to receive a total of IDR500 million (GBP35,500, USD54,800) during 2007 and 2008.

A speech by the Minister of National Education in April 2010 (Kompas 2010c) presented a modified picture. This indicated that junior secondary schools received IDR400 million in 2007 and then a further IDR300 million per year in 2008, 2009 and 2010, giving an overall total of IDR1,300 million (GBP92,300, USD142,500) over four years, as Table 7 shows. Slightly different grants were made available for senior secondary schools but no information was given for the funding allocated to primary schools.

Table 7: Block grants for SBI schools					
Source of information	**Funding source**	**Purpose**	**IDR (Rp000,000)**	**GBP (£000)**	**USD ($000)**
Ministry of National Education (interview 06 April 2009)	Central government	Refurbishment	350	24.9	38.4
		Staff development	100	7.1	11.0
		n.a.	50	3.6	5.5
	Total over two years		**500**	**35.5**	**54.8**
Ministerial speech (**Kompas** 2010c)	Central government	Junior secondary, 2007	400	28.4	43.8
		Junior secondary, 2008–2010	300 p.a.	21.3 p.a.	32.9 p.a.
	Total over four years		**1,300**	**92.3**	**142.5**
Primary school, Banda Aceh, Aceh (interview 16 April 2009)	Central government	n.a.	800	56.8	87.7
	District government	n.a.	100	7.1	11.0
	Total over two years		**900**	**63.9**	**98.6**

Junior secondary school, Makassar, South Sulawesi (interview 20 April 2009)	Central government	n.a.	700	49.7	76.7
	District government	Staff development	160	11.4	17.5
	Total over two years		**860**	**61.1**	**94.3**
Junior secondary school, Bekasi, West Java (Fahturahman 2009)	Central government	n.a.	300	21.3	32.9
	Provincial government	n.a.	240	17.0	26.3
	District government	n.a.	160	11.4	17.5
	Total per year		**700**	**49.7**	**76.7**

Individual schools in different parts of Indonesia reported that the funds which they received from central government were actually more generous than either the interview with the Ministry official or the Ministerial speech indicated. In addition, schools reported receiving additional grants from their district government. In some cases schools said that they had also received further grants from their provincial government. This can be illustrated by the following three case studies.

Case study one, state primary school, Banda Aceh
The headteacher of an ISS state primary school in Banda Aceh, the capital of the province of Aceh, reported that over the first two years of participation in the scheme his school had received a block grant of IDR500 million from central government in the first year and IDR300 million in the second year. The provincial government had added a further IDR100 million. As Table 7 shows, the total over two years came to IDR900 million (GBP63,900, USD98,600). The headteacher was expecting that there would be a further payment in 2009 for the 2009–2010 school year. (Interview 16 April 2009)

Case study two, state junior secondary school, Makassar
The headteacher of an ISS state junior secondary school in Makassar, the capital of the province of South Sulawesi, also reported figures which were markedly higher than those suggested by the Ministry official. The school had received IDR400 million from central government in 2007 followed by IDR300 million in 2008. The Makassar city government had also made available IDR160 million, earmarked specifically for staff training, bringing the total over two years to IDR860 million (GBP61,100, USD94,300). Further payments were expected. (Interview 20 April 2009)

Case study 3, state junior secondary school, Bekasi
Fahturahman (2009) reports that an ISS state junior secondary school in Bekasi, a city in the province of West Java, received ISS funds from three sources in its first year of being associated with the ISS scheme. Central government provided IDR300 million, the West Java provincial government granted IDR240 million and the Bekasi city government allocated a further IDR160 million. As Table 7 shows, the total funding received by this school in just one year was IDR700 million (GBP49,700, USD76,700).

We noted earlier that there has been uncertainty regarding several aspects of the ISS scheme and that policy development has been an ongoing process. From these three case studies it appears that a similar degree of uncertainty is a feature of the funding arrangements for ISSs. Nevertheless, what is undeniable is that schools receive extremely generous financial allocations, especially in comparison with the modest value of the standard BOS grants which are given to all schools. Indeed the non-government organisation (NGO) Koalisi Pendidikan (Coalition for Education) has estimated that the average annual subsidy received by ISSs from central and local government in 2010 was actually IDR1.5 billion (GBP107,000, USD164,000). This is even more than the figures in Table 7 would suggest, although the basis for Koalisi Pendidikan's estimate is not explained.

But the story does not stop there. State primary and junior secondary schools are forbidden from charging fees (however disguised). An exception is made for ISSs, however. Consequently, state primary and junior secondary ISSs are free to charge additional fees, on top of the BOS and ISS grants which they receive from government.

According to a 2010 study by the NGO Koalisi Pendidikan, the average monthly fee charged by ISS primary schools was IDR200,000 (GBP14, USD22) with an additional annual 'development contribution' of IDR6 million (GBP426, USD658). In the same year the average monthly fee charged by ISS junior secondary schools was IDR450,000 (GBP32, USD49), also with an annual development contribution of IDR6 million. On top of these, there are also entrance examination fees and fees for international study tours (Kompas 2010d).

In comparison, among the ISSs surveyed in 2009 by the author of this chapter, monthly fees ranged from as little as IDR20,000 (GBP1.42, USD2.19, primary school, Banda Aceh) to as much as IDR1 million (GBP71, USD110, senior secondary school, Jakarta). Although these fees may appear to be modest, if they are set alongside the per capita income figures for Indonesia discussed above (Table 1) it becomes clear that the ISSs are way beyond the financial capacity of the majority of the population.

All in all, therefore, ISSs are extraordinarily well funded, with funds from the routine BOS programme, with ISS funds from central, provincial and district governments and with substantial monthly and annual fees which have to be paid by parents. It is not surprising then that the ISSs have been described as 'overflowing with cash' (kucuran dana melimpah, Kompas 2010d). As further evidence of this wealth, a Ministry of National Education official reported in early 2011 that a group of ISSs in Jakarta were planning to draw on their own funds to send a delegation of teachers and headteachers on a study tour to the UK; in 2010 the same group of schools had sent a similar delegation of teachers and headteachers to Australia at a cost of IDR600 million (GBP43,000, USD66,000) (Samto, personal communication, 24 January 2011).

Summary

In this section we have seen that:

- ISSs receive government grants over and above the routine funding which is given to all schools.

- The ISS grants from central government are very generous. They are supplemented by further grants from district governments and in some cases by grants from provincial governments as well.

- Some schools report receiving grants which are even more generous than those announced by government.

- State ISSs are also permitted to charge admission and tuition fees. This makes them accessible only to the most prosperous sector of society.

Globalisation as a rationale for International Standard Schools

This section examines the arguments which have been proposed for the establishment of the ISS scheme in Indonesia.

One justification for the establishment of ISSs is that they prepare pupils for studying abroad. An example is the following statement made by the headteacher of a private primary ISS in Tangerang, one of Jakarta's satellite cities:

> It's for the long term, so that the pupils can study abroad.
> *(Interview 08 April 2009)*

Other informants felt that the rationale for the ISS scheme lay in the use of English as the medium of instruction, as the following somewhat confused argument suggests:

> *International Standard School means 'bilingual' lessons. That means teaching through English. But unfortunately sometimes two languages are used.*
> *(Interview with headteacher, state senior secondary school, Banda Aceh, 17 April 2009)*[14]

But overwhelmingly the justification put forward – both in official documents and by individual stakeholders – for the establishment of ISSs is that of 'globalisation' and 'competition' with other nations. A Ministry of National Education background document, produced in 2007 as the ISS scheme was about to be introduced, stated (emphasis added):

> *Education will produce people of [high] quality who can compete locally and internationally. This is important in the era of globalisation and the free market, in which competition between nations is becoming ever more transparent and uninhibited. (Hadi et al. 2007:1)*[15]

The 2008 guidebook for junior secondary schools working towards ISS status makes a similar statement:

> *The provision of international standard education at the primary and secondary levels ... is based on the following argument ...: The era of globalisation demands competitive competence in engineering, management and human resources.* ***(Depdiknas 2008b:3)***[16]

A senior official in the Ministry of National Education interviewed in Jakarta in 2009 repeated the same formula:

> *This is the era of globalisation. We need to be prepared so that the Indonesian nation can compete with other nations.* ***(Interview, Jakarta, 06 April 2009)***[17]

And a very similar comment was made by the headteacher of a state primary school in Aceh:

> *Actually I don't know what the rationale [for establishing ISS] is, only 'global competition'.* ***(Interview, Banda Aceh, 17 April 2009)***[18]

The same concept is expressed in a government decree on the management and implementation of education issued in 2010:

> *The quality of education must be constantly improved ... so that the future generations who will take the nation forward can be prepared well in advance such that [they] will be in a high ranking and competitive position in national life and globally.* ***(Republik Indonesia 2010:1)***[19]

And so it goes on, with the terms 'globalisation' and 'competitiveness' repeated time and again like a mantra. Even individual primary schools claim to be producing graduates who are 'globally competitive':

> *Vision: Leading towards a school which is innovative, prestigious and religious such that its graduates are innovative, possess high morals and are competitive globally.* ***(SDS Model Islamic Village 2008)***[20]

One can only wonder just how 'globally competitive' twelve-year-old children can be expected to be ...[21]

The use of English as a medium of instruction also frequently collocates with 'globalisation' in government and school documents concerning the ISS system. The relationship is never spelt out explicitly, but it is approximately as shown in Figure 1. The Figure shows that globalisation is perceived as being synonymous with international competition; international competition in turn is assumed to involve the use of English; and using English appears to necessitate the learning of other subjects through English.

Figure 1: Perceived relationships between 'globalisation' and other concepts

Of course, this formulation can be challenged in a number of ways. First, globalisation need not imply competition. An alternative interpretation of globalisation, which celebrates the opportunities which it offers for co-operation between the peoples of the world, is very rarely encountered. The only exception which we have found is contained in the Indonesian Ministry of National Education's 2008 Handbook on International Standard Primary Schools:

> The aim of international standard primary schools is to improve the professionalism of primary schools ... based on national standards and an international perspective ... Graduates of international standard primary schools are world class, able to compete and to collaborate globally with other nations in the world, and this requires understanding of people and cultures across the world. (Depdiknas 2008a:3, 23)[22]

Although 'competing globally' makes an appearance here as well, the formula is leavened to some extent with references to an 'international perspective', 'collaborating globally' and the need for cross-cultural understanding.

The second way in which the formulation shown in Figure 1 can be challenged is simply to question whether the need for English in international contacts (whether those contacts are competitive or collaborative in nature) necessarily implies that the learning of mathematics, science and vocational subjects in school should take place in English. There is no obvious link.

Summary
This section has shown that:

- The most common explanation for the establishment of the ISS scheme found in official documents and given by stakeholders is 'globalisation'. This is almost always interpreted in terms of competing against other nations.

- Globalisation and competitiveness are associated with a need for English and then with a need to use English as a medium of instruction, although the logical relationships between these different concepts remain unclear.

Another constituency

But there is another constituency in Indonesia which, it can be argued, is actually experiencing the impact of globalisation in a direct way. These are Indonesia's migrant workers. According to Indonesian government figures, in the period January to September 2010 there were 428,000 Indonesian migrant workers in other parts of the world (Kompas 2010e). However, the International Labour Organisation claims that the figure is much higher, with 700,000 registered migrant workers from Indonesia working in other parts of the world in 2008 (ILO 2008). Meanwhile, a report produced for the United Nations High Commission for Refugees calculated that in 2007 there were 'more than two million illegal [= unregistered] migrant workers' from Indonesia in other countries (Sidel 2007). We can conclude, then, that at any one time there are possibly between 2.5 and 3.0 million Indonesians working abroad.

The principal characteristics of Indonesia's migrant workers are that they are 83 per cent female, aged 14–40, generally unskilled and for the most part educated only to primary school level (World Bank 2006). The majority come from rural backgrounds in East and Central Java, East Kalimantan, Riau and West Nusa Tenggara (World Bank 2007). Many are employed as domestic servants in the Middle East, Malaysia and Hong Kong. Registered migrant workers are given minimal basic skills training before they leave Indonesia but the unregistered migrants receive no pre-departure training at all. Once they arrive at their destination they face many obstacles and are vulnerable to exploitation and abuse.

The scale of the difficulties experienced by migrant workers can be gauged from an Indonesian government announcement in early 2011 in which it was revealed that 25,000 migrant workers in Saudi Arabia were 'experiencing problems' (bermasalah) and would need to be repatriated. The repatriation programme was expected to take until the end of the year and would cost IDR120 billion (GBP8.5 million, USD13.2 million), a sum which will be charged to the public purse (Co-ordinating Minister for the People's Welfare, quoted in Kompas 2011).

Another indicator of the hardship experienced by Indonesia's migrant workers is the number who die abroad. For example, the Chair of the Indonesian Migrant Labourers' Union was reported in 2010 as saying that the airport of Surabaya, capital of East Java, receives on average one coffin a day containing the remains of a migrant worker from the East Java region who has died abroad (Sawabi 2010). It is likely that similar events occur in those other parts of the country which are home to large numbers of migrant workers.

No research has been undertaken to investigate why Indonesia's migrant workers experience problems on such a scale but it appears that a major factor is likely to be the difficulty which they have in communicating with their employers. Cultural misunderstandings between workers and their employers are also likely to be contributing factors.

Despite these appalling problems, migrant workers remit very large amounts of money back to their families in Indonesia. The World Bank estimated that in 2005 USD2.5 billion (GBP1.6 billion, IDR22 trillion) was transferred back to Indonesia through formal routes (World Bank 2006) but by 2008 the International Labour Organisation estimated that this sum was actually USD6.1 billion (GBP4.0 billion, IDR54 trillion; ILO 2008). By 2010 the World Bank estimated that USD9.1 billion had been remitted back to Indonesia by migrant workers in the first nine months of the year (Kompas 2010e); if the flow of remittances continued at the same rate for the rest of the year then the total for 2010 would be approximately USD12.1 billion (IDR108 trillion, GBP7.8 billion).

Summary

- There may be up to 2.5 million migrant workers from Indonesia in other countries producing an annual capital inflow of IDR108 trillion in remittances. The majority of these people receive no language tuition or any other sort of training before going abroad. Many of them appear to experience communication problems while they are away.

Discussion

This survey of the ISS scheme in Indonesia and the context in which it operates has found that:

- Education at the primary and junior secondary levels in Indonesia is compulsory and free. The national language, Bahasa Indonesia, is the medium of instruction while English is a compulsory subject in the second school curriculum. Primary and junior secondary schools receive a modest capitation allowance from government, in return for which they are not allowed to levy fees. About 30 per cent of the population of Indonesia live on less than USD1.25 per day.

- The ISS scheme was introduced in 2007. The ISSs are excused from the requirement to use Bahasa Indonesia as the medium of instruction and in fact are expected to use English, at least for the teaching of mathematics and science and at least in secondary schools. ISSs appeal primarily to the prosperous middle class. By early 2011 fewer than 0.5 per cent of the country's schools had been given ISS (or 'fledgling ISS') status.

- ISSs receive extremely generous additional funds from central and local government; they are also permitted to charge fees. They have been described as being 'overflowing' with money.

- 'Globalisation' is referred to repeatedly as the reason for the ISS scheme to be established. This concept is interpreted in terms of 'global competition' which supposedly requires children to have a mastery of English and therefore (although the link has not been demonstrated) there is a need for English to be used as the medium of instruction.

- Indonesia's migrant workers constitute a neglected constituency. They are calculated to generate IDR108 trillion in foreign exchange but are given minimal – if any – language training or other pre-departure preparation.

The picture which has been created reveals a number of anomalies. The first is that the ISSs – which serve a privileged and prosperous minority – receive a massive financial reward from government on top of the modest grant which is given to all schools. In other words, the ISSs constitute a considerable subsidy to the most prosperous sector of society which is not available to the rest of the community.

The second anomaly is that the ISS scheme claims to be preparing students for a 'globally competitive' world. But there is a very large group of Indonesians who go abroad and face 'global competitiveness' in a direct and often painful way: the migrant workers. Migrant workers are mostly female, are generally poorly educated, do not speak any foreign language and are not being prepared at all for the 'globally competitive' world which is waiting for them.

A third anomaly is that this second group – despite being so poorly prepared before leaving the country – generates a very large inflow of funds to Indonesia.

What, then, are the implications of these findings?

At one level, it is possible to argue that the Indonesian government's English medium ISS scheme, presumably established with the best of intentions, seems to be focusing on a sector of society which already has a high level of awareness of the importance of English. As Lamb (2011, Chapter 9 this volume) shows, the Indonesian middle classes will always find a way to achieve their aspirations. Consequently, this sector of society does not require a substantial state subsidy.

On the other hand, it is also appropriate to suggest that the migrant workers, who make an enormous contribution to the Indonesian economy, are being neglected even though they would actually be able to benefit substantially from pre-departure language training (and other forms of preparation, including cross-cultural awareness training). Such language training would have to include both English and the language of the host community where the workers are to be placed: Colloquial Arabic in the Middle East, Cantonese in Hong Kong, Malay in Malaysia, etc.[23]

More broadly, the ISS case appears to confirm the suspicion, already aired by Lamb and Coleman (2008) – in a paper written before the ISS scheme had been launched – that the Indonesian education system is perpetuating social inequalities, particularly through the way in which English is offered and taught. Those who can afford to purchase English language tuition privately are enjoying access to a heavily subsidised school system which gives high priority to the use of English as a medium of instruction. On the other hand, those who urgently need English (and other languages) for survival while working abroad are left to fend for themselves without access to language tuition of any kind.

More broadly still, this case highlights the difficulties which many governments have in planning the allocation of resources for language development (particularly English) in a manner which supports national development objectives, maximises economic benefits, is transparent, is equitable and, crucially, empowers citizens to make of their lives what they will. In this regard, Sayers' proposal for a 'human rights typology' of language acquisition planning is extremely thought provoking (Sayers 2010).

Perhaps we can conclude by adapting Amartya Sen's celebrated statement about starvation and the availability of food: 'Ignorance is the characteristic of some people not having enough access to good education. It is not the characteristic of there being not enough good education.'[24]

Notes

1. This is a modified and updated version of one section of an earlier paper (Coleman 2010) which also looked at similar types of school in South Korea and Thailand. I am grateful to Martin Lamb and Danny Whitehead for comments on an intermediate version. The views expressed here are those of the author and are not those of the British Council, which commissioned the original study (Coleman 2009) on which the chapter is based.

2. Published figures are indicated in **bold**; other figures are extrapolated from these. Figures are rounded to the nearest 1000 rupiah and to the nearest dollar and pound (except for the daily rates for batik dyers and those living below the poverty line where they are given to the nearest hundredth of a dollar and hundredth of a pound).

3. The rupiah figures were announced by the Minister for National Education on 27 December 2010 (Kompas 2010f).

4. 'Pemerintah dan/atau Pemerintah Daerah menyelenggarakan sekurang-kurangnya satu sekolah pada semua jenjang pendidikan untuk dikembangkan menjadi sekolah yang bertaraf internasional.'

5. 'Pemerintah bersama-sama pemerintah daerah menyelenggarakan sekurang-kurangnya satu sekolah pada jenjang pendidikan dasar dan sekurang-kurangnya satu sekolah pada jenjang pendidikan menengah untuk dikembangkan menjadi sekolah bertaraf internasional.'

6. 'Untuk meningkatkan daya saing bangsa ... pemerintah dengan pemerintah kabupaten/kota yang bersangkutan [perlu] mengembangkan SD, SMP, SMA dan SMK yang bertaraf internasional sebanyak 112 unit di seluruh Indonesia.'

7. 'Sekolah/Madrasah yang sudah memenuhi seluruh Standar Nasional Pendidikan dan diperkaya dengan mengacu pada standar pendidikan salah satu negara anggota Organisation for Economic Co-operation and Development dan/atau negara maju lainnya yang mempunyai keunggulan tertentu dalam bidang pendidikan sehingga memiliki daya saing di forum internasional.'

8. Literally, rintisan means a 'new shoot' on a plant. In the context of the ISS scheme the term is used metaphorically to indicate schools which are leading towards full ISS status. 'Fledgling' therefore seems to be a more appropriate translation.

9. The total number of primary, junior secondary, senior secondary, vocational secondary and special schools (both state and private) in 2007–2008 was 189,284. This was the most recent figure available on the website of the Ministry of National Education (*www.kemdiknas.go.id/list_link/statistik-pendidikan.aspx*) in February 2011. This figure does not include Islamic schools operated or overseen by the Ministry of Religious Affairs.

10. 'Depdiknas menargetkan pada tahun 2014 paling tidak satu SD dan satu SMP pada masing-masing kabupaten/kota sudah dirintis menjadi ... sekolah bertaraf internasional ... Pengembangan sekolah berkeunggulan ... menargetkan paling tidak satu SMA/SMK pada masing-masing kabupaten/kota akan menjadi sekolah berkeunggulan lokal dan/atau bertaraf internasional pada tahun 2014.'

11. 'Kemampuan mengkomunikasikan ide dan informasi kepada pihak lain dalam bahasa Indonesia dan bahasa asing (utamanya Bahasa Inggris).'

12. 'Profesionalisme pendidik dan tenaga kependidikan ditunjukkan oleh penguasaan bahasa asing bahasa Inggris khususnya ... Pengembangan guru-

guru SDBI dilakukan secara bertahap dan berkelanjutan, melalui ... peningkatan kemampuan salah satu bahasa asing, utamanya bahasa Inggris.'

13. '... pembelajaran mata pelajaran kelompok sains dan matematika menggunakan bahasa Inggris, sementara pembelajaran mata pelajaran lainnya, kecuali pelajaran bahasa asing, harus menggunakan bahasa Indonesia ... dalam proses pembelajaran selain menggunakan bahasa Indonesia dan bahasa Inggris, juga bisa menggunakan bahasa lainnya yang sering digunakan dalam forum internasional, seperti bahasa Perancis, Spanyol, Jepang, Arab dan Cina.'

14. 'SBI artinya pembelajaran bilingual. Artinya mengajar dengan Bahasa Inggris. Tetapi sayang sekali kadang-kadang dua bahasa dipakai.'

15. 'Melalui pendidikan akan dicetak manusia-manusia berkualitas yang memiliki daya saing lokal maupun internasional. Ini menjadi penting pada era globalisasi dan pasar bebas, di mana persaingan antar negara semakin terbuka bebas.'

16. 'Penyelenggaraan pendidikan yang bertaraf internasional pada jenjang pendidikan dasar dan menengah ... dilatarbelakangi oleh alasan ... berikut: Era globalisasi menuntut kemampuan daya saing yang kuat dalam teknologi, manajemen dan sumberdaya manusia.'

17. 'Ini era globalisasi. Siap-siap supaya bangsa Indonesia bisa bersaing dengan negara lain.'

18. 'Sebenarnya saya tidak tahu kenapa mesti ada SBI, hanya "persaingan global".'

19. 'Pendidikan harus secara terus-menerus perlu ditingkatkan kualitasnya ... agar mampu mempersiapkan generasi penerus bangsa sejak dini sehingga memiliki unggulan kompetitif dalam tatanan kehidupan nasional dan global.'

20. 'Visi: Menuju sekolah yang inovatif, prestatif dan religius sehingga mampu menghasilkan lulusan yang inovatif dan berakhlak mulia serta kompetitif di dunia global.'

21. This concern with competitiveness and relative standing vis à vis other countries can be seen also in the importance which both government and press in Indonesia attach to achievements in the various international 'olympiads' in different school subjects. Examples include the International Mathematics Olympiad (www.imo-official.org/), which has up to 100 participating countries, and the International Earth Science Olympiad (www.ieso2009.tw/main/home/home.html), with just nineteen participating nations. Every medal won by an Indonesian high school student in these competitions is reported in the national press, almost always with the phrase anak bangsa ('child of the nation') appearing somewhere in the report to indicate the nation's pride in the achievements of its sons and daughters in their competition against representatives of other countries.

22. 'Tujuan SDBI adalah untuk meningkatkan keprofesionalan satuan pendidikan SD ... berdasarkan standar nasional dan wawasan internasional ... lulusan SDBI berkelas dunia, mampu bersaing dan berkolaborasi secara global dengan bangsa-bangsa lain di dunia, dan itu memerlukan pemahaman orang dan budaya lintas bangsa.'

23. Most Indonesian migrant workers are native speakers of Javanese, Sasak and other Indonesian languages, not of Bahasa Indonesia. Their school education will have been through Bahasa Indonesia but, as the majority come from rural workers, they may not have had much experience of using Bahasa Indonesia on a daily basis. Moreover, colloquial Bahasa Malaysia differs sufficiently from Bahasa Indonesia for communication difficulties to arise.

24. 'Starvation is the characteristic of some people not having enough food to eat. It is not the characteristic of there being not enough food to eat.' (Sen 1981:1)

References

Antara News. 2010. *Continued Economic Growth Seen for RI in 2011.* Uploaded 20 December 2010. Available online at: *www.antaranews.com/en/news/1292832746/continued-economic-growth-seen-for-ri-in-2011*

Bax, S. 2010. *Researching English Bilingual Education in Thailand, Indonesia and South Korea. Kuala Lumpur: British Council East Asia.*

BPS (Badan Pusat Statistik, Central Board for Statistics). 2009. *IHK, Upah Nominal, Indeks Upah Nominal dan Riil Buruh Industri Berstatus di bawah Mandor Menurut Wilayah, 2004-2009, Triw III.* [CPI, Nominal Wage and Nominal and Real Wage Index of Industrial Labourers below Supervisory Level, 2004-2009, 3rd Quarter]. Available online at: *www.bps.go.id/tab_sub/view.php?tabel=1&daftar=1&id_subyek=19&notab=2*

Coleman, H. 2009. *Teaching Other Subjects through English in Three Asian Nations: A Review.* Unpublished report for the British Council.

Coleman, H. 2010. *Are 'International Standard Schools' really a response to globalisation?* In N.Supriyanti (ed.), *Responding to Global Education Challenges: Proceedings of an International Seminar on Education*, 11-35. Yogyakarta: Yogyakarta State University.

Darmaningtyas. 2010. *Mendesak, Revisi UU Sisdiknas.* [Revision of the Law on the Education System Urgently Needed.] **Kompas** 16 August 2010. Available online at *http://edukasi.kompas.com/read/2010/08/16/12043080/Mendesak.Revisi.UU.Sisdiknas*

Depdiknas (Departemen Pendidikan Nasional). 2005. *Rencana Strategis Departemen Pendidikan Nasional 2005-2009*. [Department of National Education Strategic Plan 2005-2009.] *Jakarta: Departemen Pendidikan Nasional.*

Depdiknas (Departemen Pendidikan Nasional). 2007. *Pedoman Penjaminan Mutu Sekolah/Madrasah Bertaraf Internasional Jenjang Pendidikan Dasar dan Menengah.* [Quality Assurance Handbook for Primary and Secondary

Level International Standard Schools/ Madrasahs.] *Jakarta: Direktorat Tenaga Kependidikan, Direktorat Jenderal Peningkatan Mutu Pendidik dan Tenaga Kependidikan, Departemen Pendidikan Nasional.*

Depdiknas (Departemen Pendidikan Nasional). 2008a. *Panduan Penyelenggaraan Rintisan Sekolah Dasar Bertaraf Internasional.* [Guidelines for Implementation of 'Fledgling' International Standard Primary Schools.] *Jakarta: Direktorat Pembinaan Taman Kanak-Kanak dan Sekolah Dasar, Direktorat Jenderal Manajemen Pendidikan Dasar dan Menengah, Departemen Pendidikan Nasional.*

Depdiknas (Departemen Pendidikan Nasional). 2008b. *Panduan Pelaksanaan Pembinaan Rintisan Sekolah Menengah Pertama Bertaraf Internasional (SMP-SBI).* [Guidelines for Mentoring of Fledgling International Standard Junior Secondary Schools.] *Jakarta: Direktorat Pembinaan Sekolah Menengah Pertama, Direktorat Jenderal Manajemen Pendidikan Dasar dan Menengah, Departemen Pendidikan Nasional.*

Depdiknas (Departemen Pendidikan Nasional). 2008c. *Draf RENSTRA 2010-2014, 18 November 2008. [Draft Strategic Plan 2010-2014, 18 November 2008.]* Unpublished document.

Depdiknas (Departemen Pendidikan Nasional). 2009. *Peta Kemampuan Bahasa Inggris Pendidik dan Tenaga Kependidikan Rintisan Sekolah Bertaraf Internasional Berdasarkan Test of English for International Communication (TOEIC).* [Mapping of English Language Competence of Teachers and Other Education Personnel in Fledgling International Standard Schools Based on TOEIC Results.] *Jakarta: Direktorat Tenaga Kependidikan, Direktorat Jenderal Peningkatan Mutu Pendidik dan Tenaga Kependidikan, Departemen Pendidikan Nasional.*

Fahturahman. 2009. *Decentralisation of Education Finance in Indonesia: Perceptions of Policy Makers.* Unpublished PhD thesis, University of Birmingham, UK.

Hadi, D.W., Supriyadi T., Yufridawati, Handayani, M., Karmidah dan Relisa. 2007. *Model SMA Bertaraf Internasional: Hasil Refleksi dari Penyelenggaraan yang Ada.* [A Model for International Standard Senior Secondary Schools: A Reflection on Current Practice.] *Jakarta: Pusat Penelitian Kebijakan dan Inovasi Pendidikan, Badan Penelitian dan Pengembangan, Departemen Pendidikan Nasional.*

ILO (International Labour Organisation). 2008. *Press Release: Utilising Remittances of Migrant Workers for Productive Investment.* 21-11-2008. *Jakarta: International Labour Organisation.*

Kemdiknas. 2009. *Statistik Pendidikan 2007-2008.* [Education Statistics 2007-2008.] *Jakarta: Kementerian Pendidikan Nasional.* [Ministry of National Education.] Available online at: *www.kemdiknas.go.id/list_link/statistik-pendidikan.aspx*

Kompas. 2010a. *Bahasa asing di sekolah langgar undang-undang.* [Foreign languages in schools is against the law.] *Kompas* 8 November 2010. Available online at *http://cetak.kompas.com/read/2010/11/08/04275014/bahasa.asing.di.sekolah. langgar.undang-undang*

Kompas. 2010b. *Harus bangga gunakan Bahasa Indonesia.* [(We) should be proud of the Indonesian language.] *Kompas* 10 November 2010. Available online at *http://cetak.kompas.com/read/2010/11/10/04224694/harus.bangga.gunakan.. bahasa.indonesia*

Kompas 2010c. *Dana RSBI akan dievaluasi.* [Funding for fledgling International Standard Schools to be evaluated.] *Kompas* 30 April 2010. Available online at *http://cetak.kompas.com/read/2010/04/30/04464922/dana..rsbi.akan.dievaluasi*

Kompas. 2010d. *Konsep RSBI tak jelas.* [Fledgling International Standard School concept is unclear.] *Kompas* 6 November 2010. Available online at *http://cetak.kompas.com/read/2010/11/06/03001614/.konsep.rsbi.tak.jelas*

Kompas. 2010e. *Remitansi besar, perhatian kurang.* [(Migrant workers send) large remittances, (receive) little attention.] *Kompas* 27 December 2010. Available online at *http://cetak.kompas.com/read/2010/12/27/04230572/.remitansi.besar.perhatian. kurang*

Kompas. 2010f. *Mekanisme BOS diubah.* [Mechanism for school operational support grant to be modified.] *Kompas* 28 December 2010. Available online at *http://cetak.kompas.com/read/2010/12/28/02291970/mekanisme.bos.diubah*

Kompas. 2011. *190 pengusaha sepakat: Perlindungan TKI di Arab Saudi diharapkan bisa membaik.* [190 business people reach agreement: Protection of Indonesian migrant workers in Saudi Arabia expected to improve.] *Kompas* 17 February 2011. Available online at *http://cetak.kompas.com/ read/2011/02/17/04061363/190.pengusaha.sepakat*

Kroll, L. and Miller, M. 2010. *The World's Billionaires. New York: Forbes.com.* Available online at: *www.forbes.com/lists/2010/10/billionaires-2010_The-Worlds-Billionaires_CountryOfCitizen_12.html*

Lamb, M. 2011. *A 'Matthew Effect' in English language education in a developing country context.* Chapter 9, this volume.

Lamb, M. and Coleman, H. 2008. *Literacy in English and the transformation of self and society in post-Soeharto Indonesia. Bilingual Education and Bilingualism* 11(2), 189-205.

OECD (Organisation for Economic Co-operation and Development). 2010. *PISA 2009 Results: What Students Know and Can Do – Student Performance in Reading, Mathematics and Science, Volume I*. Paris: OECD. Available online at: *http://dx.doi.org/10.1787/9789264091450-en*

Ratna, M. 2010. *Keindahan gentongan Tanjungbumi.* [The beauty of gentongan batik from Tanjungbumi.] *Kompas* 21 November 2011.

Republik Indonesia. 2003. *Undang-Undang No 20 Tahun 2003 tentang Sistem Pendidikan Nasional.* [Law No 20, 2003, on the National Education System.]

Republik Indonesia. 2005. *Peraturan Pemerintah No 19 Tahun 2005 tentang Standar Nasional Pendidikan.* [Government Decree No 19, 2005, on National Standards for Education.]

Republik Indonesia. 2010. *Penjelasan atas Peraturan Pemerintah No 17 Tahun 2010 tentang Pengelolaan dan Penyelenggaraan Pendidikan.* [Clarification of Government Decree No 17, 2010, on Management and Implementation of Education.]

Sawabi, I. 2010. *Tiap hari satu TKI pulang jadi mayat.* [Every day one Indonesian migrant worker returns home in a coffin.] *Kompas* 10 September 2010. Available online at *http://bisniskeuangan.kompas.com/read/2010/09/18/13533921/Tiap.Hari. Satu.TKI.Pulang.Jadi.Mayat*

Sayers, D. 2010. *A human rights typology of language acquisition planning.* (Unpublished paper.) *Abertawe/Swansea: Prifysgol Abertawe/University of Swansea.* Available online at *http://swansea.academia.edu/DaveSayers/ Talks/17027/A_Human_Rights_Typology_of_Language_Acquisition_Planning*

SDS Model Islamic Village. 2008. *Handbook SDS Model Islamic Village 2008-2009. Tangerang: SDS Model Islamic Village (RSBI).*

Sen, A.K. 1981. *Poverty and Famines: An Essay on Entitlement and Deprivation. Oxford: Clarendon Press.*

Sidel, J.T. 2007. *Indonesia: Minorities, Migrant Workers, Refugees and the New Citizenship Law. (Report commissioned by Status Determination and Protection Information Section, United Nations High Commissioner for Refugees.) London: Writenet.* Available online at *www.unhcr.org/refworld/pdfid/463ae6272.pdf*

UNDP (United Nations Development Programme). 2010. *The Real Wealth of Nations: Pathways to Human Development. (Human Development Report 2010, 20th Anniversary Edition.) Basingstoke and New York: Palgrave Macmillan for UNDP.* Available online at *http://hdr.undp.org/en/*

UNESCO (United Nations Educational, Scientific and Cultural Organisation). 2010. *UIS Database Table 5: Enrolment ratios by ISCED level. Paris: UNESCO.* Available online at *http://stats.uis.unesco.org/unesco/TableViewer/tableView. aspx?ReportId=182*

World Bank. 2006. *Fact Sheet: Migration, Remittance and Female Migrant Workers. Jakarta: Female Migrant Workers Research Team, World Bank.*

World Bank. 2007. *Indonesian Overseas Migrants (Outflows) and Remittances (Inflows) Based on Migrants' Place of Origin for the First Quarter 2007. (Map.) Washington DC: East Asia Social Development Unit, Financial Market Integrity Unit, The World Bank.*

Perceptions of English

6

English education, local languages and community perspectives in Uganda[1]

Juliet Tembe and Bonny Norton

Introduction

Over the past two decades, there has been a growing number of researchers who have provided convincing support for the promotion of mother tongue education in the early years of schooling (Cummins 1981, 1993, 2000, Klaus 2003, Obondo 2007, Williams 1996). These researchers make the case that knowledge and skills gained in the mother tongue can transfer across languages; they also argue that multilingual children perform well at school when the school teaches the mother tongue effectively. Literature on literacy development attests to the benefits of using a child's mother tongue even when the goal is learning a second language. Further, research in second language acquisition has shown that the level of proficiency in the first language has a direct influence on the development of proficiency in the second language. For example, in two experimental studies of bilingual education in Guinea-Bissau and in Mozambique (Benson 2000), the students in the bilingual programme performed better when tested in the second language than their monolingual counterparts.

Research in Africa suggests, however, that multilingual language policies have met with limited success, partly due to a lack of appreciation of the context in which such policies are implemented (Bamgbose 2000, Kwesiga 1994, Oladejo 1993, Parry et al. 2005, Stein 2007). For example, many African parents assume that mother tongue policies have been imposed for political rather than sociolinguistic or demographic reasons (Muthwii 2002). In addition, parents want their children to master the official language, or the language of wider communication (LWC), early in the education process (Bergmann 1996). There is a common (though mistaken) belief that African languages are not equipped to deal with scientific and technical concepts (Obanya 1995, Prah 2010).

Like many countries in Africa, Uganda, which gained independence from Britain in 1962, has been struggling to develop and implement effective multilingual policies in its schools. English is the official language of the country, but there is as yet no national language because none of the Ugandan languages has been considered demographically strong enough to take on this role. After a period of political turmoil in the 1970s and 1980s, the government appointed an education review commission to carry out a comprehensive analysis and suggest a blueprint for the future. The report of the commission culminated in the publication of a Government White Paper (GWP) on education (Government White Paper 1992). One of the major curriculum-related changes introduced by the GWP was the language education policy, which distinguished between policies in rural and urban areas. It was noted that the majority of the Ugandan population (90 per cent) is rural based, such that extensive areas may have people who speak the same language living together. However, the increasing rural–urban migrations in search of a better life have resulted in a growing number of urban centres with populations that are highly mixed linguistically. Therefore, against this background, the GWP stipulated that, in rural areas, the 'relevant local languages' would be used as the media of instruction from Primary 1 to Primary 4. English then becomes the medium of instruction in Primary 5. Primary 4 is a transition year, in which teachers use both the local language and English. In urban areas, English would be the medium of instruction from Primary 1 onwards, with the 'local language' taught as a subject. Kiswahili, 'as the language possessing greater capacity for uniting Ugandans and for assisting rapid social development' (GWP 1992:19), would be taught as a compulsory subject in both the rural and urban schools from Primary 4 to Primary 7. See Table 1.

Table 1: Languages in primary schools in Uganda						
Location	Class	Local language as medium	Local language as subject	English as medium	English as subject	Kiswahili as subject
Rural	1	✓			✓	✓
	2	✓			✓	✓
	3	✓			✓	✓
	4	✓			✓	✓
	5		✓	✓		✓
	6		✓	✓		✓
	7		✓	✓		✓
Urban	1		✓	✓		✓
	2		✓	✓		✓
	3		✓	✓		✓
	4		✓	✓		✓
	5		✓	✓		✓
	6		✓	✓		✓
	7		✓	✓		✓

It should be noted that policy and practice often differ. For example, although Kiswahili is emphasised, few schools are actually teaching it because there are not enough trained teachers or instructional materials.

Although the Education Review Commission, on whose report the 1992 White Paper on education was based, had recommended that the medium of instruction in the first four years of primary schooling should be the mother tongue, the government changed this to 'the relevant local language'. As mentioned above, urban centres had highly linguistically mixed populations. But similar situations were also found in some rural areas, especially where there were no distinct boundaries as one moved from one language group to another. Thus there may be a dominant language in a rural village, but trade with neighbouring villages might lead to the use of other languages. Therefore, it was practical to speak of a local language that would be used perhaps as a lingua franca by people whose mother tongue was different. (See, for example, Mukama 1991.)

In response to the proposals in the GWP, the National Curriculum Development Centre (NCDC) developed a curriculum that was eventually introduced into primary schools in two parts, in 2000 and 2002. One of the challenges facing the NCDC was how to address the government language policy in the context of Uganda's linguistic landscape, which includes 63 main languages spoken by 24 million people (NCDC 1999). Exacerbating the challenge of deciding which language constitutes the most dominant 'local language' in any given area was the acute shortage of funding and human resources to support materials development and teacher education. The primary curriculum review of 2004 drew attention to the low literacy levels in both English and local languages, especially outside Kampala and in rural areas, and stressed the need to promote mother tongue literacy to address this perennial concern (Ministry of Education and Sports 2004).

Against this background, this chapter reports on a study of multilingual language and literacy policy conducted in eastern Uganda from 2005 to 2006. The two central questions we address are as follows:

i.   To what extent is the local language policy in rural primary schools supported by members of a rural community in eastern Uganda?

ii. To what extent do urban perspectives on the local language policy resonate with the perspectives of the rural community?

The community was included in this study because ultimately the community is the beneficiary of the language policy, especially with regards to the development of multilingual literacy for their children. As Bamgbose (1991) and Muthwii and Kioko (2004) have observed, implementation of language education policies can fail if the targeted population is not supportive of the policy.

Theoretical framework

The theoretical framework for this chapter is based on recent work in multilingual literacies (Hornberger 2003, Martin-Jones and Jones 2000, Street 1984, 2001), which is centrally concerned with the intersection of research on multilingualism, on the one hand, and literacy, on the other. For many years, Goody's (1977) universalising theory influenced the views of many educators regarding literacy development, which was regarded as involving reading, writing and the mastery of grammar as separate individual skills. It was also viewed as an autonomous technology of modernity, leading to the rational, psychological and cultural transformation of people. However, a growing body of literature posits a divergent view of literacy embedded within a cultural context (Barton 1994, Barton and Hamilton 1998, Baynham 1995, Gee 1990, Heath 1983, Purcell-Gates 2007, Prinsloo and Breier 1996, Stein 2007). These studies have examined the literacy practices of individuals and groups, including people's uses and meanings of literacy and the value it holds for them. As a result, they have contributed to a theory of literacy as a social practice and collective resource.

Street (1984), for example, argues that the meaning of literacy cannot be separated from the social institutions in which it is practised or the social processes whereby literacy is acquired. In Street's ideological model, the focus on literacy development shifts from individual, discrete skills to reading and writing as cultural practices. This formulation is concerned with the extent to which literacy tasks are jointly achieved in the context of collaborative activities in particular social circumstances (Prinsloo and Breier 1996). This, therefore, calls for a conception of literacy that takes into account the people involved and the places in which it occurs. We need to understand literacy both locally and historically and with reference to the social relationships in which speakers, readers and writers find themselves (Barton and Hamilton 1998).

However, studies that have shown the importance of the role of community and parental support to children's early literacy development have hitherto been mostly associated with the print-rich cultures of the western world (Anderson et al. 2005, Hannon 1995, Kendrick 2003, Wolfendale and Topping 1996). The present case study was carried out in two under-resourced schools in two communities in Sub-Saharan Africa. Such research is relevant to a wider international audience not only because there are complex relationships between unequally-resourced global communities (Adejunmobi 2004, Lin and Martin 2005, Makoni and Meinhof 2003), but because even in wealthy regions of the world there are communities that have been historically and educationally marginalised (see Garciá et al. 2006, May 2001).

The theory of 'community' that we brought to this study is drawn in particular from the work of Kanu (2006), who defines 'communalism' as one of the central tenets of African social philosophy. In this view, 'an individual's involvement in the interests, aspirations and welfare of the group is the measure of that individual's worth' (Kanu 2006:210). What this suggests is that the success of the wider society is of paramount importance and that the meaning of an individual's life is constructed with reference to the group. In this spirit, communalism is characterised by practices of solidarity, interdependence, co-operation and reciprocal obligations. In our study, therefore, we defined 'community' as those people in the wider community with an investment in the student population of a particular school. We considered, for example, people such as the elders and opinion leaders interested in issues of development, as well as members of the Parent Teacher Association (PTA), the School Management Committee (SMC) and the Lunyole Language Association (LLA). Further, because we were interested in both rural and urban school communities, we selected communities within the catchment area of Bugagga Rural Primary School (BRPS)[2] and Tiriri Urban Primary School (TUPS), both in eastern Uganda. However, given that the local language policy targeted rural schools, we focused our data collection on the rural community, drawing on data from the urban school community for comparative purposes.

Methodology and data collection

The rural community where the research was undertaken is located in the newly formed Butaleja District, with a population of approximately 230,000 people (Uganda Bureau of Statistics 2002). Butaleja District is in southeastern Uganda and the people speak Lunyole, one of the Bantu languages. The urban community selected for comparative purposes was Tororo Municipality in Tororo District in eastern Uganda. Tororo District has a population of approximately 400,000 people (Uganda Bureau of Statistics 2002). Common languages in this area include Dhopadhola, Ateso, Samia, Lugwere, Lunyole, Lumasaba and Lusoga, the first two belonging to the eastern and western Nilotic language families respectively, while the rest are Bantu languages. In TUPS, while all local languages are represented in the school, the languages used most commonly as lingua franca, according to the headmaster, are Luganda and Kiswahili.

It is important to note that although Lunyole is the dominant language in Butaleja district, formal education was first introduced using Luganda as the language of instruction. Luganda is one of the Bantu languages spoken in central Uganda and is one of the six languages that the colonial government selected to be used in education (the others being Runyakole/Rukinga, Ateso, Luo, Runyoro/Rutooro and Ng'akirimojong). The use of Luganda in Butaleja District goes back to the period when the people from Buganda were used as administrative agents by the colonial government. The language was and still is used in churches, the lower courts and health centres. The orthography of Lunyole, in contrast, was only developed in 2003, through the Lunyole Language Association in partnership with the Summer Institute of Linguistics (SIL). In 2004, calendars were published in Lunyole and to date some primers have been developed through the efforts of this community language association. However, there are as yet few literacy materials that can be used in schools to promote mother tongue literacy in Lunyole.

Tembe collected the data for the study between October 2005 and June 2006. In the rural community, Tembe administered a questionnaire to 18 participants in early October 2005 and held follow-up focus group discussions (FGD) with all of these participants, as well as one additional participant, later in the month. Another focus group discussion was held in June 2006 with nine participants, two of whom had participated in the October 2005 discussions. There were thus a total of 25 participants in the FGD. Because the questionnaires were in English, not all participants were comfortable with the questionnaire format, thus the FGD provided participants with the opportunity to discuss their views in the familiar Lunyole language, also spoken by Tembe. Interviews were then transcribed and translated into English.

Table 2: Participants who responded to the questionnaire

	Counsellors	SMC	PTA	LLA	Total
Female	1	1	1	0	3
Male	2	2	5	6	15
Total	3	3	6	6	18

Of the 18 rural participants who completed the questionnaire, three were Counsellors at the sub-county where the BRPS was located, three were members of the SMC, six were members of the PTA and six were members of the LLA. Three of the participants were female and 15 were male. (See Table 2.)

To ascertain comparative views from an urban community, Tembe also interviewed nine participants in the Tororo district in June 2006, six women and three men. Four of these participants gave individual interviews while the remaining five were involved in two focus group discussions. The languages spoken by these participants were Dhopadhola, Ateso, Lusamia, Lugwere, Lunyole, Lugbara and Somali. Interviews were conducted primarily in English, with the occasional use of translators. The participants had diverse occupations in the community, including farming, housekeeping, teaching, business and administration.

Our research sought to investigate the extent to which participants, both rural and urban, were aware of the new language policy and the extent to which they supported it. In addition, in the questionnaire administered to the rural community, participants were asked the following specific questions regarding the languages used for different purposes and the preferred language for teaching their children:

i.   What is the main language that you use to interact with your children?

ii. What languages are used for homework for your children in Primary 1–4?

iii. What languages do you prefer teachers to use in teaching your children the following subjects: social studies, science and mathematics?

iv. What other language would you like your children to be able to speak, read and write?

Responses to these questionnaires were tabulated, but additional insight was gained through the focus group discussions that followed the administration of the questionnaire.

Findings

The rural community as stakeholder

As mentioned in the Introduction, we raised two central questions to guide our study. In this section, we present the findings of the first of these questions, which was: To what extent is the local language policy in rural primary schools supported by members of a rural community in eastern Uganda?

Language profile and practices of the community

From the questionnaire and FGDs, we learnt that all participants except one spoke Lunyole as their mother tongue. This latter participant came to live in this area after getting married to a Munyole man and spoke Lugwere as her mother tongue. As indicated by all participants, Lunyole was also the common language spoken in the villages they came from. Furthermore, for all participants, Lunyole was the language used at home to speak with their children.

However, English and Luganda were the languages commonly used for reading and writing; a few participants indicated that they were able to read and write using both English and Lunyole. (See Table 3.)

Table 3: Language use by participants						
Languages used	Lunyole	Luganda only	English only	English and Lunyole	English and Luganda	Other
Language used for writing	1	7	2	4	4	0
Language used for reading	1	5	3	4	5	0
Mother tongue/L1	17	-	-	-	-	1*

*Lugwere, one of the Bantu languages spoken by the neighbours to the north of Butaleja district

Awareness of language policy

As indicated in Table 4, there was general awareness of the new language policy by most participants. In the FGDs, the participants said they had heard about the new language education policy through school meetings, the media and during burial ceremonies.

Table 4: Awareness of the new language education policy		
Category	Yes	No
Counsellors	1	1
School Management Committee	2	1
Parent Teacher Association	5	1
Lunyole Language Association	6	0
Total	14	3

However, with respect to their specific understanding of the new language policy, there was some uncertainty. For example, four members of the LLA responded as follows in response to the question 'Are you aware of the government's language education policy? If yes, what does it say?':

■ It says Kiswahili language should be taught as a national language.

■ Go to school all of you.

■ Mother tongue should be taught as subject in primary or as a medium of instruction for P1–4.

■ Every person should learn and promote his mother tongue to ease learning/communication.

In focus group discussions, participants noted that the purpose of the mother tongue policy was aimed at facilitating easy understanding, identity and maintenance of their culture, which are objectives associated with schools in wealthy regions of the world. As one of the participants pointed out:

> You see we normally say that the English (omuzungu[3]) is intelligent. Why is this? This is because right from the beginning, the child is taught in his language. In this way they learn quickly. But for us here, we want to teach English to our children and at the same time they are learning Lunyole. It becomes a bit of a problem to the child.

Some of the participants noted that when a child is first taught in their mother tongue, they would still be able to learn English. After all, as one participant said, many countries that have developed, such as China and Japan, do not teach in English but have advanced greatly technologically.

In the implementation of language policy, the participants also raised the issue of the language of assessment, especially to the children being taught in Lunyole. According to the policy, when the mother tongue ceases to be used as a medium of instruction in Primary 4, it would continue as a subject up to Primary 6. During this period, the participants were concerned that the language of examination should also be that used as medium of instruction. However, the following quote highlights what often happens in schools, which was a major cause of concern for the participants:

> There are some teachers who try to teach in Lunyole and Luganda. But at the time of examinations, they examine in English. So the child who would have performed well, but because the examinations are in English, which he may have not quite grasped well, that child performs poorly. Therefore, examinations should be in the language in which they would have been taught, that is from P1–4, this should be Lunyole.

Insights on school language practices

With respect to languages used for homework in Primary 1–4, we learnt from the questionnaires that 15 participants indicated that English was the language in which homework in science and social studies was set for their children in Primary 1–4; two said that it was in both Lunyole and English; and one said that it was in English and Luganda. With respect to the languages parents preferred teachers to use in teaching social studies, science and mathematics, there were varied opinions. Eight of the 19 participants in the October 2005 FGDs indicated that Lunyole was the preferred language to use for teaching all the subjects to their children in lower primary, as children would be able to learn concepts in their own language. As these parents reasoned, science begins with things that are near, those they see and are known in the mother tongue. Therefore, by using Lunyole, the children were able to apply their knowledge and share it with the parents. The same would apply in social studies. The parents further explained that by using Lunyole to teach reading and writing, the child is able to write what they read; for example, by learning about the environment through reading and then explaining to others what they have found through writing.

For the other 11 participants in the October 2005 FGDs, however, while they indicated that for mathematics, science and social studies, Lunyole was preferred,

Luganda was the language preferred for reading and writing. The reasons given for their preferences varied. On the one hand, while Lunyole was the language commonly used and therefore facilitated easy understanding, they preferred Luganda for reading and writing because they believed spelling and combining sounds was easier in Luganda than in Lunyole. In addition, their perception was that Luganda 'integrated' many of the Bantu languages.

Language as resource

Ruiz (1984) draws a useful distinction between the diverse orientations that a community has towards particular languages, their speakers and the roles that the language plays in society. The three fundamental orientations address language as a resource, language as a problem and language as a right. For this reason, one of the questions the participants were asked concerned their preference for languages other than the mother tongue. Although Luganda and Kiswahili were mentioned, English was the predominant 'other language' which the participants wanted their children to be able to speak, read and write. (See Table 5.)

Table 5: Language preferences other than mother tongue					
Language use	Luganda	English	Kiswahili	Not definite	Total
Speak	2	9	4	3	18
Write	1	11	1	5	18
Read	1	10	2	5	18

It is interesting to note the different resources that participants associated with each of these languages. Some of the participants felt that there was a need to teach students in English, because for them a child being able to speak English is proof that learning is taking place. As one parent said:

If you get a child of P2 speaking English, it pleases you, or a P1 child speaking English. Then you actually prove that the child is actually learning.

For many rural parents, then, knowledge of English represents progress and justifies the many financial sacrifices they make to send their children to school.

In addition, participants hoped that their children would be able to speak English at an early age, like their counterparts in urban areas. For example, one of the participants commented:

I usually admire children who come from outside this area; you can see a child of P1 speaking English. Therefore, they should teach more of English first, then the other languages after that.

The issue of learning Kiswahili also came up in the discussions. It was pointed out that while it was good to learn English, there were situations that required knowledge of Kiswahili. The participants cited an example of when one travels to other parts of the country and encounters security personnel. During such times, they pointed out, people have had problems because they could not speak Kiswahili, the lingua franca of the army and the police force. One of the participants explained thus:

> Kiswahili is very important. You may study but if you do not speak Kiswahili, then you have learnt nothing. Because when travelling you might meet someone in the security [police, army] who may ask you something in Kiswahili and if you happen not to understand – my friend you are in trouble, because you have not understood what he has asked. My friends, there are times when knowing Kiswahili is helpful.

Finally, Luganda was also seen to be a useful resource. For many participants, Luganda had been used in their schools for instruction and therefore, according to them, was easier to use for reading and writing than Lunyole. They noted further that if a child went to live with a relative such as a paternal uncle or auntie (a common practice) where their mother tongue, Lunyole, was not the majority language spoken, the child would feel isolated. In such situations, some of the participants argued that it was therefore necessary to learn another language like Luganda. As one participant remarked:

> My reason is that a child may leave this place and travel to another place like to Buganda where Luganda is spoken. So if a child has learnt Luganda, then it becomes easy for the child to cope.

In summary, then, the community of Bugagga Rural Primary School was aware of the new language education policy. While they were happy that the new policy would promote language and literacy in the mother tongue, they had a strong desire for their children to be able to speak English at an early age. The participants also acknowledged that Kiswahili and Luganda were important languages in their community and that their children needed to learn these at school. The former, they pointed out, was particularly important for security purposes; however, some were supportive of Luganda because most participants had learnt it when they were at school and took the position that it was easier to develop literacy in Luganda than in Lunyole.

The urban community as stakeholder

As discussed in the Introduction, according to the new policy for urban areas, a local language was to be taught as a subject from Primary 1, while English was used as a medium of instruction. We therefore sought to gain comparative views from the urban community towards the teaching of a local language. To this end, the question we raised was: How do urban perspectives on the local language policy resonate with the perspectives of the rural community? Our findings are discussed with respect to participants' preference for English, their ambivalent support for local languages and their general resistance to Kiswahili.

Preference for English

In the urban community, all nine participants had heard about the new language education policy. However, they were generally opposed to teaching a local language at school. While a local language was appropriate for use in the home and community, they expressed a preference for the use of English at school. The following examples illustrate this point of view:

- I use my language Lunyole. However, when he goes to school he should begin with English.

- For me, I say as the child grows, from two to five years, it should use the mother tongue, but at school – no it should be English. Because a child knows where it belongs by learning the mother tongue at that age and then adopts another one.

- For me, we are not from the same language background with my wife. So we use English right from childhood for my family. I am Lugbara [from the Central Sudanic language family] and she is a Musoga [from Bantu language family]. I have told my wife to let the children learn whatever language, Kiswahili, Luganda, Lusonga, etc. These are for communicating to our people in the village. But I say English is preferable.

The participants noted, in particular, that the multiplicity of languages within their environment made the choice of a designated local language at school extremely difficult. Consider, for example, the following participant's linguistic history:

We speak – both of us speak Ateso. I am from Soroti and my husband is from Tororo. However, we moved to Kenya and the children picked up Kiswahili from the house help we had, so they forgot the mother tongue. After three years we came back to Uganda, they again picked up Dhopadhola from the neighbours. So, right now they speak English, Kiswahili, Dhopadhola and a little of the mother tongue, that is Ateso.

For many of the parents, English provided an enhanced set of opportunities for the future. The following quote captures the views of these parents:

Children ... should learn a language which helps them in the future. Not put them in brackets of second community.

Recalling their experiences while in school, the participants were happy that they had been encouraged to use English and had not resisted punishment for speaking the mother tongue:

We used to carry a badge in primary schools for speaking the mother tongue so that at the end of the day if you had the badge you would be punished. So this was used to encourage us to speak English.

This, according to them, worked well and they were able to learn to speak English. They therefore felt the same practice should still work for their children. Indeed, there were some who felt that parents could support their children by introducing English in the home. As one said:

Try to introduce English even at home. The emphasis here we are saying that let mother tongue be taught from home. Meanwhile, the child is picking English from home partly from parents. However, at the school level let it be English.

Ambivalent support for local languages

Although, for this group of parents, there was much resistance to the use of the mother tongue in the school, some ambivalence was detected as community members continued to debate the relative merits of local languages and international languages. For example, one participant observed as follows:

> There are languages that are international than our own local languages as Ugandans. Learning our own languages would not matter. However, at the same time we need to know the future of the child. Use international language so that the world can get closer to you by communication, French, Arabic and English. Nevertheless, at the same time we should also encourage them with our own culture, local languages. We should not say we do not need our own languages. No, we need them.

In addition, as exemplified in the following quote, the participants recognised that a child's mother tongue is an important mark of identity:

> [The mother tongue] puts them to where they belong in the community. They come to know about their roots, who they are. They do not go back and start looking for our roots after 40 or so years of our life.

Ambivalence towards Kiswahili

Uganda, together with Kenya and Tanzania, is a member of the East African region. The three countries have a common past in that at one point they were linked to Britain, leading to the adoption of English in commerce, government, administration and education. Given this past, the participants were aware that both Kenya and Tanzania had attempted to implement a policy of Kiswahili medium of instruction. However, the participants argued it had not benefited these countries. For example, they pointed out that the Kenyans were unable to make 'good' public addresses due to the fact that, according to these participants, they did not speak good English:

> Look at Kenya, Kiswahili is their [basic right] from childhood, so it is easier for them to learn. But it has brought them problems – they cannot address people properly because they have been brought up in Kiswahili.

According to the participants, Uganda was privileged in comparison to the other East African states, particularly Tanzania, in that the colonial administration introduced the use of English in schools. Consequently, they remarked on the good standard in Ugandan education, which was an attraction to people in other East African states:

> Even our standards in east Africa are the best – Kenyans and Tanzanians are coming to Uganda because of the language we are speaking.

Further, the participants were of the opinion that Kiswahili was not a sufficiently international language to be taught in schools. As one noted:

> For me, I prefer English. Kiswahili is like a local language the way I see on my side.

At the same time, however, the participants also noted that both Kiswahili and Luganda could serve as national languages in their school community. As one noted:

> Why not use a national mother tongue like either Kiswahili or Luganda, where it can be general?

Further, the participants recognised that the use of a local language had helped to unite Tanzanians of different linguistic backgrounds. Nevertheless, according to these participants, the Tanzanians were now struggling to catch up with the rest of the world by having to learn English. It was therefore advisable that in Uganda children are taught English right from the beginning. As one said:

> They say we are Africans and we should speak our African languages but now it is also causing them problems. Those are practical examples from Kenya and Tanzania. Why don't we go straight to something that is international?

The other East African countries had made the mistake of teaching in the local language. Therefore, Uganda should take heed and not fall into a similar trap.

In summary, the findings from the urban school community suggest that, in general, community members were aware of the education policy promoting local languages in primary schools. However, the participants were opposed to the implementation of this policy, saying that the teaching of a mother tongue was the responsibility of the parents at home. The schools ought to be concerned with the teaching of an international language such as English, for the future of their children. The fact that many languages were spoken in the community further complicated the possible implementation of the policy. The government, for example, had not been able to decide on a national language to unite the country, though it hoped Kiswahili might serve this role. The language problems experienced in the neighbouring countries, which had implemented local language policies, were not desirable and provided lessons that were relevant to Uganda.

Analysis and discussion

Batibo (2005) observes that speakers of minority languages are in a dilemma, particularly in relation to choice of language of instruction. On the one hand, there is the desire to maintain their linguistic, cultural and ethnic identity. On the other hand, the wish to access education in a language that will enable them to interact at international level is equally strong. Okombo and Rubagumya (1996) make the case that if European children are faster and more assertive in learning than African children, this is due not to race or culture but to linguistic and economic conditions. As Skutnabb-Kangas (1988) and Phillipson (1992) contend, it is the responsibility of education to boldly advocate the use of indigenous languages and to offer practical strategies. Similarly, Fishman (2000) and Tsui and Tollefson (2003) argue that the medium of instruction is the means by which languages and culture are maintained and revitalised. At the same time, however, Bamgbose (2000) observes that because language policies in Africa tend to ignore minority languages, it leads speakers of these languages to devalue them and assume that they are not useful for social and economic advancement. Perhaps, as Batibo (2005) points out, this is because the minority languages are used within the confines of their speakers' territories and speakers are forced to learn and use one of the dominant area languages or the respective ex-colonial language for purposes of wider communication. Our findings as outlined above support Batibo's assessment of the ambivalence of minority language speakers. In this section, we explore this ambivalence in greater detail, highlighting our findings from both rural and urban school communities with regard to Lunyole as a local language, English as an international language, Luganda as an area language and Kiswahili as a regional language. We conclude with a consideration of the role of assessment in language planning.

First, with respect to the promotion of local languages, we found that there was ambivalence in both the rural and urban school community. The community of Bugagga Rural Primary School was concerned that a local language policy was a regressive step to the past, rather than a progressive step to the future. Because of their past, in which Luganda and English were promoted, the participants in the study had mixed feelings towards the implementation of a language policy that would promote the minority Lunyole language. While some appreciated it, there were those who were concerned about using it as a language of instruction. Similar sentiments as those expressed by the rural community were prevalent among the stakeholders of the urban school. Indeed, the participants observed that because of the many languages spoken by the pupils in the school, selecting only one to be taught as a subject would be difficult. Therefore, for these participants, there was no place in their school for the local language policy. The participants were adamant that it was the role of parents, not the school, to teach the mother tongue to their children.

However, the issue of identity and cultural maintenance was also an important consideration for parents in both the rural and urban communities, though the rural community held stronger views in this regard. To the rural participants, it was important that they spoke Lunyole and identified themselves as such. Therefore, to have their children learn in Lunyole was one way they could be proud of their language and identity, a position supported by much current research (see, for example, Norton 2000). From this point of view, the participants did appreciate that the government had sanctioned the teaching of their language. Not only would it promote their language, but their culture as well, something they considered to be of great significance for their children and for development in their area (see Kramsch 1993).

Nevertheless, and this is our second major finding, both the rural and urban communities were particularly concerned about the need to expose their children to an international language and to English in particular. They had observed problems with local language policies in other countries within the region, which now faced the challenge of reversing negative effects associated with this policy. In the literature, Bamgbose (2000) has observed that using African languages as a medium of instruction has been notoriously unstable in several African countries. He identified dissatisfaction with the practical outcome of a particular policy as one of the reasons for this instability. Furthermore, such factors as the status of English as an international language, internal and external migrations and the need for economic survival are raised as constraints to the use of African languages in education.

This view that the stakeholders have towards the value of English was also observed in a study on the returns on English language skills in India (Azam et al. 2010). The researchers observed that in India, from an individual's perspective, there are several economic incentives to learn English. For example, English has value as a lingua franca. Knowledge of a common language facilitates communication. A common language is especially useful in linguistically diverse places, where the chances of meeting someone with the same native language are relatively low. In India, there is considerable variation in languages spoken even within narrowly defined regions, such as the district. A common language is also useful for international trade.

Participants in our study also argued that due to ongoing globalisation in terms of technology, there was no need to insist on using their mother tongue; to catch up in this fast-moving world, children needed to start with an international language, which was English. The place for the mother tongue was the home and the parent was the rightful person to handle that. Further, English was also viewed by these participants as a lingua franca within the country, given the multiplicity of languages in Uganda. It was a necessity and therefore an advantage that the colonial administration decided to promote English in the country. This is undoubtedly a common perception expressed by many in multilingual communities. In Nigeria, as Adedimeji (2004) points out, English plays an integrative role. It is a language of nationism concerned with political integration and efficiency (Bamgbose 1991:20); and also a language of nationalism.

Our third major finding addresses the relationship between local languages and more dominant 'area' or regional languages. As we mentioned above, the colonial government used Buganda agents as administrators in eastern Uganda. Consequently, when formal education was introduced in the eastern region, Luganda, in which the Bible had already been translated, was used as the medium of instruction. Thus in Butaleja district, Luganda continued to be used up until the launching of the new policy. This confirms what Batibo (2005) observed as the fate of minority languages in the face of the area languages used in education. The community from the rural school preferred the use of Luganda to teach reading and writing, arguing that this was the language that had been used in the past and that they were now accustomed to. When many participants were growing up, there was no orthography available for Lunyole while the only reading materials that were available were in Luganda. Some participants therefore struggled to conceive of Lunyole as a medium of instruction.

Like the community of the rural school, the use of Luganda was often mentioned among the urban community stakeholders at TUPS. As the participants pointed out, they were taught in Luganda as the local language in their time at school. It was therefore interesting that even for TUPS, where the spoken languages within the municipality were predominantly from the Nilotic language family, Luganda was regularly mentioned as a possible compromise if the policy of teaching a local language was to be enforced. As with the participants from the rural school, Luganda was preferred because it had been used in the past. As Batibo (2005) notes, a historical legacy of domination by the dominant area languages tends to make speakers of minority languages feel inadequate in comparison to those who speak the widely used languages. This observation applies to the speakers of Lunyole as a minority language, given the experiences narrated by some of the participants. However, although speakers of Luganda account for 17 per cent of Uganda's population (Uganda Bureau of Statistics 2002), Luganda has failed to attain national status. Nevertheless, its hegemonic influence now seems to constrain the implementation of the new policy, especially within the communities in which minority languages had hitherto not been used in education and therefore did not have written resources.

Our fourth major finding addresses the ambivalent status of Kiswahili, a language that is extensively used within the Great Lakes region (Uganda, Burundi, Rwanda and the Democratic Republic of Congo) and which serves as a national language in Kenya and Tanzania. Several attempts were made from 1903 to 1971 to develop Kiswahili in Uganda both as a national language and a medium of instruction, but as Kasozi (2000) explains, there were no strategies for implementing such policies. Thus the use of Kiswahili in Uganda was mainly in the security forces. It also became a language of commerce as result of its use with traders from the coast of Kenya and it was developed into a lingua franca, particularly among those poorly educated, just as English is for those well educated. Thus, while Uganda has no national language, according to the new policy Kiswahili has been introduced as a subject in both rural and urban schools with a view to eventually developing it as a national language. It is against this background that the community of the rural school acknowledged that, although it was good to learn English and the mother tongue, Kiswahili was also a useful resource. However, to some of the stakeholders in the urban community, Kiswahili was also regarded as a local language and therefore not acceptable to be taught to their children. Others, however, were supportive of the teaching of a local language that was designated as a national language. In this regard, the two possible languages were Kiswahili or Luganda.

Our fifth major finding, particularly with regard to the rural school community, was the issue of assessment. The community was greatly concerned about the language that was used to assess their children. It would defeat the objective of teaching in the local language if assessment were carried out in another language. However, as long as the available materials are in English – which the teachers translate when teaching in the mother tongue – there is a concern that the examinations will be conducted in English. Furthermore, much as the policy was being implemented in the lower classes, there was no mention by the school administration of continuing to teach local languages in the upper classes, as stipulated in the policy. Continued teaching of local languages as a subject to the upper classes would compel the administration to work out appropriate strategies for assessment since they would have to ensure that assessment of local languages as subjects was done through the local languages themselves and not through English.

Conclusion

When Uganda's new policy promoting local languages was launched, it generated much debate in the media and there was general concern that the policy was misguided. Comments by the journalists Mbekiza and Kamanzi, whose 2006 articles appeared in one of Uganda's leading daily newspapers, the *New Vision*, are illustrative of the Ugandan public's concerns. Mbekiza, for example, attacked the policy on the grounds that parents, rather than schools, should be the guardians of the mother tongue. As he said:

> Mother tongues are vital, but they should be developed independently. And this lies primarily on parents. **(Mbekiza 2006)**

Kamanzi, on the other hand, focused on economic considerations, particularly with regard to the Kyeyo sector (Ugandans in the diaspora), who are a major contributor to Uganda's national income. The local language policy, according to Kamanzi, was 'inward looking' and 'cannot sell', because:

> In order for one to qualify for a 'Kyeyo' job, he or she must be fluent in one of the three international languages. These are English, French and Spanish. **(Kamanzi 2006)**

This is confirmed by Coleman (2010) in his discussion of the English language in development. Coleman identifies many roles that English plays in development, one of which is international mobility of workers. Indeed, the fact that English is taught as a second language in Uganda has enabled many young people to seek employment at international level with ease. As mentioned earlier, the participants did recognise the fact that the world has become a global village, therefore it was necessary to learn an international language. While there were languages like French or Arabic that can also play this role, they singled out English as the most important. Within Uganda, a good command of English is a prerequisite to getting professional employment. Azam et al. (2010) too observe that in India, to be a government official or teacher (other than at low levels), one needs to be proficient in English.

In this article, we have sought to determine to what extent the participants in two Ugandan school communities, one rural and one urban, supported the new local language policy. Our research was framed by theory supporting the view that literacy must be understood both locally and historically and with reference to the social relationships in which speakers, readers and writers find themselves (Barton and Hamilton 1998, Hornberger 2003, Martin-Jones and Jones 2000, Street 2001). In this view, a language policy needs to be supported by families and communities if it is to be successful. Although the findings indicate that the participants were generally aware of the new local language education policy, there was ambivalence concerning the implementation of local languages in the school context. The participants' desire to have their children learn a local language for purposes of identity and cultural maintenance was often overshadowed by factors considered to be more urgent. Among these was the parents' desire that their children be part of the international community and thereby increase their opportunity for employment. In this regard, learning an international language such as English was considered very important; there was concern that learning a local language was a regressive step, compromising childrens' progress. In addition, many participants, especially from the urban community, took the view that the mother tongue should be relegated to functions in the home.

There were important differences of orientation in the two school communities, however. In the rural area, unlike the urban area, the community shared a common mother tongue and so there was little problem regarding the selection of a relevant local language for instructional purposes. However, the community appreciated that the learning of other, more widely spoken languages would facilitate mobility across the country, observing that they would not be able to communicate easily outside of their area if they spoke only their mother tongue, Lunyole. In the urban community, the linguistic diversity prevalent in the Tororo District was a major challenge for the community, as no one language could be identified for instructional purposes. Indeed, English served as a lingua franca in some contexts. Further, the urban community tended to be more mobile and cosmopolitan, looking beyond local borders for personal and professional advancement. Hence they were in favour of their children learning languages of wider communication like English, French and Arabic.

During the colonial period in Africa, the acquisition of literacy in the colonial language was the main tool for upward mobility and economic gain; this view has survived the colonial era. The views of the urban community, in particular, can be traced back to the colonial education system, in which only a tiny minority of Africans who attended the colonial education system gained access to European languages. As a result, it placed them in a better position in their own society (Alidou 2004, Wolff 2006), creating sharp divisions within African communities. Further, Benson (2004) notes the inequalities in schooling, within the development context, between rural and urban areas and between elite and subordinate social groups. These inequalities, as she demonstrates, correspond to ethnolinguistic heritage and conditions of language access.

The new language policy empowers rural communities to select a relevant local language to use as a medium of instruction while urban communities can teach local languages as subjects in their schools. However, from our case study, it was clear that the community was not adequately informed of the pedagogical advantages of using a mother tongue or local language as the medium of instruction, particularly in the first years of developing their children's literacy. Further, the lack of instructional materials in the local language was a major impediment to the success of the policy. Indeed, materials in English were often translated by teachers and frequently used for assessment purposes. There was some support for the use of Luganda and Kiswahili as languages of wider communication, but it was English that received unequivocal support. We conclude with the observation that the community needs to be adequately informed about research that demonstrates not only that mother tongue literacy promotes effective learning, but that it enhances second language acquisition as well. Without adequate resources in the local language, as well as appropriate teacher training, however, local language policies are greatly compromised. Further, it is clear that parents and communities need convincing evidence that instruction in local languages will not compromise desires for global citizenship.

Notes

1. We would like to acknowledge the generous contribution made by the participants in our research; they brought great insight to our project. We would also like to thank the Social Sciences and Humanities Research Council of Canada for its financial support. This chapter is a modified version of an article which was published in the *Canadian Modern Language Review* in 2008 (Tembe and Norton 2008). Permission to modify the article is gratefully acknowledged.

2. Pseudonyms are used for schools, places and people.

3. Muzungu is the common word used in Lunyole and other Bantu languages in Uganda to refer to a European.

References

Adedimeji, M.A. 2004. *The unifying role of English in a multilingual nation: The case of Nigeria.* In O.Ndimele (ed.), *Language and Culture in Nigeria: A Festschrift for Essen Okon,* 67-86. *Aba: National Institute for Nigerian Languages.*

Adejunmobi, M. 2004. *Vernacular Palaver: Imaginations of the Local and Non-native Languages in West Africa. Clevedon: Multilingual Matters.*

Alidou, H. 2004. *Use of African Languages and Literacy: Conditions, Factors and Processes. Biennale on Education in Africa. Libreville: ADEA.*

Anderson, J., Kendrick, M., Rogers, T. and Smythe, S. (eds). 2005. *Portraits of Literacy Across Families, Communities and Schools: Intersections and Tensions. Mahwah, NJ: Lawrence Erlbaum.*

Azam, M., Chin, A. and Prakash, N. 2010. *The Returns to English-Language Skills in India. CREAM Discussion Paper Series CDP No 02/10. London: Centre for Research and Analysis of Migration (CREAM), University College London.* Available online at *www.econ.ucl.ac.uk/cream/pages/CDP/CDP_02_10.pdf*

Bamgbose, A. 1991. *Language and the Nation. Edinburgh: Edinburgh University Press.*

Bamgbose, A. 2000. *Language and Exclusion: The Consequences of Language Policies in Africa. Hamburg: LIT.*

Barton, D. 1994. *Literacy: An Introduction to the Ecology of Written Language. Oxford: Blackwell.*

Barton, D. and Hamilton, M. 1998. *Local Literacies: Reading and Writing in One Community. London: Routledge.*

Batibo, H. 2005. *Language Decline and Death in Africa: Causes, Consequences and Challenges. Clevedon: Multilingual Matters.*

Baynham, M. 1995. *Literacy Practices: Investigating Literacy in Social Contexts. London: Routledge.*

Benson, C. 2000. *Real and potential benefits of bilingual programmes in developing countries. International Journal of Bilingual Education and Bilingualism* 5(6), 303-317.

Benson, C. 2004. *Bilingual schooling in Mozambique and Bolivia: From experiment to implementation. Language Policy* 3(1), 47-66.

Bergmann, H. 1996. *Quality of education and the demand for education: Evidence from developing countries. International Review of Education* 42(6), 581-604.

Coleman, H. 2010. *The English Language in Development. London: British Council.* Available online at *www.teachingenglish.org.uk/transform/books*

Cummins, J. 1981. *The role of primary language development in promoting educational success for language minority students. In California State Department of Education (ed.), Schooling and Language Minority Students: A Theoretical Framework. Sacramento CA: California State Department of Education.*

Cummins, J. 1993. *Bilingualism and second language learning. Annual Review of Applied Linguistics* 13, 51-70.

Cummins, J. 2000. *Language, Power and Pedagogy: Bilingual Children in the Crossfire. Clevedon: Multilingual Matters.*

Fishman, J.A. 2000. *Reversing language shift: RLS theory and practice revisited. In G.Kindell and M.P.Lewis (eds), Assessing Ethnolinguistic Vitality: Theory and Practice; Selected Papers from the Third International Language Assessment Conference*, 1-25. *Dallas: SIL International.*

García, O., Skutnabb-Kangas, T. and Torres-Guzmán, M.E. 2006. *Imagining Multilingual Schools: Languages in Education and Glocalisation. Clevedon: Multilingual Matters.*

Gee, J.P. 1990. *Social Linguistics and Literacies: Ideology in Discourses. London: Falmer Press.*

Goody, J. 1977. *The Domestication of the Savage Mind. Cambridge: Cambridge University Press.*

Government of Uganda. 1992. *Education for National Integration and Development. Government White Paper on the Education Policy Review Commission. Entebbe: Government Printers.*

Hannon, P. 1995. *Literacy, Home and School: Research and Practice in Teaching Literacy with Parents. London: The Falmer Press.*

Heath, S.B. 1983. *Ways with Words: Language, Life and Work in Communities and Classrooms. Cambridge: Cambridge University Press.*

Hornberger, N. (ed.). 2003. *Continua of Biliteracy. Clevedon: Multilingual Matters.*

Kamanzi, S.B. 2006. *Vernacular policy will affect Kyeyo sector. New Vision* 12 July 2006. , July 12). Available online at *www.newvision.co.ug*

Kanu, Y. 2006. *Reappropriating traditions in the postcolonial curricular imagination.* In Y.Kanu (ed.), *Curriculum as Cultural Practice: Postcolonial Imaginations,* 203-222. *Toronto: University of Toronto Press.*

Kasozi, A.B.K. 2000. *The failure to develop a national language in Uganda: A historical survey.* In K.Parry (ed.), *Language and Literacy in Uganda: Towards a Sustainable Reading Culture,* 23-29. *Kampala: Fountain Publishers.*

Kendrick, M.E. 2003. *Play, Literacy and Culture: Converging Worlds.* Bern: Peter Lang.

Klaus, D.A. 2003. *The Use of Indigenous Languages in Early Basic Education in Papua New Guinea: A Model for Elsewhere? Washington: World Bank.*

Kramsch, C. 1993. *Culture and Context in Language Teaching. Oxford: Oxford University Press.*

Kwesiga, J.B. 1994. *Literacy and the language question: Brief experiences from Uganda.* In D.Barton (ed.), *Sustaining Local Literacies,* 57-63. *Clevedon: Multilingual Matters.*

Lin, A.M.Y. and Martin, P. 2005. *Decolonisation, Globalisation: Language-in-Education Policy and Practice. Clevedon: Multilingual Matters.*

Makoni, S. and Meinhof, U. (eds). 2003. *Africa and Applied Linguistics. AILA Review 16. Amsterdam and Philadelphia: John Benjamins and AILA.*

Martin-Jones, M. and Jones, K. (eds). 2000. *Multilingual Literacies: Reading and Writing Different Worlds. Amsterdam: John Benjamins.*

May, S. 2001. *Language and Minority Rights: Ethnicity, Nationalism and the Politics of Language. London: Longman.*

Mbekiza, A. 2006. *Mother tongue policy flawed. The New Vision 12th July 2006.* Available online at *www.newvision.co.ug*

Ministry of Education and Sports. 2004. *Uganda Primary Curriculum: Final Report. Kampala: Ministry of Education and Sports.*

Mukama, R.G. 1991. *Getting Ugandans to Speak a Common Language, Changing Uganda. Kampala: Fountain Publishers.*

Muthwii, M. 2002. *Language Policy and Practices in Education in Kenya and Uganda. Nairobi: Phoenix.*

Muthwii, M. and Kioko, N. 2004. *New Language Bearings in Africa. Clevedon: Multilingual Matters.*

NCDC (National Curriculum Development Centre). 1999. *Circular Reference CD/P/MT/14, 30 September 1999. Kampala: National Curriculum Development Centre.*

Norton, B. 2000. *Identity and Language Learning: Gender, Ethnicity and Educational Change. London: Longman/Pearson Education.*

Obanya, P. 1995. *Case studies of curriculum innovations in Western Africa. International Review of Education* 41(5), 315-336.

Obondo, M.A. 2007. *Tensions between English and mother tongue teaching in post-colonial Africa.* In J.Cummins and C.Davison (eds), *International Handbook of English Language Teaching,* 37-50. *New York, NY: Springer.*

Okombo, O. and Rubagumya, C.M. 1996. *A Synopsis of Research Findings on Languages of Instruction and their Policy Implications for Education in Africa.* (Working paper prepared for the Pan-African Conference on Problems and Prospects of the Use of African Languages in Education, Accra, 26 – 30 August 1996.) *Paris: ADEA* (Association for the Development of Education in Africa). Summary available online at *www.adeanet.org/adeaPortal/adea/newsletter/Vol8No4/ en_n8v4_3.html*

Oladejo, J.A. 1993. *How not to embark on a bilingual education policy in a developing nation: The case of Nigeria. Journal of Multilingual and Multicultural Development* 14(1-2), 91-102.

Parry, K., Andema, S. and Tumusiime, L. (eds). 2005. *Teaching Reading in African Schools. Kampala: Fountain Publishers.*

Phillipson, R. 1992. *Linguistic Imperialism. Oxford: Oxford University Press.*

Prah, K.K. 2010. *Language, literacy and knowledge production in Africa.* In B.V.Street and N.H.Hornberger (eds), *Literacy: Encyclopedia of Language and Education Volume 2,* 29-39. *Berlin: Springer.*

Prinsloo, M. and Breier, M. 1996. Introduction. In M.Prinsloo and M.Breier (eds), *The Social Uses of Literacy: Theory and Practice in Contemporary South Africa,* 11-29. *Cape Town: Sached Books.*

Purcell-Gates, V. (ed.). 2007. *Cultural Practices of Literacy: Complicating the Complex.* Mahwah, NJ: Lawrence Erlbaum.

Ruiz, R. 1984. *Orientations in language planning. National Association of Bilingual Education Journal* 8(2), 15-34.

Skutnabb-Kangas, T. 1988. *Multilingualism and the education of minority children.* In T.Skutnabb-Kangas and J.Cummins (eds), *Minority Education: From Shame to Struggle,* 9-44. *Clevedon: Multilingual Matters.*

Stein, P. 2007. *Multimodal Pedagogies in Diverse Classrooms. New York: Routledge.*

Street, B.V. 1984. *Literacy in Theory and Practice. Cambridge: Cambridge University Press.*

Street, B. (ed.). 2001. *Literacy and Development: Ethnographic Perspectives. New York: Routledge.*

Tembe, J. and Norton, B. 2008. *Promoting local languages in Ugandan primary schools: The community as stakeholder. Canadian Modern Language Review* 65(1), 33-60.

Tsui, A.B.M. and Tollefson, J.W. 2003. *The centrality of medium of instruction policy in the sociopolitical process.* In J.W.Tollefson and A.B.M.Tsui (eds), *Medium of Instruction Policies: Which Agenda? Whose Agenda?,* 1-18. Mahwah, NJ: Lawrence Erlbaum.

Uganda Bureau of Statistics. 2007. *Uganda Population and Housing Census 2002. Kampala: Uganda Bureau of Statistics.* Document UGA-UBOS-PHC-2002-v1.0. Available online at *www.ubos.org/nada/ddibrowser/?id=2*

Williams, E. 1996. *Reading in two languages in Year Five in African primary schools. Applied Linguistics* 17(2), 182-209.

Wolfendale, S. and Topping, K. (eds). 1996. *Family Involvement in Literacy: Effective Partnerships in Education. London: Cassel.*

Wolff, E. 2006. *Language politics and planning in Africa.* In ADEA (Association for the Development of Education in Africa), *Optimising Learning and Education in Africa: The Language Factor.* ADEA-GTZ and UNESCO Institute for Education Working Document. *Tunis: ADEA.*

Student perceptions of English as a developmental tool in Cameroon[1]

Gladys Ngwi Focho

Introduction

The central concerns of this chapter are to describe the ways that students in a Francophone context in Africa look at the English language and to see whether it is possible to influence those perceptions.

The chapter consists of five sections. It begins with a general overview of the role of English in the developing world. This leads into a detailed discussion of four significant roles which English may be expected to play in developing countries. These are as a key to academic success, as a means of obtaining international job opportunities, as a way of facilitating international communication and as a medium for achieving global education leading to global understanding. The following section discusses the position of English in Cameroon. Next, the method used in the research reported here is described and this is followed by a detailed discussion of the research findings. The chapter ends with a summary and conclusions.

English in the developing world

The teaching of English as a Foreign Language (EFL) in many developing countries has always been problematic because students may fail to see its relevance to their immediate and future needs except for examination purposes. And because many students continue to sail through different levels of their educational career without proficiency in English, the tendency is to pay little attention to the subject. Generally, English is viewed as a subject imposed on the school curriculum for reasons undefined to them; after all, all the other subjects necessary for their future careers are taught in another language in which they are proficient. Approaches to the teaching of EFL seem to perpetuate this perception; recent trends, however, strongly indicate that proficiency in English is linked to development.

Although the perception of what development is differs across nations and cultures, the general consensus is that it is the reduction of poverty which incorporates the enhancement of human rights, universal freedom and self-esteem (Markee 2002, Coleman 2010). This implies the general wellbeing of the individual, economically, physically, socially and psychologically. The above is emphasised by the Millennium Development Goals (MDGs; see Appendix 3 for a summary) which target the reduction of extreme poverty, through education, gender equality, health, the environment and international co-operation. In analysing why the MDGs matter, Fukuda-Parr (2004) posits that these goals address the central objectives of human wellbeing. He sees a common vision between the MDGs and human development such as freedom, dignity, tolerance and solidarity.

The notion that education as a whole contributes enormously to the development of individuals and nations is not contested. Each subject in the school curriculum contributes to that, including English, which has its own particular role to play in the development process. This view is stressed by Ekpoki (2009) who observes that the target beneficiaries of the MDGs are underdeveloped countries, many of which prioritise English as a common communication tool because of the multilingual nature of their societies. He observes too that English plays an important role in enabling nations to become engaged with the MDGs and to achieve them.

In view of the above, the place of English in development can hardly be minimised. It has been established that development is sustained by technological and scientific advancement. According to Seidlhofer (2003), English is the language of science, technology and economics worldwide. It is also acknowledged to be the working language of medicine and aviation. Graddol (2000) pointed out that English is the language of the global economy, most scientific publications, international banking, advertising for global brands, internet communication, technological transfer and international law. Looking at the last of the eight MDGs – developing a 'global partnership for development' – we can see that English has a central role to play here for it is considered an international language for international communication, collaboration and co-operation (Coleman 2010).

Even though some researchers like Iman (2005) and Rogers (1982) dispute the claim that proficiency in English guarantees economic development, or a better future, it is obvious that it has a great contributory effect. For instance, Grin (2001) demonstrates that salaries increase with proficiency in English. Globalisation encourages migrant workers to look for decent or better paying jobs abroad, notably in the USA, UK, Australia, South Africa and Canada, which are all English-speaking countries. Moreover, many multinational companies open branches in developing countries (whose national language may not be English) due to cheap labour and this demands workers to have some proficiency in English. Even in non-English-speaking countries where job migration is high like Saudi Arabia, Oman, UAE and Malaysia, English is often a shared language among migrant workers.

The role of international bodies like the United Nations (UN) and the Commonwealth in development cannot be underestimated. The fact that English is one of the official languages of the UN and of many international bodies and conferences underlines the hypothesis that it has a positive correlation with development. As Hasman states (2004), English has a very important role in the 21st century since governments, industries, corporations and international organisations need it to progress. Coleman (2010) perhaps best summarises the role of English in development under these main categories: English for employability, English for international collaboration and co-operation, English for access to research and information, English as an impartial language and English for facilitating international mobility of students, tourists and workers.

Four roles for English

For the purpose of this study, four areas in which English may have important roles to play are examined in detail here. These are English for academic success, English for international job opportunities, English for international communication and English for global education leading to increased global understanding.

English for academic success

In many countries the world over, English is either taught as a school subject or used as a medium of instruction across subjects. Its importance lies not only in success in examinations (Fakeye and Yemi 2009, Graham 1987) but also in research through books and the internet. Hasman (2004) contends that English has been established as the language of science and technology. He further states that, at the beginning of the 21st century, 90 per cent of information in electronic retrieval systems was stored in English, which was generally recognised as the language of the internet. This trend has since weakened, according to Coleman (2010, quoting Crystal 2006), but compared to other languages English still has a dominant role.

There is also the increasing phenomenon of student migration. Forty-five per cent of the world's international students are in four English-speaking countries: USA, UK, Australia and Canada (Coleman 2010). Dickson and Cumming (1996) indicate that even in non-English-speaking countries, English is the most popular foreign language as a subject for students worldwide. Furthermore, all over the world, the number of universities using English as a medium of instruction is increasing. Foreign students going to these countries and universities necessarily need to be proficient in English. As proof of this, they usually have to take an international English language test such as TOEFL (Test of English as a Foreign Language) or IELTS (International English Language Testing System) before registering at the overseas university.

Students who seek to study in English medium universities despite language difficulties must be convinced of the potential gains. Proficiency in English thus seems to be an important gateway (though not the only one) to an education that is easily recognised and valued internationally (especially in the job market). For example, it is a common occurrence for employers to request that certificates be translated or their equivalences given in English.

English for international employment opportunities

The relationship between English and employability is a significant one. Employability can be viewed as the ability to get a job, maintain it or get a new one (Kirubahar et al. 2010). In some cases, this will depend on ability to speak English fluently and to effectively communicate one's ideas orally. Coleman (2010) argues that several early studies have failed to find convincing evidence linking English to the economic development of the individual or nation. However, some recent studies are starting to show that there may indeed be a positive relationship between English and employability.

From the economic point of view, the 21st century is characterised by globalisation of economies and high job mobility. Millions of non-native speakers of English work in foreign countries where the use of English in the workplace is a necessity. Even in newly industrialised nations like China, Japan and India, English is becoming more and more necessary at work. As Warschauer (2000) observes, many non-native speakers of English need to use English daily in workplaces for presentations, negotiations and international collaboration. Besides, migrant working is a common phenomenon of this age and English plays a central role because it acts as a shared or link language among migrant workers from other countries (Coleman 2010).

International companies, industries and organisations pay the best salaries in many countries. They often seek to hire those who are bilingual in the indigenous language plus English. In China, for example, proficiency in English helps in getting well paid jobs, especially those with international connections (Cortazzi and Jin 1996). Similarly, Kossoudji (1988) demonstrates that in the United States deficiency in English has a negative impact on migrant workers; they tend to have lower earnings and less job mobility compared to those with greater competence in English. Today, the job market, for both migrant and international workers, is more competitive due to the large number of people who are proficient in English. Moreover, there is increasing emphasis on English for the workplace, necessitating the design of language courses for various professionals (businessmen, medical doctors, nurses and those working in technology, agriculture, aviation, etc.) The growing demand for proficiency in English opens thousands of job opportunities for English language teachers worldwide. Take the case of a multilingual country like Uganda, where English is a preferred language because parents believe that it provides wider opportunities for their children in the future (Tembe and Norton 2011, Chapter 6 this volume). Similarly, Hailemariam et al. (2011, Chapter 11 this volume) report that in Eritrea English plays no official role in the workplace, for professional promotion or for business; yet the demand for the language is high because people are convinced that it is important for job mobility worldwide, travel and socialising.

English for international communication

English is an international language used by many people across the world as a native language (ENL), second language (ESL), foreign language (EFL) or lingua franca (ELF). Jenkins (2003) refers to Kachru's categorisation of the use of English into the inner, outer and expanding circles (Kachru 1992). The inner circle is made up of those who use English as a native language or mother tongue like the UK, USA, Ireland, Australia, New Zealand, part of Canada and some Caribbean Islands. The outer circle includes Commonwealth nations who use English as an official language though it is a second language to its citizens. This includes countries like India, Pakistan, Nigeria, Philippines and South Africa. In the expanding circle, English has no official role but is important especially for business. China, Japan and the rest of the world fall into this category.

It is thus obvious that in every continent of the world English is spoken in one form or other, giving rise to many models such as native speakers, nativised speakers or lingua franca users (Kirkpatrick 2006). This justifies its status as a world or global language. Moreover, as Seidlhofer (2003) points out, bilingualism is a popular trend and English has a stabilisation role in bilingualism since most people speak their language and English.

In terms of the global spread of English, Hasman (2004) postulates that one out of five people in the world speak English and 85 per cent of mails are in English. According to him, pilots, physicists, executives, tourists and pop singers who speak other languages use English to communicate with colleagues in other countries. This transcontinental use of English is succinctly illustrated by Hasman thus:

> When Mexican pilots land their airplanes in France, they and the ground controllers use English. When German physicists want to alert the international scientific community to new discoveries, they first publish their findings in English. When Japanese executives conduct businesses with Scandinavian entrepreneurs, they negotiate in English. When pop singers write their songs, they often use lyrics or phrases in English. When demonstrators want to alert the world to their problems, they display signs in English. **(Hasman 2004:19)**

The above underlines the point made by Jenkins (2006) that English is a means of international communication across linguistic boundaries. It is a shared foreign language used by people of different nations and languages to communicate with each other. Whitehead (2011, Chapter 16 this volume) points to the fact that even in fragile states like the Democratic Republic of Congo, where reconstruction seems axiomatic, attention is still given to the teaching of English to the military. This aids communication with peace-keepers and facilitates effective participation in peace-keeping missions abroad.

From Hasman's (2004) point of view, this international spread in the use of English is facilitated by the fact that 80 per cent of English vocabulary has foreign origins and has cognates from all over Europe. It continues to borrow from Spanish, French, Hebrew, Arabic, Hindu-Urdu, Bengali, Malay, Chinese and West African languages.

In this communication age, audio-visual products abound in English (Graddol 2000). The most popular international films and pop music are in English. Many films in other languages have subtitles scripts in English. Such international television channels as CNN and Eurosport are in English. The development of 'net English' has spread worldwide and has been incorporated into other languages. Many radio stations, magazines, newspapers and journals in English have gained international readership. For safety purposes, instructions and warnings on drug leaflets, processed food and in airplanes (to name a few) have an English version.

The point has already been made that English as a language for international communication is one of the main languages of the United Nations, other international organisations and conferences. The emphasis here shifts from the employability factor to that of interpersonal communication and understanding.

English for global education

Development incorporates personal empowerment. Knowledge, which is often equated to power, is a catalyst for gaining positive self image and confidence. A global education is key to such knowledge gain since it empowers students with information in the following areas synthesised by Focho (2010) as constituting the global curriculum: cross-cultural awareness, global issues, universal values, critical thinking/leadership skills and experiential learning.

According to Roux (2001), students must be aware of traditions and beliefs which are different from their own. Such understanding fosters cross-cultural co-operation, tolerance and peace and helps minimise hatred, tribalism, racism and violence which inevitably lead to war. Kennett (2011, Chapter 15 this volume) reiterates that teaching conflict resolution, the value of dissent and the importance of consensus in the English class are especially relevant in multicultural countries with ethnic tensions. There can be no development without peace.

Awareness of the state of the world (or global issues) is important in pricking the student's conscience on such global concerns as:

> *environmental protection and sustainable development, globalisation and world economies, human rights and social justice, gender and discrimination, conflict resolution and peace building, population and food security, democracy and good governance, health, sanitation and HIV/AIDS, rural development and poverty reduction, war and natural disasters, uses and misuses of ICTs, volunteering and community service ...* **(Focho 2010:138)**

Such concern for the state of the world will provoke the building of a culture of peace and respect for human rights (Mansilla and Gardner 2007, Osler and Starkey 2005). All of the above touch on the MDGs and students need to be sensitised on what it takes to achieve these goals.

Universal human values include truth, honesty, love, sacrifice, hard work and striving for excellence. These factors also contribute to peace and development by reducing social ills like fraud, oppression and apathy. Proponents of global education hold that the goal of education should be to develop social responsibility and global citizenship (Merrifield and Kai 2004). Experiencing learning in various forms of interaction and community service leads to greater understanding of the state of the world and the living conditions of others. In Schattle's (2008) opinion, this will build a culture of responsibility for the welfare of others and the planet. Besides, global education in general builds self-confidence and a feeling of being well informed since the student is able to participate in discussions on global issues. This all relates to personal empowerment and development.

The English class is an ideal location for developing such knowledge because there are few constraints on the subject matter discussed during language learning activities. Interesting topics from the global curriculum can be used to teach listening, speaking, reading, writing, grammar and vocabulary. Regular classroom activities like dialogues, role plays, debates, speeches, essay writing, group work, interviews and projects improve proficiency in English. A further incidental benefit of learning English in this way is that students are prepared for interaction in the workplace.

To summarise, there are many reasons for considering that English is valuable for students. It helps them to achieve academic success, makes it easier for them find employment, enables them to communicate internationally and gives them a broader perspective on the world in which they live. There is only a minimal risk of raising unrealistic expectations in the minds of students regarding the importance of English because what is being emphasised is not only the economic benefit of mastering the language but also a wide range of other social and personal advantages.

English in Cameroon

As documented by Breton and Fohtung (1991), Cameroon is a multilingual entity with over 247 local languages, two official languages (French and English) and one lingua franca (Cameroon Pidgin English). Historically, Cameroon was divided into two and ruled by the French and the British. These colonial powers imposed their languages as the official languages in the two parts of the country. After reunification in 1961, both French and English were adopted as official languages, thus earning Cameroon the title of a bilingual country.

In the Francophone part of the country, French is the main language for school, work and communication generally. The reverse is true in the Anglophone regions. Because the Francophone region is larger, many more Cameroonians speak French than English. This situation is often referred to as state bilingualism with French being the first official language and English the second. To encourage individual bilingualism, the government language policy is for both languages to be taught in schools at all levels. English is taught to Francophones as a foreign language (EFL) and to Anglophones as a second language (ESL) and vice versa with French. Language centres have also been opened all over the country for the same objective. These language centres were created by the government to promote the learning of both French and English by the general public and are open to all categories of people.

In Francophone secondary schools, students study English as a foreign language for three to five hours per week depending on their level. Tamba (1993) and others observe that many Francophones are resistant to the study of a second official language. (The same is true of Anglophones and their attitude to French.) One of the reasons, according to Tamba, is that Francophones do not envision any material gains in learning English. Given that French is spoken by the majority of Cameroonians and is a more popular working language, Francophones in general and Francophone students in particular have no intrinsic motivation to be proficient in English. Because Anglophones are in the minority, English has a lower status than French. For example, all official decrees and communiqués are initially prepared in French before being translated into English. From the standpoint of Gardner and Lambert (1972) and Ushioda (2008), the socio-cultural context – including attitudes to and the perceived status of particular languages – influence motivation to learn those languages. This view is confirmed in the Cameroonian situation by research carried out by Dyers and Abongdia (2011). Moreover, German and Spanish are also taught as foreign languages to Francophone students, which they consider more useful since many of them travel to Europe. Thus it is not uncommon to hear students ask On part ou avec l'anglais? (Where will English take one to?).

Another factor which contributes to the lack of motivation is the nature of examinations in Francophone schools. Because their curriculum is geared towards a comprehensive education, students study all the subjects offered and an average of all the subjects is the minimum required to be considered successful. Students can always pass without necessarily having a pass mark in English. Besides, there is no test for oral proficiency and many test items are written in multiple-choice format. This situation encourages many students to depend on chance in the examinations; the popular impression is that C'est Dieu qui donne l'anglais (It is God who can make you pass in English).

An additional factor that can hardly be ignored is the teaching approach. A good number of teachers fail to be creative in making English language teaching (ELT) dynamic and related to real-life experiences. They are still glued to the textbook, moving from one unit to the next without any attempt to integrate experiential learning or global issues to make learning interesting. Besides, the large class size is a real handicap to the use of various activities, individual attention and effective evaluation. Furthermore, there is little emphasis on oral skills and this discourages many students who are more interested in speaking English. There are some students who believe it is more important to speak fluently even with very little accuracy in writing. So they lose motivation when they can neither speak nor write English, nor pass tests and examinations.

Francophone students are unaware of the potential of English as a developmental tool because teachers fail to educate them about this. Teachers hardly ever explain to students why they should study English (beyond success in examinations). Probably the teachers themselves know no better. The Inspectorate General of Pedagogy for Bilingualism (1994) signed an order defining the English syllabus for Francophone secondary general schools which states as general objectives the acquisition of the four language skills, communicative skills and extensive reading skills. Nothing is mentioned about the long-term gains of proficiency in English.

However, it is obvious that, even in Cameroon, the stakes are changing. The fact that the government is putting more emphasis on bilingual education indicates its renewed interest in individual, not only state, bilingualism. In some universities and all professional schools there is a significant number of Anglophone lecturers. With regards to the civil service, the government policy now is to post workers to any part of the country irrespective of linguistic orientation. Students should be made to understand that they could be sent to work in an interior part of Anglophone Cameroon where nobody understands a word of French. Moreover, Francophones are being appointed ambassadors, governors (and to other posts of responsibility) in purely Anglophone countries abroad or regions within the country.

There are indications that in the future, as Tamba (1993) proposed, appointments to posts of responsibility (ministers, governors, directors, etc.) in the country will be reserved for those proficient in both official languages. A lot of companies, industries and non-government organisations in Cameroon now tend to hire workers who are bilingual. And, as will be discussed below, the global trend indicates that English is becoming an international language with immeasurable opportunities for those proficient in it. One pertinent example is the fact that today many Francophone Cameroonian students are going for further studies in the USA, UK, Canada and South Africa. There are many Cameroonians working with international organisations needing people who are bilingual.

Conscious of the need for Cameroonians to be bilingual, the government has created a special bilingual education programme for secondary schools which is in its second year of experimentation in some pilot schools (50 schools across the country). Beginning from 2009, one class of first year students in both the Anglophone and Francophone sections are chosen and are taught intensive French and English respectively. Furthermore, the content and language integrated learning (CLIL) model is used where some social studies subjects like history and citizenship education are taught in the other official language. In this partial immersion programme, Francophones are taught these subjects in English and Anglophones in French. This programme has some similarities with the International Standard Schools in Indonesia as described by Coleman (2011, Chapter 5 this volume) but with the difference that, in Cameroon, the programme is imposed by the government on all schools; it is therefore not an elitist innovation as appears to be the case in Indonesia.

While waiting for this project to go fully operational at some point in the future, the Ministry of Secondary Education has instituted the 'Bilingual Game' which requires teachers of all subjects to use the other official language within the last ten minutes of their lessons. This implies that the Francophone teacher of Mathematics, for example, will use the last ten minutes to explain the key concepts of his lesson in English to his Francophone students. The reverse holds for the Anglophone teachers.

A further perspective is that English language teaching should empower people to survive in, respond to and influence the context in which they find themselves. For example, Ayuninjam (2007) recommends that ELT in Cameroon should equip speakers to exploit the technological age. Mutaka (2008) also suggests that the course content of EFL in Cameroon needs to be reshaped to address the immediate needs of students, which include economic, health and environmental education. He says emphasis should be put on oral skills, which are presently neglected.

Method
The survey examined the perceptions of a class of 70 Francophone science-oriented students who study English as a foreign language. This class consists of 30 girls and 40 boys ranging from 17 to 21 years of age. These are final year science students of a seven-year secondary school programme who have two hours of English a week. Being in a purely Francophone school in a Francophone town, the students have limited opportunities to speak English out of the classroom.

Box 1: Questionnaire on student perceptions of English as a developmental tool

Section I: Biographical data

Name of school: _____

Student name: _____

Class: _____

Sex: _____

Age: _____

Level of English: Oral (Poor, Average, Good); Written (Poor, Average, Good)

Future Profession: _____

Section II: English for academic success

Please indicate the degree to which you perceive English to be important for academic success. Use the rating scale below:

VGE = Very Great Extent (4 points)
GE = Great Extent (3 points)
LE = Little Extent (2 points)
VLE = Very Little Extent (1 point)

No.	Items	VGE	GE	LE	VLE
1	English is important for promotion to the next class				
2	English is important for university studies in Cameroon				
3	English is important for university studies abroad				
4	English is important for library research				
5	English is important for internet research				

Section III: English for international job opportunities

Use the same rating scale above to indicate your perception of the importance of English for international jobs.

No.	Items	VGE	GE	LE	VLE
1	English helps you get an international job in Cameroon				
2	English facilitates your appointment to work in a diplomatic service				
3	English helps you get an international job abroad				
4	English helps you get a job in an English-speaking country				
5	Being bilingual in English/French helps you to get promoted at your job				

Section IV: English for international communication

Use the same rating scale above to indicate your perception of the importance of English for international communication.

No.	Items	VGE	GE	LE	VLE
1	English is important for communication with non-native English speakers (e.g. tourists)				
2	English is important for watching popular TV stations				
3	English is important for listening to popular international musicians				
4	English is important for watching popular movies				
5	English is important for reading popular international newspapers and magazines				
6	English is important for playing favourite video games				
7	English is important for social networking like Facebook or Twitter in English				

Section V: English for global education

Use the same rating scale above to indicate your perception of the importance of English for global education.

No.	Items	VGE	GE	LE	VLE
1	The English class gives the opportunity to know much about other cultures				
2	The English class gives the opportunity to learn a lot about global issues				
3	From the English class, one can learn a great deal about universal human values				
4	The class provides a lot of opportunity to experience learning through varied projects.				

Section VI: Global perception (for post responses only)

Give your opinion on the following by stating 'yes' or 'no':

1. Generally, do you think English is important for development?

_____

2. Are you willing to make a conscious effort to be proficient in English?

_____

Data on student perceptions of English as a developmental tool were collected using a structured questionnaire designed by the investigator with input from the available literature. Because development is a multifaceted concept, items for the questionnaire were generated under four different facets of English and development: English for academic success, English for international job opportunities, English for international communication and English for global education. (The questionnaire can be seen in Box 1.) The purpose was to find out students' perceptions of the importance of the English language to the different aspects of development. The questionnaire used a Likert scale requiring respondents to choose from four options to indicate the degree of their perception. Responses were graded from 4 to 1 (Very Great Extent, Great Extent, Little Extent, Very Little Extent). The mean for each item for all respondents was obtained by summing the numerical value of each and dividing by the number of respondents. Contrary to the general practice of anonymous respondents, students were required to write their names for the purpose of subsequent individual follow up. Other biographical data such as age, expected future profession and self-perceived level of English were requested for the same purpose. After whole class, group and individual discussions plus inspirational activities, further data was collected by monitoring class participation, attitude towards homework and scores in class tests.

Validation of the questionnaire was done by colleagues in this area. Reliability was tested using the Cronbach alpha technique with a sample of ten students from another final year science class. The results for Sections II, III, IV and V of the questionnaire are 0.75, 0.69, 0.81 and 0.85 respectively.

The study took place during the 2009–2010 academic school year from September 2009 to June 2010. According to the school programme, the first test normally takes place in early October. The results were very poor with an average score of 42 per cent. Student engagement in class activities up to this point was quite timid. There was reluctance to ask or answer questions or to be fully engaged in oral or written tasks. This gave us the idea for an action research study to try to find out students' views about English and to look for ways to motivate them. The questionnaire was initially administered in mid-October and then during the year student motivation was monitored through observation of class participation, attitudes towards homework and performance in tests. The same questionnaire was given again at the end of the school year in June 2010 to see if there had been any changes in students' perceptions of English as a developmental tool. The mean was used to analyse the questionnaires and percentages used to assess the other aspects of student motivation.

Meanwhile, extra activities were designed to increase student motivation in the learning of English. Attempts were made to integrate experiential learning. Such activities included discussions (group and plenary), internet searches, exposés, debates, interviews and essays on the four main research questions identified above. Some of the topics for these activities are shown in Box 2.

Box 2: Topics for activities

- Why are Francophone students not interested in English?

- Many Francophone parents now send their children to Anglophone schools. Find out why.

- Apart from being one of the official languages, how else is English useful to Francophones in Cameroon?

- If you were given an American scholarship and a Russian scholarship, which would you prefer and why?

- From the internet, find out the following:

  i. the most widely used languages in terms of number of speakers and their international spread;

  ii. why English is acclaimed as an international language;

  iii. Obama's inaugural speech and Martin Luther King's 'I have a dream' and identify at least two catch expressions;

  iv. what the MDGs are;

  v. at least ten UN organs, their full names and principal activities.

- What inspiration do you draw from Obama's election as the first black president of the US?

- Dramatisation of excerpts from 'I have a dream'.

- Interview teachers on one of the following:

  i. their dream for Cameroon;

  ii. their view on gender equality;

  iii. environmental pollution in their town;

  iv. democracy in Cameroon

In order not to deviate too much from the school curriculum, these activities were integrated with the teaching of the various language skills and were used as an opportunity to contextualise grammar and vocabulary. The focus, however, was to lead students to the realisation that English is important in many more ways than one, while helping them to learn the language simultaneously.

Results and discussion

The responses to the questionnaires – before and after awareness raising about the importance of English as a developmental tool – were analysed and are presented below.

English for academic success

Analysis of data on student perceptions of English as a tool for academic success is presented in Table 1.

The results indicate that students' views of English as important for academic success strengthened on all the items. The most important role of English for the students was success in examinations, enabling promotion to the next class, both before (mean 3.54) and again after (mean 3.75) the awareness-raising activities. In terms of the degree of change, however, students' views on this point increased by under six per cent.

Table 1: Student perceptions of the importance of English for academic success N=70			
English is important for:	**Mean (scale 1–4)**		**Change (%)**
	Pre	**Post**	
... university studies in Cameroon	2.75	3.64	+32.4
... university studies abroad	2.41	2.89	+19.9
... library research	2.26	2.63	+16.4
... internet research	2.53	2.88	+13.8
... promotion to the next class	3.54	3.75	+ 5.9
Cluster	**2.69**	**3.15**	**+17.1**

The largest change in views occurred with regard to the importance of English for university studies in Cameroon (2.75 before, 3.64 after, an increase of 32 per cent). Further discussions with students revealed that before the programme they had been unaware of the fact that up to a quarter of university lecturers in Cameroon lecture in English.

With regards to studying abroad many students at first dismissed the possibility because of the poor economic status of their parents but, after discussions, they recognised that they might be eligible for scholarships to study in universities abroad where English would be the medium of instruction; views here strengthened by almost 20 per cent. In relation to library and internet research, students still felt that they could get most of the information they needed in French, but as science students they came to understand that English has been acclaimed as the language of science and technology; views strengthened by 16 per cent (library research) and nearly 14 per cent (internet research). Generally, students expressed a need for more hours for the study of English and more emphasis on enabling students to speak the language.

English for international employment opportunities

Table 2 summarises students' perceptions of English as a means of gaining international employment.

Item:	Mean (scale 1–4)		Change (%)
	Pre	Post	
English helps you get a job in an English-speaking country	1.22	2.55	+109.0
Being bilingual in English/French helps you to get promoted at your job	1.51	1.98	+31.1
English facilitates your appointment to work in a diplomatic service	1.63	2.13	+30.7
English helps you get an international job in Cameroon	2.15	2.50	+16.3
English helps you get an international job abroad	1.47	1.56	+6.1
Cluster	**1.59**	**2.14**	**+34.6**

Table 2: Student perceptions of the contribution of English to international employment N=70

The results show that by the end of the programme students were not convinced about the contribution that English might play in helping them to find employment abroad. For example, by the end of the course the mean score regarding competence in English helping people to find a job in an English-speaking country was still only 2.55. Nevertheless, it is important to note that at the beginning of the programme the average perception had been extremely low, only 1.22. In other words, there had been a dramatic increase of more than 100 per cent with regard to this item.

The likely reason for students' general lack of conviction regarding the value of English in seeking employment is that, living as they do in a rural area, they do not yet envisage having international jobs. Their responses about their likely future professions showed that no student expressed a desire to be a diplomat, an international businessman or businesswoman or to work with an international organisation such as the World Bank or the UN. From their oral responses, the students' immediate plans were to pass their final examinations, enter university, graduate and then get whatever job they could find to earn a living. Some said that, when the time came to look for international jobs, they would study some more English to improve on their proficiency. Awareness raising or sensitisation here dwelt on the fact that opportunity favours those who are well prepared.[2]

English for international communication

Table 3 summarises student perceptions of the importance of English for international communication and the changes in those perceptions which took place during the programme.

Table 3: Student perceptions of the importance of English in international communication N=70

English is important for:	Mean (scale 1–4)		Change (%)
	Pre	Post	
... watching popular TV news stations	1.54	2.11	+37.0
... communication with non-native English speakers	2.78	3.64	+30.9
... playing favourite video games	2.42	2.76	+14.0
... reading popular international newspapers and magazines	1.10	1.25	+13.6
... watching popular movies	3.19	3.57	+11.9
... listening to popular international musicians	3.22	3.52	+9.3
... social networking like Facebook or Twitter	2.45	2.57	+4.9
Cluster	**2.38**	**2.77**	**+16.4**

For this group of students, it appears that English is significant for them for communicating with non-native English speakers (mean score 3.64 at the end of the programme), for watching popular movies (mean 3.57 at the end of the programme) and for listening to popular international musicians (mean 3.52 at the end). But the largest increase in perceptions took place regarding television news stations (an increase of 37 per cent).

In discussion, students expressed the view that Standard English was more important in employment contexts than in informal or entertainment contexts (where it was likely that it would be replaced by a lingua franca such as Pidgin English). Students indicated that they regularly watched only music, sports and movie channels in English (MTV, Eurosport and Africa Magic respectively). Their reason for not reading much in English was that it was more difficult to understand the printed word than the spoken language. As for social networking, many students revealed that they used the English-named sites but even when using them they actually communicated mostly in French. By the end of the year, though, they had discovered that a lot more communication through the media and interpersonally is done in English worldwide; overall their mean score in this area increased from 2.38 to 2.77 (a small change of +16 per cent).

English for global education
Results regarding students' perceptions of English as a way of gaining access to global education are presented in Table 4.

The results suggest that, initially, students had been largely unaware of the contribution that English could make to a global education. For example, at the start of the course the idea that one might learn about universal human values in the English class was given an average score of just 1.43, while the suggestion that an English class could provide a chance to learn through a variety of projects received an average of 1.51. By the end of the course, however, students' perception of being able to learn about universal human values in the English class had risen to 2.17 on average (an increase of nearly 52 per cent). Meanwhile, students' view that English could be delivered through a variety of projects jumped to 2.88, an increase of almost 91 per cent.

Item:	Mean (scale 1–4)		Change (per cent)
	Pre	Post	
The class provides a lot of opportunity to experience learning through varied projects.	1.51	2.88	+90.7
The English class gives the opportunity to know much about other cultures	1.54	2.62	+70.1
The English class gives the opportunity to learn a lot about global issues	1.63	2.74	+68.1
From the English class, one can learn a great deal about universal human values	1.43	2.17	+51.7
Cluster	**1.52**	**2.60**	**+71.1**

Table 4: Student perceptions of the contribution of English to global education N=70

During discussions, students explained that apart from some global issues which they occasionally came across in textbooks, other global issues were hardly ever part of English lessons. Besides, previously they had felt that they could get such information from other subject areas or the media, although at the same time they confessed that they almost never watched, read or listened to the news (even in French). The students also admitted to never previously having experienced a class project in English; however, by the end of the programme they recognised the value of having such activities within the framework of the language class.

After the innovative approach to teaching English in this class – which integrated a global curriculum with the teaching of English – many students felt the impact, such that their overall perception increased by over 70 per cent (from an average of 1.52 at the start to an average of 2.60 at the end). Nevertheless, it should be noted that students still had some reservations and expressed the view that English does not have a prerogative over other languages. Since Francophones in Cameroon study English, French and either German or Spanish, they felt that the other international languages could play a similar role of raising awareness of global issues.

Motivation

To monitor student motivation through class participation, a checklist was used to record the number of students who participated orally, who finished written tasks in class and who handed in assignments and projects on time. Table 5 shows the results term by term.

From Table 5 it is clear that at the beginning of the academic year, student motivation was very low. Oral participation and engagement in assigned tasks in and out of class were limited. Low motivation was reflected in their poor performances in class tests.

Type of activity	per cent participation			Increase in percentage points over one year
	Term 1	Term 2	Term 3	
Oral participation	26	64	91	+65
In-class written tasks	48	78	86	+38
Assignments	69	75	93	+24

Table 5: Student participation in activities N=70

However, gradual improvements took place. For instance, students making spoken contributions in class increased by 65 percentage points from 28 per cent in Term 1 to 91 per cent in Term 3. These improvements can be attributed to students' increasing awareness of the importance of English in various domains and to the student-centred approach to teaching which was adopted. Activities such as exposés, dramatisations, the use of the internet, television and radio, interviews and personal experiences helped to boost student motivation. Students participated more in oral than in written tasks. Students themselves reported that it was more important or 'necessary' for them to speak than to write and, besides, they found speaking easier (even if they made a lot of errors).

Conclusions

Students' perceptions of English became more positive after awareness raising had taken place. A summary of the results can be seen in Table 6.

Table 6: Overall student perceptions of the importance of English for development N=70

three items with which students agreed most strongly plus three with which they agreed most weakly at end of course	Mean	three items showing largest change plus three showing smallest change during course	Change (%)
English is important for promotion to the next class	3.75	English helps you get a job in an English-speaking country	+109.0
English is important for university studies in Cameroon	3.64	The class provides a lot of opportunity to experience learning through varied projects	+90.7
English is important for communication with non-native English speakers	3.64	The English class gives the opportunity to know much about other cultures	+70.1
Being bilingual in English/French helps you to get promoted at your job	1.98	English helps you get an international job abroad	+6.1
English helps you get an international job abroad	1.56	English is important for promotion to the next class	+5.9
English is important for reading popular international newspapers and magazines	1.25	English is important for social networking like Facebook or Twitter	+4.9

By the end of the experiment, the three areas in which students could see most clearly that English was valuable were for promotion to the next class (mean score 3.75), for studying in university in Cameroon (mean score 3.64) and for communicating with native speakers (also 3.64). However, discussion with students revealed that 'communicating with native speakers' was widely interpreted to mean communicating with Anglophone Cameroonians using Pidgin English! Nevertheless, students came to understand that one person in every five in the world speaks English (Hasman 2004); as they graduate and move out of the confines of their small town they will need English more and more for interpersonal communication within the country and abroad.

The three areas in which students' views had developed most markedly were the perception that English language competence may help in looking for work in English-speaking countries (an increase of 109 per cent), an awareness that English language lessons can provide a range of different learning opportunities (increase of 91 per cent) and an understanding that it is possible to learn about other cultures through English lessons (increase of 70 per cent). Students appreciated the fact that the English class could host any subject matter, especially current trends and issues not anticipated in the official curriculum of the various subjects. This open space was also experienced as ideal for multiple and varied activities, the result being that learning the language and global knowledge gain took place simultaneously.

By the end of the experiment, the areas where students were still least convinced of the value of English were the ideas that being bilingual in French and English can lead to promotion (mean score 1.98), being competent in English can lead to 'international' employment abroad (mean 1.56) and English is valuable for reading international newspapers and magazines (mean 1.25).

Meanwhile, the areas where the smallest changes were observed lay in English helping to gain 'international' employment abroad (a small increase of six per cent; the students remain unpersuaded about this), English being important for promotion to the next class (almost six per cent increase; they are already very aware of this and can hardly become more aware) and English helping students to participate in Facebook and Twitter (less than five per cent increase; they already use these social networking media but use French rather than English to participate).

It was interesting to note that students in this study were realistic and were conscious of the fact that proficiency in English was not a guarantee for getting an international job or a bright future on a global basis. They expressed the view that the best jobs were more accessible to the children of the rich whose parents lobby and guarantee these jobs for them. Thus, contrary to the fears of Iman (2005) and Rogers (1982), the danger of raising false hopes and eventual disillusionment is minimised. Students debated whether there was hope for those who excel academically and have dual or multiple language proficiency.

Generally, discussions on the various issues surrounding English and development increased student motivation. By the end of the programme the majority of students were positive that English has a significant positive role to play in their future development and were committed to taking up the challenge to become proficient in it. Furthermore, the role of the teaching approach in raising motivation cannot be ignored. This approach was experimental in the fact that there was a deliberate effort to 'teach' the importance of English to development and a conscious use of various activities often ignored by teachers due to difficult teaching conditions.

In conclusion, one can say that, in many cases, the teaching and learning of English in schools has been viewed mainly as a means of immediate academic advancement. Learners are not informed about other potential gains resulting from proficiency in the language such as access to jobs, international communication and global education. The purpose of studying English should go beyond success in examinations. Apart from course objectives, teachers should come up with general goals and educate students on the contributions of English to development in all its ramifications. More emphasis should be laid on spoken English and, if possible, the number of hours for studying English should be increased. Coupled with creative teaching methods and experiential learning approaches, students will be highly motivated to learn English. Wedell (2011, Chapter 13 this volume) also proposes that teachers should view the communicative approach to ELT as an opportunity to try out new ideas, techniques and materials.

The case for English for development is a compelling one. According to Seargeant and Erling (2011, Chapter 12 this volume), simply viewing English as an international language for communication across linguistic and cultural barriers is outmoded. The big questions should be these: As a pre-eminent global language, what does this entail for the users of English? Of what benefit is it? Even though Seargeant and Erling suggest that there are inequalities perpetuated by the promotion of English for economic progress in poor countries, they also affirm that English helps people build their capacity to fight poverty and increases people's choices for increased participation in world economies and sustainable development.

Therefore, if English helps students to progress academically, this will lead to good jobs (even at the local level) and improved standards of living. If it leads them to international jobs the impact is even greater. Those who can use English to acquire more knowledge and information and to relate with others all over the world become personally and socially empowered. However, Coleman (2010) cautions that the importance of English to development should not be exaggerated, especially for those who have little access to it. Evidently, English is by no means the only route to development but it definitely plays a significant role.

Notes

1. Thanks are due to Adrian Odell for comments on an earlier version of this chapter.

2. Respondents appear to be able to make a distinction between 'getting a job in an English-speaking country' and 'getting an international job abroad'. The first seems to be interpreted as migrant work and is within the bounds of probability for the respondents. The latter is interpreted as gaining employment with an international agency such as the UN or the World Bank and remains inconceivable for them.

References

Ayuninjam, F.F. 2007. *Language education in Cameroon: From the colonial era to the 21st century. Springer International Handbook of Education,* 19(1), 49-74.

Breton, R. and Fohtung, B. 1991. *Atlas Administrative des Langues Nationale du Cameroon. Yaounde: CERDOTOLA, CREA-ACCT.*

Coleman, H. 2010. *The English Language in Development. London: British Council.* Available online at *www.teachingenglish.org.uk/transform/book*

Coleman, H. 2011. *Allocating resources for English: The case of Indonesia's English medium International Standard Schools.* Chapter 5, this volume.

Cortazzi, M. and Jin, L. 1996. *English teaching and learning in China. Language Teaching* 29(2), 61-80.

Crystal, D. 2006. *Language and the Internet. 2nd edition. Cambridge: Cambridge University Press.*

Dickson, P. and Cumming, A. 1996. *Profiles of Language Education in 25 Countries. Slough: NFER.*

Dyers, C. and Abongdia, J. 2011. *An exploration of the relationship between language attitudes and ideologies in a study of Francophone students of English in Cameroon. Journal of Multilingual and Multicultural Development* 31(2), 119-134.

Ekpoki, H.A. 2009. *The place of English language in the achievement and sustenance of the MDGs. The Voice of Teachers* 1(2), 138-140.

Fakeye, D.O. and Yemi, O. 2009. *English language proficiency as a prediction of academic achievement among EFL students in Nigeria. European Journal of Scientific Research,* 37(3), 490-495.

Focho, G.N. 2010. *Language as tool for global education: Bridging the gap between the traditional and a global curriculum. Journal of Research in Innovative Teaching* 3(1), 135-148.

Fukuda-Parr, S. 2004. *Millennium Development Goals: Why they matter. Global Governance* 10, 395-402.

Gardner, R.C. and Lambert, W. 1972. *Attitudes and motivation in second-language learning. Rowley: Newbury House.*

Graddol, D. 2000. *The Future of English. Revised edition. London: The British Council.* Available online at *www.britishcouncil.org/learning-elt-future.pdf*

Graham, J.G. 1987. *English language proficiency and the prediction of academic success. TESOL Quarterly* 21(3), 505-521.

Grin, H. 2001. *English as economic value: Facts and fallacies. World Englishes* 20(1), 65-78.

Hailemariam, C., Ogbay, S. and White, G. 2011. *English and development in Eritrea.* Chapter 11, this volume.

Hasman, M.A. 2004. *The role of English in the 21st century. TESOL Chile* 1(1), 18-21.

Iman, S.R. 2005. *English as a global language and the question of nation-building education in Bangladesh. Comparative Education* 41(4), 471-486.

Inspectorate General of Pedagogy for Bilingualism. 1994. Order No. 1751/D55/MINEDUC/SG/IGPBIL *To define the English syllabus for Francophone secondary schools.*

Jenkins, J. 2003. *World Englishes: A Resource Book for Students. London: Routledge.*

Jenkins, J. 2006. *Current perspectives on teaching world Englishes and English as a lingua franca. TESOL Quarterly* 36(3), 265-274.

Kachru, B. 1992. *Teaching World Englishes. In B.Kachru (ed.), The Other Tongue, English across Cultures, 355-366. 2nd edition. Urbana: University of Illinois Press.*

Kennett, P. 2011. *English as a tool for conflict transformation.* Chapter 15, this volume.

Kirkpatrick, A. 2006. *Which model of English: Native-speaker, nativised or lingua franca? In M.Saraceni and R.Rubdy (eds), English in the World: Global Rules, Global Roles, 71-83. London: Continuum Press.*

Kirubahar, J.S., Santhi, V.J. and Subashini, A. 2010. *Personal and labour market environment factors in English for employability: A case study of KSA. Language in India* 10(4), 21-29. Available online at *www.languageinindia.com*

Kossoudji, S.A. 1988. *English language ability and the labour market opportunities of Hispanic and East Asian immigrant men. Journal of Labor Economics* 6(2), 205-225.

Mansilla, V.B. and Gardner, H. 2007. *From teaching globalisation to nurturing global consciousness. In M.M.Suarez-Orozco (ed.), Learning in the Global Era: International Perspective on Globalisation and Education, 47-66. Berkeley: University of California Press.*

Markee, N. 2002. *Language in development: Questions of theory, questions of practice. TESOL Quarterly* 34(3), 511-535.

Merrifield, M. and Kai, M. 2004. *How are teachers responding to globalisation? Social Education* 68, 354-360.

Mutaka, N.M. 2008. *Building Capacity: Using TEFL and African Languages as Development-oriented Literacy Tools. Bamenda: Langaa Research and Publishing Common Initiative Group.*

Osler, A. and Starkey, H. (eds). 2005. *Citizenship and Language Learning: International Perspectives. Stoke on Trent: Trentham Books.*

Rogers, J. 1982. *The world for sick proper. English Language Teaching Journal* 36(3), 144-151.

Roux, J. 2001. *Re-examining global education's relevance beyond 2000. Research in Education* 65, 70-80.

Schattle, H. 2008. *The Practices of Global Citizenship.* Lanham MD: Rowman and Littlefield.

Seargeant, P. and Erling, E. 2011. *The discourse of 'English as a language for international development': Policy assumptions and practical challenges.* Chapter 12, this volume.

Seidlhofer, B. 2003. *A Concept of International English and Related Issues: From 'Royal English' to 'Realistic' English? Strasbourg: Council of Europe.*

Tamba, T.P. 1993. *Motivation in language learning- The case of Francophone Cameroon learners of English. The English Teacher* 22, 18-23.

Tembe, J. and Norton, B. 2011. *English education, local languages and community perspectives in Uganda.* Chapter 6, this volume.

Ushioda, E. 2008. *Motivation and good language learners.* In C.Griffiths (ed.), *Lessons from Good Language Learners,* 19-34. *Cambridge, Cambridge University Press.*

Warschauer, M. 2000. *The changing global economy and the future of English teaching. TESOL Quarterly* 34(3), 511-535.

Wedell, M. 2011. *More than just 'technology': English language teaching initiatives as complex educational changes.* Chapter 13, this volume.

Whitehead, D. 2011. *English language teaching in fragile states: Justifying action, promoting success and combating hegemony.* Chapter 16, this volume.

English in Africa:
An impediment or a
contributor to development?

Nigussie Negash

Introduction

The African continent is a vast region with a huge resource, both material and human (cultural and linguistic). However, it is one of the neglected regions in the world. Even in the field of English language teaching (ELT) we do not hear about as much activity in Africa as we do in other regions of the world. David Graddol, whose influential books address diverse ELT contexts (Graddol 1997, 2006), says almost nothing on English in Africa. So it is high time that voices from the region are heard.

This paper takes an African (insider) look at the role of English in development in Africa. My inspiration to grapple with the topic comes from attending conferences dealing with language policy, language and development, and reading sources in the area (Graddol 1997, 2006, Coleman 2010). Another source of inspiration is the experience of working as a British Council and Hornby School teacher trainer in East Africa and West Africa, which are geographically far apart but struggling with similar issues concerning the role of English and indigenous languages. Similar to Coleman (2010), my chapter deals with English in development but focuses on Africa's complex political, social and linguistic context.

There is insufficient space in this chapter to delve into too much detail concerning development. However, it is clear that there has been a movement among development thinkers away from the conventional conception of development simply as economic growth, meaning a sustainable process that expands the quantity and variety of goods and services that people use to satisfy their material wants. Instead, development is seen now as 'a process enlarging people's choices' (UNDP 1990:1).

From this perspective, African countries, which are traditionally associated with war, famine and poverty, seem to have made some progress (Mwabu and Fosu 2010, quoted by UNDP 2010a). A press release from UNDP (UNDP 2010b) states that 'most developing nations made dramatic, yet often underestimated, progress in health, education and basic living standards in recent years.' UNDP actually ranks Ethiopia 11th out of 135 countries in terms of improvement in its relative position in the Human Development Index (HDI) between 1970 and 2010.

Among other things, Africa's economic and political interconnectedness both within the continent and beyond it to other parts of the world has contributed to these achievements. Africans have begun to engage more openly and critically. There are some initial talks to unite African states into one strong entity like the European Union or the United States of America. There are economic and political forums at the sub-regional level such as IGAD (Intergovernmental Authority on Development, with seven member states), ECOWAS (Economic Community of West African States, with 15 members), COMESA (Common Market for Eastern and Southern Africa, with 19 members) and more recently NEPAD (New Partnership for Africa's Development, a forum which African leaders have established to provide a peer review mechanism). Africans are beginning to negotiate with one voice on trade and development issues, for example at the Copenhagen Climate Conference, in which African governments appointed a team led by the Ethiopian Prime Minister as the chief negotiator.

As an official language of the African Union (AU) and an international language, English is important for the continent. The question then is what concrete roles does English have in development in Africa? Is it a detractor or a contributor to Africa's development endeavours?

Coleman (2010) addresses a similar question by reviewing the functions of English in development. He identifies four areas where English has often been given a role to play:

- for employability

- for international mobility

- for unlocking development opportunities and accessing information

- as an impartial language.

In this chapter, I have adopted a more or less similar categorisation to help me to analyse the role played by English in African development, but I have made several modifications to Coleman's categories.

Because of its association with colonialism, English is often stigmatised as the language of imperialism or oppression (Phillipson 1992). Many writers on language policy (e.g. Ouane and Glanz 2010) lament that the emphasis on foreign languages like English (Graddol 2006, Batibo 2007) has led to Africa making an insignificant contribution to knowledge production and creative writing because this has led to a dependency syndrome among educated people. However, it is not rational to blame every ailment in Africa (political, economic, educational) on these foreign languages. After all, as Phillipson (1996) observes, after independence it was African leaders, such as those in Nigeria, who were responsible for the choice of

English over local languages. This was done with the intention 'to de-emphasise ethnicity and build up a sense of nationhood' (Phillipson 1996:162).

In spite of their historical association with colonial rule and the fact that they have limited the development of indigenous languages, the former colonial languages are useful now in several ways. As an African, I will try to answer the question as to whether English is helping or hindering development. This is a complex issue that does not have a straightforward answer, so I will look at the challenging co-existence of English with other indigenous languages and foreign languages. I will also try to comment on some recent challenges presented by China's desire to dominate economic activities in Africa.

Arrival of English in Africa

The continent of Africa has a population of about 460 million who speak more than 2,000 languages (Lodhi 1993). English was introduced to Africa with the arrival of Europeans as slave traders and colonisers. Despite the departure of Europeans after independence, English has remained in the continent and today it is used as one of the official or working languages in the AU. It is used for different communicative purposes in 52 African countries (possibly 53 when Southern Sudan becomes independent), depending on the language and education policy of each country. Of these, six countries are listed by Graddol (1997:10) as territories where English is used as the L1 but where there is greater L2 use or significant use of another language. About 20 sub-Saharan countries, usually known as Anglophone, use English as an official language exclusively (for example Ghana, Nigeria, Namibia and Zambia) or with another African language (Kenya, South Africa, Uganda and Zimbabwe). In the Lusophone (Portuguese speaking) and Francophone (French speaking) countries and in Ethiopia – none of which were British colonies – the status of English is also very high. In Ethiopia, for example, English was introduced in the 1940s as a language of science and education and to facilitate knowledge and technology transfer from the developed West (Haile-Michael 1993, Bogale 2009, Negash 2005).

Roles of English in Africa's development

English is a major international language with multiple functions and roles for Africans within Africa and in interaction with the people of other continents. It plays a critical role in entertainment and the media, in diplomacy, in commerce and tourism, in migration and in education. In fulfilling these roles, English creates development opportunities for individuals and communities in Africa. We will look at each of these aspects individually below.

English in entertainment and media

One of the areas where English is most accessible in Africa is probably entertainment and the media. Video films produced in Hollywood have inundated African urban areas. Football is another popular social event to which Africans have access through English, the English Premier League being the most famous programme. Television has played a significant role in captivating Africans' attention. Despite some countries' unwillingness to privatise their state-owned television companies (Shinn 2008) or expand the range of their broadcasts, many international news and entertainment programmes are available for free or fee through private satellite dishes.

During the Cold War many African countries were aligned with either the West or the Soviet Union; the citizens of countries in the Communist bloc were denied access to information from inside or outside. As relatively more liberal regimes have come to power, the use of English in the print media has grown rapidly in Africa.

In Ethiopia, print media appeared for the first time in the period of Emperor Menelik. For example, *Aimero* was published in Amharic between 1902 and 1903 and *Le Semeur d'Ethiopie* in French from 1905 to 1911 (Bekele 2003:14). Television and radio broadcasts – in Amharic – began during the rule of Haile-Selassie. By the 1990s English was still rarely used in the media: there was only one official newspaper, *The Ethiopian Herald*, one television programme and one radio broadcast in English (which was limited to one hour per day). Today, radio broadcasts have still not changed much, apart from FM stations transmitting music in English. But we now have far more English language newspapers than ever before. The total number of newspapers has increased dramatically from three to more than 15. They are published in Amharic, other indigenous languages and English, despite having a somewhat uneasy relationship with the government. A simple internet search generates the list of current print and online English newspapers and magazines shown in Box 1. Some of these publications are pro-government, others are independent.

Box 1: English language media in Ethiopia (World-Newspapers 2010)	
Addis Fortune: Quality business newspaper	**Ethiopian Reporter:** Daily newspaper based in Addis Ababa
Addis Tribune: Private weekly newspaper from the Ethiopian capital Addis Ababa	**Ethiopian Review:** News site publishing wide range of dissident views
allAfrica.com: Ethiopia: Daily news articles related to Ethiopia from African sources	**Helm:** Ethiopian fashion and entertainment magazine
BBC Country Profile: Ethiopia: Features country overview, news, key facts and events, timelines and leader profile	**Jimma Times:** Independent online newspaper run by reporters both in Ethiopia and the Ethiopian diaspora
Capital: Newspaper striving to promote free enterprise in Ethiopia and inform the public at large about economic events	**Nazret.com:** US-based news portal with headlines from various sources
Ethiopian Commentator: Opinion-based online magazine	**Tadias:** Lifestyle and business publication devoted exclusively to the Ethiopian–American community
Ethiopian Observer: Provides news and commentaries regarding current issues on Ethiopia	**Walta Information Centre:** Government-affiliated site providing daily news in Amharic and English from all regions

Furthermore, in public libraries we can now find foreign magazines such as *The Economist*, *Newsweek*, *Focus on Africa*, *NewAfrica* and so on.

Internet-based communication has also grown rapidly over recent years, thanks to the expansion of IT facilities. In the past, people in some parts of Africa had difficulty accessing newspapers published in the West because they were banned, due to ideological differences during the Cold War. Now anyone can access online international news outlets, including the BBC and CNN. Despite the relatively small number of citizens who are literate in English, it is amazing to observe the eagerness of many – especially young people – to chat in English. Several websites are available (including BBC opinion columns) where Africans can debate politics, economics and so on.

English as the language of diplomacy
African countries use English as one of the major working languages at AU meetings, seminars and conferences. The leaders, policy makers and experts meet in different cities in Africa to debate multifaceted issues, mostly using English. For instance, AU parliamentary meetings are often conducted in English with parallel translations into other international working languages such as Arabic, French or Portuguese. Similar to the way that the Association of Southeast Asian Nations (ASEAN) works, African leaders come together to debate development issues (such as climate negotiations) using English. In October 2007 I attended an African Parliamentary meeting in Addis Ababa which was chaired by Ethiopia; the language of discussion was English. Agendas for AU meetings are also prepared in English; for an example, see *www.africa-union.org/root/au/Conferences/Past/2006/July/summit/summit.htm*

University professors who participated in the 5th International Conference on Federalism, held in Ethiopia in December 2010, reported that – although participants came from many countries where languages other than English are spoken – all the sessions were conducted in English. (See, for example, the opening speech by the Ethiopian Prime Minister, Meles Zenawi, at *www.waltainfo.com/index.php?option=com_content&task=view&id=24625&Itemid=52.*)

English for commerce and tourism
Though it is not well developed and its potential has not been fully exploited, tourism is an attractive sector for Africa's development. In its own ways, Africa's tourism industry has already grown significantly:

> Africa attracted just about four per cent of total international tourists and received two per cent of international tourist expenditure ... in 2001. However, tourist arrivals in Africa increased from 15 million in 1990 to 29.1 million in 2002. **(Naudé and Saayman 2005:367)**

Today, African countries formerly known for civil war, such as Sierra Leone, Mozambique and Ethiopia, are growing to be tourist destinations. As the tourism sector continues to expand, which it definitely will, there will be many African industries, airlines, hotels, handicraft manufacturers, tour operators and travel agencies that will reap dividends. This sector creates job opportunities for many people, even for the low-skilled ones. However, its success in packaging and selling of products and services for tourists depends on competence in one of the international languages. English is an important tool of communication between Africans and visitors from all parts of the globe. The importance of English will therefore increase as African countries gear up to attract the growing tourist numbers from Asia (especially from China). For example, a report from the Information Office of the State Council of the People's Republic of China (English Xinhua.net 2010) indicates that in 2009 alone about 381,000 Chinese tourists travelled to Africa and about the same number of Africans (401,000) visited China.

The demand for English does not arise from language policy only. It arises also from outward-looking economic development strategies; for example, through attracting foreign investors and tourists or selling products abroad. To bring their citizens out of poverty, African governments encourage their citizens to produce goods and crops for foreign markets. Navuri (2010) gives the example of Tanzanian farmers being challenged to produce cotton to export to the hungry textile industries of Turkey. The cash crops which Africans export include coffee from Ethiopia and Kenya, cotton and sugar from West and Central Africa and cocoa from West Africa. These are produced by a mix of large- and small-scale farming operations (mainly the latter).

Since the world economy has become more and more interdependent, price fluctuations and subsidies by the West have had an immediate impact on the wellbeing of poor farmers (who constitute the majority of producers and are the backbone of the economy in many countries). For example, Gumisai Mutume reported for *Africa Recovery* magazine in 2003 that the price of cotton had plunged because of the billions of dollars that the EU and the US was spending on subsidising their local farmers (Mutume 2003). Similarly, in the coffee market, the farmers who have laboured for so many years remain poor, earning less than USD0.25 (GBP0.16, ETB4.11) per kilo for their export standard coffee which is then sold for at least USD12 (GBP8, ETB197) in the USA:

> ... [We must be aware of] the pain that Western subsidies cause poor African farmers. One of the main criticisms against agricultural subsidies is that they work directly against efforts by donor nations, including the US, to combat poverty in developing countries. An estimated 96 per cent of the world's farmers live in developing countries, with some 2.5 billion people depending on agriculture for a livelihood. Many seek an opportunity to trade their way out of poverty through a fair trading system. But over the years, unfavourable trade terms have been a major factor in the erosion of the market share of poor nations. According to the WTO, the share of developing countries in world agricultural exports fell from 40 per cent in 1961 to 35 per cent last year. **(Mutume 2003:4)**

The security of millions of African farmers depends on the negotiation and marketing skills – including their command of English – possessed by the leaders and exporters who represent them. The extent to which developing country representatives possess these skills determines the effectiveness or otherwise of their participation in multilateral and bilateral negotiations, such as the 2006–2008 dispute between Ethiopia and the American company Starbucks regarding the branding of Ethiopian speciality coffees in the States. A biodiversity academic who has participated in many negotiations and conferences in Africa, Europe and Asia expressed the importance of English as follows:

> We feel the importance of English when we participate in international negotiations that involve people from Africa and other regions. Usually the ones from English-speaking countries express their ideas very clearly and dominate debates. I remember one negotiation event in Nagoya, Japan, on biodiversity. We spent an unnecessarily long time on understanding the word 'eminent'. In our debriefing after the event, we talked about lack of mastery of English as the main challenge. We concluded that our children should learn English properly for us to make our contributions and take our rights. **(Interview/DM/December 2010)**

But Africans do not trade or negotiate only with the West. Asian markets, such as China, India, Japan and Thailand, are becoming the major trading partners for Africans. An official report from China put the value of trade between Africa and China in 2010 at USD114.81 billion (GBP74.38 billion, ETB1,886 billion), a 43.5 per cent increase on the previous year. Furthermore, China's exports to Africa:

> ... from the 1980s to the 1990s were mainly light industrial products, food chemical products, native produce, animal by-products. Since 2000 the export of machinery, automobiles and electronic products has been dramatically increasing, with product quality and technology markedly improved.
> **(English Xinhua.net 2010)**

The report adds further that Africa–China economic relations also involve direct investment. That is to say, the Chinese government provides financial support for Chinese enterprises to expand their investment to Africa. The Chinese government has signed investment agreements with 33 African countries:

> So far 13 companies have moved in; they engage in mining, prospecting, non-ferrous metal processing, chemical engineering and construction.
> **(English Xinhua.net 2010)**

Many Chinese people come to Africa as investors and as employees in various industries. Experts have different estimates for the size of the Chinese workforce in Africa, but *Xinhua,* China's official newspaper, put the figure at 750,000 in 2008 (Politzer 2008).

Traditionally, Africans used to export primary products such as cotton and phosphate to China. Of late, these have diversified to include steel, copper, chemical fertilisers and electronic items manufactured in Africa, as well as agricultural products like oranges, wine, cocoa beans, coffee, olive oil and sesame. The official report referred to above (English Xinhua.net 2010) also indicates that Africa–China trade is more or less evenly balanced, probably due to China lifting the tariff of almost 95 per cent which used to apply on African products.

To effectively manage such a huge and growing economy the main language which Asian and African businessmen, investors, experts and leaders have in common is English. This is likely to continue to be the case for the foreseeable future.

English and African migration

Migration is not a new phenomenon for Africa. Africa has perhaps been the region of the world which has been most affected by migration, both negatively and positively. The phenomenon of African migration has various forms and causes, including forced migration due to conflicts arising from ideological differences, economic migration due to poor working conditions and remuneration, and legal migration for study purposes. There is a commonly held belief that people migrate only from developing to developed countries. In fact, the largest numbers of migrants are found in internal displacement (within the same country) caused by wars or disasters and in 'low HDI to low HDI' migration between neighbouring countries (UNDP 2009). That means internal and intraregional movements far outnumber migration from the developing to the developed world.

Another important aspect of African migration is the movement of skilled workers and professionals from their home countries to other African countries, the West (Europe and North America) and Asia. Traditionally, Europe and North America have been the major destinations for skilled and professional African migrants. In 2005 the BBC (BBC 2005) carried a story from the Institute for Public Policy Research (IPPR) on Africans' success in the UK which noted that 'African-born immigrants are doing better than many other migrants.' The IPPR report stated that the employment rate of South Africans in the UK was 81 per cent, Zimbabweans 73 per cent and Nigerians 61 per cent but only 12 per cent of skilled Somalis were in employment. Although we cannot be sure whether the same situation applies today following the economic crisis, we can deduce from these figures that English language competence almost certainly plays an important part in African professionals' ability to find employment in the UK.

Figures are hard to come by, but Australia, the Middle East and Asian countries such as Japan, China and India have also become destinations for African professionals. Former US ambassador David Shinn estimates that about 300,000 African professionals work and live outside Africa, making it a continent which is losing 20,000 of its highly trained persons annually (Shinn 2008). The medical profession has been the most active in seeking employment abroad. Parker (2009) notes that there has been a huge influx of African doctors into Canada; the main reason for this being the big gap in remuneration. For instance:

> Physicians in developing African countries like Ghana and Nigeria are estimated to earn between CAD3,600 [GBP2,300, USD3,600] and CAD12,000 [GBP7,700, USD12,000] per year, which is in stark contrast to the average physician salaries of CAD162,000 [GBP105,000, USD161,000] in developed countries such as Canada. **(Parker 2009:22)**

Parker also identifies other cases of professional migration, including the case of Ethiopian Airlines losing 150 of its most highly skilled personnel in 2007 to other higher paying Gulf Airlines.

Shinn (2008) observes that African skilled worker migration takes place not only to the West but within Africa as well, from poor and politically unstable parts to the relatively peaceful and prosperous countries. Surprisingly, African countries pay USD4 billion (GBP2.6 billion) annually to employ expatriate professionals.

Migration (albeit temporary) for study purposes is also a significant phenomenon. A Hong Kong-based newspaper reports that:

> In 2001, there were 1,224 African students in China; by 2010, it is hoped that scholarship and sponsored students alone will be about 4,000 and total numbers may well exceed 12,000, many of them in private and/or independent institutions. **(Simons 2009)**

African migration has been associated with many negative phenomena. In the developed countries, it puts pressure on resources and consequently has become a serious political issue. In Africa, on the other hand, it is an issue of a 'brain drain', a serious loss of the most highly skilled and best qualified people that African nations possess. These issues, however, are rarely seen from the perspective of the individuals involved or the migrants' contribution to development. As the former UN Secretary General, Kofi Annan, put it:

> We cannot ignore the real policy difficulties posed by migration ... But neither should we lose sight of its immense potential to benefit migrants, the countries they leave and those to which they migrate. **(Cited in Mutume 2006:15)**

Mutume (2006) laments the irony that the developed countries create a conducive environment for the flow of goods and services but they restrict the flow of labour from developing countries. Increasingly, however, professional and other forms of labour migration are being interpreted in terms of 'human development' (UNDP 2009), as creating opportunities for individuals and adding value to both the host and sending nations.

The most conspicuous way in which this can be seen is that migrants send remittances home. Several African countries have benefited in this way. For instance, a World Bank report (World Bank 2010) has estimated that worldwide migration remittances to developing countries, including Africa, totalled USD336 billion (GBP218 billion) in 2008 and USD316 (GBP205 billion) in 2009. These sums exceed direct capital flows to developing countries through private investment and donations. They account for 1.9 per cent of GDP for all developing countries and 5.9 per cent for the lowest income countries (which include most of the African nations). In spite of the high cost of transferring remittances (in some cases as much as 25 per cent), a report from the International Fund for Agricultural Development (IFAD) indicates that:

> More than 30 million Africans live outside their countries of origin, sending more than USD40 billion [GBP26 billion] to their families and communities back home every year. **(IFAD 2009)**

The money remitted has a particularly important impact on rural communities, where it may be used for a range of different purposes. According to UNDP (2009:7):

> Moving generally brings benefits, most directly in the form of remittances sent to immediate family members. However, the benefits are also spread more broadly as remittances are spent – thereby generating jobs for local workers – and as behaviour changes in response to ideas from abroad. Women, in particular, may

be liberated from traditional roles. The nature and extent of these impacts depend on who moves, how they fare abroad and whether they stay connected to their roots through flows of money, knowledge and ideas.

I have interviewed a number of people who have travelled outside Africa to find out about their experiences of using English.

Mr Samabat (not his real name) is a male taxi driver who has lived in Washington DC in the USA for 15 years. He said:

Life in US is difficult and easy but for some time I had difficulty because I didn't understand English very well, I didn't pay much attention to English in school: So I suffered. I think I have had enough now, I want to come back and establish some business. (Translated from Amharic)

Ms Firewinta is a female who spent five years in Dubai and Qatar as a domestic servant. She said:

To communicate with my employers was very difficult. One of the problems was language. I only learnt a few Arabic words before leaving my country. So my only option was to talk to them in English. Although I didn't understand them well, they also spoke to me in English. Slowly I increased my Arabic. The employers want to talk to me in Arabic always but still there is difficulty.

Ms Abebasori is a female who lived in the UK for two years, working as a cleaner in a hospital. She said:

When I first arrived I was afraid because in my country I only met foreigners as a secretary but they speak clear English. But in the hospital people from UK but also other countries, it was difficult to understand their accent.

Finally, Mr Nega Alem, a male academic who wanted to pay a short visit to Cairo in Egypt, had this to say:

I was coming back from Europe and I wanted to visit an Egyptian friend in Cairo for some three days. When I was trying to get through security I had a problem. The security officers processed the other European tourists but they refused to allow me in. I heard them using English with the others, but when I tried to talk to them in English they were speaking in Arabic which I didn't understand completely. I was kept in the airport for long hours and travelled to my country when the plane arrived.

The above extracts are real-life instances of Africans encountering English in English-speaking countries and elsewhere. The examples illustrate how much these people needed English for everyday survival and yet, at the same time, how one can be subject to indifference for using English in certain contexts. Living in a foreign country presents many challenges and not knowing the language makes things even more complicated: the individual is disempowered and may be unable to understand what is happening. But still English as an international language is usually available to facilitate interaction between Africans and people with other cultures and languages.

Recently, there have been some creative new projects established by the International Organisation for Migration (IOM) which encourage professional migrants to return to their home countries for the short or long term to support development in different sectors. These returnees are also becoming major investors by setting up new businesses, especially hotels and agricultural industries.

Some African countries, such as Ivory Coast, Nigeria, Ghana and Ethiopia, have established their own mechanisms to encourage their diaspora to return long term or short term to provide professional assistance or to invest in their countries. Although these programmes still have a long way to go there are some encouraging results.

The BBC has also reported on a trend which has been observed in nine African countries 'from Mali to South Africa, from Ghana to Ethiopia' for Africans to return to their home countries after working or studying abroad, either for patriotic reasons or because of 'the growing opportunities back home' (BBC 2010). The report shows how committed professionals can make a significant contribution to their home country by using the knowledge, skills and experience they gained through employment, research and education in developed countries. A case in point is that of Ms Elleni Gebre-Medhin, a US-educated Ethiopian who spearheaded the establishment of the Ethiopian Commodity Exchange and which, in 2010, she was still leading. However, another aspect of this phenomenon, the BBC report indicates, is that even without physically dislocating from their host country the African diaspora are transferring their expertise to their countries and the region as a whole 'helping universities, schools or individuals ... to bridge the skills gap with the West' (BBC 2010).

We can see, therefore, that English language competence is important in all of these aspects. Professionals need to know English both to gain new experience in their host countries and to transfer their knowledge and skills back to their home countries.

There is yet another dimension to work-related migration. Africa is not only sending its citizens abroad; it is also increasingly becoming an attractive destination for global investment companies and professional migrants from other continents (predominantly from China, as we noted above). People from countries in Asia and Europe are beginning to arrive in Africa looking for jobs. The current job creators include the construction, oil, mining, and horticulture industries, international organisations and non-government organisations.

Language policies and English in education
The most important contribution which English has made in Africa is in education. However, this contribution has been challenged because of the limiting effect which it has had historically on the use of the indigenous languages, especially in primary education (Batibo 2007). Many writers (for example, Clegg 2007 and Williams 2011, Chapter 3 this volume) argue strongly for adopting the mother tongue as the medium of instruction, especially in early childhood education, because it facilitates cognitive, communicative and social skills development. Indeed, Ouane and Glanz

(2010) go so far as to observe that 'Africa is the only continent where the majority of children start school using a foreign language'. Language policy analysts hold the view that the lack of development in Africa is associated with failure to exploit the potential of indigenous languages. Despite their independence from colonial rule, African states have failed to come up with effective language policies:

> *The most challenging realities that most of these states had to grapple with were the prevailing multilingual and multiethnic phenomena. Most of them took a shortcut by adopting an exoglossic language policy, in which the ex-colonial language was adopted as official language and, in some cases, served also as national language.* **(Batibo 2007:15)**

More recently, African states – as well as the regional organisation AU – have tried to recognise the indigenous languages as official languages (Chimhundu 2002) and they have formulated laws and policies that encourage the use of L1 as medium of instruction at least up to the primary level. Good examples are South Africa and Ethiopia, which have adopted constitutions that stipulate that all languages should be accorded equal esteem. In South Africa, eleven languages, including the previously marginalised ones, are now recognised as official languages (Fisseha 2009). The provincial governments can select any of these languages for administrative functions, based on 'usage, practicality, expense, regional circumstances and the balances of the needs and preferences of the population as a whole or in the province concerned' (Fisseha 2009:130). A similar approach is taken in Ethiopia. Contrary to the unification agenda of the previous rulers which promoted just one local language, Amharic (Bogale 2009, Haile-Michael 1993, Negash 2005), the current regime has promulgated a constitution that guarantees the equality of all languages and their use:

> *Every nation, nationality and people in Ethiopia has the right to speak, to write and to develop its own language; to express, to develop and to promote its culture and to preserve its history.* **(FDRE 1994, Article 39(2), 96)**

Although there is some variation at the lower levels, English is used as a medium of instruction in many African countries, from primary school up to the tertiary level. In the former French colonies of Ivory Cost, Mali and Sénégal, English is the first compulsory foreign language taught in secondary schools. In most cases there is a desire to expand the teaching of English to the primary level as well (Apia 2010, Tennant and Negash 2010).

Research indicates that adopting the first language is not a straightforward thing. Due to the many indigenous languages competing for dominance, national and local governments face difficulty deciding which language to make an official one or a language of education at primary, secondary and tertiary levels. Cohen's (2007) research in Ethiopia sheds some light on the local linguistic conflicts that come with political moves to empower local languages.

A very good instance of the challenge which Africans encounter concerning the transition from English to the mother tongue as a medium of instruction can be found in the work of Bogale (2009) in Ethiopia. In Ethiopia the transition from mother tongue to English as medium of instruction starts from Grade 5 in one region, Grade 7 in another region and Grade 9 in yet another. There is even disparity between private and public (government) schools. The private schools, usually located in urban areas, attract the children of well-to-do families, teach English as a subject and use it as the medium of instruction beginning at the kindergarten level. On the other hand, the government schools follow the national policy.

This experience is similar to that of other African countries (for example, Kenya). Despite governments seeking to enforce the national policy in the private schools, parents seem to resist because they believe that they can give their children better opportunities, educationally and economically, than are experienced by those who are taught in their mother tongue. Very often, arguments for using the mother tongue as the medium of instruction do not seem to have answers for all questions. A Ugandan academic, lecturing in the postgraduate programme in Urban Management in a university in Addis Ababa, described the situation in his home country, as follows:

> In the past the use of vernacular was discouraged in schools, children who did that were stigmatised. However, now it is better because these languages are used for primary-level education. But the lingering problem is young people who have not enough competence in English feel discriminated against in the workplace. English is a compulsory language to get jobs, even in government offices, and it is a compulsory subject one should pass to join university.
> **(Interview/TG/December 2010)**

This interview extract clearly reflects the challenges involved in using English alongside the local languages. As the Ugandan academic reflected, many job vacancies in government and non-government organisations require competence in English.

The issue from the parents' side is that they feel that they are in a better position to know what is suitable for their children, and to safeguard their children's rights, rather than the government. Further evidence concerning the perceived value of English in Africa is that many parents (even the policy makers themselves) send their children to English medium schools in their home countries or in the UK, US and Canada, if they have the financial resources to enable them to do so. I interviewed some Ethiopian parents about the idea of educating their children in private English medium schools. Here is what one educated parent said:

> Since there is still confusion, no conclusive evidence at what age a foreign language should be taught, I just followed what the public does. But I think English creates future opportunity for my child.
> **(Interview with LLSN, a law lecturer)**

We should be aware, also, that simply using the mother tongue is not a panacea for all of Africa's education and development problems (Williams 2011).

Since students in ESL and EFL contexts face difficulties in communicating effectively, some education experts (Stoddart 1986, Tekeste 1990) have argued that foreign languages such as English should be replaced by local languages since it is easier for students to acquire them. There have been attempts to do this in

Ethiopia, for example the Amharicisation programme (translation of all educational books into Amharic) during the Dergue (Haile-Michael 1993). But this did not last long due to lack of resources and a reluctance to accept the programme by various stakeholders. In Africa, it seems that we are not yet ready politically as well as economically to totally replace English as the language of education at secondary and tertiary levels.

The origin of the perception that English (in ESL/EFL contexts) is an obstruction rather than a facilitator of learning (Stoddart 1986) is the poor teaching methodology that pervades education systems (Haile-Michael 1993, Negash 2005). There are instances (for example, Ethiopia and Zambia) that show that citizens or children are not taught properly to develop communicative competence. Williams (2011) cites teacher-dominated classroom interaction which focuses on rote learning instead of meaning comprehension; this leads to lack of competence in English. The national education policy document for Ethiopia (FDRE 2002) expresses a similar kind of dissatisfaction with English language teaching methodology which does not help students achieve a meaningful or working level of proficiency even after many years of formal schooling.

To manage Africa's multilingualism and to use English effectively, it is wise to consider Batibo's proposal for a balanced or hierarchical approach to language use optimisation:

> At the top level we would have the ex-colonial or global language, which would serve as the external window of the country linking it with the outside world in international communication and diplomacy. At the second level, we would have the nationally dominant lingua franca ... as ... both the main official language and the national language ... The third level is that of the major areally dominant or provincial languages which would be used for provincial communication, particularly in primary education and localised mass media. **(Batibo 2007:21-22)**

The future of English in Africa

In his forward to Graddol's 2006 book, Neil Kinnock, a retired UK politician, made the following prediction about the future of English in the world:

> The growth of the use of English as the world's primary language for international communication has obviously been continuing for several decades. But even as the number of English speakers expands further there are signs that the global predominance of the language may fade within the foreseeable future.
> **(Kinnock 2006:3)**

English is not the only foreign language in Africa; governments have to share their budgets between the teaching of English, indigenous languages and other foreign languages. English therefore is competing for resources and status with indigenous languages (estimated at 1,000) and foreign languages such as Portuguese, still used in several African countries, and Italian, which has a relatively minor role in Eritrea (Hailemariam et al. 2011, Chapter 11 this volume) and Ethiopia. A language of major importance in certain parts of Africa is Arabic, which came to Africa in the first century AD with the migration of the Arabs and then again a few centuries later with the spread of Islam and the introduction of Quranic schools (Abdelali El Ouadghiri 2003).

Though not so dominant as English, French is also a European language which competes with it in Africa. It is used as an official language in the former French colonies in West Africa (e.g. Benin, Niger, Sénégal) and North Africa (e.g. Algeria, Morocco, Tunisia). It is one of the AU's working languages, in parallel with English, Arabic and Portuguese. An interesting phenomenon identified by Martin Plout, BBC Africa Analyst, is that just as French speakers in the Francophone countries of Africa are keen to learn English so that they can communicate with their English-speaking neighbours, so some traditionally Anglophone countries are starting to show interest in learning another European language for international communication:

> Ghana recently decided that its officials should learn French, so that they could hold their own with their West African colleagues from Ivory Coast, Burkina Faso and Sénégal. So although Paris will not be pleased by the Rwandan decision [to use English as a medium of instruction], their language is by no means about to be extinguished from the African continent. **(Plout 2008)**

The rising eastern economies like China and India, with their pragmatic philosophy of non-interference in the politics of their African partners, are challenging the economic dominance of the West. This new economic and political dominance might also lead to new linguistic and cultural influences on Africa. This will certainly be the case if China decides to maintain or expand still further its investment in the promotion of its language and culture in the same way that the Anglophone countries have been doing for many years. As in other parts of the world, including Europe, China is launching Confucius Institutes which offer free Chinese language instruction; there are already said to be 20 in different parts of Africa. Perhaps African governments want to ease the pressure which the West puts on them to introduce political reform as a precondition for aid by developing new partnerships with China. For example, in 2009 Zimbabwe instructed its universities to begin teaching Chinese history, culture and language (Mandarin) (Magaisa 2009). Meanwhile, different sources indicate that the Chinese government is financing regular conferences in African universities (see Simons 2009 and Mvogo 2010) and offering scholarships to Africans.

Even individual Chinese observers recognise that their government has adopted an aggressive policy towards Africa. I recall personal communication with postgraduate students from China whom I met in the USA while visiting the University of Michigan in the summer of 2010. These students told me repeatedly how friendly China is towards Africa. They asked me:

> Is there any Chinese language teaching or Confucius Institute in your country? Our country uses Confucius institutions to teach Chinese way of life and create peaceful relations with countries. **(Field note/UM/ELI/August 2010)**

It is interesting to observe how much effort China is putting into promoting the learning of Mandarin in Africa while at the same time investing so much to help its own citizens learn English. Magaisa (2009) remarks, however, that Chinese project workers in Africa (specifically Zimbabwe) tend not to put too much effort into learning African languages to communicate with the people they are supervising. This leads Magaisa to wonder, therefore, whether the energetic promotion of Chinese language and culture in Africa might be 'quite simply one language of power (Mandarin) being given space to dislodge another (English).'

My own belief is that English is and will continue to be an effective common language in Africa–China interaction and that Mandarin will not replace English as the dominant international language in Africa. This is because the Chinese themselves are learning English in order to spread their influence (see also Bruthiaux 2002). Evidence of this can be seen in the communication between Chinese supervisors and African construction workers. I was curious about how the Chinese supervisors communicate with labourers in Africa and so I talked to some of the latter:

> We use 'broken English', just simple words like Stop! No! ... with gestures. And sometimes we use translation from English to Amharic.
> **(Talk with Ethiopian, December 2010)**

My own and other survey studies indicate, therefore, that despite challenges from other languages English will remain the most popular or desired language in Africa. My own interview survey carried out on an ongoing basis since 2006 has involved 126 Africans of diverse careers from various countries; they include language experts, teachers, students, drivers and hotel workers, chosen randomly. The interview questions included 'How do you see the importance of English for Africa and your country's development?' and 'How do you see the role of English in your career advancement?' As Graddol (2007) has noted elsewhere, the respondents overwhelmingly talk of 'globalisation' as an explanation for the prominence of English in the continent. Many teachers I met in Burkina Faso and Sénégal in West Africa told me that individuals of their acquaintance who were educated in other foreign languages, such as French, Spanish or Portuguese, were taking private tuition in English. A group of Burkina English language inspectors described the situation in their country as follows:

> Although French is the official language, we need English to do business with non-French speakers. In Ouagadougou we have about five English language centres. One of these is the American Centre. There are also other English language centres run by Burkinas as well. **(Interview/CS/October 2010)**

Many Ethiopians I talked to (teachers, students, experts in different fields) have a very positive attitude towards English. One of the reasons for this is that English is associated with modernisation and development. Although many teachers and students feel that they have still not mastered English, they believe that the driving force behind the growing importance of English is economic and political interdependence. Here is the view of a statistics lecturer that can represent the opinion of a majority of educated Ethiopians:

> English is a de facto international language for Africa. Because of the globalisation level in trade, politics, learning we need English, we can't stay isolated. In the past, other European countries like France, Austria, Germany insisted on using their

own language in business, education. But these days, they have become bilingual, they use English to publish and to teach, because they want to reach the world citizens. Although sometimes culturally unacceptable things can be sent through the internet, 90 per cent of resources we get in Africa or Ethiopia come from the West and this is almost all in English. Even people from Francophone countries need English to access these resources.
(Interview with LMD/September 2010)

Contrary to the above perception, however, there are some experts and teachers of different subjects who may feel that the use of a foreign language like English is rather an obstruction to learning (Stoddart 1986). The following comment sums up the pain which many Africans using English as a second or foreign language have experienced:

We are confused in Ethiopia; we don't learn English and use English properly and at the same time we have it as a medium of instruction and a second official language. Sometimes I feel very frustrated, we don't use it as well as other Africans. **(Interview with MDS/December 2010)**

Another academic, however, expressed his opinion that, despite the importance of English, he is dissatisfied with the general level of proficiency in the language:

These days the level of English language has deteriorated, but this shouldn't be an excuse for wanting to resort to using local language for education. You know we tried this during the socialist regime, translate words into Amharic, but that didn't succeed. So we have to find a way of teaching the students better English. (Interview with LSE/December 2010)

And so, unlike the language specialists, many ordinary Africans believe that the problem with English language proficiency is not a reason for replacing it with indigenous African languages. In fact, there are some who believe that they communicate quite adequately in English:

I personally don't feel any obstacle in career development because of English; I would say I communicate easily in English especially with what I am doing now, reading, writing and teaching **(Interview/TG/December 2010)**

My survey results are supported by a similar study conducted in another African country, Sudan, which compared the relative importance of English, Arabic and the first language. The study concluded:

English is important as an international language; it facilitates contact with foreigners ... (they) speak Arabic mainly for instrumental and pragmatic reasons such as in formal domains, at the workplace, in education and so on ... they liked to maintain their L1 for integrative or ideological/symbolic reasons as part of their heritage and as a cultural symbol. **(Idris et al. 2007:42)**

Apart from the public interest, governments in Africa also place a high value on English. For instance, Ivory Cost and Ethiopia are currently spending money on national curriculum revisions and the preparation of new teaching materials based on recent language teaching methodologies. In Ethiopia, the present government has invested a greater amount of money than its predecessors in English language improvement projects for English and other subject teachers (Siraj et al. 2007).

Recently, Rwanda has switched from French to English as a language of post-primary education. Although there seems to be political motivation behind the change, I believe that a major factor is the continued dominance of English as the language of wider international communication in Africa and beyond. Plout has observed:

> *Conversations in the capital, Kigali, are increasingly conducted in English. A colleague who recently visited the country reported being given a brisk brush-off for asking for information in French. And the Kigali Institute of Science and Technology has for some time used English as the official medium of instruction.*
> **(Plout 2008)**

Organisations like the British Council, the Hornby Trust and USAID are also investing in English language provision, teacher training and the production of resource materials. In Francophone West Africa (and Portuguese-speaking Cape Verde), there is some significant work in progress co-ordinated and supported by the Hornby Trust and the British Council. Since 2009 the Trust and the British Council have conducted four Hornby Schools in Sénégal and Burkina Faso to train teacher trainers and teachers. A training and methodology resource book (Tennant and Negash 2009) has been published. And an ongoing discussion with senior stakeholders responsible for English and others in these countries aims 'to get better understanding of how an organisation like the British Council ... could best engage with policy makers, teachers and learners' (Tennant and Negash 2010:1).

Conclusion

Although it is often argued that English is the language of the African elite, it actually has many roles in development in Africa, the effects of which can trickle down to the masses. With good language planning, English is going to be the major international language for some time to come, which will help Africa and Africans to get connected within and beyond their national and regional boundaries.

However, since development is increasingly associated with using the L1 as a language of education, there seems to be an unhelpful labelling of foreign languages like English as languages of imperialism (Phillipson 1996). This ignores the pragmatic, sociolinguistic, economic and political realities in Africa and beyond. If an L1 is used ineffectively this cannot be blamed entirely on the dominance of foreign languages; there have also been failures in the management of multilingualism, in the teaching of the mother tongues and in the teaching methods adopted for ESL and EFL. The negative associations attached to English may also have arisen from the use of an inappropriate teaching approach and materials that give the impression that the culture of native speakers of English is in some way superior to the cultures of the countries where English is taught and used as a second or foreign language (Canagarajah 1999).

It is definitely unhelpful for Africa to continue viewing English or any other international language as the language of colonisation or imperialism. Africans need to go beyond this and see the usefulness of English without it dominating or deterring the development of our indigenous cultures and languages.

What Africa needs is an optimisation (Batibo 2007) of linguistic resources (including national, local and international languages), in the continent as a whole and in each individual country. This requires an effective language policy to manage multilingualism and the competition for resources and status between the indigenous languages themselves and between English and the indigenous languages or other international languages. There also needs to be some solid research on Africans' perceptions of the value of English, so that the debate on language planning can move beyond the whim of the elites.

English is going to be even more important as Africa, its member states and its citizens engage with the rest of the world more meaningfully. As governments and people become more confident to have their say in global economic, social and political matters, the demand for English will increase.

References

Abdelali El Ouadghiri. 2003 (1424H). *Arabic language in Sub-Saharan Africa: Past, present and future. Islam Today* 20.

Apia, K.D. 2010. *Contribution to 'Ambitions for English in Francophone West Africa' Project.* Prepared for Heads of English Meeting organised by British Council Sénégal, Ouagadougu, Burkina Faso, 1-2 October 2010.

Batibo, H.M. 2007. *Language use optimisation as a strategy for national development.* In H.Coleman (ed.), *Language and Development in Africa and Beyond: Proceedings of the 7th International Language and Development Conference,* 15-26. Addis Ababa: British Council. Available online at *www.langdevconferences.org*

BBC (British Broadcasting Corporation). 2005. *African success in UK highlighted. BBC News Online* 7 September 2005. Available online at *http://news.bbc.co.uk/2/hi/africa/4222812.stm*

BBC (British Broadcasting Corporation). 2010. *Brain gain: African migrants returning home. BBC News Online* 29 May 2010. Available online at *www.bbc.co.uk/news/10173682*

Bekele, D. 2003. *The Legal Framework for Freedom of Expression in Ethiopia. London: Article 19 Global Campaign for Free Expression.*

Bogale, B. 2009. *Language determination in Ethiopia: What medium of instruction?* In S.Ege, H.Aspen, B.Teferra and S.Bekale (eds), *Proceedings of the 16th International Conference of Ethiopian Studies, Volume 4,* 1089-1101. Trondheim: Department of Social Anthropology, Norwegian University of Science and Technology. Available online at *http://portal.svt.ntnu.no/sites/ices16/Proceedings/Volume per cent204/Volume per cent204 per cent20Complete per cent20version.pdf*

Bruthiaux, P. 2002. *Predicting challenges to English as a global language in the 21st century. Language Problems and Language Planning* 26(2), 129–157.

Canagarajah, A.S. 1999. *Resisting Linguistic Imperialism in Teaching English. Oxford: Oxford University Press.*

Chimhundu, H. 2002. *Language Policies in Africa: Final Report of Intergovernmental Conference on Language Policies in Africa, Harare, Zimbabwe, 17-21 March 1997.* (Web version edited by Karsten Legère.) Paris: UNESCO. Available online at *http://ocpa. irmo.hr/resources/docs/Harare_Language-en.pdf*

Clegg, J. 2007. *Moving towards bilingual education in Africa. In H.Coleman (ed.), Language and Development in Africa and Beyond: Proceedings of the 7th International Language and Development Conference, 49-64. Addis Ababa: British Council.* Available online at *www.langdevconferences.org*

Cohen, G.P.E. 2007. *Mother tongue and other tongue in primary education: Can equity be achieved with the use of different languages? In H.Coleman (ed.), Language and Development in Africa and Beyond: Proceedings of the 7th International Language and Development Conference, 79-96. Addis Ababa: British Council.* Available online at *www.langdevconferences.org*

Coleman, H. 2010. *English in Development. London: British Council.* Available online at *www.teachingenglish.org.uk/transform/books/english-language-development*

English Xin-hua.net. 2010. *Full text: China-Africa economic and trade cooperation. English Xin-hua.net,* 23 December 2010. Available online at *http:// news.xinhuanet.com/english2010/china/2010-12/23/c_13661632.htm*

FDRE (Federal Democratic Republic of Ethiopia). 1994. *Constitution. Addis Ababa: FDRE.* Available online at *wwwethiopar.net/*

FDRE (Federal Democratic Republic of Ethiopia). 2002. *Capacity Building Strategy and Programmes. Addis Ababa: FDRE.*

Fisseha, Y.T. 2009. *A tale of two federations: Comparing language rights regimes in South Africa and Ethiopia.* In R.Tsegaye (ed.), *Issues of Federalism in Ethiopia: Towards an Inventory,* 115-160. *(Ethiopian Constitutional Law Series Volume 2.) Addis Ababa: Addis Ababa University Press.*

Graddol, D. 1997. *The Future of English. London: The British Council.*

Graddol, D. 2006. *English Next: Why Global English May Mean the End of 'English as a Foreign Language'. London: The British Council.*

Hailemariam, C., Ogbay, S. and White, G. 2011. *English and development in Eritrea.* Chapter 11, this volume.

Haile-Michael, A. 1993. *Developing a Service English Syllabus to Meet the Academic Demands and Constraints in the Ethiopian University Context. PhD thesis submitted to Addis Ababa University, Ethiopia.*

Idris, H.F., Legère, K. and Rosendal, T. 2007. *Language policy in selected African countries: Achievements and constraints.* In H.Coleman (ed.), *Language and Development in Africa and Beyond: Proceedings of the 7th International Language and Development Conference, 27-48. Addis Ababa: British Council.* Available online at *www.langdevconferences.org*

IFAD (International Fund for Agricultural Development). *2009: Result of the Global Forum on Remittances 2009: Remittances as a development tool in Africa. FFR [Financing Facility for Remittances] Update* 4th Quarter (1), 1. Available online at *www.ifad.org/remittances/newsletter/1.pdf*

Kinnock, N. 2006. Foreword. In D.Graddol, *English Next: Why Global English May Mean the End of 'English as a Foreign Language', 3-5. London: British Council.*

Lodhi, A .Y. 1993. *The language situation in Africa today. Nordic Journal of African Studies 2(1), 79-86.*

Magaisa, A.T. 2009. *Mandarin in Zimbabwe: To learn or not to learn. NewZimbabwe.com* 11 December 2009. Available online at *www.newzimbabwe. com/pages/magaisa13.13683.html*

Mutume, G. 2003. *Mounting opposition to Northern farm subsidies: African cotton farmers battling to survive. Africa Recovery* 17(1), 18. Available online at *www.un.org/ecosocdev/geninfo/afrec/vol17no1/171agri4.htm*

Mutume, G. 2006. *African migration: From tensions to solutions. Africa Renewal* 19(4), 1. Available online at *www.un.org/ecosocdev/geninfo/afrec/ vol19no4/194migration.html*

Mvogo, R. 2010. *African academics hail Confucius institutes as a bridge of culture, partnership. Forum on China-Africa Cooperation,* 13 August 2010. *Beijing: Ministry of Foreign Affairs.* Available online at *www.focac.org/eng/zfgx/ t724757.htm*

Mwabu, G. and Fosu, A. 2010. *Human Development in Africa. (Human Development Research Paper 8.) New York: UNDP-HDRO.*

Naudé, W.A. and Saayman, A. 2005. *Determinants of tourist arrivals in Africa: A panel data regression analysis. Tourism Economics* 11(3), 365-391.

Navuri, A. 2010. *Tanzanian farmers challenged to export products to Turkey. IPPMedia.com* 25 December 2010. Available online at *www.ippmedia.com/frontend/ index.php?l=24405*

Negash, N. 2005. *Exploring Active Learning in EAP Classrooms: An Ethnographic Action Research. PhD thesis submitted to the University of Exeter, U.K.*

Ouane, A. and Glanz, C. 2010. *Why and How Africa Should Invest in African Languages and Multilingual Education. Hamburg: UNESCO Institute for Lifelong Learning.*

Parker, M. 2009. *Diagnosis brain drain: The migration of African physicians to Canada. Queens Health Science Journal* 9(2), 21-24.

Phillipson, R. 1992. *Linguistic Imperialism. Oxford: Oxford University Press.*

Phillipson, R. 1996. *Linguistic imperialism: African perspectives. ELT Journal* 50(2), 160-167.

Plout, M. 2008. *Rwanda opts for English language teaching. BBC News Online 10 October 2008.* Available online at *http://news.bbc.co.uk/2/hi/africa/7663298.stm*

Politzer, M. 2008. *China and Africa: Stronger economic ties mean more migration. Migration Information Source Online,* August 2008. Washington, DC: Migration Policy Institute. Available online at *www.migrationinformation.org/Feature/display.cfm?id=690*

Shinn, D. 2008. *African migration and the brain drain. Paper presented at the Institute for African Studies and Slovenia Global Action, Ljubljana, Slovenia,* 20 June 2008. Available online at *http://sites.google.com/site/davidhshinn/Home/african-migration-and-the-brain-drain*

Simons, B.B. 2009. *Confucianism at large in Africa. Asia Times* 7 August 2009. Available online at *www.atimes.com/atimes/China/KH07Ad03.html*

Siraj, A., Baraki, A. and Altshul, J. 2007. *Ethiopian teachers' evaluation of a language improvement programme.* In H.Coleman (ed.), *Language and Development in Africa and Beyond: Proceedings of the 7th International Language and Development Conference,* 195-212. *Addis Ababa: British Council.* Available online at *www.langdevconferences.org*

Stoddart, J. 1986. *The Use and Study of English in Ethiopian Schools. Unpublished report. Addis Ababa.*

Tekeste, N. 1990. *The Crisis of Ethiopian Education: Some Implications for Nation Building. Uppsala Reports on Education 29. Uppsala: Uppsala University Press.*

Tennant, A. and Negash, N. 2009. *English Language for Teachers: A Methodology Training Book. Dakar: British Council Sénégal.*

Tennant, A. and Negash, N. 2010. *Contribution to 'Ambitions for English in Francophone West Africa' Project. Prepared for Heads of English Meeting organised by British Council Sénégal, Ouagadougou, Burkina Faso,* 1-2 October 2010.

UNDP (United Nations Development Programme). 1990. *Concept and Measurement of Human Development. (Human Development Report 1990.) Oxford and New York: Oxford University Press for UNDP.* Available online at *http://hdr.undp.org/en/reports/global/hdr1990/chapters/*

UNDP (United Nations Development Programme). 2009. *Overcoming Barriers:Human Mobility and Development. (Human Development Report 2009.) Basingstoke and New York: Palgrave Macmillan for UNDP.* Available online at *http://hdr.undp.org/en/media/HDR_2009_EN_Complete.pdf*

UNDP (United Nations Development Programme). 2010a. *The Real Wealth of Nation: Pathways to Human Development. (Human Development Report 2010, 20th Anniversary Edition.) Basingstoke and New York: Palgrave Macmillan for UNDP.* Available online at *http://hdr.undp.org/en/media/HDR_2010_EN_Complete_reprint.pdf*

UNDP (United Nations Development Programme). 2010b. *Ethiopia is among the top development movers: The 2010 Human Development Report asserts. UNDP Ethiopia Press Release,* 4 November 2010. Available online at *www.et.undp.org/index.php?option=com_news&id=95*

Williams, E. 2011. *Language policy, politics and development in Africa.* (Chapter 3, this volume.)

World Bank. 2010. *Migration and remittances. (Topics in Development.) Washington DC: World Bank.* Available online at *http://go.worldbank.org/0IK1E5K7U0*

World-Newspapers. 2010. *Ethiopian Newspapers, Magazines and News Sites in English.* Available online at *www.world-newspapers.com/ethiopia.html*

Social and
geographic mobility

9

A 'Matthew Effect' in English language education in a developing country context

Martin Lamb

For unto every one that hath shall be given and he shall have abundance; but from him that hath not shall be taken away even that which he hath.
(New Testament, Gospel According to Matthew, XXV, 29)

Introduction

As enshrined in the second of the Millennium Development Goals (see Appendix 3), education is generally agreed to be an important engine of national development, capable of making a major contribution to the reduction of poverty and inequality within developing societies. Yet education itself has often been accused of fostering inequality. UNESCO's report on the Dakar 'Education for All' initiative highlighted 'deep and persistent inequalities' in developing country education systems, arguing that 'the circumstances into which children are born, their gender, the wealth of their parents, their language and the colour of their skin should not define their educational opportunities' (UNESCO 2008:1-2). Continuing inequity in education is not only against the spirit of the 'education for all' agenda, the report warned, but also threatens to transmit poverty across generations, in turn undermining long-term economic growth and the development of civil societies.

Educational inequality features as a central theme of several chapters in this book. Tembe and Norton (2011, Chapter 6 this volume), for example, contrast the language of education in urban and rural areas in Uganda and report the anxieties of rural parents and communities that their children are being denied access to the one language, English, which can truly facilitate their advancement; while Williams (2011, Chapter 3 this volume) makes a strong argument that African children who are not educated in their mother tongue are actually the ones suffering disadvantage. As Seargeant and Erling (2011, Chapter 12 this volume) show, these heated debates about the relative benefits of global and local languages in schools are not confined to Africa; Coleman (2011, Chapter 5 this volume), for example, describes attempts among advantaged social groups in Indonesia to establish English medium state schools to operate alongside the majority Indonesian medium education system, with a view to giving their children a competitive advantage in further education and work.

Whereas the focus in these chapters was mainly on the language of education and local people's differential access to it, in this chapter I hope to expose inequalities within the learning of one language – English – within one state system. The setting is provincial Indonesia, where in the absence of any Anglophone colonial legacy and a historical openness to external cultural influences there has long existed a consensus, both in official discourses and popular belief, that proficiency in English is beneficial for individuals and society at large (Beeby 1979, Lamb and Coleman 2008). From 2002 to 2004 I studied the motivation and learning behaviour of a small group of young adolescents starting to learn English in junior high school. The rapid divergence in experience and achievement among these learners over their first 20 months of language education was suggestive of a 'Matthew Effect', where the cumulative effects of a slight early advantage lead to the 'rich getting richer and the poor getting poorer'. The divergence became all the more striking when I returned to Indonesia in 2008 to meet the same students and learn about their progress. I will first present previous reported cases of the Matthew Effect in education, as well as theoretical perspectives on educational inequality, before presenting the case in Indonesia. I will conclude with some tentative suggestions for how English language education in Indonesia – and, by extension, other developing country contexts – might be made more equitable, so that greater numbers of young people develop and realise linguistic aspirations.

The Matthew Effect

The term 'Matthew Effect', deriving from the biblical passage quoted above[1], has been applied to many different areas of human endeavour, notably economics where a Matthew Effect has been observed in the way various factors combine to widen the wealth gap between the world's richest and poorest countries, and between social classes within states (Rigney 2010); and academia, where small differences in ability and opportunity among early career academics have been shown to result in major differences in later career achievement (Merton 1988).

In the field of school education, Walberg and Tsai (1983) used the term to characterise their research findings, which showed that the interaction of three basic factors – early educational experiences, current educational activity and motivation (see Figure 1) – meant that:

> *socio-economic and ethnic groups that scored somewhat higher than others in the early grades scored much higher in the later grades; and the gap or cumulative advantage increased steadily with grade levels.* **(Walberg and Tsai 1983:360)**

Their own research with American schoolchildren suggested that home background and associated early educative experiences were the most significant predictor of achievement in general science, contributing directly to performance at school but also indirectly by making it more likely that children from certain ethnic and socio-economic groups had higher motivation to learn and showed more adaptive learning behaviour.

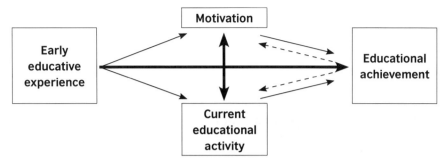

Figure 1: A diagrammatic representation of the Matthew Effect (based on Walberg and Tsai 1983)

Educational Matthew Effects have been explored in most detail in the development of children's reading skills (Stanovich 2000). It has been found that children who have a very slight edge in phonemic awareness when they start school – that is, they understand how words are made up of different sounds – are in a good position to make use of instruction in the alphabetic system; they start reading independently more quickly and therefore get more practice; as they practise, they develop automaticity and can give more attention to meaning, which in turn increases their enjoyment and encourages them to read more. By the 5th grade it is estimated that the top ten per cent of children read ten times more than the bottom ten per cent, with obvious benefits for other aspects of their education. Social background is implicated because it is often children from middle class backgrounds who come to school with slightly higher phonemic awareness, because parents have spent more time reading to them. A related example of the Matthew Effect is the TV programme *Sesame Street* in the USA, which was originally designed to increase the educational attainment of children from poor working class backgrounds who liked watching TV. Evaluation studies found that paradoxically it tended to increase gaps in achievement, because middle class parents spent more time discussing the programme with their children, enabling them to get more out of it.

In language learning, Williams et al. referred to the Matthew Effect in their study of pupils' motivation to learn French and German in UK schools. They found that by Year 9 there were already significant differences in the motivation and attitudes of high proficiency and low proficiency students and 'such differences had clearly emerged early on in these students' secondary school careers' (Williams et al. 2002:523). They speculated that pupils who were perceived as good language learners by their teachers and by themselves tended to enjoy lessons more, were thereby motivated to learn more, did better and so on, while other pupils were caught in a vicious circle of poor performance and motivation. Williams et al. also hinted at a possible role for social background in these effects, as proficient students reported their parents as being particularly supportive.

The relations between social background and education have of course been theorised at more philosophical levels. Educationalists have been aware of social class differences in educational achievement since the 1960s. Over the following decades, Bernstein (e.g. 1971) attempted to explain these differences in terms of the language ('code') used in school which, he argued, privileged the middle class children who, using the more elaborate academic codes at home with their parents, were socialised early into the educational processes of knowledge transmission.

Far more influential in contemporary theorising, however, is the late French sociologist Pierre Bourdieu, who viewed education as the means by which dominant social classes reproduced their culture and influence and sought deliberately to bring to light the usually invisible processes which underlie such social inequalities. Bourdieu's best known concept, cultural capital, was developed 'to explain the unequal scholastic achievement of children originating from the different social classes' (1986, cited by Pennycook 2001:124). All children inherit, through family and other early social practices, cultural capital along with varying levels of social and economic capital; but only the more prestigious types of cultural capital are granted legitimacy in particular 'fields' and in education those tend to be the values and priorities of the dominant social class. Further, cultural capital becomes embodied in the 'habitus', a nexus of bodily and mental habits and dispositions, including language, which causes us to feel comfortable in some environments (such as school) and uncomfortable in others (for reviews of social and cultural capital in educational research, see Dika and Singh 2002 and Lareau and Weininger 2003). Thus, in his own example, Bourdieu writes that a parent might accuse his son of being 'bad at French', yet his underperformance is actually 'a direct function of the family's cultural atmosphere' (Bourdieu and Passeron 1990:109). In many societies the English language currently represents a highly valued form of cultural (linguistic) capital and recent studies in Hong Kong (Lin 1999, Flowerdew and Miller 2008) and Spain (Block 2008) have shown how social class influences the way young people experience institutional language learning.

An Indonesian case study

In the rest of this chapter I will describe what appears to be an instance of the Matthew Effect in English language learning in provincial Indonesia, using concepts from Bourdieu as well as psychological constructs from the literature on L2 motivation to describe the contrasting trajectories of different learners. The original purpose of the research study was to investigate the motivation of Indonesian young adolescents, aged 11–13, to learn English as it evolved during their first two years of formal study in junior high school. The school was situated in what might be described as an 'emergent middle class area' of a Sumatran town which I will call 'Ajeng', and though its own facilities were basic and the intake was of mixed socio-economic background, it had a good reputation in the local community. As a provincial capital the town had experienced an influx during the Soeharto years of relatively affluent and well-educated civil servants from Java, whose offspring tended to study at this school. In more recent times, local political autonomy and laissez-faire capitalism has encouraged the rapid growth of forest-based industries, giving Ajeng something of the character of a frontier boomtown.

My research used questionnaires at the beginning of the first year and end of the second year to get a broad view of motivational trends for the whole year group (approximately 200 pupils); and then chose a 'focal group' of 12 learners to track in more detail over the subsequent 20 months, through interviews at three points, by observing them in English classes and by visiting them outside school. Eight of these learners were chosen because, on the basis of their questionnaire results and teacher comments, they had particularly high motivation. The other four were chosen, on the same basis, as being 'less motivated' to learn English, though each one stressed in their first interview with me that they did want to learn English. I also interviewed nine English teachers about their perceptions of learner motivation. In reporting my findings, I will begin by characterising the general population's motivation to learn English, before describing in more detail the learning trajectories of the 12 'focal' learners.

Learner motivation for English

On entry to the school, learners' motivation to study English was extremely high, with only one respondent out of over 200 saying that it was 'not important' to them. Their motivation could be characterised as future-oriented, blending both integrative and instrumental motives (Lamb 2004). The questionnaire responses showed that the majority of these 11- and 12-year-old learners were acutely aware of the effects of globalisation on their community and understood that mastery of English could help them gain access not only to successful careers but also to international friendships, further study abroad, new forms of technology and entertainment and to social and geographic mobility. They looked forward to the process of studying the language in junior high school.

After 20 months of study, their perception of the potential importance of English remained very high (in fact, slightly more rated it as 'very important' to them), but their enjoyment of the process had declined slightly. Fewer pupils thought that there was intrinsic pleasure to be found in learning the language, while their comments about the language tended to relate more to their classroom experiences rather than to its global role. For example, at the beginning of her studies one student wrote in her questionnaire response that she thought English was 'very important' because 'if I learn English I can gain self-confidence and many benefits ... It's the world language'; after 20 months she assessed it only as 'quite important', 'because learning English in this school is just like learning it elsewhere ... It's not so satisfying.' This general moderate fall in intrinsic motivation to learn was not unexpected; it is commonly reported in studies of learner motivation of all subject areas during the middle school years (see Wigfield et al. 1998).

Learner performance in English

I had no independent data on learners' performance in their English studies over the research period. However, besides providing a more in-depth picture of each focal learner's perceptions of their motivation, the interviews gave me insight into the development of their language competence. I started each interview in English, but quickly changed to Indonesian if the learner preferred. During the first phase of interviewing, all the learners used mainly Indonesian, though one or two of those previously identified as 'more motivated' did try to exploit the opportunity of conversation with a native speaker (in almost all cases, their first such opportunity) to use a few English words and phrases. During the second interviews eight months later, the same pattern repeated itself, though one was now able to express herself in English almost all the time. In the third interviews a further 12 months on, all seven[2] of the 'motivated' learners used English for most of the time, reverting back to Indonesian when communicatively challenged or when the conversation got very animated. One pair of girls actually spoke to each other in English[3]. In stark contrast, the four learners who were previously identified as 'less motivated' made no significant attempt to use English during the final interview. In other words, there was a striking divergence over these 20 months in the performance in English of the focal learners, with some making considerable progress and others making none at all.

To illustrate this contrast, I give below extracts from the third (2004) interviews with two pupils, the first one (who I call 'Marlina') identified initially as a 'more motivated' learner:

I: Do you feel confident now about your English?

M: Not yet

I: How do you feel about speaking in English, for example speaking in English to me?

M: Er I feel it's very hard, but I want to study it very hardly and I know in future I can speak English yang sempurna [perfectly]

I: Uh-uh right, so how do you feel when talking to me?

M: agak grogi! [rather nervous]

Clearly, as she herself recognises, Marlina's English is far from the level of perfection she demands but her determination to use the language to express herself as far as she can (as well as her high ambitions) are very evident and she has come a long way from her first interview, 20 months earlier, when she had used her L1 throughout.

The second learner, 'Krisna', was identified initially as 'less motivated'. What is striking about the beginning of the interview with Krisna – and with two of the three other less motivated learners[4] – was their reaction to my invitation to speak English; not only were they unable to respond, they smiled in amusement at the notion, as if they could not conceive of themselves as legitimate English speakers.

I: OK K, can you say something about yourself? Can you speak about K? For example, 'I am K. I live ...'

K: ... [smiles, shakes head]

Conversation continues in Indonesian:

I: How are your English studies going?

K: Not so well

I: Why is that?

K: Don't know

I: Not so ... what?

K: Don't understand well

I: ... So how do you feel?

K: Mmm ... nervous

I: That's a pity ... what makes you feel nervous?

K: Afraid of making a mistake

I: If you make a mistake, are you told off?

K: Yes

I: By who?

K: The teacher ... but she doesn't get angry

I: So why do you feel nervous?

K: I'm afraid

I: But if she doesn't get angry, why be afraid?

K: I'm ashamed

I: Ashamed oh ... Studying English for you, is it important or not important?

K: Mmm, I feel it's important

I: And your desire to learn?

K: It's less now.

As the extract indicates, Krisna still recognises the importance of English in principle, but his negative feelings about the process of learning – particularly his failure to understand what's going on in the lesson and the teacher's unsympathetic reaction to his mistakes – has reduced his desire to learn. It is also noteworthy that both learners admit to feeling nervous, yet their anxiety apparently has different origins and outcomes – for Marlina, it is a by-product of her excitement in exploiting a rare opportunity to communicate with a native speaker; for Krisna it is a symptom of his fear of failure.

Four years on, I interviewed these two and the other ten focal learners again, offering them the same choice of speaking in English or Indonesian. Now the gap in speaking performance had widened much further. As a crude measure of this gap, I counted the number of turns begun in English during the interview by six of the learners. The results are presented in Figure 2.

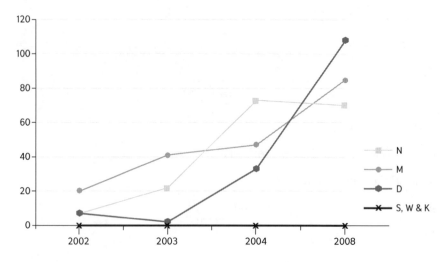

Figure 2: Number of utterances begun in English during the four interviews, for six learners: N, M, D, S, W and K.

For Marlina (M) and two of the other 'more motivated' focal learners, the graph shows a distinct upward trend[5], one that I am confident would be replicated by the other five learners. By contrast, Krisna (K) and two of the other 'less motivated' learners still showed no willingness to communicate in English with me, despite four more years of English language learning.

Of course, oral fluency is only one aspect of L2 proficiency. All the learners, including S, W and K, claimed to have learned some English grammar or vocabulary in the intervening years and all had passed school and national tests. But in terms of their willingness and ability to use the language, as they stood on the threshold of adulthood, some had not progressed at all since they were in their first year of formal study, while the others had attained sufficient functionality to hold a long conversation with a native speaker. In the next section I will argue that this widening gap in achievement can be understood in terms of the three factors which Walberg and Tsai (1983) identified as producing a Matthew Effect (see Figure 1).

How the Matthew Effect works in this context

Early educative experience
Walberg and Tsai (1983) included in their construct of 'early educative experience' several background variables such as parental education and occupation, ethnicity, household income as well as early formal education experiences. My own background data on the 12 focal learners was much more limited and I had never intended to use indicators of social or educational background to select them. However, through their survey responses, information gleaned from my interviews with them and from visits to their houses or private language schools, I was able to identify telling differences among the participants which broadly corresponded to the division between 'more motivated' and 'less motivated' learners.

By definition, learners in the 'more motivated' group had advantages over the others on entry to the school, since the teachers confirmed them as 'motivated' learners when I originally chose them on the basis of their questionnaire responses. Evidently they brought with them cultural capital which allowed them to be recognised by the teachers as potentially good learners of English. I have shown that this did not consist of any significant oral linguistic ability, at this stage, but would have manifested itself in other ways. Among them would have been their behaviour in English classes, which I discuss below (see the third sub-section below on 'learning activity'), but other possible factors which caught the attention of teachers would be their relatively neat appearance, their use of Bahasa Indonesia and some awareness of their relatively privileged family backgrounds.

These eight students' fathers were: two senior civil servants (the father of one girl was on the town council, another was head of section in the local office of agricultural affairs), two civil servants of unspecified rank, two businessmen (at least one of whom, Marlina's father, was doing extremely well as the owner of palm oil estates), one university lecturer (his daughter had actually been born in the USA while he was studying for Master's degrees there) and one doctor (two mothers were also doctors). Three had parents who spoke English to a high level, while all had other family members who spoke some English. All eight had studied some English in primary school; this was a surprise to me as the language was not (and still is not) on the national primary curriculum, but some local primary schools had begun to fit English lessons (usually no more than once a week for 45 minutes) into their provision, often asking parents to pay extra fees for the recruitment of a teacher. And on entry to the junior high school, seven of the eight had already studied English at a private language school in the town.

Meanwhile, three of the four 'less motivated' learners were disadvantaged in significant ways. Krisna's family were recipients of the school's small scholarship fund for the local poor. His older sister spoke some English and he had studied some English at primary school, but had not attended a private language school. Learner S was always very conscious of the fact that he came from a small town in the hinterland of the province – 'at primary school I didn't learn English, I was in the village and there weren't any English lessons' (fourth interview) – and during his second year in the junior high school his father, a forestry worker, died and he had to return to the village. Learner R's father was, in his words, 'an ordinary civil servant', by which he probably meant lower rank though I have no independent verification of this; he did have one year's lessons in English at primary school but did not attend a private language course. What is more, his parents were going through a difficult divorce (a fact he never revealed to me) which teachers said were the source of long-term behavioural problems which he displayed in school. The fourth 'less motivated' learner's (W) situation is harder to explain as his father was Dean of the Faculty of Education at the local university. Furthermore, W had studied some English in primary school and had been sent to a reputable private language school for over a year. Yet despite these auspicious beginnings, W never developed an interest in, or apparently put much effort into, learning English.

An unexpected source of evidence for the influence of family background on English learning came from my interviews with teachers. These covered several topics, including their own careers, perceptions of their job, their views on their school pupils and their progress in English. Eight of the nine teachers interviewed mentioned social background as a significant determiner both of pupil progress and their own job satisfaction, either at previous schools they had worked at or their current school. For example, early in my first interview the teacher commented:

> The first time I taught English in [Junior High School X] it seems to me my ability to teach English did not develop well. Teaching was difficult because the background of the students there did not support them to speak English in class. Every time I ask them questions, no response from the students.

This teacher went on to stress the importance of study outside school, for example in private language schools, as if it was a pre-condition for successful learning in the state school. Another teacher stressed the role of parents:

> Home, it [is] an important thing, I think, an important role, if their parents don't think about English, or they don't care about English, they never give suggestions to the students to study English, they never guide the students how to study English, or when they have to study at home, ah, it's impossible for the students.

Even though the majority of parents in this generation are unable to speak English themselves, it is their attitude towards their child's language learning which in turn helps to determine the child's own attitudes, this teacher implies.

A familiar problem in many parts of the developing world is that children are needed for economic activity to support their families and miss school entirely. In this part of Indonesia, the problem is not so extreme and school attendance is good, but some teachers argued that many children were disadvantaged by having to earn extra income for their family after school, as this meant there was no opportunity to attend private English courses or buy study materials. Moreover, there are suggestions that pupils from lower socio-economic backgrounds faced more subtle psychological pressures. As a teacher working at a school on the outskirts of Ajeng put it:

> Most of my students can [speak] ... English but maybe they are afraid, this is the problem ... if their friends say [speak] in English, some of their friends laughing, laughing, smile with their friends ... makes the students shamed.

She claimed that there were '15 students' in her school who could speak English, but that, despite her own encouragement, they were deterred by the mockery of their friends, who might accuse them of being 'sok-sokan' or 'kebarat-baratan' – showing off or trying to be a westerner.

Motivation

This leads us into the second of Walberg and Tsai's (1983) factors underlying the Matthew Effect. As I have written above, my survey instrument revealed generally very high levels of motivation to learn English among students in this junior high school, in terms of the importance of English, the reasons for its importance (e.g. instrumental motives, integrative motives) and their desire to learn it. In interviews, my focal learners all affirmed their desire to learn the language and its potential importance to them – this is true even of the low-achieving learners (see the extract from K's interview above), which is why I designated them 'less motivated' rather than 'unmotivated'.

However, a discursive analysis of the interviews over the period 2002–2008 has allowed me to identify revealing differences in the nature of these learners' motivation, which may help to explain the differential effort that they invested in learning English. Using Dörnyei's L2 motivational self-system as a theoretical framework (see Dörnyei 2009, also Whitehead 2011, Chapter 16 this volume), I found strong evidence in the talk of the 'more motivated' group for the development of 'ideal L2 selves' over this period and the persistence of 'ought-to L2 selves' in the 'less motivated' group (Lamb 2009, Lamb in press). In other words, some of the learners were able to develop vivid images of themselves as future users of the language, which, according to Dörnyei's theory, would make them more inclined to invest effort in learning the L2 in order to close the gap between this 'ideal self' and their 'current self'. By contrast, learners with an 'ought-to L2 self' are motivated mainly by a feeling of duty to meet the needs or desires of significant others, such as parents or teachers – a weaker form of motivation that is likely to make them more concerned to prevent failure in conventional tokens of achievement, such as exam results or school reports, rather than seek out opportunities for genuine learning.

To illustrate this distinction, I will draw on my interviews with the same two learners, Marlina and Krisna (for further examples, see my discussion of two other learners in Lamb 2009). In 2008, both learners were aged 17 and in their final year at senior high school. When asked about her immediate plans after finishing school, Marlina replied (in original English):

> I'd like to go to Padjadjaran University, Bandung, to the Communication Faculty um and I'd like to study there, after that, this is my wish, I can go to maybe in the other country I'd like to get the Magister in Broadcasting I'm very interested in broadcasting … I get a contract with Ajeng TV for one year but I don't know, I cannot do I can do it or not because after the final exam I'd like to move to Bandung or Jakarta … if I want to progress my education I have to move to the other place, Ajeng is not qualified to … progress my education.

Her long-term vision is to work in broadcasting and she has already worked out some 'proximal subgoals' (Dörnyei 2009) to help her achieve this ambition, including getting a job in the local TV station (through her parents' social connections) and studying at the prestigious private university in the cosmopolitan city of Bandung. English is implicated in these plans because, as she put it, 'it is going to be very useful for my education'. Looking further ahead, she said 'I have a lot of things that I want to [do] in ten years … I want to make my parents *naik haji ibadah haji* [go on the Haj pilgrimage] with my own money with my own money'.

Krisna's talk about the future was of a different nature, more diffident and less certain as his language here reveals. In response to my question about where he might be in ten years' time he replies (translated from Indonesian):

K: Um maybe I don't really know yet but if it's up to me, my desire is to become a computer expert in a company and maybe also, in ten years' time, because perhaps I'll already have children, maybe I'll give some basic lessons in English, so that my children will understand English from the beginning of school, because now it's already the beginning of the global era.

I: Uh-uh … you mean your own children?

K: Yeah

I: How many children will you have?

K: Haven't thought about it yet!

I: Will you live in Ajeng, or where do you want to live?

K: Or for that, I don't know yet, it's a population factor that, some places are full, we don't know what'll happen in ten years' time.

He does express a goal – to become a 'computer expert' – but at no time in his interview does he talk about what plans he has made to achieve this goal. Interestingly, he is conscious of the importance of English for the future, but rather sadly relates it to the futures of his children not himself. When later in the interview he does express a wish to learn more English himself, it is, as Dörnyei's theory would predict, with a view to preventing problems rather than expanding his personal capacities: 'if I don't master English well then maybe I'll have difficulty doing my job and also problems in accessing computers.'

To summarise, I am arguing that the focal learners who I originally designated 'more motivated' in fact had a different type of motivation to learn English than the others. As Ryan (2009) has recently written, education systems in many countries promote the value of English, such that when young people are asked about whether they like English or want to learn it, they tend to follow the 'scripted discourse' and agree that it is important for their futures. However, it is often only a minority who invest the considerable effort necessary to learn the language while at school. In the case of Ajeng, it appears that learners from more privileged, middle class backgrounds are able more easily to imagine themselves (and each other) as future users of the language and that this socially-derived 'ideal L2 self' may be the psychological mechanism which encourages self-regulation of learning.

Learning activity
One obvious way in which socio-economic background could influence the learning of English, already alluded to, is through providing the means for study at private language courses. In fact, several learners and teachers identify the private course as the primary site of learning English; at the beginning of her first interview with me in 2002, for example, Marlina responded to my question 'What do you think of your English classes?' with the statement 'I'm already nearly in level 8', referring to the institutional rankings at the LIA (Lembaga Indonesia–Amerika, Indonesian-American Institute) private English school. Six years later she is still attending the same school, now in the final level 'High Intermediate 3' and attributed the

development of her oral fluency to the speaking practice she gets there, whereas in school she only learned 'grammar, grammar, grammar'. Hamid et al.'s (2008) study in Bangladesh also found private tutoring in English to be extremely popular with students and parents (mainly because of the perceived deficiencies of the state system) and they identified a direct positive effect on students' achievement. As they argue, this huge and growing global industry, sitting 'at the interface between education and commerce' (Hamid et al. 2008:282) and offering considerable competitive advantage to children from more affluent homes, warrants more systematic attention from educationists.

Besides attending private courses, my focal learners also mentioned several other out-of-school resources that had helped them learn English. These include computer games, local English language magazines, satellite TV programmes and movies in English and English language pop songs. In Marlina's early interviews she repeatedly mentioned the books and cassettes that her mother regularly bought her ('If I go to bookstore she always buys some cassettes English, book of English', third interview) and during my visits to their homes other learners brought out English language materials (e.g. novels, dictionaries, magazines) which they said they had learned from. Apart from offering practice opportunities, such materials can also play a motivational role; Marlina again: 'all of my mother's books are in English so I realise I have to be able to understand English' (third interview, part-translated).

In addition to the economic capital necessary to fund long-term private study or learning materials, families also can provide the necessary social capital to facilitate other forms of learning. Parents and other older relatives with English proficiency may themselves be a resource for learning, or know of other opportunities through their own social networks, while older siblings or their friends can serve as 'near peer role models' (Murphey and Arao 2001) as well as English conversation partners. In her 2008 interview, for example, Marlina claims that she uses English regularly with several Indonesian friends, either in speech or through online chatting, including a house guest who is the daughter of the Indonesian ambassador to Canada. By contrast, two of the 'less motivated' group of learners deny any activity involving English outside school. As learner 'S' from the rural district told me in 2008, 'here, it seems there isn't any [English]. There aren't any people like that, using English outside school, there's none, no homework, except for private lessons, there isn't any' and as he went on to say, he had neither the means nor the desire to take private lessons. Krisna admits to an older sister and a former girlfriend who know English, but he only actually uses English when listening or singing English pop songs. The other two 'less motivated' learners may have had more opportunities to use English outside school, but neither appears to have taken them. Space does not allow a full discussion of their cases, but both had suffered from negative learning experiences inside school, not only related to English.

My observation data reveal telling differences between the behaviour of the two groups of students in their school English classes. Classrooms tended to be hot and crowded (35–45 students per class), lessons were long (90 minutes) and routine (a similar pattern of reading texts, grammar and vocabulary exercises, choral repetition and teacher–student questioning) and the textbooks were dull in content and appearance; to learn English in these circumstances demanded strategic effort. Similar to what Shamim (1996) observed in Pakistan, the more motivated learners tended to sit in prominent positions in the class, which afforded them a good sight of the blackboard and aural reception of the teacher's voice; the less motivated learners tended to sit at the back or sides of the class with like-minded peers, reducing the chances of them being called upon to contribute but increasing their chances of being distracted by friends inside or outside the class (a frequent complaint by all the learners)[6]. Teachers meanwhile, not unnaturally, tended to focus their attention on the more responsive learners seated in the central area, while those in the outer area could become quickly stigmatised as 'poor learners', a fate that befell at least two of my focal group: One learner had a placard placed around his head by the teacher labelled 'Lazy Boy', while Krisna's teacher described him as 'slow' and, during my observations, very rarely invited him to contribute.

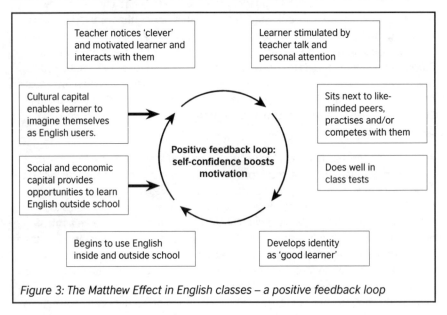

Figure 3: The Matthew Effect in English classes – a positive feedback loop

As Walberg and Tsai's (1983) model predicts, in most educational contexts there will be a strong reciprocal effect between learning activity and motivation[7]. Based on experiences in school, many learners experience either a positive or negative feedback loop, spiralling upwards towards greater achievement or downwards towards (in the worst case scenario) a state of 'learned helplessness'.

I have attempted to illustrate the kind of processes at work in this Indonesian junior high school English lessons in Figures 3 and 4 and would argue that, along with learning activity and motivation to learn English outside school (for which, perhaps, a similar diagram might be drawn), this serves to explain the observed Matthew Effect, where small early advantages are turned into large long-term differences in achievement.

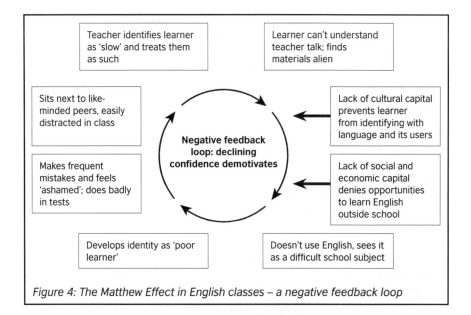

Figure 4: The Matthew Effect in English classes – a negative feedback loop

The following text boxes appear in the figure around the central circle labelled "Negative feedback loop: declining confidence demotivates":

- Teacher identifies learner as 'slow' and treats them as such
- Learner can't understand teacher talk; finds materials alien
- Sits next to like-minded peers, easily distracted in class
- Lack of cultural capital prevents learner from identifying with language and its users
- Makes frequent mistakes and feels 'ashamed'; does badly in tests
- Lack of social and economic capital denies opportunities to learn English outside school
- Develops identity as 'poor learner'
- Doesn't use English, sees it as a difficult school subject

Of course, this is a gross simplification of the factors operating in any particular class or for any particular individual and there are many other possible factors which may work to accelerate or slow down the process. There will also be exceptions to the pattern presented. For example, almost all the 'more motivated' learners had complaints to make about their school English classes, indicating that they were not always positive experiences that fuelled their self-confidence and motivation. Marlina, for instance, expressed severe criticisms of her English teacher, angrily denouncing her as 'an irritable person' who was always angry in the class. On further discussion, with both Marlina and the teacher concerned, it appeared that the teacher had become tired of Marlina's own criticisms of her teaching style and English language. The teacher herself lacked the cultural capital – above all, she lacked oral fluency in English – to convince Marlina that she could help her learn English. As a consequence, Marlina decided to focus her energies on her private school.

I should report one further complicating factor: some of the 'more motivated' learners were selected for elite 'acceleration' or 'excellence' classes while in junior high school, where they received slightly more intensive English classes, better classroom conditions and more competent teachers. This policy of selection is part of the trend towards English language elitism reported by Coleman (2011). These one or two years of preferential treatment probably contributed towards their motivation – by boosting their self-confidence – and their progress in the language (though some of them complained that the extra tuition was simply 'more of the same' and did not actually help them learn English).

A Matthew Effect could probably be found for almost all school subjects. But there are several reasons why it might afflict languages more than others. As Gardner (1985) has long argued and as a recent UK report (CILT 2005) confirms, school pupils' attitudes to languages are uniquely susceptible to influence by attitudes at home: if parents value foreign language learning, there is a high likelihood their children will too and parents' attitudes are in turn deeply influenced by socio-cultural factors in the local community. Related to this, Tsui (1996) has pointed out how language learners are more vulnerable to criticism and negative evaluation than other subject learners because there are so many chances of making mistakes or, one might add, of sounding pretentious when successful. A third reason why Matthew Effects may be more of a problem in language education is suggested by Jones and Jones (2001), who argue that underachievement is very difficult to correct in language classrooms because of the cumulative nature of the subject matter. With some other school subjects, a new week brings a new topic and a fresh opportunity to perform well; in language classes, especially those using a grammatical and/or lexical syllabus, failure to learn material in one week is likely to cause poor task performance the following week, potentially leading to the spiral of poor performance and demotivation presented in Figure 4. Finally, in education systems where language teachers are strongly encouraged to teach in the L2, the subject is also the medium of instruction in a way that it is not in other lessons. In the questionnaire responses in this study, a frequent complaint about school English lessons was that they were incomprehensible: 'I can't catch the main point when the teacher explains something,' said one pupil.

Does a Matthew Effect in English language education matter?

My argument in this chapter is that, in this small-scale case study of teenagers learning English in provincial Indonesia, I found a striking divergence in competence in the language over the six years of schooling, whereby some appeared to make no progress at all in oral communicative ability while others achieved quite a high level of functionality. There is sufficient evidence to attribute this divergence to a Matthew Effect, in which the social, economic and cultural capital provided by home background and early educative experiences enabled some learners to benefit more from the state provision of English language education, as well as to exploit opportunities to learn the language outside school, leading to a massive competitive gain over six years.

Like all case studies, its findings are unique and no claims can be made for general validity. I have no reason to believe, however, that this school was significantly different from other 'good' schools in other provincial towns in Indonesia. In more 'average' schools, I would speculate that the pool of advantaged learners would be fewer but that similar processes may be at work, though further research is necessary to confirm this. This type of mainly qualitative study also needs to be complemented by larger-scale quantitative research, in which specific background variables are correlated with learning outcomes as in Walberg and Tsai (1983) and that reported in Stanovich (1986).

If a Matthew Effect does exist in English language education, it is possible that it will contribute in the very long term to a widening economic and cultural class divide. If Marlina's academic and work aspirations materialise, she can be expected both to achieve even greater fluency in English and to earn a good income. When she has children herself, she will be able to provide them with even greater advantages than she had, giving them an even bigger head start over their peers. Already it is not unusual to find private 'pre-school English' courses being advertised in larger Indonesian towns. On the other hand, Krisna's expressed wish to ensure his own children learn English (echoed by one of the other 'less motivated' learners) is perhaps a small sign of hope that such a cycle of cumulative advantage is not inevitable.

It may also be claimed that Indonesia, like other developing countries, would not significantly gain from having a majority of the population proficient in English (Coleman 2010 quoting Thandika Mkandawire, Professor of African Development at the London School of Economics) and that therefore educational policy should prioritise the small minority who do have a chance of gaining proficiency. Yet this argument ignores the fact that English, as a form of cultural capital, has considerable currency within Indonesia and is used as a common gate-keeping device in both academia and the jobs market (cf. Seargeant and Erling 2011). To ensure equal opportunity to acquire English skills therefore becomes a moral issue, for as Lin has argued in the context of Hong Kong, 'ignoring the children's varying amounts of initial linguistic [and] cultural capital contributes to the reproduction of existing social stratification and the lack of social mobility of children from disadvantaged groups' (Lin 1997:24). Moreover, if it is true that large sections of the population are currently being denied a reasonable chance of learning English, this represents a vast loss of potential talent not only in language specialisms but in all the other occupations for which English ability is an entry requirement.

How can a Matthew Effect be alleviated?

UNESCO (2009:235) warns that 'one of the central lessons to emerge from this report is that there is no quick fix for enhanced equity' in educational provision in developing countries. The innate desire of parents to give their children all possible advantages means there will never be a completely level educational playing field, as parents themselves have differential advantages to offer. Nevertheless, for the moral and economic reasons suggested above, governments need to minimise inequality in provision of English language education. In relation to the development of L1 reading, Stanovich (1986) argued that early intervention was essential to prevent the cycle of disadvantage from generating momentum. Policies such as Head Start in the USA and Sure Start in the UK were designed precisely to increase early educational attainment among disadvantaged social groups.

In Indonesian English language education, the equivalent focus would be on the first years of junior high school when the language is introduced into the formal curriculum. It is essential that all children are given the best possible foundation in their language study, even if some of their peers have already benefitted from primary level English language services. Space prevents a full elaboration of curricular implications, but among the most important may be these:

- Lin (1999) and Flowerdew and Miller (2008) discuss the need for disadvantaged learners to develop 'creative discursive agency', by which they mean the will to expand their own discursive repertoire by finding opportunities to engage with English in the social environment. This may, they point out, lead to learners developing strategies of resistance to English (such as those documented in Sri

Lanka by Canagarajah 1999), though even this, they argue, is better than the passive submission and exclusion induced by heavily unequal social structures. In the Indonesian context what this implies is using classroom time to critically engage with the English already in the local environment, for example in consumer product labels, billboard advertisements, popular TV programmes, magazines and songs. As Seargeant and Erling (2011) point out, the rapid expansion of the internet in Asian countries has the potential to democratise access to English and provide vastly increased opportunities for practice.

- From a self-psychological perspective, young people need to develop an 'ideal L2 self', such that they can one day imagine the possibility of 'being an English speaker' and using English socially, academically or professionally to their own advantage. There are many ways in which this could be done, but it argues against current policy moves towards streaming English language classes and establishing elite English medium schools as this potentially designates the excluded or lower-ranked students as future 'non-users' of English, with resultant demotivational effects.

- Teachers themselves need to become aware of prejudices they may carry towards pupils from a rural or urban poor background and resist the temptation to associate lack of early achievement in English with lack of potential to learn. A good starting point would be a recognition of the pupils' existing language skills – especially where, as here, most are at least bilingual in a regional and national language by the time they reach puberty – and working together to analyse how they gained these skills. Further, use of diagrams like Figure 1 in training seminars could raise awareness about how teachers' own behaviour may unwittingly contribute to the underachievement of some learners and about the need to create a more inclusive atmosphere in the class. This could be achieved by, for example, more use of the L1 to scaffold the learning of weaker pupils and by encouraging stronger pupils to work alongside weaker peers. The young people in this study were very conscious of how English could benefit their country as a whole; the learning of English has the potential to be a 'class project' rather than an individual pursuit, where all can take satisfaction from seeing less advanced pupils catching up with the majority.

Notes

1. The conventional religious interpretation of the passage is that people who strive to make the most of their resources, both wealth and talents, will be properly rewarded while those who merely sit on what they have will lose even that. Presumably the interpretation may differ in non-capitalist societies. One respondent had moved to Jakarta so there were only 11 learners left.

2. Interviews were individual except for one pair of girls who preferred to be interviewed together.

3. The fourth 'less motivated' learner from the focal group presented a rather unusual case as he remained confident he would succeed in English in the long term, in spite of making little visible progress and being held back in the first year of school for persistent misbehaviour in class.

4. N's flat trajectory between 2004 and 2008 is slightly misleading as her turns in 2008 were much longer and she did not revert to Indonesian so often.

5. So prevalent did this strategic seating become that the school has recently introduced a policy of enforced rotation.

6. And in fact a 'strident' socio-cultural approach to motivation would not wish to separate the two (cf. Hickey 2003).

References

Beeby, C.E. 1979. *Assessment of Indonesian Education: A Guide in Planning. Wellington: Oxford University Press.*

Bernstein, B. 1971. *Class, Codes and Control, Volume 1. London: Routledge and Kegan Paul.*

Block, D. 2008. *EFL narratives and English-mediated identities: Two ships passing in the night? In P.Kalaja, A.-M.Barcelos and V.Menezes (eds), Narratives of Learning and Teaching EFL,* 141-154. *London: Palgrave Macmillan.*

Bourdieu, P. 1986. *The forms of capital.* In J.Richardson (ed.), *Handbook of Theory and Research for the Sociology of Education,* 241-258. New York: Greenwood.

Bourdieu, P. and Passeron, J.-C. 1990. *Reproduction in Education, Society and Culture. London: Sage.*

Canagarajah, A.S. 1999. *Resisting Linguistic Imperialism in English Teaching. Oxford: Oxford University Press.*

CILT (Centre for Information on Language Teaching). 2005. *Languages in Key Stage 4 2005. London: CILT.*

Coleman, H. 2010. *The English Language in Development. London: British Council.* Available online at *www.teachingenglish.org.uk/transform/books*

Coleman, H. 2011. *Allocating resdources for English: The case of Indonesia's English medium International Standard Schools.* Chapter 5, this volume.

Dika, S.L. and Singh, K. 2002. *Applications of social capital in educational literature: A critical synthesis. Review of Educational Research* 72(1), 31-60.

Dörnyei, Z. 2009. T*he L2 Motivational Self System. In Z.Dörnyei and E.Ushioda (eds.), Motivation, Language Identity and the L2 Self,* 9-42. *Bristol: Multilingual Matters.*

Flowerdew, J. and Miller, L. 2008. *Social structure and individual agency in second language learning: Evidence from three life histories. Critical Inquiry in Language Studies* 5(4), 201-224.

Gardner, R. 1985. *Social Psychology and Second Language Learning: The Role of Attitude and Motivation. London: Edward Arnold.*

Hickey, D.T. 2003. *Engaged participation versus marginal non-participation: A stridently sociocultural approach to achievement motivation. The Elementary School Journal* 103(4), 401-429.

Jones, B. and Jones, G. 2001. *Boys' Performance in Modern Foreign Languages. London: CILT.*

Lamb, M. 2004. *Integrative motivation in a globalising world. System* 72(1), 3-19.

Lamb, M. 2009. *Situating the L2 self: Two Indonesian school learners of English.* In Z. Dörnyei and E.Ushioda (eds.), *Motivation, Language Identity and the L2 Self,* 229-247. *Clevedon: Multilingual Matters.*

Lamb, M. In press. *Future selves, motivation and autonomy in long-term EFL learning trajectories.* In G.Murray, T.Lamb and X.Gao (eds), *Identity, Motivation and Autonomy: Exploring their Links. Bristol: Multilingual Matters.*

Lamb, M. and Coleman, H. 2008. *Literacy in English and the transformation of self and society in post-Soeharto Indonesia. International Journal of Bilingual Education and Bilingualism* 11(2), 189-205.

Lareau, A. and Weininger, E.B. 2003. *Cultural capital in educational research: A critical assessment. Theory and Society* 32, 567-606.

Lin, A.M.Y. 1997. *Hong Kong children's rights to a culturally compatible English education. Hong Kong Journal of Applied Linguistics* 2(2), 23-48.

Lin, A.M.Y. 1999. *Doing-English-Lessons in the reproduction or transformation of social worlds? TESOL Quarterly* 33(3), 393-412.

Merton, R.K. 1988. *The Matthew Effect in Science II: Cumulative advantage and the symbolism of intellectual property.* Isis 79(4), 606-623.

Murphey, T. and Arao, H. 2001. *Reported belief changes through near peer role modelling.* TESL-EJ 5(3). Available online at http://tesl-ej.org/ej19/a1.html

Pennycook, A. 2001. *Critical Applied Linguistics.* Mahwah, NJ: Lawrence Erlbaum.

Rigney, D. 2010. *The Matthew Effect: How Advantage Begets Further Advantage. New York: Columbia University Press.*

Ryan, S. 2009. *Ambivalence and commitment, liberation and challenge: Investigating the attitudes of young Japanese people towards the learning of English. Journal of Multilingual and Multicultural Development* 30(5), 405-420.

Seargeant, P. and Erling, E.J. 2011. *The discourse of 'English as a language for international development': Policy assumptions and practical challenges.* Chapter 12, this volume.

Shamim, F. 1996. *In and out of the action zone: Location as a feature of interaction in large ESL classes in Pakistan.* In K.M.Bailey and D.Nunan (eds), *Voices from the Language Classroom,* 123-144. *Cambridge: Cambridge University Press.*

Stanovich, K.E. 1986. *Matthew Effects in reading: Some consequences of individual differences in the acquisition of literacy. Reading Research Quarterly* 21, 360-407.

Stanovich, K.E. 2000. *Progress in Understanding Reading. New York: The Guilford Press.*

Tembe, J. and Norton, B. 2011. *English education, local languages and community perspectives in Uganda.* Chapter 6, this volume.

Tsui, A.B.M. 1996. *Reticence and anxiety in second language learning.* In K.M.Bailey and D.Nunan (eds), *Voices from the Language Classroom,* 145-167. *Cambridge: Cambridge University Press.*

Walberg, H.J. and Tsai, S. 1983. *Matthew effects in education. American Educational Research Journal* 20, 359-373.

Whitehead, D. 2011. *English language teaching in fragile states: Justifying action, promoting success and combating hegemony.* Chapter 16, this volume.

Wigfield, A., Eccles, J. and Rodriguez, D. 1998. *The development of children's motivation in school contexts. Review of Research in Education* 23, 73-118.

Williams, E. 2011. *Language policy, politics and development in Africa.* Chapter 3, this volume.

Williams, M., Burden, R. and Lanvers, U. 2002. *'French is the language of love and stuff': Student perceptions of issues related to motivation in learning a foreign language. British Educational Research Journal* 28(4), 504-528.

UNESCO (United Nations Educational, Scientific and Cultural Organisation). 2008. *Inequality Undermining Education Opportunities for Millions of Children.* (Press release No.2008-115.) Available online at *www.unesco.org/education/gmr2009/press/GMR2009_pressrelease_EN.pdf*

10

Language and migration: The social and economic benefits of learning English in Pakistan

Tony Capstick

Introduction

In this chapter I contrast the educational experiences of four learners of English in Pakistan, all of whom were hoping to migrate to the UK in the near future. This constitutes part of a wider study of language testing legislation for migrants in the UK. Based on semi-structured interviews and classroom observations, I look at these learners' opportunities to learn English alongside the larger socio-political context in Mirpur (a city in Azad Jammu and Kashmir, AJK), in AJK itself (a state which is administered by but is not formally part of the Islamic Republic of Pakistan), in Pakistan more broadly and in the UK. Following Julia Menard-Wright's work with adult ESL Latina immigrants in California (Menard-Wright 2005), I situate the four Mirpuri learners' experiences of studying English within the social and economic history of immigration from AJK. The reason for choosing this approach is that migration continues to be responsible for not only dramatic social changes in Mirpur but also some of the most striking economic changes in the contemporary world (Ballard 2008). This is revealed through an investigation of the impact of remittances on the local Mirpuri economy throughout the various stages of migration from the area. Whereas Ballard was concerned with the migration of peasant farmers from northern Pakistan who migrated to Britain and the Middle East during the 1960s, 1970s and 1980s, this chapter investigates the increasing role which English language proficiency plays in chain migration at the end of the first decade of the 21st century. By tracing access to English language courses and tests, this study demonstrates how English contributes to transnational family life at a time when the West is experiencing a tightening of the relationship between language, immigration, citizenship and national security (Cooke and Simpson 2008). Interviews carried out in Mirpur weeks before the introduction of language testing legislation for migrants wishing to settle in the UK highlight the current dilemma:

The response to post-colonialism and globalisation by governments – in the UK and elsewhere – is sometimes contradictory: they must attract inward investment by offering skilled low-wage labour while also appealing to certain sections of the electorate by being seen to be 'tough' on asylum and immigration.
(Cooke and Simpson 2008:8)

The introduction of language testing legislation for migrants is a result of this contradiction and has begun to represent the kind of immigration controls which Werbner has argued:

strike at the very roots of British Pakistanis' deepest loyalties: to close kinsmen, dependents and in relation to unquestionable family obligations
(Werbner 2008:6)

thereby denying members of transnational families the right to marry by choice. Government limits on immigration from outside the European Economic Area (EEA) and investment in the training and recruitment of UK workers have led to English language proficiency being linked to issues of employment, welfare, cohesion and 'integration'.

Theoretical framework

The theoretical framework which underpins this study draws from research on transnational migration and the economy and, more specifically, the nexus of marriage, migration, kinship and gender. The role of language here is analysed alongside social anthropologists' work investigating the relationship between migration and the development of economies with specific reference to the experience of migrants from Pakistan.

Relationship between migration and the development of local and national economies

In his study of migration and the local economy in Mirpur, Ballard has argued that it is migrants' remittances that have had the greatest impact on Mirpuri society given the many millions of pounds that have been remitted to the area over the last 60 years. But this has not led to significant economic development of what is a predominantly agricultural area. Rather, Ballard argues that after the building boom of prestigious houses in Mirpur by migrants in the UK in the 1970s, there was little interest in investing in agriculture due to the lack of status associated with the sector, low prices and little development of infrastructure by the state. The result has been that Mirpur is now heavily dependent on the remittances, a condition which Ballard argues:

is primarily a consequence of the way in which Pakistan's whole economy is structured. It is no fault of the Mirpuris themselves that agriculture has been rendered completely unprofitable as a result of central pricing policies, nor that the Government of Pakistan has done next to nothing to mobilise local resources, nor even to provide the infrastructural facilities around which migrants could more profitably and productively invest savings. **(Ballard 2008:36)**

The remittances, however, are not only of great importance in Mirpur but also contribute significantly to the national economy. Gazdar (2003) found that remittances from international Pakistani migrants constitute the single largest source of foreign exchange earnings for the country, where an estimated USD2.4 billion (GBP1.54 billion) – four per cent of the country's GNP – is currently remitted annually by international migrants (Mansuri 2006). On a global scale, these contributions sent home by the 70 million migrant workers from developing countries around the world have been estimated at USD192 billion (GBP123 billion) in 2007 – the equivalent to four times the total amount of official aid received by developing countries (UNDP 2009 quoted by Coleman 2010a).

Experience of migrants in the UK

Given the significance of the above in the household finances of Mirpuris, the status of transnational marriages means that they are an important commodity in Pakistan. It is not uncommon for young British Pakistanis to marry into Mirpuri families, particularly if their parents have rural origins and have not excelled in the British school system (Harriss and Shaw 2008). In a previous study, Shaw argued that for these young British men and women, transnational marriage allows for a diversification of assets through the consolidation of links to properties in Pakistan as well as the UK (Shaw 2000). Moreover, transnational marriage enhances the reputation of the kin group by demonstrating solidarity and by providing British parents with opportunities to import tradition and religion into the marriages of 'culturally confused' British Pakistani families.

Katherine Charsley's work here is particularly relevant for an understanding of the case studies in this chapter as she draws on the experiences of the 'imported husband' who is unable to assert his authority when settled in the UK due to conflicts with his father-in-law. Language here plays a key role as husbands are further emasculated by experiencing a reduction in their economic status as a result of poor English while their Pakistani qualifications and employment experience go unrecognised in the UK (Charsley 2005). Harriss and Shaw argue that the gender relations in the marriages of Pakistani women marrying British-born husbands are significantly different from those in marriages with local Pakistani husbands (Harris and Shaw 2008). While transnational marriage provides opportunities to raise the status of women within their Mirpuri family, their status in the family home in the UK will still require negotiation. Understanding gender relations and the transnational context in this way provides for a more thorough understanding of the decisions being made by the four respondents in each of the case studies presented here.

'Sense of agency'

Given that the emphasis in this chapter is on the socio-cultural aspects of language testing for migrants, the study draws on the concept of 'agency' as described by the linguistic anthropologist Laura Ahearn where 'agency refers to the socio-culturally mediated capacity to act' (Ahearn 2001:112). Put another way, 'agency' in this study refers to 'how an individual takes control over some aspect of his or her life' (Cooke and Simpson 2008:13). 'Action' is central to both definitions, but what is particularly important to the transnational context is that:

*within different cultures, human beings and the material world might exhibit
capacities for action quite different from those we customarily attribute to them.*
(Pickering 1995:245)

I use the term agency therefore to focus not only on the socio-culturally mediated
capacity to act in relation to language learning and migration but in order to
emphasise how that sense of agency will differ in Pakistan and the UK.

Context

The context of this study is described by looking, first, at the economy of the
United Kingdom and the history of its reliance on migrant labour over the last 60
years. Next, background information on Pakistan is provided with reference to its
current geopolitical significance alongside indicators of the poverty which fuels
much of the current unrest. Understanding education and the economy in Pakistan
and the AJK region in this way then provides the context for a description of the
history of Pakistani, especially Mirpuri, migration to the UK. In order to understand
the dramatic changes taking place in how language is becoming central to these
historical patterns of migration, a final section explains recent UK policy and the
role of English language proficiency in immigration controls.

The UK economy and its reliance on migrant labour

The UK's economy became increasingly reliant on migrant labour from the 1950s
onwards. Mike Raco argues that government policy focused on the promotion of
international immigration as a means of balancing immigration with emigration
from the UK, thereby providing the foundations for the modernisation of the British
economy. Shortages were particularly acute in 'essential' sectors such as agriculture,
coal mining, textiles, construction, foundry work, health services and international
domestic service. To meet the labour shortage which the country was facing and
to encourage immigration from the Commonwealth, the UK government passed the
1948 British Nationality Act, which essentially established an open borders policy
between the UK and Commonwealth countries (Raco 2007). However, following the
introduction of micro-chip technology in the 1980s, a large manual labour force
was no longer a prerequisite of industrial production, hence there was a reduction
in migratory flows, particularly under the Conservative governments of the 1970s
and 1980s and a shift in the kinds of migrants looking to settle in Britain. It is these
current flows of migration that this chapter seeks to investigate given that the effects
of earlier movements will remain with us (Ballard 2008).

The stricter controls of the 1980s gave way to what became known as managed
migration from 1997 onwards under the Labour governments of Tony Blair. Layton-
Henry (2004) argues that the strong economy that Labour inherited from the
Conservatives in 1997 allowed for a re-evaluation of immigration policy which saw
skilled and unskilled workers welcomed to the UK as part of New Labour's initial
commitment to more open borders. However, this government became increasingly
inclined towards immigration controls and was planning to introduce language
testing for migrants in 2011. The new Conservative–Liberal Democrat coalition
government then brought forward the language testing of migrants to 2010 soon
after its election in May of that year. This shift in immigration policy sees the

welcoming of skilled workers from inside the European Economic Area, rather than low-skilled workers and their spouses from poor areas of the Commonwealth who were once encouraged to settle.

Basic facts about Pakistan in general and AJK in particular

At the time this study was carried out, Pakistan was continuing to receive considerable attention from across the world due to increased militancy in its tribal areas and the US-led war against the Taliban in neighbouring Afghanistan. Alongside this a debate about 'radical' versus 'moderate' Islam in a country which is still known as one of the US's closest allies in the 'war on terror' continued. Western imperialism has a long history in the region, modern-day Pakistan having been carved out of British India in 1947. Since this time, the country has grown rapidly, with a population of 185 million (UNDP 2010). But in terms of development, the country ranks as 125 out of 169 countries, whilst 23 per cent of the population live on less than USD1.25 (PKR106, GBP0.81) a day (UNDP 2010). Pakistan has one of the lowest figures for public expenditure on education at only 2.9 per cent of GDP yet one of the highest figures for military expenditure at 2.6 per cent of GDP (UNDP 2010). These and other key development indicators can be seen in Appendix 2 at the end of this volume. The geopolitical consequences of Pakistan's strategic importance in the region can be seen alongside the poverty indicators, which mark it out as one of the most vulnerable in the region. This vulnerability is compounded by the high level of division between the language of schooling and the languages of the home. As we shall see in the following section, the increasing instability in the country has been attributed to this disjuncture between home languages and the languages of education.

Also of significance for this study, major gender disparities in Pakistan are revealed in the difference between male and female earning capacity where attitudes across socio-economic groups in Pakistan see less value in educating girls than boys, since girls will not be able to earn as much as boys even if they are educated (Coleman 2010b). This is reflected in participation rates for schooling in Pakistan. According to the UK's Department for International Development (DfID), the net primary enrolment rate for boys in Pakistan is 73 per cent whereas for girls the figure is closer to 59 per cent. These figures drop to 36 per cent of boys and 28 per cent of girls participating in secondary schooling. By the time students reach higher education, only six per cent of boys and five per cent of girls remain in education (DfID n.d.).

The context of schooling in Pakistan is particularly complex given the variety of non-governmental schools which operate in both urban and rural areas. Good quality English medium schools serve the country's small wealthy elite. Meanwhile, lower quality private schools also claim to provide English medium instruction but with very limited success. The military provides good schooling through to tertiary level while schools operated by charitable organisations also provide primary and secondary schooling in Pakistan on a large scale, particularly in AJK. An Islamic education – sometimes supplemented with the state curriculum – is provided by networks of madaris (madrasahs) across the country. Some of these also teach English as a subject.

However, the majority of school children who make it into school attend Urdu medium government schools. For example, data derived from the National

Education Census of 2005 and analysed for a review of teacher education in the AJK region (Coleman 2010c), shows that 35 per cent of pupils study in private schools; this indicates that the government education system is able to accommodate only 65 per cent of the demand for schooling in AJK. (Incidentally, the situation regarding language of instruction in state schools is changing. The Federal Government and some provincial ministries of education, notably Punjab, are moving towards English as the medium of instruction for mathematics and science at the primary level.)

Prior to Partition in 1947, the Maharaja of Jammu and Kashmir agreed to join India after initial attempts at independence. Within a matter of months India and Pakistan were at war over the territory and a 1949 ceasefire left approximately two-fifths of the former state in the control of Pakistan (adapted from Coleman 2010c). AJK has its own legislative assembly with a prime minister and a president. The territory consists of eight districts, with a total population of about 3.3 million (Rensch 1992). Mirpur district is the fourth smallest district in AJK with a population of 371,000, though the town of Mirpur has the largest population of any urban area.

The education context in AJK is very similar to that in Pakistan. According to the Azad Jammu and Kashmir Council, in 2006 there were 5,866 government schools in AJK (AJK Council 2010). In Pakistan in general, 44 per cent of teachers have no post-school qualification; 37 per cent hold a Primary Teaching Certificate or a Certificate of Teaching and only 19 per cent of teachers hold higher qualifications including diplomas, Bachelors and Masters degrees (Pre-STEP 2010:6 and MOE 2005). Though these statistics cover Pakistan as a whole, they provide an indication of the quality of teacher education across the country, including AJK, and the context within which the four respondents from the case studies went to school.

History of Mirpuri migration to the UK
Azad Kashmiris are often subsumed within the label Pakistanis in the migration literature, although they are in fact numerically dominant among people of Pakistani origin in the UK (Kalra 2008). Harriss and Shaw (2008) have defined three phases of migration from Pakistan: male labour migration, family reunion and marriage migration. The initial migrants in the chain were linked by family membership and consisted mainly of single men looking for the promise of higher wages. The 'pioneer' male labour migrants later married or called over their wives and children to the UK; this represented:

> a shift in orientation towards Britain as a place of temporary residence, where they would work and earn money for their families back home, to one in which they are sufficiently rooted to settle. **(Harris and Shaw 2008:119)**

As a result of immigration controls in the 1970s, this second phase gave way to a third phase – known as marriage migration – in which spouses and dependent children became some of the few remaining groups eligible for entry to the UK. This phase remains in force today, although with some modifications. The largest component of migration from Pakistan during the third phase has been young second- or third-generation British Pakistanis who marry 'back home' – i.e. in Mirpur – and who, on their return to Britain, bring brides or bridegrooms, particularly cousins, with them (Shaw 2000).

Harriss and Shaw (2008) argue that since the 1970s, government controls on family immigration have increasingly tightened the grip on transnational marriage. An example is the primary purpose rule which was in place in the UK from 1980 to 1997. This ruled that marriage should not be for the purposes of economic migration. Given that this rule appeared specifically designed to discourage immigration from South Asia through marriage – and was thus discriminatory – it was abolished in 1997 by the New Labour government. Since this time, the number of husbands gaining visas to Britain has increased to the extent that there have been almost equal numbers of male and female migrant spouses in recent years (Home Office 2001).

Recent UK government policy regarding language and immigration

The period of managed migration overseen by the Labour government was dramatically cut short within weeks of the election of the Conservative–Liberal coalition government in May 2010. Immigration was clearly put back at the top of the political agenda by the new Home Secretary in an early interview with the BBC:

> I believe being able to speak English should be a prerequisite for anyone who wants to settle here. The new English requirement for spouses will help promote integration, remove cultural barriers and protect public services. *(Casciani 2010)*

Here the Home Secretary refers to legislation that was eventually introduced in November 2010 that requires spouses of UK citizens to be able to demonstrate English proficiency by having passed an approved English language test before applying for their visa. The argument about the protection of public services is not new and can be traced back to similar arguments over competition for scarce resources such as those Ballard (1996) identified behind the racial polarisation of the 1980s, then, as now, often most acute during periods of economic recession. However, Home Office figures collected over the previous ten years reveal that the pressure put on public services by 'ethnic minorities' continues to be something of a myth in the UK. Between 1999 and 2000, migrants contributed approximately GBP31.2 billion (USD48.30 billion) in taxes and consumed an estimated GBP28.2 billion (USD43.6 billion) in benefits 'resulting in a net contribution of GBP2.4 billion [USD3.72 billion] to the economy' (Layton-Henry 2004).

In August 2010 the United Kingdom Border Agency (UKBA) announced that, from 29 November that year, partners of migrants would be required to take and pass an English language test:

> The minimum standard that applicants will need to meet is in speaking and listening at level A1 of the Common European Framework of Reference[1]. The list of approved tests and providers includes some tests above A1 level – this is because we will also accept tests in speaking and listening, or in speaking and listening with additional skills such as reading or writing, that are taken at a higher level with an approved test provider. *(UKBA 2010)*

However, in Pakistan – as in many other countries – speaking and listening are rarely practised or assessed in state sector schooling. In response to the move towards English language testing for non-EU migrants applying under the UKBA Points-based System, Dr Nick Saville, Director of Research at Cambridge ESOL (English for Speakers of Other Languages) identified two measures as prerequisites for testing for migrants. Firstly, he emphasised the importance of procedures for monitoring test outcomes which ensure that the test does not lead to discrimination; and secondly, he identified the need for a clear purpose for the test with clarity on how the purpose influences the level, content, administration and use of results (Saville 2009). At the time of writing, neither of these is in place for the UKBA list of approved tests. Given that there is still a distinct lack of empirical evidence to back up the appropriate use of the UKBA tests for the purpose of migration (Charles Alderson, email communication 09 July 2010), it would seem that there is still a great deal of basic validation work to be carried out.

Methodology and data collection

It is within this context that the four respondents in this study were preparing for their visa applications and would, if successful, migrate to the UK to join their wives and husbands already living there. These narratives illustrate each participant's perspective on how their English language learning has been influenced by their families' messages about marriage and migration, as well as UK immigration policies and language planning.

Throughout the data collection period (June to November 2010) I observed several classes at two language schools in Mirpur town. The courses at the first school fall into two types. The first is the 'IELTS class' which prepares learners for the IELTS (International English Language Testing System) administered by the British Council and one of the few of the UKBA's approved tests available in Pakistan. The second is the 'Spoken English' course which is specifically aimed at young men and women with low levels of education wishing to migrate. Research was also carried out at a second private language school in the town which offers a more diverse range of English language courses and information and communications technology (ICT) courses. The majority of interviews were held with students of the 'Spoken English' class in the first school. However, interviews with a learner from the second school are also included in the analysis which follows. This particular respondent's interviews provide a vivid account of the role of English in migrants' lives. They also provide an alternative picture of how fluency in English leads to increased opportunities for migration.

Given that little research exists on Pakistani migrants' pre-departure English language learning, the aims of this part of the study were (i) to identify the factors which influence access to English in Mirpur for migrants and (ii) in the light of the Mirpur case studies, to investigate the assumptions about language learning that are being made in the recent language testing legislation.

The case studies

Seema

At the time of the interview Seema was 20 years old and lived with her two brothers and two sisters (all of whom were still at school) and her mother, a housewife. Before his death, Seema's father had encouraged his daughter to agree to marry the son of a friend of his in the UK as he had wanted to 'join the two families'; the father was keen for her to settle in the UK, though none of Seema's siblings had plans to migrate.

Seema reported that she spoke Urdu, Pahari, Punjabi and a little English. All of her interview responses were given in Urdu apart from a few words in English. Although she was very much at beginner level at the time of the interviews, during the final interview her teacher revealed that Seema had shown 'amazing improvement though she is the least educated in the class'. Previously she had studied English at private school for one month. She left government school at the age of 18 when she was in Class 7 but without taking the Class 7 exam.

Throughout the data collection period, Seema attended English classes for two hours every morning. She planned to continue studying for a total of two months or possibly longer. She explained that she was learning English because she was planning to join her husband there after their marriage in Mirpur in February 2011.

Seema said that she was planning to have the nikah ceremony (signing of the Islamic marriage contract) in February 2011 and that she would apply for the visa after that. She had no plans to take an English language test before making the application and indeed by the time of my final meeting with her she was still unaware that under the new legislation she would need to pass a language test. In our final interview she said that the only information which she had been given by her family-to-be in the UK was that she would need English in order to be 'comfortable' there.

Seema did not know yet whether she would work outside the home or be a housewife in the UK; she would make a decision after arriving there. She wanted to see the country before deciding which role was preferable, although she added that all her female relations in the UK were housewives.

When Seema was asked directly about how her migration might help her family in Mirpur she responded by asking, 'How am I able to help them?' She explained that her brothers support the family. Furthermore, since her father's death a cousin in the UK had also been sending a sum of money each month to Seema's family. When asked whether her future husband would be able to provide financial support for the family in Mirpur she explained that they would have to wait to see; at the time of the research he was training to become a teacher. (The interpreter interjected at this point in the interview to add that generally speaking it was not possible to predict what the nature of the 'co-operation' between the individual families would be before migration took place.) Finally, Seema said that she had no plans to return to Pakistan after migrating to the UK; however, she was determined that she would use Urdu with her children because this is the language that they would need when visiting relatives in Pakistan.

Bushra

Bushra was studying English 'for a visa' as she had been told by her husband, who was living in the UK but whom she had married in Mirpur, that there would be a new visa rule in 2010 which would mean she would need to learn English. Bushra was aware that she would need to take a test. However, she did not yet know when she would be leaving for the UK and so, at the time of the interviews, she had not begun the visa application process. Bushra's father's brother, mother's brother and her own brother and sister lived in the north of England, but her plan was to join her husband in London where he worked as a taxi driver.

Like Seema, Bushra had left school at the end of Class 7, although unlike Seema she had passed the Class 7 examination with the second highest score in the school that year. Since leaving school she had neither worked nor studied. She thought that she would like to study English in the UK but she had no plans to work. Bushra said that she could not see how she would be able to help her family financially once she was in London, as it was the responsibility of her father and brothers in Mirpur to do that. Finally, she claimed that she wished to stay in England for the rest of her life, because her life must be where her husband is.

Salman

Salman, aged 23, planned not to leave Mirpur for at least another two years because he wished to learn English slowly rather than 'waste two years there [in England] with no knowledge.' Salman had left school when he was in Class 6 because he did not want to study and he started work at a young age. At the time of the interviews, he was running a shop and driving a van. His UK-born spouse had recently completed her studies and was looking for work in the UK. Salman said that he would be going to the UK for the sake of his mother and father; he was planning to earn money there and would send it back to his parents.

Regarding his feelings about going to the UK, Salman mentioned two things. Firstly, England was where his wife was (and so by implication he had no alternative but to go there). Secondly, in order to change his life for the better, he would need to leave Mirpur. His plan was to settle in the UK; he had already 'spent a lot on this purpose' and would need to recoup the expenditure by working once he arrived there. His plan was to take the UK driving test and become a taxi driver, but he was willing to do 'anything' if that plan did not succeed. Salman added that he had also spent a lot of money – as much as 50,000 Pakistan Rupees (approximately GBP382, USD590) – on his marriage nikah. This money had come partly from the grocery store which he ran and partly from his father who worked as a driver in Dubai.

Usman

Usman's father was a member of the Pakistan armed forces and so Usman himself had been educated through the medium of English in schools operated by the military; this was the case in each of the three cities in which his family had lived as he was growing up. As a result, Usman was fluent in English and, unlike the three previous respondents, the interviews with him were all in English. Earlier in 2010 Usman had passed the IELTS test with a score of Band 6[2]. Although IELTS Band 6 is well above the Council of Europe's A1 level, as required by UKBA, Usman was rather disappointed with his result. He attributed this to the fact that he had been entered for the 'academic' version of IELTS rather than the 'general training' version.

Usman had recently married a 'British girl' whom he speaks to in English. His brother-in-law had already explained to him the forthcoming legislation on language testing for spouses wanting to enter the UK. Usman demonstrated a clear sense of agency when he described how he had found out more about the language requirements for migration and the visa application procedure by checking a blog on the internet.

Usman was planning to leave for the UK before mid-January 2011 (two months after my last interview with him), which was when his wife was due to give birth to their first child. It was during this final interview that Usman described his desire to become a police officer in the UK. This decision was probably influenced by his father's role in the military; Usman himself had tried to join the Pakistani military but had been rejected. Usman also reported that he had been doing well at university in Mirpur but had dropped out in order to migrate to the UK.

Discussion

A number of important issues arise from these case studies. The first is that there are certain significant similarities and differences between the experiences of the four individuals, an examination of which provides the opportunity to move towards understanding recent UK policy changes in light of these experiences. By drawing on the earlier theoretical discussion of the relationship between migration and the economy, the case studies will then be used to analyse several assumptions that lie at the heart of language planning for migrants.

Similarities and differences between the four cases

Fifteen respondents were interviewed over the course of three months. Four have been selected for presentation and analysis here because they are in different ways representative of the thousands of migrants who leave Mirpur for the UK each year. However, the differences between these four narratives also serve to reveal the complexity and variety of factors that influence migrants' and their families' decisions about moving to the UK. The most striking difference here lies in the very different approaches adopted by the two men and the two women in planning their moves. Regardless of socio-economic background and education, both men had clearly defined roles for themselves as economic migrants, settling in the UK to enhance their own employment opportunities while at the same time sharing with their families back in Mirpur some of the financial rewards which they would reap by working abroad. On the other hand, Seema was unsure whether she would work after arriving in Britain while Bushra was sure that she would not work. This raises questions about the role of English for learners who are not necessarily looking to work, particularly in light of the fact that English language courses in the public sector in the UK generally have employment-related curricula and state funding for such courses is often linked to assessment based on the enhanced employability of students (Cooke and Simpson 2008).

A closer look reveals that despite the initial similarity between Bushra and Seema there is also a significant difference between them. Bushra wants to continue to learn English but she does not wish to work; she therefore requires an English language programme with a different curriculum from the employment-related courses which are available. Seema, on the other hand, has not ruled out the possibility of working but she has no plan to continue studying English. Given that Bushra excelled at school but dropped out of school at the end of Class 7, we can see how significant the learning opportunities of an English course might be for her new life in the UK. The sense of agency which Bushra demonstrates here may not be linked to English for employment, but it provides an alternative rationale for ensuring that recent migrants have access to English courses as these may be their only means of continuing their education.

Another major difference between the four respondents is the role which education has played in their lives. Looking at their experiences inside and outside formal schooling as children and young adults and the way in which education has shaped and influenced decisions about their futures in the UK helps us to develop a more nuanced understanding of the role which education plays for them. For example, Salman left school while still quite young (Class 6) yet he demonstrates a strong will to work. It is quite likely that only access to English classes in the UK will help him to achieve his objectives, since he has no formal qualifications and he is vulnerable to the challenges faced by 'imported husbands'.

Usman is much less likely to face such challenges because he already knows English well and is confident that this will help him to achieve his plans to become a policeman. English quite clearly offers opportunities for social mobility in his case. Usman's education background is markedly different from the other three respondents and is representative of not only military families in Pakistan but also the majority of middle class families who choose private English medium schooling for their children. Usman's case reveals the huge disparity in Pakistan between those families (or their employers) who can afford this type of schooling and the majority who have no option but to send their children to Urdu medium schools. Graduates of English medium schools will gain access to a range of job opportunities in Pakistan, including the civil service and most white collar jobs. Not only does the gate-keeping role of English provide Usman with access to higher education in Pakistan but it will possibly also provide him with employment opportunities in the police force in the UK should his visa application be successful.

By identifying similarities and differences between the four respondents, the diversity of their needs in learning English has become clear; this has been done particularly in relation to their ability to find, take and pass a test which meets standards of fairness and reliability (Saville 2009). These case studies reveal the importance of taking language, education, employment and immigration status into account when considering testing for migrants. The following discussion covers the issues that are currently referred to by the UK government as reasons for introducing language testing for migrants: speaking English in order to integrate and to find work. Seema's opportunities to learn English are viewed alongside the language in education context in Mirpur and how this positions learners who wish to learn to speak English. Bushra's desire to continue to learn English in the UK is examined as a central theme in the debate around language and cohesion. The notion of the 'imported husband' with low levels of English is explored through the barriers to employment and education that Salman may face should his English not improve before departure, as well as the effect that this may have on any children he has in the UK. Finally, Usman's decisions about employment and education both before and after departure are examined in relation to the English he has learned in Pakistan.

Analysis of recent UK policy in the light of the case studies
Seema, who dropped out of school at the end of Class 7, revealed in interviews that she speaks to her husband in the UK in Urdu and Punjabi, that she would speak to her children in the UK in Urdu, that their grandparents would speak to them in Pahari and that she does not feel a need to learn any more English once she has

settled in the UK. These languages are in addition to the Arabic that she uses to read the Koran. (Seema was the only respondent who mentioned this as a regular activity.) What these comments on language highlight is the multilingual repertoire which Seema employs across the different domains of her life and which will hold significant influence over how she learns English. Though no detailed language profile for AJK has been carried out, in his review of teacher education in the region Coleman (2010c) found that the language continuum of Potwari, Pahari and Mirpuri is complicated given that Mirpuri speakers often refer to their language as Pahari. Furthermore:

> *since Pahari is the language of the majority of Kashmiris and since Kashmiris constitute the majority of the Pakistan-origin community in the UK, there must therefore be approximately one million Pahari speakers in the UK. This would make Pahari the most widely used language in the UK after English.*
> *(Coleman 2010c:5, quoting Ali n.d.)*

As well as revealing how little is known about the languages of AJK and the gaps in our knowledge of the languages spoken in the UK, Coleman's observations indicate how central language is to education. Although Pakistan wishes to move to English medium instruction in its primary schools, the respondents in Coleman's AJK study acknowledged that even in the teaching of English the languages used are mostly Urdu and Pahari. Given that 'there is little specialist teacher education for English language teachers across the country in the state sector' (Coleman 2010c:10) and little English is used in the classroom, it is not unlikely that learners would struggle to reach the A1 target of the UKBA. Not only does the lack of mother tongue education have profound implications for how learning more generally takes place (see Cummins 1981, 2000, UNESCO 2003), but it also creates obstacles to the way in which foreign languages are learned. These barriers, therefore, to quality English language teaching that learners like Seema face are ignored both in the level that the UKBA has identified and the style of tests that are available in Pakistan. IELTS, which is available in Pakistan, does not test at the lower levels of proficiency. Moreover, the UKBA tests aim to assess listening and speaking competence but this does not take into account the fact that little listening and speaking practice is provided for learners of English in government schools in AJK. This demonstrates the difficulty in achieving the Home Secretary's desire that 'being able to speak English should be a prerequisite for anyone who wants to settle here' (Casciani 2010).

Seema's account of dropping out early from school and her low educational attainment highlight the generally high school dropout rate among girls in Pakistan and the fact that girls in AJK are less likely to be schooled than boys:

> *In AJK, then, it can be said that, after the age of nine, participation in education is a minority activity. In particular for girls after the age of 12, going to school is an extremely unusual activity undertaken by fewer than one in ten.*
> *(Coleman 2010c:17)*

Poor participation rates in education can often be attributed to the lack of mother tongue education and this certainly seems to be the case in Pakistan in general and in AJK in particular. A Save the Children report argues:

Large-scale analysis of participation in education is showing that whether or not a child is taught in their first language, or mother tongue, often has a strong effect on whether or not a child attends school, particularly in rural areas. The language used to deliver the school curriculum pulls down the educational performance of many of those who do not use it at home, particularly those who do not have regular access to it outside school. (Pinnock 2009:8)

It is within this context that Seema is expected to learn English from teachers who have had no English language teacher training and in classes that do not provide opportunities to practise speaking the language. Moreover, Seema is also expected to pass an approved test, such as IELTS, which, according to Professor Charles Alderson (who was responsible for the design of IELTS), was never validated for migration purposes and is not appropriate for testing at the lower levels of English (personal correspondence 2010).

English to 'integrate'

As we have seen, Bushra felt that she would like to continue learning English in the UK even though she had no plan to work once she had settled there. The legislation regarding language testing for migrants has been justified in terms of the need for 'integration'; in this context, Bushra's aim to continue learning English is significant. In 2008, a study carried out for the National Institute of Adult Continuing Education (NIACE) interviewed women of Pakistani, Bangladeshi and Somali origin who were resident in Britain. It was found that a significant number of women only began to consider learning for themselves after their children had grown up. Moreover, the women in the study illustrated a strong sense of cohesion within their own community:

The vast majority of women described strong bonds and links in their communities. They valued these strong communities, supported neighbours and helped each other with childcare. Few were active citizens outside their own community primarily because of language, low confidence and lack of information. (Ward and Spacey 2008:3)

It would appear, then, that proficiency in English would help these women to overcome the barriers to cohesion (language, confidence and access to information) beyond their immediate community and there is thus a strong argument for the provision of English classes to aid 'integration'. Moreover, education and work outside the home play an important role in changing the balance of gender relations which women experience after they arrive in the UK, enabled by the kind of practical support which they receive from the strong bonds and cohesion with their communities (Harris and Shaw 2008). However, though the issue of language for cohesion is often identified in the national press as a means to 'integrate', Sheila Rosenberg reminds us that the issue of women's contribution to cohesion remains under-researched. Although the Ward and Spacey (2008) study for NIACE demonstrates that English language proficiency can bring individual benefits such as a feeling of empowerment, Rosenberg argues emphatically that:

A glib generalisation which links women and language to successful settlement and community cohesion ignores the history of all the previous groups who have settled and thrived, despite the fact that women at home have often not learned a great deal of English. Such a generalisation makes some unpleasant stereotypical assumptions about gender and culture, ignores class and poverty as powerful determinants and does not begin to recognise the wider social and political factors influencing attitudes and actions among our communities.
(Rosenberg 2009:43)

Here, unequal access to education and English in the home country can be compounded if women are not provided with opportunities to learn in the UK. At the same time we have to recognise that understanding English alone does not ensure community cohesion. However, there is evidence from a consultation carried out by the UK's Department for Business, Innovation and Skills (DBIS) that those who access learning generally (including learning English) do reap wider benefits both in terms of individual development and from social engagement (DBIS 2010). The DBIS report found that social and civic engagement increased with learning; individuals also enjoyed better health as well as increased social inclusion. Given that Bushra clearly wanted to continue learning English in the UK, it could be argued that, initially, this may in fact be the only type of learning she engages in, thereby linking learning (English) to the benefits of social and civic engagement.

However, a direct connection between English proficiency and cohesion continues to be challenged, as was recognised in a consultation report produced by the government's Department for Innovation, Universities and Skills (DIUS):

Some felt that there was not necessarily an automatic link between ESOL and community cohesion and that ESOL is not necessarily a solution on its own: i.e., increased language skills implying that people can play a fuller part in society but this doesn't mean that they will value or believe the same things. **(DIUS 2009:7)**

Moreover, Rosenberg claims that:

it must also be acknowledged that if settling and thriving are to be used as tests, then it is true that some of the members of certain ESOL communities have not done so well, especially if we use levels of employment and education as measures of success. But as ethnic, gender and social class monitoring carried out first by the ILEA [Inner London Education Authority], now widely practised, demonstrates, such failures are also true of long-term settled English-speaking groups, particularly white working class boys. **(Rosenberg 2009:42)**

The integration argument, then, is far from clear cut. Nevertheless, it provides English language teachers with an opportunity to contribute to the debate (through research projects with learners and their families) as to whether social cohesion increases in tandem with language proficiency.

English and the family
As we have seen in the previous section, cohesion has a direct link with employment. Thandi (2008) has argued that high unemployment and a widening earnings gap is a result of certain ethnic groups being disadvantaged in the British

labour market, which in turn has a negative effect on economic opportunities and social mobility for these groups. Thandi argues that there are specific factors of labour market achievement for Pakistani men in the UK, one of the most striking being that they are over-represented in some sectors. As we saw earlier, the first wave of migrants came to the UK from Mirpur to work in specific 'essential' sectors. Today, Pakistani men are still over-represented in textiles/clothing and taxi driving. Of Pakistani male employees and self-employees, 12 per cent are taxi drivers compared with the national average of one per cent. Thandi claims that this data illustrates the point that most British Asians are disproportionately concentrated not only in declining sectors but also sectors with large labour turnover which are low paid. It is this environment that Salman is preparing to enter as a taxi driver.

Thandi's analysis looks at the structural characteristics of the labour markets in which Pakistanis operate in order to shed light on British Asian labour market disadvantage. On the supply side of the labour market he demonstrates that different British Asian communities have:

> different endowments of human capital – level of education, skills, language fluency and so on. Research reveals that differences in labour market outcomes are linked to educational qualifications. **(Thandi 2008:219)**

Thandi's analysis, however, does not go further in helping us to understand the link between language fluency and success in the labour market. However, the work of Tahir Abbas with Pakistani and Azad Kashmiri groups in Birmingham does explore the link between language and educational attainment. Abbas argues that these groups 'lead excluded lives, existing near or at the bottom of local area economic and social contexts' since 'the fact that one in eight of working Pakistani men in Britain is a taxi driver ... indicates the marginal nature of these communities' (Abbas 2008:288). This research from the late 1990s looked at the educational achievement of South Asians in Birmingham. By working with eight secondary schools, some of which were populated almost entirely by Pakistani-heritage children, Abbas found that:

> achievement was strongly related to social class (measured by both occupational positions and educational levels of parents) and to the effect of schools per se. **(Abbas 2008:289)**

Moreover, Abbas' research found that:

> for many Pakistanis in education it was parents who did not possess formal education and tended to have a limited comprehension of the English language and the education system itself who were least able to assist their children. **(Abbas 2008:290)**

As Pakistani children attended inner city schools areas in the UK, which are known to have lower outcomes of educational achievement than those in other parts of the country, Abbas argued that:

> It is the combination of adverse home and school factors which negatively impact upon Pakistanis and provide the main reasons for relative educational

underachievement. Indeed, South Asian children with parents who are not just motivated but educated too, combined with learning in stronger schools, are the main reasons why other South Asian groups achieve above Pakistanis.
(Abbas 2008:290)

It can be concluded, then, that taking part in learning activities – and learning English in particular – has positive benefits for community engagement. But the children of Pakistani adults – like Salman – who access English language courses in the UK also benefit because motivated parents who engage with their children's school work and home work are likely to have a positive impact on the educational attainment of those children. In the light of Abbas' findings, schools and education authorities have an opportunity to provide compensatory English language provision for those children whose parents are not proficient users of English.

Migration to the UK and family responsibilities in Mirpur
As we saw, for Usman migration to the UK is the alternative to a career in the Pakistan military. We also noted that Usman had left his BSc programme in IT during the fifth semester to marry and migrate to the UK where his new wife lives. Rather than look at Usman's English language education, this final sub-section investigates the way in which Usman understands his forthcoming migration in terms of family responsibilities and the employment opportunities that English provides him with outside of Mirpur.

Usman met his fiancée for the first time in Mirpur in April 2010 when she arrived from the UK to marry him. The nikah was held five days after her arrival in AJK and she returned to the UK a month later. Usman planned to join his wife in the UK before she was due to give birth to their first child in January 2011. This case neatly illustrates the process of arranging transnational marriages through what Mooney (2006) calls 'transmigrant kin networks' which continue to offer a means to economic migration and citizenship abroad.

Usman's account also demonstrates an ideology of responsibility felt towards his family. He explained how, once settled in the UK, he would need to help support his family back in Mirpur. His family in Mirpur consisted of two brothers and one sister while his father, who ran a shop, was not doing very well financially. Usman felt that, after putting aside funds for his living expenses and savings in the UK, he would be able to send some money to his family in Mirpur each month. He added:

They are not totally expecting me to send something but I am, will, 'cause they are doing good for their, you can say, for their own sake, their own livelihood, but there are some things, you know, my dad took some er, er, credit from the bank so we have to pay in your language we can say 200 pounds [USD311, PKR27,000] every month, it's due so we have to pay it, we have to find that money every month, so at least I'm gonna help with that one, at least.

When asked whether his siblings would migrate, Usman revealed a great deal about the economic reasons behind migrating to the UK. He suggested first that his brother who plans to become a doctor would not need to migrate whereas he felt the need to arrange a marriage in the UK for his second brother:

one of my younger brothers he is, er, he will become a doctor because he is,
you know, very bright, very bright, and he's choose the biology subjects and he's
gonna be a doctor so obviously he's not gonna go over there but, er, one of my,
the brother who is next to me, so he's a ... I think I'm gonna find him a, I'm gonna
find a girl, somebody to, you know, somebody you know to marry her and he will
inshallah [God willing] come there.

It is clear that for Usman there was no need for the 'bright' brother to migrate
because working as a doctor in Pakistan guarantees financial security. Given that
Usman had dropped out of university in order to migrate, it seems that the family in
general and Usman in particular perceived there to be greater economic benefits –
and possibly greater social standing – in migration rather than graduation. As with
Seema and Bushra, but for very different reasons, there was considerable risk in
Usman's decision to become an 'imported husband' (Charsley 2005). For Salman
the risk was even greater because while also planning to become an 'imported
husband' he lacked the social capital which being competent in English would have
given him. English will protect Usman from the downward economic mobility that
Salman may face. Usman's IELTS Band 6 score will be crucial for him, not only in
obtaining a visa but also in enhancing his opportunities to join the police in the
UK. This seems to indicate that it will be men from urban areas in AJK who have
already had substantial access to English and who have enjoyed good educational
opportunities who will find it easier to join their spouses in the UK, in comparison
with poorer candidates and particularly female candidates from rural areas.

Conclusions

The language learning histories, educational backgrounds and future plans of
a small group of prospective migrants to the UK from Mirpur demonstrate the
complexities of learning English to a level that allows them to join their families
in the UK. The unprecedented gate-keeping role that English has acquired in
the UK's immigration controls assumes that English can be fairly and reliably
tested in contexts such as Mirpur. As we have seen, ideologies of obligation and
responsibility towards kin 'emerge as utterly central to the experience of migration
between Britain and Pakistan' (Harriss and Shaw 2008:106). The extended kinship
networks which have been identified in this study demonstrate how overseas
communities must find the means with which to study English and also gain access
to certain approved tests, so that those family obligations can be fulfilled. The same
challenges face transnational communities who merely wish to choose whom to
marry and where to live. Simpson (2010) describes this as linguicism, discrimination
against people on grounds of the language they speak or do not speak. He argues
that this type of discrimination contravenes Article 2 of the Universal Declaration of
Human Rights, which states:

Everyone is entitled to all the rights and freedoms set forth in this Declaration,
without distinction of any kind, such as race, colour, sex, language, religion,
political or other national or social origin, property, birth or other status.
(UN 1948)

Furthermore, Simpson suggests that the home language is also protected by Article 16(3) which recognises the family as 'the natural and fundamental unit of society' which is entitled to protection by society and the State' (UN 1948).

In addition to this threat to family life, language is also an organising principle in national life. In 1971, when East Pakistan (now Bangladesh) broke away from West Pakistan, language was a central component of the unrest which divided the different political interests in the country. Today, language continues to play a significant role in the construction of a national identity in Pakistan, where the official language of Urdu, spoken as a mother tongue by approximately seven per cent per cent of the country, is used as the medium of instruction in government schools (Rahman 2002). A growing body of evidence suggests that in linguistically diverse countries such as Pakistan, where a national or international language is used for schooling, a significant proportion of children are out of school owing to the mismatch between the language of the home and the language of school. Pinncok (2009) has argued that the 'high linguistic fractionalisation' in Pakistan leads to long-term political, social and economic instability and divisions along linguistic and ethnic lines. The challenges of access to English and international tests that prospective migrants face must be seen, then, within a context of broader threats that national language policy poses to the social and economic prosperity of an increasingly unstable part of the world.

Notes

1. Common European Reference Levels were developed by the Council of Europe to describe standards at successive stages of language learning. A1 is a basic speaker who can understand and use everyday expressions and phrases and can interact in a simple way provided the other person is prepared to help.

2. Band 6 describes a competent user who has a generally effective command of the language despite some inaccuracies, inappropriacies and misunderstandings. He or she can use and understand fairly complex language and can understand detailed reasoning.

References

Abbas, T. 2008. *Multiculturalism, Islamaphobia [sic] and the city.* In V.S.Kalra (ed.), *Pakistani Diasporas: Culture, Conflict and Change,* 285-298. *Oxford: Oxford University Press.*

Ahearn, L.M. 2001. *Language and agency. Annual Review of Anthropology* 30, 109-137.

AJK Council (Azad Jammu and Kashmir Council). 2010. *Azad Jammu and Kashmir.* Available online at *www.ajkcouncil.com/AJKAdministration.asp04/08/2010*

Ali, D. n.d. *Educational underachievement of Kashmiris in Britain. Alami Pahari Adabi Sangat.* Available online at *www.pahari.org/index.php?option=com_content&t ask=view&id=1060&Itemid=1*

Ballard, J. 1996. *Desh Pardesh: The South Asian Presence in Britain. Delhi: DK Publishers.*

Ballard, R. 2008. *The political economy of migration: Pakistan, Britain and the Middle East.* In V.S.Kalra (ed.), *Pakistani Diasporas: Culture, Conflict and Change,* 19-42. *Oxford: Oxford University Press.*

Casciani, D. 2010. *English rules tightened for immigrant partners. BBC News UK,* 9th June 2010. Available online at *www.bbc.co.uk/news/10270797*

Charsley, K. 2005. *Unhappy husbands: Masculinity and migration in transnational Pakistani marriages. Journal of the Royal Anthropological Institute* 11(1), 85-105.

Coleman, H. 2010a. *English and Development . London: British Council.* Available online at *www.teachingenglish.org.uk/transform/books/english-language-development*

Coleman, H. 2010b. *Teaching and Learning in Pakistan: The Role of Language in Education. Islamabad: British Council.* Available online at *www.britishcouncil.org/pakistan-ette-role-of-language-in-education*

Coleman, H. 2010c. *English Language Teacher Education in Azad Jammu and Kashmir.* (Unpublished report.) *Islamabad: British Council.*

Cooke, M. & Simpson, J. 2008. *ESOL: A Critical Guide. Oxford: Oxford University Press.*

Cummins, J. 1981. *The role of primary language development in promoting educational success for language minority students. In California State Department of Education (ed.), Schooling and Language Minority Students: A Theoretical Framework,* 3-49. *Los Angeles CA: National Dissemination and Assessment Center.*

Cummins, J. 2000. *Language, Power and Pedagogy: Bilingual Children in the Crossfire. Clevedon: Multilingual Matters.*

DBIS (Department for Business, Innovation and Skills). *2010. Skills for Sustainable Growth: Consultation on the Future Direction of Skills Policy. London: DBIS.* Available online at *www.bis.gov.uk/assets/biscore/further-education-skills/docs/s/10-1073-skills-consultation*

DfID (Department for International Development). n.d. Flag A: *Briefing paper on DfID's education plans in Pakistan.* (Unpublished paper.) *Islamabad: DfID.*

DIUS (Department for Innovation, Universities and Skills). 2009. *Focusing English for Speakers of Other Languages (ESOL) on Community Cohesion: Consultation Report.* London: DIUS. Available online at *www.bis.gov.uk/assets/biscore/corporate/migratedD/publications/E/esol_consultation_report*

Gazdar, H. 2003. *A Review of Migration Issues in Pakistan. (Mimeo.) Washington DC: Development Research Group, World Bank.*

Harriss, K. and Shaw, A. 2008. *Kinship obligations, gender and the life course: Re-writing migration from Pakistan to Britain.* In V.S.Kalra (ed.), *Pakistani Diasporas: Culture, Conflict and Change,* 105-128. *Oxford: Oxford University Press.*

Home Office. 2001. *Control of Immigration: Statistics United Kingdom 2000. London: The Stationery Office.*

Kalra, V.S. (ed.). 2008. *Pakistani Diasporas: Culture, Conflict and Change. Oxford: Oxford University Press.*

Layton-Henry, Z. 2004. Britain: *From immigration control to managed migration.* In W.A.Cornelius, T.Tsuda, P.L.Martin and J.F.Hollifield (eds), *Controlling Immigration: A Global Perspective,* 297-333. 2nd edition. *Stanford: Stanford University Press.*

Mansuri, G. 2006. *Migration, School Attainment and Child Labor: Evidence from Rural Pakistan.* (Mimeo.) *Washington DC: Development Research Group, World Bank.* Available online at *www.iza.org/conference_files/worldb2008/mansuri_g3386.pdf*

Menard-Wright, J. 2005. *Intergenerational trajectories and socio-political context: Latina immigrants in Adult ESL. TESOL Quarterly* 39(2), 165-185.

MOE (Ministry of Education). 2005. *National Education Census Report. Islamabad: Ministry of Education.*

Mooney, N. 2006. *Aspiration, reunification and gender transformation in Jat Sikh marriages from India to Canada. Global Networks* 6(4), 389-403.

Pickering, A. 1995. *The Mangle of Practice: Time, Agency and Science. Chicago: University of Chicago Press.*

Pinnock, H. 2009. *Language and Education: The Missing Link. Reading: CfBT Education Trust and Save the Children.*

Pre-STEP (Pre-Service Teacher Education Program). 2010. *Rationalisation of Pre-Service Teacher Education Programs in Pakistan. Islamabad: Pre-STEP/USAID.*

Raco, M. 2007. *Building Sustainable Communities: Spatial Policy and Labour Mobility in Post-War Britain. Bristol: Policy Press.*

Rahman, T. 2002. *Language, Ideology and Power. Karachi: Oxford University Press.*

Rensch, C.R. 1992. *The language environment of Hindko speaking people.* In C.R.Rensch, C.E.Hallberg and C.F.O'Leary (eds), *Hindko and Gujari, 1-90. (Sociolinguistic Survey of Northern Pakistan, 3.) Islamabad: National Institute of Pakistan Studies, Quaid-i-Azam University and Summer Institute of Linguistics.* Available online at *www.sil.org/sociolx/pubs/abstract.asp?id=32846*

Rosenberg, S. 2009. ESOL: *Plus ça change? Reflections from a life in ESOL. Language Issues* 20(2), 38-49.

Saville, N. 2009. *Immigration: The test case. The Guardian Online* 12th December 2009. Available online at *www.guardian.co.uk/commentisfree/2009/dec/12/ immigration-uk-border-agency-english-test*

Shaw, A. 2000. *Kinship and Continuity: Pakistani Families in Britain. Amsterdam: Harwood.*

Simpson, J. 2010. *Language testing for prospective migrants.* Message to *baalmail@lists.ac.uk*, posted 14 June 2010.

Thandi, S.S. 2008. *Brown economy: Enterprise and employment.* In N.Ali, V.S.Kalra and S.Sayyid (eds), *A Postcolonial People: South Asians in Britain,* 211-230. *New York NY: Colombia University Press.*

UKBA (United Kingdom Border Agency). 2010. *New Language Requirement for Partners. London: United Kingdom Border Agency, Home Office.* Available online at *www.ukba.homeoffice.gov.uk/sitecontent/newsfragments/26-english-language-partners*

UN (United Nations). 1948. *Universal Declaration of Human Rights. New York: General Assembly of the United Nations.* Available online at *www.un.org/en/ documents/udhr/index.shtml*

UNDP (United Nations Development Programme). 2009. *Overcoming Barriers: Human Mobility and Development. (Human Development Report 2009.) Basingstoke and New York: Palgrave Macmillan for UNDP.* Available online at *http://hdr.undp.org/en/media/HDR_2009_EN_Indicators.pdf*

UNDP (United Nations Development Programme). 2010. *The Real Wealth of Nations: Pathways to Human Development (Human Development Report 2010, 20th Anniversary Edition.) Basingstoke and New York: Palgrave Macmillan for UNDP.* Available online at *http://hdr.undp.org/en*

UNESCO. (United Nations Educational, Cultural and Scientific Organisation). 2003. *Education in a Multilingual World. (UNESCO Education Position Paper.) Paris: UNESCO.* Available online at *http://unesdoc.unesco.org/ images/0012/001297/129728e.pdf*

Ward, J. and Spacey, R. 2008. *Dare to Dream: Learning Journeys of Bangladeshi, Pakistani and Somali Women. Leicester: NIACE (National Institute of Adult Continuing Education).*

Werbner, P. 2008. *Chains of migrants: Culture, value and the housing market.* In V.S.Kalra (ed.), *Pakistani Diasporas: Culture, Conflict and Change,* 189-211. *Oxford: Oxford University Press.*

English and development in Eritrea

Chefena Hailemariam, Sarah Ogbay and Goodith White

Introduction

A number of chapters in this volume (e.g. Williams 2011, Chapter 3 this volume) reiterate the currently held view of development as encompassing both economic growth and human development, with economic growth as one means by which human development can be achieved rather than an end in itself. Djité (2008) notes that the concept of human development has become progressively wider in statements made by the United Nations Development Programme (UNDP), and now includes not only education, health care and good governance, but also issues such as empowerment, sustainability, co-operation, culture and language, together with a recognition that human development is concerned not just with individuals but also with how they interact in communities. Djité points out that: 'language constitutes the common thread that links all of these aspects together' (2008:175). In its 1996 and 2000 reports, the UNDP warned that the imposition of a dominant language in the name of nation-building could be seen as a culturally repressive form of development leading to the destruction of other cultures and the favouring of an elite, and called for a 'three-language formula' for multilingual states, which would allow for mother tongue use in education and government, as well as a national lingua franca and an international language (UNDP 1996, 2000; see also Laitin 1992).

In Eritrea, this 'three-language formula' can be seen in operation, but it appears to be working in a different way to that described in a number of the other chapters in this book, and if English is the 'international language' in this trilingual system, its role in development is harder to define in the light of the particular economic and social conditions in the country. We will argue that in addition to, and in many cases rather than, fulfilling instrumental needs such as employability, international collaboration, accessing information and international mobility (Coleman 2010) it is acting in a more nebulous, less easily described fashion as a channel for global cultural flows (with their attached values and practices), as a means of lessening isolation and linking local and diasporic Eritrean communities, and to fulfil future aspirations as much if not more than current needs. We will argue that the impetus for learning English is happening more as part of an individually motivated, bottom-up grass roots movement rather than at a macro governmental level. We will also show that the connections made by individuals between learning English and their own development differ from the connections they make between development and the country of Eritrea.

The current linguistic landscape in Eritrea

Eritrea has nine indigenous languages, including Semitic languages such as Tigrinya, Cushitic languages such as Bilen and Bedawiyet, and Nilo-Saharan languages such as Nara and Kunama (Lewis 2009). Arabic is also spoken along the Red Sea coast and on the border with Sudan. Tigrinya is spoken as a first language by at least half the population. There is no official language, though Tigrinya and Arabic predominate in commerce and public life and are de facto working languages. In the capital, Asmara, Tigrinya predominates in public life while Arabic is used as a second language by many people living in the lowlands. Arabic plays an important role in the public sphere, particularly in the western lowlands, and is taught as a subject in schools in that area. The government has an ambivalent attitude to Arabic, possibly because it is perceived as possessing the potential to polarise Eritrean society, although it is also viewed as a useful communicative resource (Kibreab 2009). As our data will show, English is currently used to some extent in public life within Eritrea, mainly to communicate with foreigners encountered during the course of work and to read manuals written in English. A number of older Eritreans can still speak some Italian, a legacy of Italian colonisation until 1941, and there is an Alliance Française in Asmara where people can study French, which accounts for references to these languages in the data we will refer to later in this chapter.

If we match the 'three-language formula' which we mentioned at the beginning of this chapter to language use in Eritrea, the 'mother tongue' is clearly linked to local areas, villages and neighbourhoods and to elementary education. The use and development of all nine of Eritrea's indigenous languages are encouraged at the local level, and children at elementary school are taught in their mother tongue. This has involved quite a lot of expenditure by the government as languages such as Bilen and Nara have needed to be standardised and written down, and textbooks produced. The policy of teaching local languages at primary school has been and remains contentious with some parents feeling that, as children learn their mother tongue at home, school time would be better devoted to teaching children through the medium of Tigrinya or Arabic, the latter especially in areas that border on regions where Arabic is spoken. One of our interviewees felt that 'we are imprisoning ourselves and our children by teaching the mother tongue at primary school' and this topic is hotly debated in English, Tigrinya and Arabic on internet sites such as Asmarino and My Awate (*www.asmarino.com* and *www.awate.com* respectively) as well as by writers such as Woldemikael (2003) and Hailemariam (2002). English is the medium of instruction in all junior and high schools. There a few elite private schools in Asmara which teach through the medium of English, only accessible to the very rich, but all children have access to state secondary education through English. Parents realise the importance of education, although the final years of high school may be less well attended for a number of reasons. The English proficiency of teachers, teaching methodology and student participation were good, even in very remote areas, when observed by one of the writers some five years ago (Belay et al. 2007), although there have been recent changes in teacher training and school administration which may have changed the picture.

In terms of the 'three-language formula', Tigrinya has operated as the lingua franca between different ethnic groups ever since Eritrea was established as an independent nation state in 1993. In order to secure government jobs or indeed jobs in the commercial sector English is not a necessity, and it is not a language associated with political power. Trade with other countries is currently very low and the World Bank (2009) reports that 'the risk of macroeconomic instability, the use of price controls, regulations and rationing, particularly of foreign exchange, create an unfavourable business environment'. This economic situation does not encourage the growth of commercial enterprise on anything more than a very small local level and this lessens the need for international communication in English, or indeed any other international language, for business purposes. Very few students go abroad to study in English-speaking countries. It could therefore be argued that English does not have very high actual capital in the present 'linguistic market' (Bourdieu 1991) of Eritrea. Yet the number of adults wishing to learn English at the British Council in Asmara has increased significantly since 2006; it seems then that the perceived capital of English is very high. So what precisely are the attitudes to English in Eritrea, and why do individuals and organisations voluntarily seek to improve their proficiency in it, if it appears that it is not essential for employability, study or business?

To answer this question, we need to consider a number of recent historical events in Eritrea and also to consider the wider African and global context for English use. Many of the chapters in this book (e.g. Williams 2011) as well as many of the articles in a forthcoming special issue of the *International Journal of the Sociology of Language* (e.g. Omoniyi forthcoming) have alluded to the dangers of using exoglossic European languages which are ill understood by the majority of the population for development purposes in African countries, particularly in the fields of education and access to research and information. Yet even the most powerful arguments for the use of indigenous languages in these spheres acknowledge that ex-colonial languages such as English have a part to play in a multilingual African state:

> African linguistic identity has never been affirmed through the denial of linguistic difference, and the richness of diversity must not be limited to indigenous languages. It will have to be extended to the European languages.
> **(Djité 2008:178)**

European languages have been part of the fabric of everyday life in Eritrea for a long time. Italian, the language of colonisers from 1896 to 1941, seems to have lost any repressive connections today and operates instead as a rather fashionable language in the capital Asmara, preserved in the names of many institutions such as the 'Casa degli Italiani', the 'Cinema Impero' and 'Pace Electronics', in the pasta and cappuccinos available everywhere, and the presence of a small Italian community. English has been used as a medium of education in Eritrea through successive periods of colonisation in the 20th century by the Italians, the British and the Ethiopians. People became even more interested in learning English during the period when the United Nations Mission to Ethiopia and Eritrea (UNMEE) had a number of peacekeepers in Eritrea (2000–2008) who communicated among themselves and with the local population through the medium of English.

But by 2009 the peacekeepers had departed as had most NGOs and tourists, meaning that the number of foreigners in Eritrea with whom the local population might use English is now negligible. Moreover, following recent political events such as the UN sanctions imposed in December 2009, many outside agencies have remarked on Eritrea's increased isolation from the global community: the *Financial Times* called it 'the insular state' (Jopson 2009) while the International Crisis Group has referred to it as 'the siege state' (ICG 2010). A number of our interviewees have commented on a growing 'anti-Western stance' on the part of the government, who 'undoubtedly feel let down by the paucity of the international efforts to secure Ethiopian compliance with the boundary decision' (Reid 2009:154) and have felt that this may affect its attitude to English as being associated with the West. Yet how isolated can any country truly be in today's global village, and why are increasing numbers of Eritreans seeking to learn English, including larger numbers of self-financing students from private enterprises, given the restrictions placed on economic development and foreign trade? Why is the government still concerned to maintain the quality of English teaching, as evinced for example in the National Conference for Improving the Quality of English Teaching in 2005, in its language policy for secondary education, and also its support for government officials learning English at the British Council?

Isolated or part of global cultural flows?

For us, the answer seems to lie in the strength of the imagined Eritrean community and in the global cultural flows which travel by means of satellite TV and the internet, linking territorial Eritrea to its diaspora and to global networks and discourses. These cultural flows in Eritrea through Appadurai's (1996) 'mediascape' are effected very largely through the medium of English (Sky, CNN, BBC, Fox), although also to an increasing extent through Arabic (e.g. Al Jazeera). Every bar and restaurant in the capital and many homes throughout Eritrea (and also in community spaces such as schools in remote rural areas) have satellite TV broadcasting programmes in English as a gentle background to all the other activities happening in these spaces, although internet access outside the capital is almost non-existent. Within Asmara every street has innumerable internet cafes which are patronised by large numbers of young people, even if the connections are painfully slow. Much has been made of the fact that the internet is increasingly in other languages than English (Crystal 2006), and yet the informal observations of one of the writers, who frequented a number of internet cafes in Asmara over a 48-hour period in October 2010, showed that the greatest amount of internet use was in English and focused on networking sites such as Facebook, which enabled global contacts to take place. Many of these appeared to be with attractive Eritrean members of the opposite sex who lived in other countries! When we speak of 'Eritrea', we are speaking of an 'imagined community' in which four million people may be in Eritrea, but at a conservative estimate, a figure of over one million are living abroad, mainly in North America and Europe (Hepner and Conrad 2005). A large number use Sudan and Ethiopia as a first staging post, but their ultimate goal is to settle in the West. The World Bank estimated that in 2005 the diaspora accounted for 19.3 per cent of the population, the highest percentage per capita in Africa (Kifle 2009). Five years on, it is now likely to be a larger percentage. According to one writer, Jopson (2009):

> At least 43,000 people voted against the regime with their feet last year ... Eritrea was the second-biggest source of asylum seekers in the world, according to the UN, a striking position for a country with the world's 113th biggest population.

At the present time Eritrea is at the top of the league of migrant-generating countries and therefore has one of the fastest growing diasporas in the world (Kheir 2010).

A study by Koser (2002) found that most Eritreans living abroad maintained contact with their relatives, while Kifle, in a recent survey of 208 Eritreans living in Germany, found that over 50 per cent sent remittances in cash or kind back for altruistic reasons to close family members still living in Eritrea. As Anderson says (1991:6):

> A nation is imagined because the members of even the smallest nation will never know most of their fellow members, meet them, or even hear of them, yet in the minds of each lives the image of their communion.

This is doubly true if many of your friends and family, as well as fellow Eritreans unknown to you, but still part of your nation, are living separated from the homeland in space and time, although you are connected with them by phone and internet. The 'imagined community' might be far from the reality. The streets are definitely not paved with gold for recent migrants, who, since 2000, have been younger and less well educated, have left for political as well as economic reasons and have had a tougher time in their journey than earlier waves of immigrants (Arnone 2008). However, for those still in Eritrea, the Western consumer world which reaches them via satellite TV, combined with their memories of less isolated times, may well colour their views of what it is like 'out there' for Eritrean migrants.

It is obvious that language proficiency plays a part in employability in the receiving country. Language proficiency is also linked to level of education, especially since tertiary education is conducted in English in Eritrea. The 2009 UNDP Human Development Report states that 36 per cent of Eritrean migrants are educated to less than upper secondary level, 39 per cent have been educated to post-secondary level and 21 per cent to tertiary level (UNDP 2009:153). The UNDP report goes on to state that tertiary educated migrants from Eritrea have a much better chance of finding work (under eight per cent are unemployed as opposed to 15 per cent of migrants educated to less than upper secondary level).

In this respect it is instructive to look at the experiences of Eritreans in the UK. Many Eritrean migrants recently arrived in the UK are young and have not completed secondary school; they experience difficulties accessing social services and finding jobs because of their lack of English. Berhane (2009) noted that in Greater Manchester 50 per cent of the demand for interpreting services comes from Eritrean refugees. Hailemariam informally interviewed a number of Eritrean immigrants in Greater Manchester for the purposes of this chapter; many of the people he interviewed remarked on how proficiency in English (or the lack of it) had affected their employment opportunities. (Names have been changed to preserve anonymity.)

- Tirhas (female): She didn't complete her high school while in Eritrea. She has been in the UK for a year and hasn't yet got any job. Her ESOL lessons haven't helped her much. She still has to depend on interpreters.

- Aster (female): She has been an asylum seeker in the UK for ten years. She has had very little education. She got her refugee status about six months ago. She has all kinds of difficulties because of her very low level of English.

- Lily (female): Works as a cook in a charity. She thinks her English has improved dramatically over the last three years which is why she has been able to get a job at the charity. She says 'proficiency in English or a qualification from the UK can help one get a job not only here in the UK but also elsewhere.'

On the other hand interviews with three Eritrean migrants with a higher initial level of education and corresponding proficiency in English reveal a more encouraging picture (but note the gender divide):

- Wolde (male): has lived in the UK for ten years now. He had completed the first year of university when he left Eritrea. He got a degree from a UK university in Business Management. He now works for a banking management company. He says 'without good English daily life would be difficult and jobs such as the one I have, in a bank would be unthinkable. I had to compete to get this job and needed good English.'

- Tesfay (male): has been in the UK for four years. He got his MA from a UK university. He works as an adviser for a charity that assists refugee communities. He says 'I improved my English in the first years, although I had some proficiency in English before coming to the UK. My job involves talking to refugees from all over the world. I have to attend to their problems and give proper advice in the language they understand. So language plays a very important role in my job.'

- Negusse (male): has lived in the UK for about five years. He works for one of the biggest charities sponsored by the Home Office. He works as a case manager assisting refugees in the early stages of their resettlement. He has completed secondary school. 'English builds one's confidence. It helped me to be confident from the time I was interviewed up to now. I was recruited as a temporary employee but became permanent after a while. Because my job requires speaking good English, it could be because of my English that I was able to maintain my job. My English proficiency was also the main reason for my educational advancement. I have been accepted as a mature student by a university after my interview and English language proficiency assessment.'

One could speculate with some certainty that word gets back to the homeland from people such as these concerning the need for good language skills if they wish to join the diaspora.

Appadurai (1996) extends Anderson's 'imagined community' and places it within the context of global cultural flow: 'an important fact of the world today is that many persons on the globe live in ... imagined "worlds" and not just in imagined communities' (1996:28). According to Appadurai, global flows are mediated through five dimensions; one of these is the 'mediascapes' we have already referred to, i.e. the dissemination of information and images by means of electronic communication, in which 'the world of commodities and the world of news and politics are profoundly mixed' (1996:30). Appadurai also proposes the dimensions of 'ethnoscapes' ('the landscape of persons who constitute the shifting world in which we live: tourists, immigrants, refugees, exiles, guest workers and other moving groups and persons'), 'technoscapes' which link people across boundaries of time and space through technology, 'finanscapes' through which money is moved on a global scale and 'ideoscapes' which have to do with the diffusion of ideologies (1996:29-31). These 'scapes' overlap in complex and often disjunctive and unpredictable ways, which 'cannot be any longer understood in terms of existing centre-periphery models (even those that might account for multiple centres and peripheries)' (1996:28). For us, this makes discussion about the use of English in Africa rather more complex than simply a colonial relic or a necessary means of accessing the knowledge and resources of the West; English appears to be an inevitable conduit for global cultural flow. The fluctuating nature of that English in terms of variety (regional or international, acrolectal or basilectal) is determined by the needs of particular contexts and audiences, rather than being tied or identified with a particular 'centre' variety used by a 'developed' country such as the USA, Australia or the UK. Pennycook, for example, using the example of how hip-hop culture was transmitted in a variety of contexts from Sénégal to Malaysia through the medium of English, talks of the 'translocal' nature of English:

> English is a translocal language, a language of fluidity and fixity that moves across, while becoming embedded in, the materiality of localities and social relations.
> **(Pennycook 2007:6)**

Evison and White (2011, forthcoming) also found this to be true in Malaysian 'celebrity culture' in which a variety of Englishes, as well as Bahasa Melayu (Malay), were used by the same individual at different times depending on audience and identity needs. Such a view of English would portray it as more 'neutral' than it is often deemed to be in discussions of its role in Africa, and as a tool for the user to manipulate rather than imposed top-down by government policy, always provided of course that the user has access to and proficiency in English (e.g. Focho 2011, Chapter 7 this volume).

It may also be that in generalising about groups of language users in particular African states, we have neglected to focus on individuals and their motivations for language use. Ricento and Hornberger (1996) and, more recently, Hornberger and Johnson (2007) have gone some way to show the role which individual local educators can play in implementing and influencing macro-level language policies in school contexts, at a much more 'grass roots' level of agency than is usually considered. However, at the most 'grass roots' level possible, the motivation of post-education adult language learners in Eastern Africa does not appear to have received much attention from researchers. In Eritrea, English is not an official language and proficiency in English does not appear to be crucial for political advancement or employability within the country. However, most people have some degree of competence in English because it has been taught in school and it provides a hope for self-development and progress in an otherwise static situation. These factors suggest that individual motivation to learn languages is an important feature of the Eritrean context and that learning English is a matter of choice rather than imposition.

A *Financial Times* article (Jopson 2009) captures the dissonances caused by the juxtaposition of Appadurai's 'scapes' when small sections of the more affluent (and earlier) diaspora meet home-based Eritreans when returning to Asmara for the summer holidays. The disjunctures occur in all kinds of ways – language use, financial situation, dress and cultural behaviour – even the attitudes to the fruit, which Asmarinos would not be able to associate with mangoes:

> *On the sun-bleached heights of the Asmara plateau, July is beles season, a few weeks of wild cactus fruit and ostentatious metropolitan chic. It is when the fig cacti, the beles, yield their knobbly pellets of fruit to sure-handed children, who pick them to earn their families some cash. July is also when Eritrea's diaspora engine goes into reverse and expat families hustle through Asmara's tiny airport and out on to the tiled streets of the capital, where they parade in the Gucci glamour and hip-hop bling of London and New York. Because their arrival coincides with the ripening of the cactus fruit – and because they have disappeared by the time the fruit is gone – they, too, are dubbed beles by the compatriots they leave behind. The two cross paths on street corners in Asmara, where plastic buckets filled with the pickings from the cactus fields sit at the knees of female traders, swathed like mummies in the white cotton shawls of the Christian highlands. Some diaspora families sweep past, Dad speaking to the kids in Tigrinya, the local language, the kids replying in English or Swedish or Dutch. Others pause to buy handfuls of the fruit, whose yellow skin conceals a fleshy orange core that tastes of mango. (**Jopson 2009**)*

Further on in the article, Jopson speculates on the effect of these disjunctures on the global aspirations of ordinary people (in contrast to the government's more localised stance) and indirectly includes the English language in those aspirations:

> *[Asmara] is a place where schoolchildren are taught in English from the age of 11, and where their parents can buy satellite dishes to receive CNN and the BBC. So while the regime is turning inwards, the people have embraced globalisation. ... Many Eritreans ... want to move on, and their model is the beles diaspora: driven by betterment, not bitterness; a desire to take advantage of the world, not to prove they don't need it. (**Jopson 2009**)*

As Jopson further remarks, 'the state is not globalising, but the people are'.

English language learners

In an attempt to confirm our hypotheses, stated at the beginning of this chapter, that English learning in Eritrea is undertaken at grass roots level to pursue future aspirations more than current needs, we surveyed 62 adult language learners, ranging from elementary to advanced level, who were attending evening classes in English at the British Council in Eritrea during the month of October 2010. They received a questionnaire which asked them 1) about their previous experience of learning English, 2) about how they currently used English in their job, 3) about how they thought English would help them in their job in the future and in their personal life, 4) what other languages they felt were important for their work and 5) on a more general level, how they thought English would contribute to the development of Eritrea.

We also interviewed five employers who had sponsored students to study English, asked 22 students to write in greater depth about their reasons for studying English and did follow-up interviews with five students whose responses were particularly interesting in the light of our hypotheses.

Experience of learning English before starting the course and motivation to learn English

All the learners we surveyed, even those at Elementary level, had had previous experience of learning English, even if that experience was often not gained in conventional ways through schooling, which for many had been interrupted by war:

> I'm a fighter and while working a full day in a government office, I went to evening school to finish my high school studies ... I also attended a three-month course over a summer.

Most respondents had learnt English at secondary school but wanted to maintain and improve it:

> My educational background is, I am 12th grade completed. That means I am able to communicate a little but I have decided to upgrade my knowledge.

> We never spoke in English at school.

> I don't have self confidence to talk to others.

Some respondents were motivated to join an English course because they were afraid they would lose their proficiency in English:

> I was good [at English] when I graduated. After I joined Telecommunications as a telephone technician, I didn't use it, because all my colleagues were Tigrinya speakers. I could make an effort to keep it by reading, listening, speaking outside my job, but I did nothing.

There were more students at the 'elementary' level (17) and 'intermediate' level (34) than at an 'advanced' level (11). Many students had already taken two or more courses at the British Council. When asked whether knowledge of English was more important for operating in the public sphere than other languages, students said that it was more important to know Tigrinya than English. Arabic was also useful, although it was not as important as English. Italian, Tigre and French were also mentioned by a few respondents. The respondents confirmed that Tigrinya plays a major part in working life and that other languages such as English and Arabic play a less central role.

Types of job represented in the survey

It was clear to us that there were beginning to be more students from the private sector who were keen to learn English. The Director of the British Council confirmed that the number of private students as a proportion had been rising over the last two years. This was surprising given the fact that they had to pay for themselves and that private enterprise was economically somewhat depressed. There were roughly 242 students studying English at the British Council in October 2010, of whom 61 were from government agencies and partly sponsored by the government, 29 from foreign institutions and 152 from the private sector. Table 1 gives an idea of the jobs represented in the group of learners who replied to our questionnaire.

Table 1: Jobs performed by students	
Type of job	**Numbers**
Government jobs Office of the President, Demobilisation Commission, Immigration. Ministry of Health, Ministry of Education, Ministry of Justice, Ministry of Agriculture, Ministry of Defence, Ministry of Finance, Ministry of Information, Ministry of Health, Ministry of Foreign Affairs, Research and Documentation Centre, Election Commission, International Airport, Eritel (telephone company), radio technician	22
Foreign institutions Norwegian Embassy, Libyan Embassy, American Embassy, British Embassy, British Council	13
Private enterprise Internet cafe, insurance company, shoe shops, doctor of Chinese medicine, graphic designers, video shops, mechanics, restaurant, music and drama organiser	23
No job Unemployed, housewives, students, 'learning for fun'	4

Another surprise was the level of job which learners were currently engaged in. More than half were clerks, receptionists, security guards, gardeners, service assistants, shopkeepers and so forth, working at the lower levels in the management structure of their organisations if they belonged to one. Table 2 gives a snapshot of the level of job performed by those respondents who stated a job title. (We used our personal knowledge of the students and further interviews to draw up this table.)

Table 2: Level of job (arranged roughly in order of responsibility)	
Type of job	**Numbers**
Gardener/driver/maintenance/security guard	5
Typist/secretarial assistant/clerk/receptionist	9
Running a family shop/cashier	8
Customer service assistant/executive secretary/visa officer/accountant	15
Graphic designer/radio technician/drama organiser/journalist at ministry	4
Doctor (self employed)	1
Middle management in ministry/project co-ordinator/librarian/underwriter	10
Secretary to a minister/management of protocol	4

There did not appear to be a correlation between level of duties and level of English; the Advanced English level included a security guard, a radio technician (who needed English to read books about electronics) and a junior accountant, as well as middle and high ranking government officials. We might of course expect this unpredictable profile, given variations in motivation, differing experiences of learning English at school, amount of contact with English speakers and numerous other factors (such as the higher salary associated with working for a foreign institution, even in a lowly position).

How is English currently used in jobs in Eritrea?

There was a clear difference in the ways in which English was used in the three sectors described in Table 1 (government jobs, foreign institutions, private enterprise). Most of the responses to the question 'What do you use English for in your job?' which were provided by people working in the government sector focused on reading and writing in English (with the exception of customs and immigration officials, and some senior staff). Those working for foreign institutions and private enterprise tended to mention oral communication with foreigners. The verb 'communicate' occurred much more frequently with the last two groups. See Table 3.

Table 3: English use in the workplace	
Type of job	**Comments**
Government jobs	'we write a lot about legal issues in English'
	'to understand manuals and use computers effectively'
	'to read and write letters'
	'writing proposals'
	'writing reports, doing research'
	'attending workshops and seminars'
	'to communicate with foreigners whom I meet in my job and abroad'
	'I don't actually use English in my job but I use it in my parent's shop'
Foreign institutions	'listening for my work orders'
	'communicating with my supervisor'
	'I use it for oral communications with my boss, emails, and to transfer information and messages'
	'communicating with my neighbours'
Private enterprise	'to help my children'
	'to sell goods to foreigners who do not talk Tigrinya'
	'to communicate with reinsurers and foreign investors'
	'communicating with my patients'
	'communicating with our customers, letters, phone calls'
	'understanding letters, writing replies'

The 'helping my children' comment referred to a wish to help them with their school work and was mentioned several times by the 'private enterprise' group.

We were interested in the response of a video shop manager who said that he needed English 'for writing words on the video cassettes' and we interviewed him further. It appeared that he made wedding movies and added the English words as subtitles because they were fashionable, could be used to add the words of English songs, and were also useful for communication if the video was sent to family members who lived in the diaspora. Stationery shop owners also told us that greetings cards in English sold much better than those in Tigrinya. This shows, as did the example of the wedding video, that English is being used as a commodity (as is French) to enhance the attractiveness and saleability of goods, by association with global culture.

The symbolic use of English in selling goods, through advertisements, promotional posters, shop signs and so on, in order to represent certain values such as modernity and fashionableness, has been studied in Asian contexts (e.g. Krishnaswamy 2007) but has been somewhat ignored in African contexts; and yet it is clearly part of economic development.

It was also clear that government offices were paying serious attention to customer service in their selection of who should benefit from English classes. Employees who had close contact with foreigners (e.g. in customs and immigration) were chosen, as well as those who might benefit from distance education with foreign universities and those who might participate in workshops and short-term training.

One group of students represented in our survey had taken a one-off course in strategic communication run by the UK Centre for Political and Diplomatic Studies and organised by the British Council Eritrea. This course was aimed at the middle and upper management in ministries, and its raison d'être was to prepare them for representing the government effectively at home and abroad and providing 'professional training in international relations, diplomatic practice, policy and political work, negotiation, management, media and language skills' (*www.cpds.co.uk*).

There was an interesting group (five students) who said that they either did not have a job or did not use English in their job. Four of these had plans to study, for example:

> I am going to join a college, and since I have been away from education, I believe I need to improve and polish my English.

One respondent said that he did not use English in his job 'until now' and stated 'I am just learning for fun'.

How respondents felt English had improved their working and personal lives

There appeared to be a mismatch between how respondents felt that English had improved their work and their personal lives. Of the 49 students who had taken at least one course (13 had only just begun learning English at the British Council), only just over half the students (29) reported that it had helped them get promoted, although many stated that it had helped them communicate better with foreigners, improved their language proficiency and given them more confidence. However,

42 out of 49 respondents said that it had improved their lives outside work. This supports our theory that students perceive English to be useful for private and individual fulfilment and future goals rather than immediate instrumental objectives in their present job.

Perceived importance of English to their own future development and that of Eritrea

It is interesting to attempt to relate the comments made by our respondents on their personal development and that of the country to the roles of English in development mentioned by Coleman (2010). He suggests the following possible roles: 1) increasing employability, 2) enabling international co-operation and collaboration, 3) providing access to research and information, 4) facilitating international mobility, 5) facilitating disaster relief and 6) acting as a neutral language in contexts where there is a potential for conflict. When asked about how they thought improved proficiency in English would help them in their work life, most people said it would help them communicate with foreigners orally or in written form, or it would help them to take part in international conferences and workshops, or it would help them study (points 2 and 3 above).

However, when asked how they thought learning English would improve their personal life in the future (as opposed to their work life), some interesting motivations were revealed. Mobility (Coleman's point 4) was a major factor: 'It will help me when I go abroad' and 'I may go abroad'. English was also seen as improving one's ability to talk to others: 'It will help me to socialise easily'. There was, too, a sense of personal development: 'I can improve myself', 'I can upgrade my education' and 'I enjoy the learning process'. Furthermore there was an often mentioned desire to help the next generation: 'I can help my children'. Such personal views on self development may sometimes be missing from the bigger picture of a country's development (except in studies such as that by Focho 2011).

Table 4: Attitudes towards the role of English in Eritrean development	
Role of English	**Views of respondents**
Employability	'To improve the work skills'
Collaboration	'Experts from all fields can share experiences and projects in English'
	'Building partnerships at bilateral and international levels'
Access to information	'Most courses for development are given in English'
	'Easy access to international resources in the areas of science, medicine'
	'Most of our curriculum is based on English'
	'To cope with science and technology'
	'Books, the internet are all in the English language'
	'Every Eritrean must advertise his source of tourism'
Mobility	No comments
Disaster relief	No comments
Neutrality	No comments

Respondents were also asked how they thought English would help Eritrea to develop. All 62 respondents felt that English was important to the future development of Eritrea. Their replies covered some but not all of the roles of English mentioned above. The categories which were not mentioned are significant in terms of Eritrea's desire to be independent of outside aid agencies and its present, somewhat isolated, political stance. Mobility was mentioned on a personal development level but not on a national level. By far the largest number of responses were in the 'access to information' category, as can be seen in Table 4.

Perhaps the perceived linguistic 'neutrality' of English is not necessary in a country which encourages local languages and has two lingua francas, Tigrinya and Arabic. It may be also that the term 'international' has connotations of neutrality. Fifty out of 62 respondents wrote some variant on the 'English is an international language therefore it is important for development' mantra without really giving any concrete examples. It seems to be an accepted truism without much reflection of its implications.

One respondent even said 'Well, English is an international language, so it is important. But to be frank, I don't know how.' If people did elaborate, it seemed to be in terms of lessening isolation and enabling communication with the rest of the world:

- English language is an international language and Eritrea is part of the world, and it's important for her development.

- If the people of Eritrea can be understood by the world, it can help the development of the economy.

- English is very important for the country to develop and go global.

- It can help us communicate with the world.

- Eritrea as part of the world community should use English.

- Eritrea will be able to communicate with other parts of the world.

These comments seem to us to represent the point of view of those who are somewhat isolated from the world community to which they allude.

By way of concluding our discussion and sorting through perspectives it is useful to consider what our findings illustrate about the most recent discourses on globalisation and cultural flows and also how they focus on individual agency as a counterpoint to that large picture. The 'linguistic imperialism' paradigm equated the spread of English with the homogenisation of world culture through English (Phillipson 1992). More recent views by, for example, Pennycook (2010) would suggest that ultimately globalisation does not have a homogenising effect; rather it creates a mixture of multiple world cultures in which a large number of languages and language varieties are involved:

> To suggest that globalisation is only a process of US or Western domination of
> the world is to take a narrow and ultimately unproductive view of global relations.
> Likewise, to view culture and language in terms only of reflections of economic
> development – as with views that relate language and culture too intimately with

*nationhood – is to miss the point that new technologies and communications are enabling immense and complex flows of people, signs, sounds and images across multiple borders in multiple directions. **(Pennycook 2010:65)***

We believe that Eritreans living in Asmara do perceive that, for them, English is an important way of being part of that globalisation process and of lessening their isolation, but this does not mean that they do not value the role which other languages can play in their lives. As well as the global view, too often when discussing the role of English in development, the smaller picture of personal decisions and choice is forgotten: 'What is lacking in this [global] perspective is an account of the agency of the individual' (McKay 2010:94). So while this study cannot claim to be more than a snapshot of the aspirations of a fairly small group of individual English language learners in the capital of Eritrea, Asmara, at a particular point in time, we hope that it has offered a view of how grass roots language values and perceptions of what the English language can do for personal development can shape individual agency in this small city in the Horn of Africa . We believe that the personal decisions to improve English proficiency by taking classes show the 'expansion of many individual horizons of hope and fantasy' (our italics), in this case through the medium of English language learning, which Appadurai mentions as one of the positive aspects of global cultural flows (1996:47).

References

Anderson, B. 1991. *Imagined Communities: Reflections on the Origins and Spread of Nationalism. London: Verso.*

Appadurai, A. 1996. *Disjuncture and difference in the global cultural community. In A.Appadurai, Modernity at Large: Cultural Dimensions of Globalisation,* 27-47. *Minnesota: University of Minnesota Press.*

Arnone, A. 2008. *Journeys to exile: The constitution of Eritrean identity through narratives and experiences. Journal of Ethnic and Migration Studies* 34(2), 325-340.

Belay, A., Ghebreab, F., Ghebremichael, T., Ghebreselassie, A., Holmes, J. and White, G. 2007. *How newly qualified primary teachers develop: A case study in rural Eritrea. International Journal of Educational Development* 27(6), 669-682.

Berhane, H. 2009. *Interpreters' Workshop.* 12 June 2009. *Greater Manchester Refugee Action, Bolton Office.*

Bourdieu, P. 1991. *Language and Symbolic Power. Cambridge: Harvard University Press.*

Coleman, H. 2010. *The English Language in Development. London: British Council.* Available online at *http://.teachingenglish.org.uk/transform/book*

Crystal, D. 2006. *Language and the Internet. 2nd edition. Cambridge: Cambridge University Press.*

Djité, P. 2008. *The Sociolinguistics of Development in Africa. Clevedon: Multilingual Matters.*

Evison, J. and White, G. Forthcoming. *'Buy-lah! The English between the music on Malaysian radio stations – a case of ELF in action? In A.Archibald and A.Cogo (eds), English as a Lingua Franca. Cambridge: Cambridge Scholars Press.*

Focho, G.N. 2011. *Student perceptions of English as a developmental tool in Cameroon.* Chapter 7, this volume.

Hailemariam, C. 2002. *Language and Education in Eritrea: A Case Study of Language Diversity, Policy and Practice. Amsterdam: Aksant Academic Publishers.*

Hepner, T.R. and Conrad, B. 2005. *Introduction. Eritrean Studies Review* 4(2), v-xvii. *(Special edition: Eritrea abroad: Critical perspectives on the global diaspora.)*

Hornberger, N. and Johnson, D.C. 2007. *Slicing the onion: Layers and spaces in multilingual education policy and practice. TESOL Quarterly* 41(3), 509-531.

ICG (International Crisis Group). 2010. *Eritrea: The Siege State. Africa Report 163,* 21 September 2010. *Brussels: International Crisis Group.* Available online at *www.crisisgroup.org/en/regions/africa/horn-of-africa/ethiopia-eritrea/163-eritrea-the-siege-state.aspx*

Jopson, B. 2009. *Inside the insular and secretive Eritrea. Financial Times* 19 September 2009.

Kheir, M. 2010. *Eritreans on the run: Trends, profiles and destinations. My Awate website,* 17 July 2010. Available online at *http://awate.com/eritreans-on-the-run-trends-profiles-a-destinations/*

Kibreab, G. 2009. *Eritrea: A Dream Deferred. London: James Currey.*

Kifle,T. 2009. *Motivations of Remittance Senders: Evidence from Eritrean Immigrants in Germany. Bremen: University of Bremen Institute for World Economics and International Management.*

Koser, K. 2002. *From refugees to transnational communities? In N.Al-Ali and K.Koser (eds), New Approach to Migration,* 138-152. *London: Routledge.*

Krishnaswamy, K. 2007. *English in Tamil: The language of advertising. English Today* 23(3-4), 40-49.

Laitin, D. 1992. *Language Repertoire and State Construction in Africa. Cambridge: Cambridge University Press.*

Lewis, M.P. (ed.). 2009. *Ethnologue: Languages of the World. 16th edition. Dallas, TX: SIL International.* Available online at *www.ethnologue.com/*

McKay, S.L. 2010. *English as an international language.* In N.Hornberger and S.L.McKay (eds), *Sociolinguistics and Language Education,* 89-115. *Clevedon: Multilingual Matters.*

Omoniyi, T. Forthcoming. *Indigenous language capital and development in Sub-Saharan Africa. International Journal of the Sociology of Language.*

Pennycook, A. 2007. *Global Englishes and Transcultural Flows. London: Routledge.*

Pennycook A. 2010. *Nationalism, identity and popular culture.* In N.Hornberger and S.L.McKay (eds), *Sociolinguistics and Language Education,* 62-86. *Clevedon: Multilingual Matters.*

Phillipson, R. 1992. *Linguistic Imperialism. Oxford: Oxford University Press.*

Reid, R. 2009. *Eritrea's External Relations: Understanding its Regional Role and Foreign Policy. London: Chatham House.*

Ricento, T. and Hornberger, N. 1996. *Unpeeling the onion: Language planning and policy and the ELT professional. TESOL Quarterly* 30(3), 401-427.

UNDP (United Nations Development Programme). 1996. *Human Development Report 1996: Economic Growth and Human Development.* Basingstoke and New York: Palgrave Macmillan. Available online at *http://hdr.undp.org/en/reports/global/hdr1996/*

UNDP (United Nations Development Programme). 2000. *Human Development Report 2000: Human Rights and Human Development. Basingstoke and New York: Palgrave Macmillan.* Available online at *http://hdr.undp.org/en/reports/global/hdr2000/*

UNDP (United Nations Development Programme). 2009. **Human Development Report 2009: Overcoming Barriers: Human Mobility and Development**. Basingstoke and New York: Palgrave Macmillan. Available online at *http://hdr.undp.org/en/reports/global/hdr2009/.*

Williams, E. 2011. *Language policy, politics and development in Africa.* Chapter 3, this volume.

Woldemikael, T. 2003. *Language, education and public policy in Eritrea. African Studies Review* 46(1), 117-136.

World Bank. 2009. *Eritrea: Country Brief. Washington DC: World Bank.* Available online at: *http://go.worldbank.org/CSITZX5Z80*

Developing English in development contexts

12

The discourse of 'English as a language for international development': Policy assumptions and practical challenges[1]

Philip Seargeant and Elizabeth J. Erling

Introduction: English and international development

With English increasingly being positioned as the pre-eminent language of international communication, this chapter examines the ways in which language education policies in developmental contexts are responding to this trend and promoting English as a vital element in the skill-set necessary for successful participation in 21st century society.[1] The chapter looks at the ways in which English is conceptualised, in terms of its form and function and in policy documents, and analyses the assumptions that are encoded in such policies as they relate to the role and status of English in the world today. Drawing on policies related to the 'English in Action' project that is currently active in Bangladesh, the chapter explores the language ideologies that create the concept of 'English as a language for international development' and uses this analysis as a means of addressing the question of what sort of contribution English language education can productively make to development agendas.

While educational opportunity and literacy have long been key elements in programmes committed to human development (e.g. Street 2001, UNESCO 2005), the increased status of English within a global economy of languages has meant that English language education has also begun to be promoted as an important factor in international development programmes.[2] Indeed, Bruthiaux (2002:289) contends that development efforts have now become 'inextricably linked in governmental and academic circles as well as in the media with English language education'. In recent works exploring the relationship between development and language education, development is defined as the process of reducing poverty while also expanding people's choices, with its ultimate aim being to increase participants' control over their own development (see Bruthiaux 2000, Markee 2002, Sen 2001). In this literature, there is a growing recognition of the role that language education can play in helping people gain the resources to lift themselves out of poverty and increase their ability to participate in world economic systems from which they have previously been excluded. Given the current status of English as the pre-eminent global language, much of this stress on language education becomes, in fact, a stress on English language education.

An example of this trend can be seen in the 'English Language Teaching Improvement Project' (ELTIP) funded by the UK government's Department for International Development (DfID) between 1997 and 2008, which had as its rationale the desire 'to strengthen the human resource development efforts of the Government of Bangladesh' (NCTB 2003, Hamid and Baldauf 2008:16) and 'to develop Bangladeshi human capital' (Hamid 2009) by introducing communicative language teaching for English in Bangladeshi schools. In 2008, DfID approved GBP50 million (USD81.4 million) for a follow-up programme entitled 'English in Action' (EIA), which was designed to 'significantly increase English language skills for 27 million people in Bangladesh' (Alexander 2008). Similar ideas lie behind the British Council's 'Project English' in India and Sri Lanka, which was launched in 2007 with the aim of implementing English language development initiatives to train 750,000 English teachers in the two countries. The project rationale reads as follows:

> High proficiency in English is seen to be essential for socio-economic development in India and Sri Lanka ... The impact of globalisation and economic development has made English the 'language of opportunity' and a vital means of improving prospects for well-paid employment. **(Project English 2009)**

Initiatives such as EIA and 'Project English' are wholly structured around the conviction that English language education can play a valuable role in human development. This rationale is clearly articulated both in the above quote from 'Project English', and in EIA's project goal, which is 'to contribute to the economic growth of Bangladesh by providing English language as a tool for better access to the world economy' (EIA 2010). The precise nature of this conviction appears to be that English language education will provide skills which will allow both individuals and institutions to engage actively with the type of contemporary society which is emerging in this current era of globalisation. In other words, English language skills are seen as a resource which will allow for participation in the financial, political and knowledge economies which, today, are increasingly being conducted at a global level, and which therefore rely on modes of international communication. With the impact of globalisation likely to be felt in the organisation of the economy and of employment in almost any context – from the international to the local – having access to the resources which operate as a medium for these forces of globalisation will, it is supposed, prevent local communities from being excluded from the global distribution of wealth and welfare. It is this basic rationale which leads to our contention that there now exists, in programmes such as those cited above, an emergent ideology of 'English as a language for international development'.

A further contention which operates as a starting point for our discussion in this chapter, however, is that such a conceptualisation of the English language is often presented as a set of uncontroversial and mostly implicit assumptions around which the details of a language education policy are then constructed. That is to say, it often appears to be taken as self-evident in the broad discourse of English as a global language that English ability is equated in some (often undefined) way with economic or social development, and this axiomatic starting point then becomes a determining factor in the structuring of policy proposals. Language policies which draw upon this discourse then have real-world consequences for social practice, as these initial beliefs about the language are transferred into large-scale educational projects such as 'English in Action'. Furthermore, the influence of the presuppositions about English which structure policy can affect the pedagogical approach adopted in language education projects, as well as the success of their implementation and the processes used for their evaluation. One possible danger resulting from this is that policies which do not attempt to take specific account of the sociolinguistic realities that appertain to English use in the societies in which they apply, and are instead structured predominantly around the broad trends of the overarching discourse of 'English as a language for international development', will be less likely to achieve positive outcomes.

Following from these contentions, the intention of this chapter is to open up a space in which the above issues can be examined. To this end, the chapter will interrogate the fundamental assumptions around which the concept of the language is constructed in policies of this sort, and make explicit what it is that English is being promoted as being able to achieve in developmental contexts. The chapter will draw upon the EIA project in Bangladesh as an exemplar of this discourse in action, and will analyse the proposals and policy documents which have structured the early development and first stages of the operationalisation of this programme, with the aim being to identify the particular characters, natures or functions which are associated with the concept of English in the discourse of English as a language for international development. The chapter will also contextualise this example with a survey of the recent scholarship on language education and international development programmes, which is beginning to build a body of empirical data on many of the issues related to this subject. It is hoped that this discursive examination of the policy assumptions and practical challenges will offer a context from which scholarship in the area can go on to address the question of how language policies can best contribute to successful and sustainable development and thereby help to reduce poverty and to increase people's control over their lives.

Concepts of English

There is now an established discourse, both in the popular imagination and in academic research, of English as a 'global language' – of English being the pre-eminent language for international communication and thus an important, if not vital, element in the skill-set necessary for successful participation in 21st century society (e.g. Crystal 2003). This discourse is reflected in policy statements in various contexts and countries, where it often becomes a determining factor in proposals for the structuring of (second/foreign) language education (Erling and Hilgendorf 2006, Seargeant 2008). In academia, the spread of English, along with the promotion of the virtues of English language skills for participation in globalised society, has been documented and debated for several decades now, and the study of world Englishes has become an established sub-discipline within applied linguistics (Bolton 2005). Within the broader discourse of English as a global language, several more specific associations have been made, such as those that characterise English as the language of international commerce, of science, of technological advancement, and of human rights (see, for example, Ammon 2001, Toolan 2003, Graddol 2006 for a discussion and critique of some of these characterisations). Our contention is that a similar formulation, that of 'English as a language for international development', is emerging in the thinking and practices of academic, educational and political institutions.

When cited as a rationale for the promotion of the language in education policy, all such formulations are built on a mixture of assumptions and observations about the status and function of the language within the world system, and about the affordances that communication skills in English allow within globalised societies. What is apparent in all these formulations therefore is that it is not English in the abstract that is seen to be of benefit; rather it is English as it actually and notionally operates in contemporary global society. In other words, what is being promoted is a very specific, modern idea of English: an English that is understood to offer access to opportunity and information due to its status and role within the current world system. In a discussion of 'language ideology' theory (which examines the entrenched beliefs that groups have towards language and linguistic behaviour), Woolard (1998:3) notes that beliefs about a particular language are rarely about that language alone, but are about the associations between the language and other social dynamics. She writes: 'ideologies of language ... envision and enact ties of language to identity, to aesthetics, to morality, and to epistemology'. In the case of the English that is advanced as a valuable resource for international development, the associations being made are the perceived benefits to which the language can provide access because of its global status.

The identification, therefore, of a specific trend which we have labelled 'English as a language for international development' (ELfID) does not refer to the emergence of a distinct variety or register of English. Rather, it is the identification of a particular concept of the language which is emergent in language policies and proposals related to development contexts, and which is embedded within the politics of globalisation. In other words, policies and projects such as 'English in Action' both react and contribute to a discourse of ELfID which is born from beliefs about the status and affordances of English within globalised societies, and which has been adapted to the goals of international development.

An analysis of ideologies of English in documents related to a language development project such as 'English in Action' can, therefore, reveal the underlying beliefs about the status and affordances of English – i.e. the beliefs which suggest that such a project is both necessary and possible. By making these beliefs and assumptions explicit, it should then be possible to interrogate the extent to which they correlate with the actuality of educational practice and lived experience.

In practical terms, the examination of these ideologies involves identifying the conceptualisations of language which create a meaningful context for a project such as 'English in Action'. These conceptualisations often operate as the 'taken-for-granted' context against which the details of the policy and its rationale are articulated. The analysis is thus looking for premises upon which arguments are based, or for associations between the language and other social concepts which need not be expressed in explicit terms because the audience to which they are addressed is already likely to be familiar with the significance of their juxtaposition. By carrying out an interpretive analysis of key policy texts which is committed to identifying the patterning of these assumptions it will therefore be possible to explore the language ideologies that create the concept of ELfID. The claims and assumptions which constitute these ideologies can then be contextualised by means of a review of recent studies which have provided empirical findings related to the individual assumptions found within the discourse; and policy statements and actual practice can be compared for the purposes of drawing together a general picture of the various issues confronting the successful promotion and implementation of programmes structured around the use of English as a language for international development.

'English in Action'

Before moving to an analysis of the patterns of key assumptions and associations which constitute the discourse of ELfID, it is first worth providing some contextual background for the 'English in Action' (EIA) project, and the proposals and policies associated with it, as this will be used as the primary source of examples for the discussion. The context in terms of current educational practices and prior policy initiatives has been a shaping factor on the initiatives undertaken by EIA, and some knowledge of it will help explain aspects of the project's ambitions.

EIA is a nine-year English language development programme in Bangladesh, funded by the UK government's Department for International Development. The EIA consortium consists of five partners: BMB Mott MacDonald (the Netherlands), the Open University (UK), BBC WST (UK), the Unprivileged Children's Educational Programme (Bangladesh) and Friends in Village Development (Bangladesh). The team is composed of national and international teacher trainers, researchers and materials developers. The pilot phase began in 2008, and the programme is scheduled to run until 2017.

The stated purpose of the programme is 'to significantly increase the number of people able to communicate in English to levels that will enable them to participate fully in economic and social activities and opportunities' (EIA 2009c).[3] In this respect, it is a follow-up to the English Language Teaching Improvement Project (ELTIP) sponsored by DfID and the Government of Bangladesh which ran from 1997 to 2008, and which had as its aim the introduction of a communicative language-teaching approach to English as part of the national curriculum for English. During the period in which it was active, ELTIP succeeded in introducing a textbook series entitled English for Today, and in providing participatory-based training to several thousand secondary teachers throughout the country (NCTB 2003). However, Hamid and Baldauf (2008:17) argue that since these teachers continued teaching in the 'same classrooms, surrounded by the same external socio-economic and political realities, with the same learners, and the same generally inadequate facilities', this has meant that 'there is little evidence to suggest that the policy brought about any significant changes in the teaching practice'. There is also no sign that the changes resulted in children being better able to communicate in

English. Baseline studies undertaken during the initial phases of EIA found little evidence of English language progression through primary and secondary school, and concluded that the majority of students remain at the most basic ability levels year after year (EIA 2009a:2). While English continues to play an important gate-keeping role for access to higher education due to the fact that students must pass an exam in the subject to progress to tertiary education, this exam currently has the highest failure rate of all subjects (EIA 2009b:13).

Policy documentation for EIA recognises that the previous ELTIP programmes had 'insufficient impact' and stresses the need to address the problem 'at scale through a project that will have reach and impact and which for this reason warrants significant funding' (EIA 2008). The EIA project therefore intends not only to 'enhance and extend the necessary learning and teaching practices', but also to utilise a range of media technologies to help Bangladeshis 'overcome barriers to the effective use of communicative English' and 'increase motivation and access to appropriate resources' (EIA 2009a:5). This is being done, in part, by continuing to focus on formal English-language learning in both primary and secondary schools.

The history and sociolinguistic profile of Bangladesh, as documented by scholars such as Banu and Sussex (2001a), Hamid (2009), and Imam (2005), can help to explain the persistent low level of competence in English that is found in the country. After Partition in 1947, both Bangla and English were suppressed in favour of Urdu – this despite the fact that Bangla was the majority language in what was then East Pakistan (now Bangladesh). The vast majority of the population today are classified as speakers of the national language, Bangla (85 per cent according to Lewis 2009). According to the census of 1991 (cited in Hossain and Tollefson 2007:243), 60 language varieties are spoken in Bangladesh, many of which have a significant number of speakers (e.g. Chittagonian with 14 million and Sylheti with five million). These languages play an important role in society, particularly in rural areas and among Bangladesh's ethnic minorities.

After a long struggle for autonomy, part of which was motivated by the establishment of a Bengali[4] Language Movement, Bangladesh achieved independence in 1971. During the first phases of the establishment of the nation, as part of an effort both to decolonise and to nation-build, the use of Bangla was extended to most nationally-regulated domains, including the education system, while the use of Urdu (which was rarely spoken by the Bangla-dominant population) and, to a great extent, English were suppressed. As a result, since 1971 there has been said to be a 'serious decline in the standard and status of English in Bangladesh', despite the expansion in the wider world of English linguistic globalisation (Banu and Sussex 2001a:131). Since the 1990s, however, there seems to have been a 'renewed awareness of the importance of English ... owing to globalisation, satellite television, the growth of the IT industry and the Bangladeshi garment industry' (Hamid 2009:31). Because Bangla is of such central importance to the cultural and political identity of the nation, however, there is a concomitant fear that English might function as 'a displacer of national tradition, an instrument of continuing imperialist intervention, [and] a fierce coloniser of every kind of identity' (Imam 2005:474). Imam (2005:482) further notes that '[in] the minds of most people, national identity and learning English are positioned as antagonistic, not complementary'.

It is due to this history of ambivalence to the English language that the EIA project has sought to offer not only formal but also informal means of English education and thus to reduce barriers to people's learning of the language. This is to be achieved by the provision of learning materials delivered via television, mobile telephones, and the internet. The project is also working with the Bangladeshi media to produce television programmes, cartoons and soap operas which will give people the opportunity to hear English in context (BBC 2009). In this way, the project focuses on the learning of English as a technical skill that will allow Bangladeshis to use the language for individual and social development purposes.

English language education and development: key assumptions

Having given the contextual background for the EIA project, we now turn to an examination of the assumptions that structure the discourse of English as a language for international development as it is articulated in this project and in the wider field of development policy. By means of an analysis of the EIA policy documents, as they act as exemplars of the public discourses surrounding the project, we can explore the various ideologies of English that EIA both relies upon and promotes, and, in this way, we can identify the key assumptions that adhere to the concept of the language in a developmental context of this sort. As well as identifying these assumptions, we will then cross-reference them with a survey of relevant research findings from the academic literature which can offer evidence for or against their validity.

Assumption 1: English as a global language

As noted above, the primary and most enduring context for the concept of ELfID – and the one which in many ways functions as a covering concept for all the others – consists of general assumptions about English in the world today, and specifically the perceived benefits to which it can provide access because of its status as a 'global' language. In this context, global language implies a language which is not exclusively associated with a particular country and culture (i.e. the UK, the USA, etc.), but is of value because of its usefulness internationally. And this becomes the immediate meaning-matrix in which the promotion of English as a language for international development makes sense. It is the taken-for-granted within which ELfID then excavates its own particular meaning.

This belief in global English is now mostly accepted as a 'done deal' or a 'mainstream feature of the 21st century' (Graddol 2006:22). Indeed, it is an attitude that is so entrenched in contemporary thinking and has become such a commonsensical notion that it is rarely stated explicitly in language policy documents. Instead, the collocation of 'English' and concepts such as 'world' or 'global' – as for example in the primary rationale given on the EIA website as providing 'English language as a tool for better access to the world economy' (EIA 2010) – relate the two implicitly. The collocation of concepts – of ideas of English and ideas about the era of globalisation – results in a complex sociolinguistic profile for English in the world which recent studies are beginning to survey (e.g. Blommaert 2010, Pennycook 2010). The rather simplistic notion of English being the international language, that is, a 'neutral' code allowing for communication across linguistic and cultural borders, is being replaced by empirical and theoretical descriptions which survey the actuality of the uses and forms of, and beliefs about, the language in diverse world contexts. The findings from this research show that the emergence of English as the pre-eminent global language is not the end of the story for international communication problems, but in many ways a new beginning. Issues such as the unequal status of diverse varieties and differential access to linguistic resources in different contexts mean that even if global English is now a 'done deal' (i.e. the language is one which is popularly perceived as having a global status), we are still working our way through what, in practice, this entails for its users around the world.

What is of note in this respect in the EIA policy documents is that English is being promoted not predominantly for its affordances as an international lingua franca, but as a resource that will be of benefit at a specifically local level. The inaugural statement about the programme from the UK Secretary for International Development (Alexander 2008), for example, makes only one direct reference to the global status of the language, contending that the 'programme will also address a major skills gap in the Bangladesh workforce and will help the country become more competitive in both internal and international labour markets'. Other than this, he stresses the perceived local benefits of the programme and that it will 'make a valuable and lasting contribution to economic and social development in that country'. From this we may infer that the global status of the language is not solely a product of its role as a code for international communication, but that in addition it has functional and symbolic roles at a local level as a consequence of the ways in which the forces of globalisation are restructuring social relations at all levels. So, while some have argued that populations in development contexts require skills in the national or local languages if they wish to participate in the local economy, and that English is needed only for participation in the global economy (e.g. Bruthiaux 2002), this no longer necessarily appears to hold true, and the EIA policy reflects the expansion of the roles that English can now play in the linguistic repertoire of traditionally non-Anglophone countries. Banu and Sussex (2001b:61) argue that Bangladesh is indeed witnessing a wider embracing of English, and that there is a 'revival of English in [the country] as a language of international, and to some extent national, currency in business, education and culture'. The exact details of this expanded and multifaceted role can then be seen in the other assumptions which constitute the discourse.

Assumption 2: English and economic value
The second key context – and the one which is possibly the most salient in terms of the concerns traditionally addressed by development studies – is the association of English with economic development. Examples of the way that English is positioned in relation to economic issues can clearly be seen in the statement from the project's directors which contends that in Bangladesh 'the national bilingual deficit is regarded, both by government and development partners, as a constraint to economic development, and the English in Action project has been designed to address this constraint' (EIA 2008). A similar declaration is articulated in the ministerial statement, which says that 'The "English in Action" programme will contribute to improving economic growth and to increasing the quality of education

provision in Bangladesh' (Alexander 2008). In both these examples there is no actual explanation of why or how English language education should be able to assist with economic development, yet the project appears to be founded primarily on this basic assumption, and thus this operates as the primary presupposition for the policy.

The associations made with the language in these examples do, of course, draw upon an established relationship that exists in the contemporary imagination between language skills and economic value. This relationship has been the focus of theorising for a number of scholars in recent decades, who have gone so far as to adopt metaphors of economic enhancement for their discussions of linguistic social practice. Most salient of these is Bourdieu's notion of 'linguistic capital' (1991), and the suggestion that linguistic resources are differentially distributed among the members of society, and that possession of certain linguistic resources gives access to improved social opportunity which can, ultimately, be transferred into economic capital. Beliefs of this sort are also to be found reflected in the popular imagination. Recent research conducted in Bangladesh as part of the EIA programme, for example, claims that over 80 per cent of Bangladeshis believe that knowledge of English will help them increase their income (BBC 2009).

While primarily English-speaking countries are currently among the nations with the highest GDPs, this does not however necessarily mean that, in development contexts, there will be a direct correlation between the acquisition of English and economic advancement. In fact, Imam (2005:480) goes so far as to argue that it is 'unethical' to allow education to sustain the illusion of English as a tool of economic and social advancement. As she notes, 'by no means everyone who acquires English will join the local or global elite', and for this reason a simplistic formula which equates English competence with economic mobility can be perniciously misleading in terms of the false assumptions it promotes.

Given these concerns it can be instructive to examine the results of research which has attempted to investigate the correlations between English and economic value. Until recently there was little hard evidence linking the language to economic value. However, educational economists have of late been conducting research into this question in response to this widespread ideology. For example, Grin (2001) has found that in the Swiss labour market salary premiums rise along with competence in English, even when education and experience are controlled for. Kobayashi (2007) found that in Japan, while English does appear to provide access to enhanced economic and employment opportunities, it only does so within the pre-existing hierarchical social structure, so that certain groups, particularly women, have less access to such opportunity whatever the level of their English language competence. And in West Bengal, where English was removed from the primary school curriculum, Chakraborty and Kapur (2008:21) found that individuals who were more likely to have training in English earned significantly higher wages and gained better occupational outcomes than those who did not, even when the level of overall education was controlled for. Evidence of this sort is thus beginning to emerge that supports some sort of causal relationship between English and economic reward, yet in each case the pre-existing social environment, as it is composed of other significant variables, works to complexify any simplistic version of this formula. So for the moment the association between English and economic value which operates at the ideological level in policy and popular belief in Bangladesh is yet to be backed by firm empirical evidence.

Another economic metaphor now used in the field of second language learning is the notion of 'investment', introduced in Norton Peirce (1995) and further developed in Norton (2000). This builds on Bourdieu's (1991) notion of cultural capital, and signals the idea that if learners invest in a second language (i.e. commit emotional, financial and intellectual resources to the learning process) they do so with the understanding that they will acquire a wider range of symbolic and material resources, which will in turn increase the value of their cultural capital. Learners expect or hope to have a good return on that investment – a return that will give them access to hitherto unattainable resources (Norton 2000:10).

This aspect of the ideology of a relationship between English education and a long-term economic benefit results in patterns of social behaviour which, according to research in this area, can have ambivalent effects on communities. It is the expectation of a 'good return' on the education investment that leads parents who can afford it to enrol their children in English language classes outside the formal education system, as these tend to be perceived as offering a higher quality of teaching (or at least of exam preparation). This practice has become commonplace in many countries, including Bangladesh, and, as Chakraborty and Kapur (2008) note, it often results in a further widening of the gap between the elite and poor sections of the community. Hamid (2009) notes that it is particularly the rural poor, whose families cannot afford to make an optimal investment in education and who therefore lack access to basic educational resources such as books, who suffer particular disadvantage. Such disadvantage is often used as an argument for implementing English language courses from an early age for all children, sometimes even at the expense of the local language (see, for example, Chakraborty and Kapur 2008), despite research that suggests a correlation between mother tongue literacy and development (e.g. Trudell 2009).

The result of this core ideology about English and its perceived economic value, therefore, is a cycle of actions and counter-measures aimed at harnessing perceived (yet empirically unattested) economic benefits but which can also inadvertently create further inequality and cultural upheaval within communities. For this reason, a caveat needs to be appended to statements such as that from the ministerial announcement which reports that:

> A recent Bangladesh Government report identified unemployment and growing income inequality as two major constraints which may prevent the country from achieving the UN's Millennium Development Goals. 'English in Action' will be an important contribution in assisting Bangladesh to overcome such constraints and to improve the livelihoods of its people. **(Alexander 2008)**

The caveat would be that, according to studies of complementary communities, 'growing income inequality' can in fact result from the promotion of English as a tool for economic enhancement, and that, in reproducing this discourse, the programme needs to exhibit an awareness of the dynamics by which linguistic capital is in actuality converted into economic capital within local social structures and the constraints they produce.

Assumption 3: English as a language for education

As well as assumptions about the economic value of English, further presuppositions about language that are frequently found in development projects relate to what Grin (2003:36) calls the 'non-market value' of English; that is, the social and cultural effects that are associated with the language. One prominent example found in the discourses of EIA is the assumption that an improvement in English language education will be closely tied to an improvement in the country's overall education system. In this vein, the ministerial statement asserts: 'The "English in Action" programme will contribute to improving economic growth and to increasing the quality of education provision in Bangladesh' (Alexander 2008). The suggestion that the project does not focus solely on the learning of English, but also on changing the pedagogy, as well as attitudes towards learning, is further implied in the title of the EIA brochure itself: 'Changing learning, changing lives' (EIA 2009c).

Again, a survey of recent research studies that have examined this relationship in other contexts can be insightful for identifying and evaluating the issues associated with this assumption. Several studies of language education in development contexts have shown that countries often opt for a strong role for English in the national curriculum because of societal attitudes that equate English with education (e.g. Tembe and Norton 2008, Williams and Cooke 2002). Hornberger (2002:38) suggests that, despite evidence that shows that basic education and literacy development is best approached by means of mother tongue instruction (e.g. Benson 2004), language educators and planners are simply not able to ignore the 'popular demand for the language of power'. Programmes like EIA which promote English as a language for international development are clearly responding to the symbolic functions, or 'non-market values', that English has for students, parents, teachers and government officials. However, any discourse that equates English with education in a rudimentary way may unintentionally marginalise the role of national and local languages in education, and perpetuate idealistic notions of English being the only rational choice for education and advancement. This may be especially problematic in contexts such as Bangladesh, where over half the population is illiterate and less than a quarter have completed five years of education (Hossain and Tollefson 2007:242).

Policies supporting the teaching of English as a means of educational enhancement are not solely based on societal beliefs about the power of English to transform people's lives, however, and there is some tangible evidence that knowledge of English can correlate with a better overall education in certain contexts (Grin 2001). Moreover, links between quality education and economic growth have been clearly established in some recent studies (Williams and Cooke 2002, Hanushek and Woessmann 2008, Little and Green 2009). From this evidence, therefore, one could argue that the prominent role assigned to quality English education in the education systems of developing countries is partially justified, though again context-specific factors need to be taken into account for each actual case. As was noted above, the promotion of ELfID is not about the adoption of an abstract and culturally-neutral code, but about the cultural associations and related practices which adhere to the language in given contexts. Yet instead of drawing on the evidence that is emerging about the complex correlations between the English language, education and development, policies for ELfID tend to articulate a discourse composed of generic societal beliefs and commonsensical assumptions. One particular danger of this is that policy statements which simplistically equate effective education with English while overlooking or ignoring the importance of literacy development in national and local languages then run the risk of perpetuating the idea that people have to decide whether to invest in the national language or English. Indeed, some scholars believe that 'donor agencies have been so concerned with supporting international languages that they have hampered educational development, destroyed local textbook production in indigenous languages and weakened local cultures' (e.g. Brock-Utne 2000 cited in Crossley and Watson 2003:87). Other research (e.g. Rogers, Hunter and Uddin 2007) suggests, however, that if English language programmes were to build upon and complement successful literacy initiatives in the national language they would not necessarily present competition for the limited educational resources that exist, nor force people into choosing which of the languages is most likely to offer them the greatest opportunities. Strategies of this sort would therefore be more likely to result in empowering people by adding to their options of language use and supporting them to make their own choices – one of the central goals of development discussed above – instead of limiting these options.

Assumption 4: English as the language of technology
As well as being promoted as a key factor for economic competitiveness and educational advancement, English is also often framed within the discourse as a means of allowing access to technology, which in turn is seen as facilitating learning and supporting educational change. In this sense, the use of technology in such projects is viewed as a way to help reach the United Nations' Millennium Development Goals (UN 2000) of universal primary education and of developing global partnerships that make available the benefits of new technologies.

A discourse that simultaneously promotes English and ICT education can be found in policy statements across the globe, and is not restricted to developing countries (see, for example, CJGTC 2000:4). In the case of EIA, however, the programme promotes access to technology as a means both of connecting people to the wider world, but also as a way of securing access to learning, especially in geographically remote areas. To this end the project is making use of mobile ICTs to reach teachers across the country, particularly those in rural areas who may have limited access to training centres, and also to increase these teachers' opportunities to participate in professional development networks. In addition to this, the EIA project intends to take advantage of new developments in technology to change attitudes to both language learning and the use of ICTs, as the following policy statement records:

> 'English in Action' will make use of rapidly expanding mobile phone technology in Bangladesh. It will use television and radio to stimulate interest and debate, and to reach the maximum number of people with appropriate learning programmes.
> **(Alexander 2008)**

Like many developing nations, the Government of Bangladesh is investing heavily in technological development, with strong arguments being made for the potential of a 'Digital Bangladesh' to transform society by 2021 (see Siddiqi 2009). The provision of ICTs in schools, and training in the use of them, is thus also seen as part of the way to provide people in remote areas with opportunities to access knowledge and education skills. In development contexts, this type of strategy is mostly viewed not as a luxury, but as part of any individual's freedom (Sen 2001). In fact, Castells (1999:4) argues that exclusion from these networks is one of the most damaging forms of exclusion, as he sees access to ICT as an 'essential tool for economic development'. By drawing on this discourse, therefore, projects such as EIA promote the idea that pragmatic competence in English is intimately linked with this access to technology.

Thus within the EIA project architecture, the concepts of English and technology, both of which are fundamental mediators and symbols of globalisation, are thoroughly intertwined, and, along with education, form a triad structuring the notion of successful participation in contemporary globalised society. As Graddol (2006:72) notes, information technology and English have become 'basic skills' in education globally; and along with literacy in the national language (and perhaps the mother tongue) and numeracy, they are now seen as 'generic skills [that are] needed to acquire new knowledge and specialist skills in the future'. Moreover, research suggests that access to technology has a particular appeal in development contexts where it 'holds the allure not only of improving education and economic competitiveness, but also of allowing a nation to leapfrog to modernity' (Warschauer 2004:378). And studies such as Mutonyi and Norton's (2007) investigation into the way that access to ICT has acted as a crucial means of education enhancement in Uganda, and Warschauer's (2004) examination of a USAID (United States Agency for International Development) project carried out in Egypt which sought to effect improvements in education, English language teaching provision and the dissemination of educational technology have shown the benefits of harnessing technology for development projects. In summary, therefore, while within the discourse of ELfID the frequent juxtaposition of technology with English likely results at least in part simply from the symbolic resonance they both have as mediators of globalisation (and thus as emblems of modernity), there does seem to be a relationship of co-occurrence that stems from the separate practical affordances they can both bring in contemporary society, though whether this extends to a causal relationship is again a question which requires more context-specific empirical enquiry.

Conclusion

In conclusion, we can ask how this analysis can contribute to productive and sustainable development. The purpose of the analysis has not been to suggest that improved education in English is in some sense incapable of supporting a country in its development aims or of achieving the eight United Nations Millennium Development Goals (2000; for a summary, see Appendix 3 at the end of this volume). Educational projects that endeavour to enhance the quality of and expand access to English language teaching so as to support economic development can very likely produce many positive results, and some of the research we have surveyed demonstrates this. But in order to consider how English (and English language education) can contribute to international development through programmes such as EIA, it is necessary to explore the discourse that promotes English as a language for international development, and analyse the expectations and claims that are made about competence in the English language in the context of an increasingly globalised world. We can then investigate how these claims equate with the nuanced evidence that recent studies are providing about the correlations between situated language use, education, and development in contexts where these sort of development programmes are targeted.

The assumptions about English that have been identified in the initial policy documents for EIA point to several motivating factors behind the emergence of the ELfID discourse. Within the broader context of development studies, these assumptions marry well with the general aims of sustainable development which attempt to alleviate poverty and increase people's participation in world economic structures (cf. Sen 2001). Ultimately though, such aims can only be achieved if policy and planning are not structured primarily around a discourse that is influenced by abstract assumptions and received wisdom about the role that English plays in globalised societies, but instead draws on detailed studies of the affordances that actual English language use can achieve in specific contexts. Such studies present a complex range of what is, at times, contradictory evidence; this can be difficult for policy makers to negotiate. These studies often suggest that mother tongue-based instruction is important for educational quality (Benson 2004, Trudell 2009), and that there is a correlation between educational quality and economic development (Hanushek and Woessmann 2008). Correlations have also been discovered between competence in English and economic development (Grin 2001, Chakraborty and Kapur 2008). A further aspect of the overall picture is the long history of failure of English language education in contexts like Bangladesh and of low achievement despite large investment of resources (Wedell 2008, Hamid and Baldauf 2008). Regardless of this, however, the demand for access to English does not appear to have slowed, as English is still perceived as the language of education and power (Hornberger 2002, Tembe and Norton 2011, Chapter 6 this volume). These, plus many other factors, comprise the picture of the role played by English in development contexts as it is pieced together from contemporary applied linguistics scholarship, and it is this that can act as a refining discourse for the presuppositions about English found in many policy proclamations for development projects.

Based on a synthesis of the evidence related to the issues which comprise the key assumptions of the discourse of English as a language for international development, we can propose the following practical recommendations. Ideally, policy statements would acknowledge the complex interconnections between English and economic development, the provision of effective education and technology, and the role of national and local languages in their articulation of distinct objectives. Doing so would assist people in making informed choices about the actualities of language learning and language use, and allow them to realistically imagine themselves functioning in the multiliterate continuum that constitutes most modern societies (Hornberger 2002). In addition, policy statements would recognise the importance of people's perceptions of the power of English and its associations with economic value, educational opportunity and technology. While simplistic notions of English as a vital tool for personal and national development are best avoided, policies need to carefully negotiate people's hopes and aspirations. Vavrus (2002:373) suggests that economic hardship among the students in her study in Tanzania 'was tempered by their optimism that their knowledge of English would eventually help them find employment or opportunities for further education'. The participants felt that English was valuable as a means of connecting them to the wider world and providing access to better jobs – if not now, then perhaps in the future. Beliefs about the role of ELfID can therefore be part of the envisioned success that is required in order for actual development to occur.

Not only is it important for policies to allow for the complex realities about the role of English and its relations to economic development and education, but it is preferable also that this should be reflected in the pedagogic practices promoted within programmes that aim to teach English as a language for international development. Wedell (2007:628) has remarked that among the possible reasons for the disappointing outcomes of English language development programmes is the fact that the type of English promoted is often unsuitable for the priorities and sociolinguistic realities of the communities at which it is targeted. As such, it is necessary to examine in depth what it means for English to be a language for international development, and based on this, consider what concept of English, what variety of English, and what type of ELT would in practice be productive for such a project.

What is needed for ELT to be transformational, then, is an ongoing dialogue between practitioners (that is learners, teachers, and the surrounding community) and policy makers which will enable a dialectic which can tailor English language education to the local needs of communities attempting to engage fully in a rapidly globalising world. In many ways, the 'English in Action' project is attempting to provide such transformational language education by engaging and collaborating with local partners to provide teaching that is both practical and context–appropriate. Moreover, the project is not focusing solely upon the learning of English (despite its title), but also on changing both pedagogy and attitudes towards learning, and in this way supporting quality imperatives across Bangladesh. If the ICT-supported architecture that is being used in EIA to assist with the implementation of quality education and create interest in learning proves successful, this could have important implications for educational change in other contexts. Yet while technology offers the allure of potential success, at the same time, issues of access can create further societal divides, and this is a paradox that will have to be dealt with in the long term. Moreover, in order to be effective in increasing people's access to resources and skills, projects of this sort need to work hard to support successful literacy development initiatives so that people are able to make appropriate choices about the actual linguistic resources that will facilitate the skills and knowledge that they need for their own particular circumstances. Only by acknowledging the complex range of factors that come into play over language choice and learning – and the role that English plays in this context – will it be possible to create education policies that increase people's 'capacity to accomplish [their] desired functions through language' (Blommaert 2005:68).

Notes

1. We would like to thank the 'English in Action' project team and our funders, the UK Department for International Development, for supporting this research. Versions of this chapter were delivered at the 8th International Language and Development Conference in Dhaka and at the Cardiff Language and Communication Seminar Series at Cardiff University, and we are grateful to the audiences at these events for their feedback. We also thank Marc van der Stouwe, Frank Banks, Obaid Hamid, Fazle Rabbani and Alison Barratt for their feedback on earlier drafts of the chapter.

2. In this chapter we use the term 'international development' to refer to internationally planned, funded and/or executed projects (i.e. those involving two or more countries), while we take the term 'development' to refer to locally or nationally planned, funded and executed projects.

3. The information about the EIA project and the discourses analysed in this chapter come from a variety of public policy statements, which include: the EIA project brochure (EIA 2009c), the EIA website (EIA 2010), a statement by the project's directors (EIA 2008) and a written ministerial statement made by Douglas Alexander, Secretary of State for International Development, DfID (Alexander 2008). These documents have been chosen because they publicly represent the project and are freely distributed via the internet. Together they represent statements of intent from the architects and sponsors of the project concerning goal-orientated procedures of action. It should be noted, however, that as statements addressed to a public rather than an internal audience, they do not operate as detailed blueprints for the course of action to be taken by the project, but rather as summaries of the rationale and generalities which characterise the project. They are also all from the early stages of the project – either its inception or first years of activity – as this was the documentation available at the time of writing.

4. 'Bengali' was the English name given to the Bangla language during the colonial period. After the colonial period, the name of the language as spoken in Bangladesh was officially changed to Bangla (Banu and Sussex 2001a:126). When spoken in India, it is usually still referred to as Bengali.

References

Alexander, D. 2008. *English Language Skills, Bangladesh. Written Ministerial Statements,* 18 March. Available online at *www.theyworkforyou.com/wms/?id=2008-03-18b.61WS.1*

Ammon, U. 2001. *The Dominance of English as a Language of Science: Effects on Other Languages and Language Communities. Berlin: Walter de Gruyter.*

Banu, R. and Sussex, R. 2001a. *English in Bangladesh after independence: Dynamics of policy and practice.* In B.Moore (ed.), *Who's Centric Now? The Present State of Post-colonial Englishes,* 122-147. Oxford: Oxford University Press.

Banu, R. and Sussex, R. 2001b. *Code-switching in Bangladesh. English Today* 17(2), 51-61.

BBC (British Broadcasting Corporation). 2009. *Strengthening Media in Bangladesh: The World Debate. BBC World Service Trust.* Available online at *www.bbc.co.uk/worldservice/trust/whatwedo/where/asia/ bangladesh/2009/04/090424_world_debate_dhaka.shtml*

Benson, C. 2004. *The importance of mother tongue-based schooling for educational quality. Background paper prepared for the 'Education for All' Global Monitoring Report 2005, The Quality Imperative, UNESCO.* Available online at *http://unesdoc.unesco.org/images/0014/001466/146632e.pdf*

Blommaert, J. 2005. *Discourse: A Critical Introduction. Cambridge: Cambridge University Press.*

Blommaert, J. 2010. *The Sociolinguistics of Globalisation. Cambridge: Cambridge University Press.*

Bolton, K. 2005. *Where WE stands: Approaches, issues, and debate in world Englishes. World Englishes* 24(1), 69-83.

Bourdieu, P. 1991. *Language and Symbolic Power. Translated G. Raymond. Cambridge: Polity.*

Brock-Utne, B. 2000. *Whose Education for All? The Recolonisation of the African Mind. New York: Falmer Press.*

Bruthiaux, P. 2000. *Supping with the dismal scientists: Practical interdisciplinarity in language education and development economics. Journal of Multilingual and Multicultural Development* 21(4), 269-291.

Bruthiaux, P. 2002. *Hold your courses: Language education, language choice, and economic development. TESOL Quarterly* 36(3), 275-296.

Castells, M. 1999. *Information technology, globalisation and social development. United Nations Research Institute for Social Development (UNRISD), Discussion Paper 14.* Available online at *www.unrisd.org/unrisd/website/document.nsf/ (httpPublications)/F270E0C066F3DE7780256B67005B728C?OpenDocument*

Chakraborty, T. and Kapur, S. 2008. *English Language Premium: Evidence from a Policy Experiment in India. St Louis: Washington University in St Louis.* Available online at *www.isid.ac.in/~pu/conference/dec_08_conf/Papers/ShilpiKapur.pdf*

CJGTC (Commission on Japan's Goals in the Twenty-First Century). 2000. *The Frontier Within: Individual Empowerment and Better Governance in the New Millennium – Chapter 1 Overview. Tokyo: Office of the Prime Minister.*

Crossley, M. and Watson, K. 2003. *Comparative and International Research in Education: Globalisation, Context and Difference. London: Routledge.*

Crystal, D. 2003. *English as a Global Language. Cambridge: Cambridge University Press.*

EIA (English in Action). 2008. *Implementation Phase, Bangladesh. BMB Mott MacDonald.* Available online at www.bmb.mottmac.nl/projectsintro/southasiaprojects/

EIA (English in Action). 2009a. *Baseline Study 1: An Assessment of Spoken English Competence among School Students, Teachers and Adults in Bangladesh. Prepared for the EIA Research, Monitoring and Evaluation Team by Dr John Brown, Trinity College, London.*

EIA (English in Action). 2009b. *Baseline Study 4: An Audit of Current Materials for Teaching English in Bangladesh. Prepared for the EIA Research, Monitoring and Evaluation Team by Dr Brigid Smith.*

EIA (English in Action). 2009c. *Changing Learning, Changing Lives. Brochure.*

EIA (English in Action). 2010. *About Us.* Available online at *http://EIAbd.com*

Erling, E.J. and Hilgendorf, S.K. 2006. *Language policies in the context of German higher education. Language Policy* 5(3), 267-293.

Graddol, D. 2006. *English Next. London: British Council.*

Grin, F. 2001. *English as economic value: Facts and fallacies. World Englishes* 20(1), 65-78.

Grin, F. 2003. *Language planning and economics. Current Issues in Language Planning* 4(1), 1-66.

Hamid, M.O. 2009. *Sociology of Language Learning: Social Biographies and School English Achievement in Rural Bangladesh. Unpublished PhD thesis, The University of Queensland.*

Hamid, M.O. and Baldauf, R.B.J. 2008. *Will CLT bail out the bogged down ELT in Bangladesh? English Today* 24(3), 16-24.

Hanushek, E.A. and Woessmann, L. 2008. *The role of cognitive skills in economic development. Journal of Economic Literature* 46(3), 607-668.

Hornberger, N. 2002. *Multilingual language policies and the continua of biliteracy: An ecological approach. Language Policy* 1, 27-51.

Hossain, T. and Tollefson, J.W. 2007. *Language policy in education in Bangladesh. In A.B.Tsui and J.W.Tollefson (eds), Language Policy, Culture, and Identity in Asian Contexts,* 241-258. Mahwah, NJ: Lawrence Erlbaum.

Imam, S.R. 2005. *English as a global language and the question of nation-building education in Bangladesh. Comparative Education* 41(4), 471-486.

Lewis, M.P. 2009. *Ethnologue: Languages of the World. 16th edition. Dallas: SIL International.* Available online at *www.ethnologue.com/*

Little, A. and Green, A. 2009. *Successful globalisation, education and sustainable development. International Journal of Educational Development* 29, 166-174.

Kobayashi, Y. 2007. *Japanese working women and English study abroad. World Englishes* 26(1), 62-71.

Markee, N. 2002. *Language in development: Questions of theory, questions of practice. TESOL Quarterly* 36(3), 265-274.

Mutonyi, H. and Norton, B. 2007. *ICT on the margins: Lessons for Ugandan education. Language and Education* 21(3), 264-270.

NCTB (National Curriculum and Textbook Board). 2003. *Project Proforma (PP) for English Language Teaching Improvement Project (ELTIP): Phase 2. Dhaka: NCTB.*

Norton, B. 2000. *Identity and Language Learning: Gender, Ethnicity and Educational Change. London: Longman.*

Norton Peirce, B. 1995. *Social identity, investment, and language learning. TESOL Quarterly* 29(1), 9-31.

Pennycook, A. 2010. *Language as a Local Practice. Abingdon: Routledge.*

Project English. 2009. *British Council.* Available online at *www.britishcouncil.org/india-connecting-project-english.htm*

Rogers, A., Hunter, J. and Uddin, M.A. 2007. *Adult learning and literacy learning for livelihoods: Some international perspectives. Development in Practice* 17(1), 137-146.

Seargeant, P. 2008. *Ideologies of English in Japan: The perspective of policy and pedagogy. Language Policy* 7(2), 121-142.

Sen, A. 2001. *Development as Freedom. Oxford: Oxford University Press.*

Siddiqi, H. 2009. *Managing Digital Bangladesh 2021. The Daily Star,* 15 March. Available online at *www.thedailystar.net/newDesign/news-details.php?nid=79698*

Street, B. (ed.). 2001. *Literacy and Development: Ethnographic Perspectives. London and New York: Routledge.*

Tembe, J. and Norton, B. 2011. *English education, local languages and community perspectives in Uganda.* Chapter 6, this volume.

Toolan, M. 2003. *English as the supranational language of human rights? In C.Mair (ed.), The Politics of English as a World Language: New Horizons in Postcolonial Cultural Studies,* 53-65. Amsterdam: Rodopi.

Trudell, B. 2009. *Local-language literacy and sustainable development in Africa. International Journal of Educational Development* 29, 73-79.

UN (United Nations). 2000. *Millennium Development Goals.* 2000. Available online at *www.un.org/millenniumgoals/*

UNESCO (United Nations Educational, Scientific and Cultural Organisation). 2005. *Education for All: Literacy for Life. Paris: UNESCO.*

Vavrus, F. 2002. *Postcoloniality and English: Exploring language policy and the politics of development in Tanzania. TESOL Quarterly* 36(3), 373-397.

Warschauer, M. 2004. *The rhetoric and reality of aid: Promoting educational technology in Egypt. Globalisation, Societies and Education* 2(3), 377-390.

Wedell, M. 2008. *Developing a capacity to make 'English for Everyone' worthwhile: Reconsidering outcomes and how to start achieving them. International Journal of Educational Development* 28, 628-639.

Williams, E. and Cooke, J. 2002. *Pathways and labyrinths: Language and education in development. TESOL Quarterly* 36(3), 297-322.

Woolard, K. 1998. *Introduction: Language ideology as a field of inquiry.* In B.Schieffelin, K.Woolard and P.Kroskrity (eds), *Language Ideologies,* 3-47. *Oxford: Oxford University Press.*

13

More than just 'technology': English language teaching initiatives as complex educational changes

Martin Wedell

Introduction

Recent papers by, for example, McGrath 2010 and Brock-Utne 2007 (which review and critique a range of current development thinking from the mostly Anglophone developed world) suggest that, for the time being, degrees of success in development will continue to be judged principally through apparently straightforward and easily interpreted measurable changes to universally applicable economic indicators, rather than through analysis of more context-bound and complex processes of social change. The role of education in such materialistic views of development seems to be to enable economic growth, through forming and expanding individual, and national, human capital:

> ... the knowledge, skills, competencies and attributes that allow people to
> contribute to their personal and social wellbeing, as well as that of their countries.
> **(Keeley 2007:3)**

The rapid expansion of English language teaching into state education systems worldwide over the past 20 to 30 years has been an obvious trend. For the first time in foreign language teaching history, national governments and individuals worldwide seem to see teaching a language (English) to all learners in state schools as an important means of increasing the human capital on which future national economic development and political power depends. At national level in Kenya, for example, the Ministry of Education sees the development of communication skills in English as important because English is:

> ... the pre-eminent language of international communication. Consequently those
> who master English reap many academic, social and professional benefits.
> **(KIE 2002:6)**

Meanwhile, the Philippine government sees its English curriculum as helping to develop 'language learners aware of and able to cope with global trends' (Waters and Vilches 2008:8) while, for individual learners in India:

> English is seen more as a language of power and empowerment, a tool for career making and a practical necessity. It is now increasingly seen as necessary for upward social and financial mobility. *(Padwad and Dixit forthcoming 2011)*

At both individual and national levels in the Ukraine:

> ... the enthusiasm of ordinary Ukrainians for English coincides with the government's ambitions for integration with the European Union on the one hand and strategic and economic partnership with the United States on the other. *(Smotrova 2009:728)*

Despite a lack of hard evidence to show whether the policy of providing universal English language teaching is beneficial and/or cost effective (Coleman 2010), the perception introduced above has resulted in innumerable English Language Teaching (ELT) initiatives to try to develop citizens' English proficiency. While most such initiatives have (in name at least) been nationally instigated, there has also been considerable direct or indirect influence on and investment in ELT by governmental agencies from (mostly) English-speaking countries as part of their international aid budgets. New English curriculum documents and teaching materials proliferate in state education systems worldwide. English has become a compulsory subject for ever more years of basic schooling. High stakes English tests are increasingly important gate-keepers for entry to higher levels of education. Although there has been massive human and financial investment in such initiatives, outcomes to date have often been disappointing. Reports (Nunan 2003, Wedell 2008) suggest that there are relatively few state school classrooms anywhere in which most learners are developing a useable knowledge of English. Those learners worldwide who do succeed in developing the hoped-for communication skills have often been at private schools and/or have had extra private tuition.

It seems unlikely that prevailing views of the important role that the development of citizens' English proficiency plays in supporting national development in a globalising world will change in the immediate future. National ELT initiatives aiming to better enable the development of English proficiency are likely to continue to be introduced. This being so, then, both for the sake of social equity, and in order to use limited educational resources to best effect, it is important that such initiatives should begin to better achieve their desired outcomes.

The remainder of this chapter has three parts. In the first I introduce a number of core issues emerging from the growing educational change literature, which are increasingly agreed to need consideration when planning a major educational change and I discuss what these issues imply for implementation processes. Next, in the light of these issues and their implications, I claim that many national, large-scale ELT initiatives are examples of complex educational change and that the failure to recognise this is one important reason for their apparent frequent failure. Finally, I briefly analyse two case studies of existing or recent ELT change initiatives from developing countries, to illustrate some consequences of acknowledging or failing to acknowledge the importance of such issues. The chapter concludes with a number of questions for further consideration.

Supporting successful large-scale educational change

National-level changes to (ELT) curricula, materials, timetable weighting for particular subjects and modes of assessment in schools represent a large-scale change in any context. Planning the implementation of such changes involves consideration of the interactions between a range of people playing many different roles at many different levels of responsibility both within the overall education system and outside. The context of change implementation planning is therefore complex and it is impossible to identify all the micro-level factors that may contribute to successful implementation. The study of the process of educational change thus accepts the inherent complexity of the process and the literature (based mostly on experiences in 'developed countries') offers no simple formulas for ensuring success. Nonetheless, over time, certain issues have been seen to reoccur time and again in different educational change contexts, and in this section I discuss three factors, from a recent paper by two extremely experienced Canadian educational change thinkers, that are generally agreed to be important when considering the implementation of educational change:

> The central lesson of large-scale educational change that is now evident is the following: Large-scale, sustained improvement in student outcomes requires a (i) *sustained effort to change school and classroom practices, not just structures such as governance and accountability*. The heart of improvement lies in changing teaching and learning practices, (ii) *in thousands and thousands of classrooms*, and this requires focused and sustained effort by (iii) *all parts of the education system and its partners*.
> **(Levin and Fullan 2008:291; my italics and numbering)**

I interpret the three factors numbered above as follows:

1. Educational change requires sustained effort over time, to change what actually happens in school classrooms rather than just the surface language or appearance of the curriculum or the materials, or the manner in which schools are evaluated. The length of time for which such sustained effort will be needed will be strongly influenced by the degree of 'reculturing' (Fullan 2007) that the change entails for those whom implementation affects directly. Funding provision and the commitment of ongoing active leadership and management of change implementation needs to reflect this reality.

2. Implementation of national educational change takes place in numerous classrooms. Schools in different parts of a city, region or country are different. The classrooms within them are different. Implementation will never look identical across the whole of any education system anywhere. Any evaluation of success will need to bear this in mind.

3. Those directly affected by large-scale educational change include educational leaders, teachers and learners. However, other components and actors in the existing education system and wider society are also affected and can critically influence implementation outcomes.

The above points are discussed more fully below. Although treated as discrete points, it will be obvious that they are in fact interdependent and influence one another in more or less predictable ways.

Sustained effort over time

Despite rhetoric that might suggest otherwise, many of the education systems into which ELT initiatives have been introduced are set within societies that retain many features of what Kennedy (2011, Chapter 2 this volume) calls the 'traditional' stage of social development. The beliefs about what teaching, learning and assessment 'mean' – and so what ought to happen in classrooms within such education systems – remained 'didactic' (Kennedy 2011) until at least the very late 20th century. Many remain so still.

The last 20 years have seen an expansion of educational change initiatives (with new English curricula often in the vanguard) that have claimed to be introducing more student-centred, interactive, participative, 'open' approaches to teaching and learning. The extent to which such approaches result in genuine changes to what happens in classrooms will be strongly influenced by how fully the people whom the changes affect can cope with the significant professional and personal 'reculturing' that such changes entail.

No professional likes to feel that their existing knowledge and skills are no longer sufficient. Everyone finds it difficult to make significant changes to their settled and unquestioned professional behaviours. Van Veen and Sleegers (2006), for example, point out how vulnerable Dutch teachers felt when they sensed that their existing professional competence was no longer adequate at a time of change from a more traditional to a more learner-centred classroom. English teachers everywhere, teacher educators, those who are supposed to be training them and those who are managing and leading the change implementation process in a school or a locality may all feel uncertain when confronted with such changes. They will all need capacity-building support over time to become able to implement some form of such professional change in classrooms.

The more ambitious and demanding an educational change is, in terms of its scale, and in terms of the degree of difference it hopes to bring about in what happens in classrooms, the longer it will take. Exactly how long is difficult to judge. Fullan (2007), using examples of change mostly from North America, suggests that a large-scale change may take five to ten years to become part of normal classroom life in the majority of schools. Polyzoi et al. (2003) suggest that in other contexts, for example many countries of East and Central Europe in the 1990s, educational changes of the kind outlined above represent such an intense degree of reculturing that they may take a generation to achieve.

Whichever timescale we subscribe to, it is clear that successful implementation of educational change takes a long time. It is an ongoing process, not an event that takes place at a particular point in time. In multiparty political contexts the timescales suggest that a culturally challenging national educational change initiative – such as the introduction of a 'Communicative English curriculum' – needs to be understood from the very start as a national, not a party, political issue (Cox and Lemaitre 1999). It will continue to need economic and political support over what may be a decade or more. In many contexts this can happen only if governments can be persuaded to 'put educational investment beyond their own need for political survival' (Fullan 2001:233).

Implementation of educational change does not take place in a uniform manner

There is an implicit assumption that implementation is an event, that change occurs next Tuesday or in September. **(Hopkins 1987:195)**

What the implementation of any national educational change actually looks like in any given school classroom will be influenced by the behaviours of different people who are in turn influenced by their own differing socio-economic, geographical and historical realities. Local conditions, which may vary from one school or one region to another, include:

- Teachers' current practices: what they are familiar with and do well, how difficult they are likely to find the new practices

- Class sizes: how supportive these are of new educational practices and whether anything can be done to make them more so

- Available resources and teaching materials: whether the new educational practices require use of particular resources or teaching materials and whether these are present or could be provided

- How well the immediate community expects its learners to perform in high stakes tests and whether expected levels of performance will be affected by the introduction of new practices

- The availability of local support for capacity building

- Awareness of and attitude to any new classroom practices on the part of local leaders and parents

- Funding actually available to help support all aspects of the implementation process and understanding of how best to spend it.

Since all these (and other possible factors) may vary between different parts of the same country or even from one school to another, the route which implementation takes, the rate at which it occurs and the degree to which the 'spirit' of the change is present in its final form may all vary. Trying to evaluate success through a uniform set of (often purely quantitative) measures is unlikely to provide an accurate picture of the outcome of any implementation process.

Large-scale educational change affects the whole of the existing education system

Many attempts at policy and programme change have concentrated on product development, legislation and other on-paper changes in a way that ignored the fact that what *people* did or did not do was the crucial variable (Fullan 2001:70).

When we think about which people need to 'do' or 'not do' certain things in order for an educational change to succeed, the first group to be considered are usually teachers. As Leithwood et al. (2002) point out, how teachers think about knowledge and about learners' roles and how their ideas translate into classroom teaching and learning is central to any concept of education. However, while teachers are central figures in any change implementation process they cannot succeed alone:

> *Real reform requires sustained attention from many people at all levels of the education system. It is not enough for a state or national government to be fully committed, difficult as this is in itself. Many, if not, most schools, and, where they exist, districts or regional authorities, must also share the goals and purposes of reform and improvement. It is even better when the efforts of the school system are understood and supported by external groups such as community agencies, since this is important to the political legitimacy of the education system. There can be – indeed, there should be – room for a variety of strategies to achieve the goals, but there cannot be substantial dissent on the main purposes themselves.*
> **(Levin and Fullan 2008:294)**

For teachers to feel supported and thus motivated to invest the effort over time that is usually required for them to understand and become comfortable with the new practices, change planners need to recognise that any large-scale change affects the whole education system. Establishing systems to help teachers to become confident in new practices over time is of course one important aspect of implementation planning. However, for such systems to 'work', planning also needs to consider two further points.

First there needs to be an honest appraisal of whether adjustments will need to be made to other components of the system such as teacher education, teaching materials and methods of assessment in order to support the change process. Secondly planners need to consider which other people more or less directly affected by change (the educational leaders and administrators at many levels, the teacher educators, inspectors and supervisors, the test and textbook writers, the school heads, the learners and even the parents) may also need to be helped to change some of their practices and expectations. Both points impact directly on whether the national education system will be able to work collaboratively to make the change a success (Wedell 2009).

In the next part of the chapter I consider to what extent ELT initiatives have so far seemed to consider the issues mentioned above.

Are educational change ideas relevant to ELT initiatives?

In the introduction I noted that judgements about the success or otherwise of development initiatives often currently focus primarily on empirical measurement of economic 'product' indicators. This product orientation of much 'economics-based' development thinking also influences how the challenge of educational change in developing countries is understood.

> More money and policy effort will get children into schools and education's effectiveness can be improved by scientifically-tested investments in the 'right' instructional materials [and] teacher upgrading. **(McGrath 2010:250)**

I suggest that such a rational view of how changes in the goals of teaching and learning can be supported (very much at odds with the current consensus regarding the influence of complex 'process' factors on the outcomes of educational change initiatives) influences the planning of many ELT initiatives. In the remainder of this chapter I propose that in most contexts the transition from foreign language teaching (in our case ELT) for a small elite to the provision of ELT for everyone – and the accompanying introduction of new curricula which aim to develop learners' communication skills – together represent a very complex educational change. I also propose that the issues reviewed in the previous section are directly relevant in such complex educational change contexts. I consider each of them below in terms of the extent to which they appear to be acknowledged in the planning and implementation of ELT change initiatives.

The need for sustained effort over time

The time needed to implement change depends greatly on the degree of reculturing that the change represents for those who will be most directly involved in implementing it. I believe that despite official rhetoric to the contrary, the contexts into which many large-scale ELT initiatives are introduced remain ones in which, 'From a cultural perspective, the prevailing pedagogical approach in Tanzania can be summed up as "we teach; students listen"' (Vavrus 2009:304). In most such contexts, the lines of communication and decision-making within education systems remain strongly hierarchical and teacher–student relationships remain formal:

> Children are brought up to respect adults and those in authority. Questioning or challenging them are not often considered appropriate behaviour. Indeed, in many African societies, the relationship between adult and child is one of respect and authority. Children are not encouraged to question; they are expected to be respectful, charming and smiling in the company of elders. Consequently, the expectations raised by CCP [child-centred pedagogy] directly contradict the cultural context of African societies. **(Altinyelken 2010:167)**

Such systems rarely encourage individual teachers or schools to show much personal or professional initiative, or to develop a sense of personal agency and autonomy:

*Institutions, teachers, and learners follow centrally prescribed norms of working, evaluation and administration, and centrally designed uniform syllabuses and textbooks. Teachers do not have much freedom in choosing or dealing with their material, methods or schedule. **(Padwad and Dixit forthcoming 2011)***

Regardless of whether the main focus of the initiative is stated to be a new curriculum, new materials, new teacher education curricula, or starting English at a younger age, ELT initiatives nowadays focus on enabling learners to use English for communication. The teaching approaches which are thought to enable learners to develop English communication skills tend to be expressed in terms imported from the 'western' literature of Communicative Language Teaching (CLT), Task-Based Language Teaching (TBLT), learner- or child-centred classrooms and constructivist approaches to teaching and learning (Vavrus 2009 in Tanzania, Waters and Vilches 2008 in Philippines, De Segovia and Hardison 2009 in Thailand, Padwad and Dixit forthcoming 2011 in India). I suggest that making such a transition is potentially threatening to many implementers' existing 'key meanings' (Blackler and Shinmin 1984). Key meanings can be seen as our day-to-day perceptions of ourselves and personal and professional relationships with others. These provide us with important stability and security. If teachers have rarely been encouraged to take personal professional decisions, it can be an:

*emotionally very challenging and upsetting task for teachers to disturb their comfortable routines, to experiment and innovate, to try and err, and to risk failure and loss of face. **(Padwad and Dixit forthcoming 2011)***

In many contexts the changes of behaviour and professional practice that ELT change initiatives imply for those directly concerned with implementation do entail an adjustment of some 'key meanings'. This is true not only for teachers (and learners) but also for the educational leaders and teacher educators who share teachers' professional and cultural assumptions and, less directly, for parents and other members of the wider society.

If implementation of ELT initiatives involves significant reculturing for a wide range of implementers, national plans need to be made to support the process, flexibly, over long periods of time. In my experience, which will, I imagine, be shared by many readers, the complexity of what ELT change entails for the many people it affects is rarely acknowledged by national policy makers or international aid providers. Instead they often behave as if the implementation planning of strategic ELT change initiatives is a technological process (Blenkin et al. 1992), with implementation viewed 'as a linear, sequentially ordered industrial production line' (Pettigrew and Whipp 1991:32). Such a process requires funding over a series of discrete stages to be completed at pre-determined points, after which impact will be evaluated and the initiative will be considered complete. Sustained context-sensitive effort over enough time to enable those affected to develop sufficient genuine understanding of and confidence in new ELT practices to make some form of these practices visible in most classrooms is rare.

The need to acknowledge that implementation will never be uniform

ELT and other education initiatives in most developing countries borrow (or are strongly encouraged to adopt) ideas about appropriate approaches to teaching and learning from very different cultural contexts (Altinyelken 2010, Vavrus 2009). The literature on the importance of taking context into account when considering what will and will not be possible in English classrooms stretches back almost 30 years (to Holliday and Cooke 1982), and books like Holliday (1994) and Coleman (1996) have been widely read. Nonetheless, in official change documentation at least, an assumption that it is possible to achieve the same change outcomes (English communication skills), to the same level, through the use of the same materials in the same ways in all environments, is often apparent.

This may be unsurprising given the hierarchical and prescriptive nature of most education systems and the lack of autonomy that this engenders among classroom-level change implementers. However, for many ELT initiatives this very prescriptiveness, when applied to the planning and design of support for reculturing (of teachers, teacher educators and educational leaders), results in uniform provision that ignores the varying contextual realities that exist in different parts of a country or region. By so doing it inherently contradicts the context-bound ideas underpinning 'communicative' and 'learner-centred' classroom teaching and the need to explicitly prepare and encourage teachers to view implementation as a process of trying out new ideas, teaching techniques and materials in ways that are sensitive to the contextual realities of their own classrooms. This prescriptiveness is also often present in the (usually brief) training that may be provided for (some) teachers when a change is introduced. Such 'trainings', perhaps partly due to their brevity, rarely explicitly acknowledge the classroom realities in which change is to be implemented. They often therefore represent poor preparation for actual introduction of change practices into classrooms once the training ends (Wedell 2005).

The need for the whole system to be consistent

It seems clear that if teachers are to be able to implement a contextually realistic version of change in their classrooms then they will not be the only ones who need to change. If teacher educators are to help teachers to understand change and how to interpret change for their own contexts, they too need training and support in the planning and design of teacher support provision that reflects the need to fit the 'spirit' of change to existing realities. Similarly, school leaders within top-down systems may need to be helped to accept that implementation of new practices may mean adjustments to existing teacher and learner behaviours; school leaders will also need to understand that the more independent teachers, able to take personal professional decisions about some of what happens in their classrooms, are not a threat to leaders' status.

All of the above can be made more or less difficult to achieve depending on the extent to which the ELT change planners consider the 'whole' system within which English teaching will take place before launching their initiatives. For example, the introduction of a communicative English curriculum has implications for initial teacher education programmes, for how teacher performance will be evaluated and – critically – for the content and format of any high stakes English examinations that learners will be expected to take during their school careers. If such issues are not considered and planned for in tandem with the apparent main focus of the initiative, they can act as further contextual barriers to implementation. Again I imagine many readers will reflect on how infrequent such internal coherence between all the affected parts of the system has been in the ELT or educational change contexts which they have experienced.

In the next section I give two brief case studies of real ELT initiatives to illustrate what may happen when the above three factors are insufficiently acknowledged, or are ignored. I was personally involved in the first case from the inception of the project to its end. (The process of implementing English at primary level, of course, continues to the present.) In the second case I was continuously involved at a remove over a three-year period as a supervisor of the thesis from which the case data has been extracted.

Case 1: Introducing English at primary level

The ELT initiative in this case aimed to support the introduction of a national primary English curriculum in all schools. The cultural context in which it was situated was highly centralised, top down and hierarchical, and the educational culture reflected this. The decision to introduce English at primary level was made with minimal consultation: local educational planners and administrators were instructed to plan for English to begin to be taught in the third year of all the primary schools by a set date. An outline curriculum was provided which stated that English should not be formally assessed.

The lead-in time for the implementation of this initiative was about two years. However, few primary English teachers were available and, due to the arbitrary and non-consultative manner in which the change had been introduced, most educators, school principals, educational administrators and members of the wider society had little understanding of the implications for teaching approaches. There was a great deal to do in the time available.

The provision of 'bodies' to teach English in classrooms was a pressing concern for regional educational policy makers and their planning for implementation thus included the establishment of a group of Teaching English to Young Learners (TEYL) trainers. It was decided that four trainer training groups (approximately 100 trainers) would have three months' TEYL and trainer skills training at a British university. Each returning group would then be responsible for running a three-week TEYL training programme for up to 800 primary school teachers in the summer or winter holiday following their return. Members of later groups would each be expected to attend one such programme as 'training assistants', prior to their departure.

Participants were carefully selected and were existing district-level teacher trainers, educators from colleges specialising in the training of primary teachers or primary teachers considered to have trainer potential. Most parts of the region were represented, but the majority came from the more developed areas and had some prior TEYL experience.

The first two months of the UK trainer training courses discussed the main principles underlying the teaching of languages to young learners and the rationale for these. It demonstrated and tried out some of the most widely used classroom techniques and activities for turning principles into classroom practices suitable for young learners. Efforts were made to relate these techniques and activities to local realities as far as possible, for example, through reference to participants' prior experiences of their context and use of local textbooks.

The final month of the programme had two main foci. The first was on developing materials to use on the teacher training programmes which participants would be expected to run on their return. The second was to develop training skills that would enable them to use the materials with teachers as effectively as possible. In a recent follow-up study involving 15 members (60 per cent) of the third group, Li (2010:59), herself a member of the group and an active trainer, reports that there was a general consensus that one month was insufficient to 'grasp the [training] techniques, at least not at a level at which they can be articulated.'

Each teacher training programme which the trainers led on their return was residential over three weeks, with approximately 800 teachers divided into 20 to 25 classes of 30 to 40 teachers each. Each trainer (with an assistant) was responsible for one class. The programme content was based on the trainer-produced materials, initially heavily based on the content of the UK programme. These were adjusted in terms of weighting and examples to meet local realities in the light of experience over time The training context could be considered supportive in two ways. Firstly since the teachers were all primary school teachers some TEYL ideas about how children learn, how they learn language, and what children's characteristics imply for the sorts of activities that help them to learn were broadly familiar. Secondly many suggested techniques fitted what was said in the outline curriculum about the need for primary English learning to focus on activities involving games, stories and songs and for children not to be subjected to formal assessment.

Despite such implicit support, the prevailing educational culture in society as a whole was not at all consistent with the types of teaching and learning activities that the training programmes suggested. Most of those both within the education system (educational administrators, school leaders, learners) and outside it (parents) continued to view learning at all levels of education as a process involving first the learning of tangible and visible knowledge (which in the case of language meant mostly grammar and vocabulary) and then being assessed on this learning.

In addition the classroom environments into which primary English was to be introduced presented further challenges. In a study of 511 teachers attending the third teacher training programme, 98.2 per cent said that the techniques and activities introduced during the training could be used in their primary English classrooms (Wedell 2005). However, 85 per cent also answered 'Yes' to a question asking whether there were any factors (apart from their own lack of experience or lack of confidence) that might make it difficult to actually use these techniques and activities in their classrooms. Factors mentioned by more than ten per cent of these teachers included (in order of frequency):

- large class size, insufficient physical space and the difficulty of classroom management

- the pressure to 'finish the book' to meet the demands of the test, while having only a few lessons a week, making it difficult to find the time to use other suggested techniques/activities

- the critical role of test results in leaders' judgments of students' and teachers' performance and the incompatibility of testing content and format with the use of the suggested techniques and activities

- learners' language level making them unable to understand meanings and instructions

- learners' cultural reluctance to participate

- inappropriacy of textbooks, meaning that there was a shortage of materials to support the use of the suggested activities

- excessive teacher workloads and so lack of time to plan classes and materials which incorporate these techniques/activities.

Given these multiple visible and invisible challenges, the great majority of primary English teachers needed support beyond a single teacher training programme to feel able to introduce new teaching practices in their classrooms.

The only explicit expectation of all the newly trained trainers was that they should contribute to just one teacher training programme after their return. While a minority did contribute to more than one programme – and a small number had explicit training roles in their existing jobs – for many there was no opportunity to develop their training skills any further. Li's (2010) follow-up study reports that 12 out of the 15 members of the group that she contacted had had no formal training role since.

Similarly, Li's (2010) study suggests that availability of further support for teachers has been dependent on the attitudes and understandings of individual educational leaders and head teachers rather than being planned for all. Where such leaders themselves understand and feel positive towards the implementation of TEYL, support is provided. This may take the form of direct resource or explicit moral support:

> The education bureau support the TEYL training a lot. The vice director of the bureau responsible for teaching ... many times when having the training he came to the spot, to confirm the management. If we ask for any resources for the training course he always agrees to provide them. **(Li 2010:65)**

Alternatively, support may be more indirect, as for example through ensuring that the content and format of low stakes assessment supports the use of some TEYL practices:

> Local research bureau are writing very simple examinations so the teachers who use appropriate techniques get high marks. **(Li 2010:70)**

Case 1 in the light of the educational change principles

The case described above represented a very complex change. A high degree of reculturing at many levels was a prerequisite if teachers were to feel able to successfully introduce some recognisable version of TEYL ideas and activities into the majority of classrooms in this context. The development of such confidence would take time and depended on serious consideration of each of the three factors which we have been examining, both at the initial planning stage and when planning implementation. As will be evident from the above description such consideration was limited. Below I consider the consequences of the way in which the programme was implemented.

The need for sustained effort over time

National policy was that primary English should be introduced in all schools by a certain date. Responsibility for enabling implementation was delegated to regional educational planners. I do not know what form their 'instructions' took or the extent of regional autonomy that they allowed. In this case the regional planners were actively involved for the two years of the trainer training project. However, the lack of any longer term scheme for utilising expensively trained trainers to provide ongoing support to teachers over time suggests that planners did not have a complete understanding of what degree of change to 'normal' classroom teaching the introduction of English in primary schools entailed, or how alien it might seem to those more or less directly affected by its introduction. Consequently there was insufficient sustained and active leadership of a region-wide, ongoing process of implementation planning and support. Trainers' skills were under-utilised (outside their own institutions) and few teachers had access to the professional and leadership support over time that might have enabled them to overcome the many practical, professional and personal problems (see below) that made it difficult to implement a version of TEYL appropriate for their own circumstances.

Many of these difficulties needed long-term national-level leadership and encouragement if they were to be overcome. This too was not forthcoming. However, even at regional level planners might in the first instance have helped implementation by clarifying what was actually expected of teachers. Project evaluators noted that 'all teachers lacked direction from the curriculum whose targets were vague and non specific' (Yu and Hurst 2004:29) and that 'a significant number of teachers had problems handling the textbooks' (Yu and Hurst 2004:15). Given that curriculum targets were not clear, even if structures for ongoing teacher support had been established, it would still have been difficult to decide how best to develop teachers' confidence in using their textbooks in ways consistent with TEYL principles. Overall, insufficiently sustained effort over insufficient time (at both national and regional levels) was devoted to planning the implementation in a manner which would maximise the development of teachers' confidence in the new professional behaviours and so increase the likelihood of some version of the hoped-for changes becoming visible in most classrooms.

The need to acknowledge that implementation will never be uniform

The outline nature of the curriculum alluded to above may suggest that national planners recognised that due to wide socio-economic disparities – and consequent inequitable distribution of resources and qualified teachers – actual implementation would 'look different' in different classrooms. Li's report (2010) also suggests that the ongoing curriculum implementation support available for teachers has been dependent on the enthusiasm of individual school or administrative leaders and that there is no template for implementation at the regional level. This recognition of the need to encourage different parts of the country to implement policy in ways appropriate to their own circumstances does, if consciously planned, show a clear sense of what is realistically possible. However, a combination of the lack of sustained support (see above), the centralised nature of the education system and the strong educational culture (see below) has meant that in fact much classroom teaching of primary English has been strongly influenced by the content and format of the form-focused examinations that primary school leavers need to take to enter junior secondary schools. The uniformity of teaching and learning that result from such influences probably bear little resemblance to the outcomes which the curriculum had envisaged!

The need for the whole system to be consistent

Given the potential threats to their 'key meanings' that the introduction of TEYL posed for teachers, consistency of message regarding what was expected of them was important. In fact, existing cultural and physical classroom realities were largely inconsistent with the classroom behaviour that the implementation of TEYL might have expected. It is in the failure to address such inconsistencies that the effects of lack of sustained effort over time become most evident.

Given the largely transmission-based nature of the existing educational culture there was a need for a national or regional awareness-raising process to try to ensure that people surrounding and influencing teachers (for example, head teachers, parents and local educational administrators) understood that what the primary curriculum would like to see happening in classrooms was different in certain ways from existing primary teaching-learning norms. Instead most English teachers remained in contexts in which:

> *Most parents do not know anything about the National Curriculum ... Usually they would expect their children to learn some specific things in school each day. If the children cannot show to their parents what they have learned, the parents would question the teaching quality of the teachers or the school.*
> **(Zeng 2005:20)**

The national policy stated that primary language learning should not be formally assessed. Again, existing educational assumptions and the key role that examinations play within almost all education systems meant that this message needed serious reinforcing from the top if it was to be heeded. Without such reinforcement most members of society both outside and within the education system continued to believe that testing was the only way of ensuring learning; moreover, they were of the view that learners' performance at all ages should be evaluated (usually) through formal, objectively marked tests:

> *Parents also care about examinations. They could not understand the formative assessment. What they believed was the marks their children could show them on papers. They would worry that their children might not be able to achieve good marks at the end of term.* **(Zeng 2005:21)**

In most educational contexts worldwide schools are increasingly judged by their perceived examination success. If parents cared about examinations primary English teachers and head teachers also had to care, since, once English was available in all primary schools, it also became one of the examinations taken to determine entry to 'good' secondary schools.

As if the above were not enough to persuade most English teachers that maintaining the status quo made sense, the prevailing ethos of the education system positively discouraged teachers from being autonomous innovators or experimenters in their classrooms, even though these qualities are exactly those needed by teachers able to flexibly interpret the goals of TEYL for their own context. Most teachers have little say regarding the selection of the textbooks that they are given; they are told what point in the textbook they should reach by when; and the examinations that their learners take are based upon what is supposed to have been covered. In such working contexts teachers thus had little 'overt support and encouragement to trial new methods' (Yu and Hurst 2004:37).

Finally the physical classroom conditions were often not supportive of the implementation of TEYL techniques and activities:

> How could a teacher use different techniques like playing games in a small classroom which holds more than 60 children (my son's class)? How could they play other interesting activities to arouse every child's interest in learning English with a class of more than 80 (my nephew's class)? The mentioned class sizes are not a rare phenomenon. **(Zeng 2005:14)**

All of the above suggest that lack of sustained effort over time by policy makers and implementation planners makes it unlikely that the change environment within which teachers are trying to introduce change into classrooms will be consistent enough to support their efforts. Similar themes appear in the next case.

Case 2: Training pre-service teachers to teach the national English secondary curriculum

This case is described only briefly, but highlights many similar issues to the one above. It is based on a PhD study with which I was closely connected. The study investigated pre-service English language teacher education.

The Ministry of Education in a centralised, top-down, education system, in which the prevailing educational culture remained largely transmission based, introduced a new English curriculum. This stated that its main task was:

> ... to shift from overemphasising the transmission mode of teaching and learning based on grammar and vocabulary to the development of students' overall ability in language use. The provision of English should attach great importance to activating students' interests in learning, relating the course content to the students' life experiences and cognitive stages of development, promoting learning through their active involvement in the process of experiencing, practising, participating in activities, co-operating with each other and communicating with the language – learning through doing. **(Ministry of Education 2001:1)**

The main goal of the new curriculum was to enable school leavers to be competent communicators (Ongondo 2009:4). It recommended that English be taught using communicative language teaching methodology without providing detailed information about what implementing such a methodology might look like in terms of classroom activities and behaviours. The curriculum had two syllabus strands, language and literature, and the documents stressed the need to teach and assess these in an integrated manner. As previously stated, I consider the introduction of a 'communicative' curriculum and the methodology, activities and behaviours that it is generally understood to imply, as representing a complex educational change for English teachers. It seems reasonable to assume that the professional development and support provided during English teachers' pre-service training would reflect the understandings and skills that novice teachers would need to be able to implement the curriculum in school classrooms.

Universities are responsible for the four year pre-service training of English teachers. The study showed however that they do not seem to be aware of what the Ministry expects English teachers to know and be able to do in classrooms when they reach schools. As autonomous entities the universities make their own decisions about the content and weighting of the various courses that make up the pre-service English teacher education curriculum. Ongondo (2009) points out that in most universities this curriculum is taught by a number of different departments, often with little or no co-ordination between them. In one university which Ongondo examined, during their four years of study trainees are required to take 12 or more courses each year. Over the four years only two of these courses are specifically focused on pedagogical content knowledge, while none specifically help the development of curriculum knowledge (Shulman 1987). The university teacher education curriculum also views English language and literature as two separate subjects, taught in two different departments and assessed separately. Trainee teachers therefore receive little exemplification of how the two strands might be taught in an integrated fashion, which the curriculum expects them to do once they enter schools.

After the above pre-service training, the novice teachers investigated in this study (Ongondo 2009) were thus professionally unprepared for teaching practice in a multitude of ways. As future English teachers their lack of preparation meant that they lacked two key sets of understandings and skills: when, how and why to use a communicative methodology to teach English and when, why and how to teach English in an integrated manner.

The schools they attended were in a relatively prosperous part of the country with good communications. Their school experience demonstrated further mismatches between classroom reality and documentary rhetoric. Firstly they found that the school-based 'co-operating teachers', who they hoped might be able to help them develop the skills needed for 'integrated teaching', were themselves unclear about how to operationalise the ideas in their classrooms (unsurprisingly, since they had received the same initial training). Consequently, few examples of actual 'integrated teaching' could be observed in any of their practice schools.

Next, the novice teachers discovered that an 'alternative' English syllabus existed, devised by the National Examination Board. This syllabus identified the areas that learners needed to cover if they were to be appropriately prepared for national high stakes tests. It did not integrate the skills in the manner recommended by the Ministry's national curriculum, but instead assessed language and literature separately. The following quote suggests what usually happens in such situations:

> If people in a change context (parents, learners, teachers, institutional leaders) see an obvious lack of harmony between the behaviours/practices underlying the proposed changes and those that are perceived to help learners pass high stakes exams, it is the practices that support success in assessment that will 'win'. **(Wedell 2009:25)**

Teachers in Case 2 were no exception; their reaction of course affected teaching materials. Teachers who are judged (and whose schools are judged through league tables) on their learners' success in high stakes tests are likely to choose textbooks which they feel will help them help their learners to pass such exams. Textbook writers therefore had little incentive to produce textbooks to support teachers in implementing the integrated, national, communicative-language-teaching-based curriculum.

Case 2 in the light of the educational change principles

As in the previous case teachers would need support over time to be able to develop the understandings and skills that would enable them to make the transition from being transmitters of information about grammar and vocabulary to being developers of students' language use ability. While it is logistically difficult, time consuming and expensive to provide such support over time to practising teachers, the context of pre-service teacher education, extending over four years, would appear to be a perfectly natural setting within which to try to ensure that the nation's future English teachers become able to teach in ways that the national curriculum recommends. As the above description shows, the opportunity to make the link between what is emphasised in training and what the teacher needs to know for classroom practice is not being utilised in the case context.

The need for sustained effort over time

The curriculum was introduced in 2002. At least two cohorts of English teachers have graduated from pre-service training programmes since then. If there had been sustained effort to raise awareness of this curriculum among those affected by it (again, not only teachers but also, in this case, especially teacher educators) and to provide appropriate support over time to teacher educators working on pre-service programmes, one might by now expect to see a minority of classroom teachers able to implement a recognisable version of what the curriculum hoped for in classrooms. However, national planners and policy makers do not seem to have made any medium- to long-term effort to support the change from the top, in terms of providing guidance or material support to encourage the institutions responsible for training English teachers to adjust their pre-service programmes to better enable their graduates to implement the curriculum in classrooms.

Communication between the various levels of the education system seems very poor. There is little evidence of effort to disseminate information and raise awareness about the new curriculum, or to provide practical support for its implementation at any level of the education system. The teacher training institution level seems to be oblivious to what the new national curriculum expects and so makes little or no attempt to link the courses that it teaches for trainee English teachers to the principles and practices that the curriculum embodies. At school level neither heads nor existing teachers in the schools studied seemed to have any real understanding of what the curriculum expects of them or of how to operationalise 'communicative, integrated methodology' in secondary English classrooms. Overall, therefore the schools studied suggested that there was little sense of the national curriculum affecting what actually happened in classrooms.

The need to acknowledge that implementation will never be uniform

Given what was said above, there seems to have been no real commitment to curriculum implementation outcomes in any settings. As in the previous case, in so far as anything was being consistently implemented in the classrooms studied it was mostly those teaching and learning techniques and activities that reflect the content, formats and weighting of the high stakes English tests which influence children's academic and professional futures. Again, therefore, English language teaching in the schools studied took place in a more or less uniform manner and – rather than reflecting the teaching behaviours and activities that the curriculum recommended – it reflected the language demands of the high stakes tests.

The need for the whole system to be consistent

It is difficult to imagine how this particular system could be much less consistent. As noted above, lines of communication between the various 'power centres' – in particular the Ministry of Education and the national body responsible for high stakes tests – seem very poor. The same is true for communications between the Ministry and the universities responsible for pre-service teacher education, within the universities between the different departments responsible for teaching the English teacher education syllabus and between these universities and the schools that they send their trainees to. While there may be context-specific political and cultural reasons for this comprehensive failure to communicate, the consequences are clearly very unhelpful for any attempt to introduce English-related educational initiatives.

The financial and human resources that are being invested in national 'English language education for everyone' are clearly not being used effectively. At national level, the lack of communication between Ministry and testing authority result in the hoped-for outcomes of the Ministry's curriculum apparently being ignored in favour of the outcomes required by high stakes tests. At university level, the efforts being made by staff and students over the four-year English teacher training course are not actually preparing novice teachers to teach the national curriculum. Meanwhile, at school level, the confusion among serving teachers again means that new teachers have no examples of how to teach the integrated 'communicative' curriculum available. Learners therefore find themselves in classrooms where their teachers do not really know why they are doing what they are doing, and so seek support from the only seemingly stable element within the system as a whole, the high stakes tests.

So what?

If policy makers in developing countries continue to believe that, despite the complexity of the process, the development of citizens' ability to use English, through the introduction of culturally challenging teaching approaches remains a suitable goal for national education systems, then I feel that in the case study contexts the factors highlighted in the educational change literature all seem relevant and these are discussed below.

The need for sustained effort

We need to face up to the fact that ELT education initiatives designed to enable the majority of citizens to develop an ability to use English will take a very long time to yield visible results. This will be especially so if such initiatives hope to introduce new more interactive English teaching-learning behaviours and activities into schools without introducing similar changes in the teaching of other school subjects. Active leadership at the national level will be needed throughout the extended planning and implementation timeline, particularly during the initial planning stages, to identify potential inconsistencies within the education system and to plan how to minimise the extent to which these may hinder implementation. To be able to identify possible inconsistencies effectively, national planners anywhere need to be willing and able to be honest about the 'baseline' from which the initiative is beginning. For reasons that include politics and (misplaced) pride, such honesty seems rare everywhere.

For practical and contextual reasons, detailed implementation plans for different parts of the country or different types of school will almost certainly need to be delegated to education professionals of various kinds at other levels of the system. However, sustained active national leadership will continue to be needed, for several years at least, to retain an overview of how the system is responding to the initiative and to consider and co-ordinate responses to what is learned from the monitoring of local implementation processes. Without sustained national and local leadership it will be impossible to establish and maintain consistency.

Implementation does not take place in a uniform manner

In terms of classroom implementation, this factor did not at first seem an explicit issue in these cases. This is probably because, as reported, policy makers provided only very limited detail of what they wished to see happening in the young learner or communicative-integrated English classroom. If this was a conscious decision on their part, it suggests that they understood that uniform implementation would be impossible in their very varied countries. However, their approach to implementation support suggests that such consciousness was not likely. While no 'template' for uniform classroom implementation existed, the support that was provided was uniform, and made no reference to teachers' (or trainee teachers') contextual realities. In these cases, it was thus the inappropriacy and uniformity of implementation support, rather than some stated desire to see certain things happening in every classroom, that contributed greatly to the limited curriculum implementation.

The need for the system to be consistent

Changes to any national state education system directly and indirectly affect a majority of any national population to differing extents. In addition there are a number of components within any subject micro-system. A key issue for national leaders and planners from the very beginning of the process is to decide what can be done to ensure that as many of the people and subject components as possible are sending broadly consistent, broadly supportive, 'messages' to classroom implementers over time. If messages are seriously inconsistent (as in both the above cases) there will be little encouragement for the implementers to sustain their efforts to make the challenging professional changes that most current ELT initiatives entail.

Credible reports of cases in which national state education ELT change initiatives are successfully enabling the majority of learners to develop a degree of English proficiency are rare. Given the massive scale of the human and financial investment that continues to be devoted to the teaching of English worldwide, the continued lack of such success cannot be considered acceptable.

Evidence that such proficiency (if eventually gained) does materially add to individual – and so to national – human capital in a manner that supports national development goals, is at present equally difficult to find. An eventual reaction to the current state of affairs might be to seriously question the extent to which the investment in English for Everyone makes a genuine contribution to 'global development'. This debate is just beginning.

References

Altinyelken H.K. 2010. *Pedagogical renewal in sub-Saharan Africa: The case of Uganda. Comparative Education* 46(2), 151–171.

Blackler, F. and Shinmin, S. 1984. *Applying Psychology in Organisations. London: Methuen.*

Brock-Utne, B. 2007. *Worldbankification of Norwegian development assistance to education. Comparative Education* 43(3), 433–449.

Blenkin, G.V., Edwards, G. and Kelly, A.V. 1992. *Recent and emergent theoretical perspectives.* In G.V.Blenkin, G.Edwards and A.V.Kelly, *Change and the Curriculum,* 39-68. London: Paul Chapman. (Reprinted as Perspectives on educational change. In A.Harris, N.Bennett and M.Preedy, 1997, *Organisational Effectiveness and Improvement in Education,* 216-230. *Buckingham: Open University Press.*)

Coleman, H. (ed.). 1996. *Society and the Language Classroom. Cambridge: Cambridge University Press.*

Coleman, H. 2010. *The English Language in Development. London: British Council.* Available online at *www.teachingenglish.org.uk/transform/books*

Cox, C. and Lemaitre, M.-J. 1999. *Market and state principles of reform in Chilean education: Policies and results.* In G. Perry and D.Leipziger (eds), *Chile: Recent Policy Lessons and Emerging Challenges*, 149-188. *Washington: World Bank Institute of Development Studies.*

De Segovia, L.P. and Hardison, D.M. 2009. *Implementing educational reform: EFL teachers' perspectives. English Language Teaching Journal* 63(2), 154-162.

Fullan, M.G. 2001. *The New Meaning of Educational Change. 3rd edition. New York: Columbia University Teachers College Press.*

Fullan, M.G. 2007. *The New Meaning of Educational Change. 4th edition. New York: Columbia University Teachers College Press.*

Holliday, A. and Cooke, T. 1982. *An ecological approach to ESP. In A.Waters (ed.), Issues in ESP,* 124-144. *Oxford: Pergamon Press.*

Holliday, A. 1994. *Appropriate Methodology and Social Context. Cambridge: Cambridge University Press.*

Hopkins, D. 1987. *Improving the Quality of Schooling. Lewes: Falmer Press.*

Keeley, B. 2007. *Human Capital: How What You Know Shapes Your Life. Paris: OECD Insights.*

Kennedy, C. 2011. *Challenges for language policy, language and development. Chapter 2, this volume.*

KIE (Kenya Institute of Education). 2002. *Secondary English Syllabus Volume 5. Revised edition. Nairobi: Kenya Literature Bureau.*

Leithwood, K., Jantzi, D. and Mascall, B. 2002. *A framework for research on Large-scale reform. Journal of Educational Change* 3, 7-33.

Levin, B. and Fullan, M.G. 2008. Learning about systems renewal. *Educational Management Administration and Leadership* 36(2), 289-303

Li, Z.F. 2010. *The effects of work contexts on former PETT trainers' application of teaching and training techniques learned from the programme: An exploratory study. Unpublished MA dissertation, University of Leeds.*

McGrath, S. 2010. *The role of education in development: An educationalist's response to some recent work in development economics. Comparative Education* 46(2), 237–253.

Ministry of Education. 2001. *National English Curriculum Standards for Nine-Year Compulsory Education and Senior High School Education. Nairobi: Ministry of Education, Kenya.*

Nunan, D. 2003. *The impact of English as a global language on educational policies and practices in the Asia-Pacific region. TESOL Quarterly* 37(4), 589-613.

Ongondo, C. 2009. *Pedagogical practice and support of English language student teachers during the practicum in Kenya. Unpublished PhD thesis, University of Leeds.*

Padwad, A. and Dixit, K. Forthcoming 2011. *Continuing professional development of English teachers in India: The ETCs experience. In M.Beaumont and T.Wright, The Experience of Second Language Teacher Education. Basingstoke: Palgrave.*

Pettigrew, A. and Whipp, R. 1991. *Managing Change for Competitive Success. Oxford: Blackwell.*

Polyzoi, E., Fullan, M.G. and Anchan, A.P. 2003. *Change Forces in Post communist Eastern Europe: Education in Transition. London: Routledge-Falmer.*

Shulman, L.S. 1987. *Knowledge and teaching: Foundations of the new reform. Harvard Educational Review* 57(1), 1-22.

Smotrova, T. 2009. *Globalisation and English language teaching in Ukraine. TESOL Quarterly* 43(4), 727-732.

Van Veen, K. and Sleegers, P. 2006. *How does it feel? Teachers' emotions in a context of change. Journal of Curriculum Studies* 38(1), 85–111.

Vavrus, F. 2009. *The cultural politics of constructivist pedagogies: Teacher education reform in the United Republic of Tanzania. International Journal of Educational Development* 29, 303–311.

Waters, A. and Vilches, M. 2008. *Education curriculum factors affecting ELT reforms: The case of the Philippines Basic Education Curriculum. RELC Journal* 39(1), 5-24.

Wedell, M. 2005. *Cascading training down into the classroom: The need for parallel planning. International Journal of Educational Development* 25(6), 637-651.

Wedell, M. 2008. *Developing a capacity to make 'English for Everyone' worthwhile: Reconsidering outcomes and how to start achieving them. International Journal of Educational Development* 28(6), 628-639.

Wedell, M. 2009. *Planning for Educational Change: Putting People and Their Contexts First. London: Continuum.*

Yu, W.H. and Hurst, R.M. 2004. *Primary English Teacher Training: Project Review. Guangzhou: British Council.*

Zeng, Y.H. 2005. *Unpublished MA assignment for module ED 5991 Approaches and Contexts in TESOL. Leeds: School of Education, University of Leeds.*

14

English as the language for development in Pakistan: Issues, challenges and possible solutions[1]

Fauzia Shamim

Introduction

English as the language for development has dominated the political and official discourse in Pakistan as in other developing countries for a long time now. More recently, the discourse of 'Education for All' and the increase in the use of English in the global market have added a universalistic dimension to the teaching-learning of English in Pakistan, thus making it a complex policy issue particularly for resource distribution and achieving quality in English language education. 'English is the passport to success and upward social mobility' and 'English is the key to national progress' are some common clichés that are interspersed in the formal discourse of official planning and policy meetings; more importantly, these clichés reflect the perception of many people – both rich and poor – in discussing future life chances for their children.

To begin with, it is important to clarify what is meant by 'development' and what are the espoused relationships between education, language and development.

Education, language and development

Chabbot and Ramirez (2004) emphasise the central role of international development organisations and conferences in rationalising a discourse that strongly links development and education for national and individual development goals. According to the United Nations' Millennium Development Goals (see Appendix 3), a major goal of education is poverty alleviation. However, recent studies emphasise the social, political and cultural aspects of development in addition to economic gains from development. The declaration of Education for All[2], signed by more than 150 nations, including Pakistan, reaffirmed the close link between education and development at the individual, national and global levels. In this context, a pertinent question asked by Brock-Utne is:

'Education for all – in whose language?' Brock-Utne argues, rightly in my view, that, 'The concept "education for all" becomes a completely empty concept if the linguistic environment of the basic learners is not taken into account' (2000:141). The complex relationship between language, power and the personal and its consequences is highlighted by Chambers, a development specialist. He asks:

> whose language and whose words count[?] In whose language do we – or are we – compelled or induced to co-ordinate our behaviour? And in whose language do we together bring forth our world? *(2007:155)*

As English is now widely recognised as a lingua franca or a 'world language', it seems pertinent to examine the relationship between English and development. In a report commissioned by the British Council, Coleman (2010a) has tried to tease out this relationship using examples from language and development conferences held in different parts of Asia and Africa since 1993. He concludes that English plays many roles in development, including:

- increasing individuals' employability

- enabling international collaboration and co-operation

- providing access to research and information

- facilitating the international mobility of students, tourists, workers and others

- facilitating disaster relief and disaster preparedness

- acting as an impartial language in contexts of disharmony. (Coleman 2010a:15)

Therefore, unsurprisingly, English is considered by donor agencies as the de facto language for development in developing countries. Often a lot of aid money is spent on improving the English proficiency of people and communities in the recipient nation states before or alongside other development work, particularly in the field of education. The aim, ostensibly, is to improve the effectiveness of teaching – and therefore the overall quality of education – in non-native English speaker contexts. Examples include the ten-year English Language Teaching Support programme for Tanzanian secondary school teachers, funded by the British Council through the former Overseas Development Administration (now the Department for International Development) (Arthur 2001) and the English Language Improvement Programme for Ethiopian teachers of English and other subjects, also funded by an international donor agency (Siraj et al. 2007).

Different kinds of relationship exist between language and development. Appleby et al. (2002:327-328) identify at least four kinds:

- language in development, where English is viewed as playing an essential role in the socio-economic development of the country

- language as development, with English being taught 'as an end in itself'

- language for development, where 'English is used as a tool for other domains of development'

- language of development, 'the discourses that construct the ways in which development happens'.[3]

In Pakistan, English is viewed mainly as the language for development at both the individual and national levels. Indeed, the race for individual prosperity and economic development at the national level seem to have overtaken issues of class, identity and fear of cultural invasion from an erstwhile colonial language.

The purpose of this chapter is to critically analyse the need and current provision for the teaching-learning of English for individual and national development in Pakistan. First, I look briefly at the factors that have led to the current insatiable desire for English in Pakistan. Second, the findings of a nationwide study of the current situation regarding the teaching-learning of English in public sector universities in Pakistan are reported so as to initiate discussion on the adequacy or otherwise of provisions for the teaching-learning of English in Pakistan; Marsh's (2005) framework of 'drivers' and 'enablers' is used for this purpose. Next, I briefly examine issues and challenges in the teaching-learning of English, such as the possible consequences of current language policy on the literacy level of children in English and other languages (including Urdu, the national language of Pakistan). Additionally, the case of a donor-funded project for teaching-learning of English at a professional university is used to illustrate the issues in 'external' projects for enhancing students' English language skills in public sector institutions, in particular.[4] Finally, policy implications are drawn for developing well informed and thus more realistic language-in-education policies in Pakistan. As the demand for English and the educational provision in several other developing contexts are similar to those in Pakistan, it is hoped that the study findings and the resultant policy recommendations will be of benefit to language-in-development workers in such contexts.

Drivers: Need for English in Pakistan

In Pakistan there has been a lack of systematic analysis, debate and dialogue about the need for English. With the national literacy level being low,[5] folklore about when children learn foreign languages best and dreams of a bright future with English for their children often influence the average person's thinking and expressed desire for the teaching-learning of English from early grades. This section critically reviews the major drivers for this felt need for English in an attempt to distil the main arguments for the need of English in Pakistan.

Political gains

Pakistan is a multilingual and multicultural society. The linguistic map of Pakistan is quite complex with many languages; each of the four provinces has one or more dominant languages and a number of minority languages. The emblematic status of English, due to its historical association with the elite and proto-elite (Haque 1983, Rahman 1998, 2002), has helped in making it a prestigious language. English is the language of power in comparison with Urdu, the national language, and other regional languages of Pakistan (Rassool and Mansoor 2009). Each new government soon after it assumes power announces its policy of teaching English to the masses as a way of achieving its democratic ideals of equality of opportunity. As this decision is politically motivated, it comes as no surprise that implementation efforts fall short of the supposedly democratic intent of the policy. This official rhetoric of providing 'equal' opportunities for learning of English as a potential tool to level differences among the social classes, without a study of current provision and teachers' ability to teach English effectively, does not match the overall 'two stream' education policy in Pakistan. (We will consider the 'two-stream' policy in detail later in this chapter.) Thus the teaching of English stays as a live issue on the agenda of every successive government (also see Shamim 2008).

Economic gains

Jalal (2004:24), a former education minister, argues:

> When we subscribe to the experts' view that the economic future of Pakistan is linked with the expansion of information technology, it means that we are recognising the need for making the comprehension and use of English as widespread as possible. This is now an urgent public requirement, and the government takes it as its duty to fulfil this requirement.

This view has resulted in the English for All policy, where once again the government has instructed all public sector schools to start teaching English from class I without working out the feasibility of this policy decision or the steps and resources required for its successful implementation (Government of Pakistan 2009). In contrast, the Higher Education Commission's English Language Teaching (ELT) Reform Project aims to improve the teaching-learning of English in higher education institutions in Pakistan. Through improvement in the teaching-learning of English, the project aims to revolutionise 'the socio-economic indicators of Pakistan' and 'contribute considerably to supplement the efforts of government to improve the standard of higher education and scientific learning'. More specifically, improving the teaching and learning of English 'will help the graduates of public sector universities and institutions of higher learning to compete for good jobs in Pakistan'.[6]

Advancement in learning English is unequivocally linked to technological development, particularly in the field of information and communication technology (ICT). However, the main argument revolves around learning English for long-term economic gains. The official viewpoint resonates with the current discourse of promoting education for poverty alleviation, a discourse initiated by development agencies and also embodied in the Millennium Development Goals. The majority of people in Pakistan also subscribe to the view that English is the tool for individual and national economic prosperity. These beliefs are in sharp contrast with the arguments put forward for using the mother tongue for economic development, particularly in rural communities in developing countries (e.g. Bruthiaux 2002, UNESCO 2005).

Two streams of education

In Pakistan, there are two distinct systems of education identified mainly in terms of medium of instruction, i.e. English medium and Urdu medium. The English medium schools are privately owned and cater to the upper class as well as some sections of the middle class. In contrast, the Urdu medium schools are mainly public sector schools catering to the lower income groups and they offer free education in addition to other incentives such as free textbooks (at least at the primary level). Private schools offer 'quality' education to elite children in highly resourced classrooms through the medium of English. The outcomes for these children, who also have acquisition-rich home environments, are higher levels of proficiency in English compared to those children studying in poorly resourced classrooms who have little or no exposure to English outside the 30–35-minute English class every day in school.

Thus the two kinds of school systems, public and private, are distinguishable by their quality of standards and learner achievement, particularly in terms of the their ability to use English for oral and written communication. With the level of proficiency in English being a major indicator of social class, quality of educational standards and learning outcomes, it is not surprising that for many people there is a fuzzy boundary between being educated and knowing English (see also Ramanathan 2005). Thus, the aspiration of most parents is to provide English medium education for their children to improve their future life chances.[7]

The huge promise of English as a 'world language' for economic and personal development seems to be a major driving force for the younger generation's desire to learn English in Pakistan. Literacy in English is considered a prerequisite, similar to ICT skills, for participating in the current trend of globalisation and becoming part of the global village. For example, Rahman (1999), in his survey of student attitudes towards English in different school types in Pakistan, found that the desire to learn English occurred among students from all school types including the deeni madrassah (religious schools) which represent the most conservative element of Pakistani society. Similarly, Mansoor's case study of language planning in higher education in Pakistan (2005) provided further evidence of an overwhelming 'need' for learning English among Pakistani students in tertiary education.

It should be noted that the existing proficiency level in English of school and university graduates does not match this popular demand for English in Pakistan. This raises an important question: Is the current provision for the teaching-learning of English adequate to meet this growing demand for English in education in Pakistan.[8] This issue is explored in the following section.

Enablers: A study of the current provision for the teaching-learning of English in higher education in Pakistan

As we saw above, there exists in Pakistan an insatiable desire to learn English for individual and national development. How can the goal of English for All be achieved? To what extent is the current provision for the teaching-learning of English sufficient for the masses to learn English (which is often their third or fourth language)? In this section, I will report the findings of a research study commissioned by the National Committee on English and funded by the Higher Education Commission as part of its ELT reform project.[9]

The objectives of the study were two-fold:

a) to review and evaluate the English language teaching capacity of a national sample of general and professional universities in Pakistan; and

b) to make recommendations for the reorganisation of English language teaching departments in public sector institutions of higher education.

A two-stage research design was used. In the first stage, a survey of the current provision for the teaching-learning of English was conducted in a nationwide sample of public sector universities. In the second stage, case studies were conducted of three selected institutions to understand, in depth, how the current organisation of English language teaching impacts on a) the allocation and utilisation of resources for teaching English, and b) teaching, learning and assessment practices for English in these institutions. This chapter reports the results of the nationwide survey and one case study of a donor-funded ELT centre established at a professional university in the province of Sindh.

The sample for the survey comprised 21 public sector universities located in various regions of Pakistan. Overall, 3,552 learners in these universities responded to a questionnaire that was administered to them on a cohort basis in English classes that were selected using pre-defined criteria. A total of 84 teachers also responded to the teachers' version of the same questionnaire. The aim was to get both student and teacher perspectives on various aspects of the teaching-learning of English in the sample institutions. In addition, the Head of Department in each university was interviewed using a structured interview schedule. The data from the general universities was analysed separately from that of the professional universities, for comparative purposes.

Major findings of the study are discussed in the following paragraphs.

Socio-economic profile

The socio-economic profile of teachers and learners in both the general and the professional universities is largely similar. The majority of teachers do not have formal qualifications or training in English language teaching. Few teachers engage in ongoing professional development activities or dialogue with the wider ELT community through membership of teachers' organisations or by presenting papers at ELT conferences at home and abroad. Fewer than one quarter of the teachers in the sample had one or more publications in the field.

English language programmes

English language courses are offered mainly at the undergraduate level but there are also some courses in postgraduate programmes in certain departments such as Business and Management Sciences. In the general universities, the undergraduate English programmes are normally managed by the Department of English in each institution. However, visiting teachers are hired to teach English, since the core business of the English departments is perceived to be the teaching of English literature and/or Linguistics to English majors. There is usually a prescribed syllabus for teaching English at the undergraduate level. In the professional universities and in the postgraduate departments offering English language programmes in the general universities, where there are no core English teaching lecturers, the English language programme is managed by the department concerned or by the department or faculty of Social Sciences, if there is one. In such cases, teachers design the curriculum for the English courses themselves. The assessment practices in all cases focus on assessing content knowledge such as 'major barriers to communication' or 'characteristics of a good paragraph' instead of language skills.

Educational resources

In terms of physical provision, the findings of the study indicate that the majority of learners study English sitting in rows in large classes. The normal duration of the English programme is 48 hours or one semester during the first year of their study programme. Very little use is made of educational technology, even where it is available in the institution. Students are given few opportunities to develop academic literacy since teaching and learning focuses mainly on getting good grades in the content-based examination. Additionally, there are few expectations that learners will use English in the classroom. Similarly, there is only a low level of feedback, both oral and written, on assigned written work. Thus opportunities for learning English to the high levels of proficiency required both for higher education and professional work are quite limited. It is not surprising, then, that there is a general sense of dissatisfaction with the current level of English proficiency of the graduates of public sector universities.

Teachers' and learners assessment of the current programmes

Surprisingly, we found that the majority of learners rated their current English language courses highly in terms of meeting their future needs. Similarly, more than 50 per cent of teachers agreed or strongly agreed that the current English language courses would help students in meeting future needs. This apparently optimistic picture could be the result of two things: a) teachers' and learners' limited experience of alternative pedagogies and assessment practices and b) a focus on gaining high grades in English as short-term goals for success in their respective educational programmes.

Unequal inputs, unequal outputs

A comparison of learners' socio-economic status with their English language scores in the most recent public examination revealed that learners in the higher income bracket (upper third of the population) consistently outperformed learners in the lower income bracket (lower two-thirds of the population). The positive correlation of high family income with students' higher levels of proficiency in English, as seen in Figure 1, may be attributed to their earlier education in private English medium schools compared to students in the lower income bracket (also see Rassool and Mansoor 2009). (The two streams of education in Pakistan have already been discussed above.)

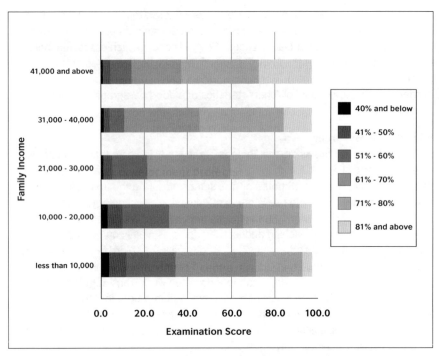

Figure 1: Students' family income (in Pakistani rupees) and proficiency in English (most recent public examination scores) adapted from Shamim and Tribble 2005

Similarly, in students' assessment of their current language skills, as used in the academic domain, the upper group was about twice as heavily represented in the categories of 'good' and 'excellent' compared to the lower third of the population. Hence, there seems to be a positive relationship between students' socio-economic status and their proficiency in English, probably due to the difference in opportunities available outside the classroom in the home and community for learning and using English. This indicates the urgent need for developing relevant and high quality English language programmes for learners in public sector universities to enable them to compete with their more fortunate counterparts.

It was concluded that the need to provide enhanced teaching-learning facilities in public sector universities cannot be over-emphasised, particularly in terms of the huge demand for English in the employment market (Mansoor et al. 2005) and the relatively low levels of proficiency of graduates from public sector higher education institutions in Pakistan.

In public sector schools, English is mainly taught using the grammar-translation method through Urdu and/or the local language in crowded and under-resourced classrooms. In private schools, while English is 'officially' the medium of instruction, bilingual discourse is commonly used in the classroom (Shamim and Allen 2000; see also Cleghorn and Rollnick 2002 for similar findings from African classrooms). However, as the use of one or more shared home languages is not legitimised, the teachers do not admit to using them in the classroom.

Issues and challenges

Three main issues can be identified: the quality of education, the tension between local and global needs and the 'language apartheid' which Pakistan is experiencing. Additionally, there is the issue of sustainability and therefore long-term impact of donor-funded projects. Each of these issues will be discussed briefly in this section.

Quality and standards of achievement

English medium education is widely assumed to be synonymous with high quality education. Is it, therefore, surprising that parents prefer an English medium education for their children? This can be seen in the proliferation of private English medium schools even in the remote areas of Pakistan.

As mentioned earlier, the decision to start teaching English from grade I is taken by all elected governments soon after they come into power as a political gesture rather than as an expression of their political will to provide opportunities for gaining widespread literacy in English (Shamim 2008). This decision is taken without any feasibility study or a well-researched and coherent implementation plan. The most recent Education Policy (Government of Pakistan 2009) also recommends the teaching of English as a subject from grade I and use of English as the medium of instruction for Science and Mathematics from class IV onwards. However, as Coleman (2010b) points out, there is lack of clarity about several aspects of this policy. Coleman also notes that there are some internal contradictions in the policy documents; for example, the policy directive of using English for Science and Mathematics from classes IV and V is at odds with earlier statements about schools choosing any language as medium of instruction between classes I and V.

Unsurprisingly, there is an ever widening gap between the 'unwritten' language policy and practice of the teaching-learning of English in Pakistan. This has led to a situation whereby the majority of school and university graduates from public sector institutions enter the job market with only limited literacy skills in English.

Tension between local and global needs

Language is a marker of identity and a tool for representing local values and culture. On the one hand, the right to study one's own language is now considered a basic human right (cf. Segota 2001). On the other hand, there is an urgent-felt need, particularly among the younger generation, to identify with the global world culture. Universities in Pakistan are also faced with the challenge of achieving internationally recognised academic excellence and status, mainly through the medium of English, while at the same time serving the needs of the local population.

The patterns of language use in society point to the use of Urdu as the lingua franca in Pakistan. Urdu is used by most people in rural contexts mainly in addition to their local language. Similarly, while English is used for official written documentation and communication, Urdu and/or the local languages are mainly used for oral interaction in government offices. In the cities, only a small part of the population, the educated elite, use English (or English and an indigenous language) for their everyday communication. The challenge is to maintain an appropriate balance in the choice of language-in-education among individual, societal and national development needs.

A state of language apartheid

In Pakistan, familiarity with and use of English are indicators of social class and educational and family background. For example, the terms 'Urdu medium' and 'English medium' in Pakistan are heavily loaded with economic and socio-cultural connotations. Hence their use denotes more than just the medium of instruction through which a person has studied in school or in an institution of higher education. In fact, a person with an 'English medium' education is considered superior in all dimensions compared to someone with an Urdu medium educational background. Thus we seem to be moving towards a state of language apartheid.

Sustainability of ELT development projects[10]

Kenny and Savage (1997:5) define development activities in development contexts such as countries in South East Asia or Sub-Saharan Africa, as the 'burden' of donor nations, where 'taxes paid by the citizens of donor countries are channelled to recipient countries as foreign aid through either multilateral organisations or national agencies, ending up as the financing of development projects'. However, the case study of a donor-funded ELT centre, established in the early 1980s at a professional public sector university in Pakistan's province of Sindh, indicates that such development projects are often not sustainable and, therefore, cannot have a long-term impact on the development of English language skills of the peoples of recipient nations.

This five-year development project aimed to enhance the English language skills of engineering students through setting up an ELT Centre at a public sector university in Pakistan. Project funding included staff and counterpart development through training courses in the UK, the provision of resources such as books and equipment and the development of learning materials and a self-access centre. The Centre was given a building by the university authorities; this was refurbished using project funds. More important, unlike other university departments, the Centre, as a donor-funded project, had financial independence with its own bank account. This greatly facilitated the work of the project and initial success was reported in several reports and studies (e.g. Ilyas 1992, Bamber 1994). However, a few years after the exit of the project (i.e. at the time of the study), the Centre presented a state of neglect and deprivation. The faculty interviewed showed low morale and uncertainty about the future of the Centre as other University departments vied for the space which had been allocated earlier to the Centre.

Why did the Centre, which seemed to flourish well during the life of the project, reach this state after its exit? If the ELT Centre was able to provide effective teaching-learning of English to the students, why could these gains not be sustained? Two issues seem to be at work here.

First, the Centre, as a development project, had been set up outside the organisational and financial structure and governance mechanisms of the university. Hence, soon after the donor agency left the ELT Centre – which was neither a department nor a centre of excellence (the two recognisable organisational units in the university) – it was bereft of support from the relevant authorities. For example, there were no funds for repair of equipment and/or its replacement and the expansion of library resources. Also, when new computers were given to all the departments, the Centre did not get its share.

Second, and more importantly, interviews with senior management of the university revealed a lack of sense of ownership of the Centre; it was described as an external project that had had its life. More important, the Centre with its limited staff and outdated resources was clearly seen as being unable to meet the growing and changing needs of its clientele. Hence, the earlier system of teachers going to different departments to teach English was revived. The university administration refused to heed the teachers' request for smaller classes for the teaching of English. Moreover, at the time the study was being carried out, the classrooms which had been given to the Centre were in the process of being appropriated by different departments.

A major lesson learnt is that there is an urgent need – in the planning of English language teaching projects – for considering 'maintenance strategies' (for example, negotiating and establishing a place in institutional hierarchies and budgetary allocation for downstream and development costs for continuous improvement) in addition to 'development strategies' (focusing on capacity building of human resources and/or the development of learning materials and resources). This is in addition to what Holliday (1996) refers to as 'means analysis' for the success of development projects. Otherwise, the efforts invested in these projects are likely to go to waste.

The challenges faced by language planners, policy makers and practitioners in Pakistan are many. These include:

- Achieving quality in education for all, irrespective of the medium of education

- Balancing language needs and provision for the teaching-learning of English and other languages for local, national and global use

- Combating linguistically defined social stratification and

- Ensuring sustainability and continuous improvement after the project ends.

We must remember that Pakistan is not alone in facing these challenges. These and similar challenges abound in the majority of African countries and many other countries in Asia (see, for example, Vavrus 2002, Brock-Utne et al. 2003, Mansoor et al. 2004, Rasool 2009, Seargeant and Erling 2011, Chapter 12 this volume, and Wedell 2011, Chapter 13 this volume). In the next section, I will take a brief look at how some nations of the world have tried to address these challenges.

Multilingualism

A current trend identifiable in policy documents in many countries seems to be that of multilingualism. Multilingualism is espoused as the preferred approach to language policy-making for recognising and celebrating linguistic diversity and for intercultural communication. For example, in India the need for the three-language formula of state, national and international language has once again been reiterated by the National Focus Group on Indian languages (NCERT 2005).

Similarly, there is a growing awareness, among the more recently established Central Asian states such as Kyrgyzstan, of the need for multilingual education for increased interethnic understanding (Korth and Schulter n.d.). This is in sharp contrast to the policy of having just one national language as a marker of unity and nationhood, prevalent among nations in South Asia and Africa during the early years of their independence.

UNESCO's position paper titled 'Education in a multilingual world' (2003) urges a change in attitudes towards multilingualism as it is a reality in many nations of the world. At the same time, the paper highlights the complexities involved in imparting education through multiple languages:

> Education in many countries of the world takes place in multilingual contexts. [In these countries] multilingualism is more a way of life than a problem to be solved. The challenge is for education systems to adapt to these complex realities and provide a quality education which takes into consideration learners' needs, while balancing these at the same time with social, cultural and political demands.
> **(UNESCO 2003:12)**

Interestingly, even in Europe, during the last two decades, efforts to facilitate trade, travel and interaction among the nations within the European Community have led to the development of policy guidelines favouring plurilingualism (differentiated from multilingualism mainly in terms of its broader view of the purposes of learning more than one language). The aim of language education, according to this view, is no longer to:

> achieve mastery of one, two or even three languages, each taken in isolation, with the 'ideal native-speaker' model. Instead the aim is to develop a linguistic repertory in which all linguistic abilities have a place. This implies, of course, that the languages offered in educational institutions should be diversified and students given the opportunity to develop a 'plurilingual competence'.
> **(Council of Europe 2001:5).**

We would do well to remember that English is the language of instruction in only three European states: the United Kingdom, Ireland and Malta.[11] And even in these countries the indigenous languages of Welsh, Gaelic, Irish and Maltese are also used as languages of instruction.[12]

Policy implications

This analysis of drivers and enablers for the teaching-learning of English in Pakistan, on the one hand, highlights current perceptions about the role and status of English in individual and national development in developing countries. On the other, it gives rise to two important questions for consideration by language planners and policy makers:

1. Is English here to stay? If yes, how can we, in developing country contexts, strategically plan for managing English for All with limited resources?

2. In order to achieve our goal of Education for All, whose language should be selected and for whose development?

The first question is a simple one addressing the pragmatics of the current situation as it exists in many developing countries of the world. That is to say, the need for English is far beyond the current resources available for the teaching and learning of the language. If we agree, through debate and discussion at local and national levels, that literacy in English is vital for individual and national development, then it must have high priority on the list of educational reforms for any government. In fact, a growing trend is to go beyond the basic question of whether to teach or not to teach English. The preferred question now seems to be whether all subjects should be taught through the medium of English.[13]

Content and Language Integrated Learning (CLIL) and the use of English have moved from experimental research to the centre of global education. As pressure grows on governments and education planners to raise English language levels, the promise of teaching the language while teaching other subjects is hard to resist. However, at the same time we need to consider whether CLIL is a Trojan horse which will drive English 'ever deeper into the heart of national education systems', as one of the participants in the Guardian-Macmillan debate wondered.

At the beginning of the chapter we noted that Brock-Utne, a leading advocate of education through indigenous languages in African countries, asks, 'Education for all – in whose language?' She also asks (in the title of a chapter in Brock-Utne 2000), 'Whose language and for whose development?' In this way, she challenges the view that English should be used as a medium of instruction particularly in early years. Accordingly, she raises issues of learning and intellectual dependency through the use of English in education in Africa and other developing countries. Several educators have voiced their concerns about using English as the medium of instruction in post-colonial contexts in Asia and Africa. In particular, they urge us to consider carefully the effects on personal and national development of using the former colonial languages in education:

> As long as African countries continue to educate the continent's future leaders primarily through foreign languages, they will remain dependent. Education for liberation and self reliance must begin with the use of languages that do not impede the acquisition of knowledge. This is a challenge for the 21st century.
> **(Roy-Campbell 1998 cited in Brock-Utne 2000:173)**

Similarly, Fanfunwa (1990 cited in Brock-Utne 2000:153), questioning the use of an imposed foreign language for communication instead of a 'familiar' language, postulates a relationship between underdevelopment and the use of a foreign language as the official language of a given country. Though there is no research evidence to substantiate his claim, the relationship between language and development is certainly worthy of attention from linguists and researchers in the field. (See also Williams 2011, Chapter 3 this volume.)

A careful consideration of these two questions tells us that it is neither politically correct nor possible for education systems dependent on large amounts of money from international donor agencies in developing countries such as Pakistan to reverse the current trend of promoting literacy in English, similar to literacy in ICT skills, for development. As long as English remains the dominant language of power, a gate-keeper to higher level jobs and a 'window to the world of opportunities' at home and abroad, all the research evidence in the world will not convince parents of the usefulness of imparting education to their children in the mother tongue. A more pragmatic approach to addressing the growing state of language apartheid between English medium and Urdu medium education in Pakistan would be to develop bilingual programmes for achieving proficiency in both English and Urdu. A second step should be to strive for a balance between felt needs and available provision for the teaching-learning of English based on research evidence. Finally, debate and dialogue should be initiated with the involvement of linguists, policy-makers, practitioners and the public media on language rights and the relationship between language and development, with the aim of working towards a practicable language policy for individual and national development.

Conclusion

I would like to conclude with two questions that I hope will be taken up for discussion elsewhere.

1. Do we, in developing country contexts, really have the right to choose our own language for development? If not, how can people in developing country contexts be enabled to choose one or more languages for individual, societal and national development?

2. How can coherence be achieved between language policy and its implementation in developing countries?

The first question seeks to initiate a debate on linguistic rights in developing countries and indicates the need for empowerment in determining the choice of language for development. Linguistic rights, or more specific to this discussion, the right to the choice of language for education is meaningless and turns into a symbolic act if there is lack of coherence between the language policy and its implementation plan, as is illustrated by Taylor (2002) through his review of language-in-education programmes in Estonia and Africa. The second question, therefore, aims to remind us – language planners, policy makers, linguists and practitioners – of our responsibility to take up the challenge of drafting viable language polices and workable implementation plans for language-in-education programmes that aim to promote individual, societal and national development.

Notes

1. An early version of this chapter was presented at the 7th International Language and Development Conference in Addis Ababa in October 2005 and published in the Proceedings of that conference (Shamim 2007a).

2. For an overview of the Education for All movement and links to the text of the Education for All Declaration (Jomtien, Thailand, 1990) and subsequent documents see the UNESCO Education for All website at *www.unesco.org/education/efa/ed_for_all/*.

3. See Pennycook (1999) for a similar discussion of language in relation to development.

4. This was a follow-up study focusing on selected cases identified for in-depth examination in the earlier study (Shamim and Tribble 2005). The author was the principal investigator for this study.

5. The adult literacy rate in Pakistan is 57 per cent, according to the Economic Survey of Pakistan (Farooq 2010:145). For other key development indicators relating to Pakistan, see Appendix 2 below.

6. This information was retrieved from the Higher Education Commission website at *www.hec.gov.pk* on 12 July 2005 is but no longer available at that location. Details about the second phase of the ELTR are available at the same website.

7. In response to this popular demand for English, the number of so-called 'English medium' schools has mushroomed, even in the rural areas of Pakistan (Harlech-Jones et al. 2005). Parents prefer to send their children to these private schools, which do not offer high quality education, in the hope that their children will learn English. Literacy in English and the ability to interact confidently in the language are perceived to have more value than, for example, learning basic concepts in Mathematics and Science.

8. We need to remember that higher education in Pakistan, particularly in public sector institutions, is considered to be a right for everyone, not a privilege for the selected few.

9. For details see Shamim and Tribble 2005.

10. This section is based on a case study reported in Shamim 2006 and discussed further in Shamim 2007b.

11. 'Languages of instruction throughout the world: Europe.' Available at *www.unesco.org/education/languages/europ.pdf*

12. Phillipson (2009) claims that English is no longer a foreign language in Europe. While, according to him, all 'domestic functions' are carried out in the 'key' national languages, the massive influx of Hollywood and other American entertainment products as well as the requirement for English in higher education and employment in many countries have strengthened the position of English in Europe in recent years.

13. This is reflected in a 2005 debate sponsored by the *Guardian*, a leading UK newspaper, and Macmillan Education, a major UK and international publishing house; see *www.guardian.co.uk/guardianweekly/story/0,12674,1395532,00.html*

References

Appleby, R., Copley, K., Sithirajvongsa, S. and Pennycook, A. 2002. **Language in development constrained: Three contexts. TESOL Quarterly** 39(3), 323-346.

Arthur, J. 2001. **Perspectives on educational language policy and its implementation in African classrooms: A comparative study of Botswana and Tanzania. Compare** 31(3), 347-362.

Bamber, B. 1994. *Project evaluation report of the English Language Centre. Karachi: The British Council.*

Brock-Utne, B. 2000. *Whose Education for All? The Recolonisation of the African Mind. London: Falmer Press.*

Brock-Utne, B., Desai, Z. and Qonno, M. (eds). 2003. *Language of Instruction in Tanzania and South Africa. Dar es Salaam: E. and D. Ltd.*

Bruthiaux, P. 2002. *Hold your courses: Language education, language choice and economic development. TESOL Quarterly* 36(3), 275-296.

Chabbot, C. and Ramirez, F.O. 2004. *Development and education. In J.H.Ballantine and J.Z.Spade (eds.), Schools and Society,* 427-438. 2nd edition. *Belmont, CA: Thomson Wadsworth.*

Chambers, R. 2007. *Words, power and the personal in development. In H.Coleman (ed.), Language and Development: Africa and Beyond: Proceedings of the 7th International Language and Development Conference,* 155-168. *Addis Ababa: The British Council.* Available online at *www.langdevconferences.org*

Cleghorn, A. and Rollnick, M. 2002. *The role of English in individual and societal development: A view from African classrooms. TESOL Quarterly* 36(3), 347-372.

Coleman, H. 2010a. *The English Language in Development. London: British Council.* Available online at *www.teachingenglish.org.uk/transform/books.*

Coleman, H. 2010b. *Teaching and Learning in Pakistan: The Role of Language in Education. Islamabad: British Council.*

Council of Europe. 2001. *Common European Framework of Reference for Language: Learning, Teaching, Assessment. Cambridge: Cambridge University Press.*

Fanfunwa, B.A. 1990. *Using national languages in education: A challenge to African educators. In UNESCO-UNICEF, African Thoughts on the Prospects of Education for All: Selections from Papers Commissioned for the Regional Consultation for Education for All, Dakar, 27-30 November,* 97-110. Paris : UNESCO.

Farooq, O. 2010. Education. *In Ministry of Finance, Pakistan Economic Survey 2009-2010,* 145-162. *Islamabad: Ministry of Finance.*

Government of Pakistan. 2009. *National Education Policy. Islamabad: Ministry of Education.*

Haque, R. 1983. *The position and status of English in Pakistan. World Language English* 2(1).

Harlech-Jones, B., Baig, M., Sajid, S. and ur-Rahman, S. 2005. *Private schooling in the Northern Areas of Pakistan: A decade of rapid expansion. International Journal of Educational Development* 25(5), 557-568.

Holliday. 1996. *Dealing with Tissue Rejection in EFL Projects: The Role of an Ethnographic Means Analysis. Unpublished PhD thesis, University of Lancaster, UK.*

Ilyas, R. 1992. *Case study on the evaluation of the English Language Centre. Unpublished MEd dissertation, School of Education, University of Leeds, UK.*

Jalal, Z. 2004. *Language policy in Pakistan. In S.Mansoor, S.Meraj and A.Tahir (eds), Language Planning, Policy and Practice: A South-Asian Perspective. Karachi: Aga Khan University and Oxford University Press.*

Kenny, B. and Savage, W. (eds.). 1997. *Language and Development: Teachers in a Changing World. Harlow and New York: Addison Wesley Longman.*

Korth, B. and Schulter, B. n.d. *Multilingual education for increased interethnic understanding in Kyrgyzstan. Geneva: CIMERA.* Available online at *www.cimera.ch/ files/biling/en/MLG_Text1.pdf*

Mansoor, S. 2005. *Language Planning in Higher Education: A Case Study. Karachi: Oxford University Press.*

Mansoor, S., Meraj, S. and Tahir, A. (eds). 2004. *Language Planning, Policy and Practice: A South-Asian Perspective. Karachi: Aga Khan University and Oxford University Press.*

Mansoor, S., Zafar, M., Hussain, N., Sikandar, A., Azam S.I. and Tatari, S.K. 2005. *English and employment in pakistan. Unpublished summary report. Karachi: Aga Khan University, Centre of English Language.*

Marsh, D. 2005. *Contribution to the debate 'Learning English or learning in English: Will we have a choice?' IATEFL Conference, Cardiff.* Available at *www.guardian.co.uk/guardianweekly/story/0,12674,1395532,00.html*

NCERT (National Centre for Educational Research and Training). 2005. *Position paper by national focus group on Indian language. New Delhi: NCERT.*

Pennycook, A. 1999. *Development, culture and language: Ethical concerns in a postcolonial world. In J.Shaw, D.Lubelska and M.Noullet (eds), Partnership and Interaction: Proceedings of the Fourth International Conference on Language and Development, Hanoi, Vietnam, October 13-15 1999, 3-22. Bangkok: Asian Institute of Technology.* Available at *www.languages.ait.ac.th/hanoi_proceedings/ pennycook.htm*

Phillipson, R. 2009. *Linguistic Imperialism Continued. Hyderabad, India: Orient BlackSwan.*

Rahman, T. 1998. *Language and Politcs in Pakistan. Karachi: Oxford University Press.*

Rahman, T. 1999. *Language, Education and Culture. Karachi: Oxford University Press.*

Rahman, T. 2002. *Language, Ideology and Power. Karachi: Oxford University Press.*

Ramanathan, V. 2005. *The English-Vernacular Divide: Postcolonial Language Politics and Practice. Clevedon: Multilingual Matters.*

Rassool, N. and Mansoor, S. 2009. *Contemporary issues in language, education and development in Pakistan. In N.Rasool (ed.), Global Issues in Language, Education and Development: Perspectives from Post-colonial Countrie,* 218-244. *New Delhi: Orient Longman.*

Roy-Campbell, Z.N. 1998. *Language as the repository of knowledge and culture: Deconstructing myths about African languages. Paper presented to the Comparative and International Education Society (CIES) annual meeting, Buffalo, New York,* 18-22 March.

Seargeant, P. and Erling, E.J. 2011. *The discourse of 'English as a language for international development': Policy assumptions and practical changes.* Chapter 12, this volume.

Segota, J. 2001. *Board of Directors reaffirms position on language rights. TESOL Matters* 6 February.

Shamim, F. 2006. Case studies of organisation of English language teaching in public-sector universities in Pakistan. Research report for the National Committee on English, Higher Education Commission, Islamabad, Pakistan.

Shamim, F. 2007a. *English as the language for development in Pakistan: Issues, challenges and possible solutions. In H.Coleman (ed.), Language and Development: Africa and Beyond: Proceedings of the 7th International Language and Development Conference,* 97-116. *Addis Ababa: The British Council.* Available at *www.langdevconferences.org*

Shamim, F. 2007b. *Sustainability of ESP projects: A case study from Pakistan. Paper presented at the IATEFL Conference,* Aberdeen, 19-22 April 2007.

Shamim, F. 2008. *Trends, issues and challenges in English language education in Pakistan. Asia Pacific Journal of Education* 28(3), 235-249.

Shamim, F. and Allen, P. 2000. *Activity types and patterns of interaction in language classrooms in Pakistan. Unpublished research report. Karachi: Institute for Educational Development, Aga Khan University.*

Shamim, F. and Tribble, C. 2005. *Current provision for English language teaching in higher education in Pakistan. Unpublished research report. Karachi: Institute for Educational Development, Aga Khan University.*

Siraj, A., Baraki, A. and Altshul, J. 2007. *Ethiopian teachers' evaluation of a language improvement programme.* In H.Coleman (ed.), *Language and Development: Africa and Beyond: Proceedings of the 7th International Language and Development Conference,* 155-168. *Addis Ababa: The British Council.* Available at *www.langdevconferences.org*

Taylor, S.G. 2002. *Multilingual societies and planned linguistic change: New language-in-education programmes in Estonia and South Africa. Comparative Education Review* 46(3), 313-338.

UNESCO (United Nations Educational, Scientific and Cultural Organisation). 2003. *Education in a multilingual world. Education Sector Position Paper. Paris: UNESCO.*

UNESCO (United Nations Educational, Scientific and Cultural Organisation). 2005. *First Language First: Community-Based Literacy Programmes for Minority Language Contexts in Asia. Bangkok: UNESCO.*

Vavrus, F. 2002. *Postcoloniality and English: Exploring language policy and politics of development in Tanzania. TESOL Quarterly* 36(3), 373-397.

Wedell, M. 2011. *More than just 'technology': English language teaching initiatives as complex educational changes.* Chapter 13, this volume.

Williams, E. 2011. *Language policy, politics and development in Africa.* Chapter 3, this volume.

English in
fragile contexts

15

English as a tool for conflict transformation[1]

Psyche Kennett

Introduction

Armed conflict remains the number one cause of poverty in developing countries. In the past decade the number of armed conflicts between countries has declined but the United Nations High Commissioner for Refugees claims in the annual Global Trends report for 2008 (UNHCR 2009) that the number of people affected by internal conflicts is at an all-time high. Ethnic, religious and territorial conflicts are tearing Gaza, Afghanistan, Pakistan, Sudan and Iraq apart (Robinson 2006). Social inequality and conflict over democracy affect countries like Sri Lanka, Burma, Iran and Tibet. Kosovo, Timor Leste, Nepal and even Northern Ireland have emerging post-conflict status but maintain a fragile peace punctuated by violent incidents. Global warming and the energy crisis exacerbate conflicts over resources – in Bolivia, South Africa and Ghana over water (OECD 2005); in Russia and Georgia over gas; in Iraq and most recently Peru, over oil. Hyperinflation and economic recession have created conflict in Somalia and Zimbabwe while the international financial crisis is forecast to feed conflict over unemployment in China and Russia (Hollerman 2008).

The war may be over in Sri Lanka but the issues behind the conflict remain unresolved. Language is one of them. In the aftermath of the fighting, victims of conflict, military authorities, civil servants and international relief agencies struggle to restore basic services and keep food distribution and de-mining on track. The soldiers do not speak Tamil, the refugees do not speak Sinhala and the doctors from Médecins Sans Frontières do not speak either language. They all communicate in English.

In the past, English was considered divisive. The Sinhalese called it kaduwa – the sword that cut between the classes – a colonial legacy that they sought to remove, along with Tamil, in the Sinhala Only legislation that followed Independence. But more recent amendments to the constitution have brought English back as a link language and English continues to be used as the language of management in public service and of international development. In addition, English continues to be the second language that people in Sri Lanka most want to learn.

Recognising this fact, the Performance Improvement Project, implemented by German International Cooperation (GIZ) – on behalf of the German Federal Ministry for Economic Cooperation and Development (BMZ) and the Australian Government (AusAID) – works with Sri Lanka's Northern and Eastern Provincial Councils to encourage English as a link language and a tool for conflict transformation and development. This is part of the project's mandate to build capacity for provincial and local government and community-based organisations, so that they can work together towards sustainable socio-economic development in a participatory and conflict mitigating way. The project's main stakeholders are decision-making public servants in key offices in the Northern and Eastern Provincial Councils and local government as well as community leaders with an emphasis on Women's Rural Development Societies. Through these actors the project seeks to create a critical mass of change agents who will work towards building peace and social cohesion for good governance and development in the country. For this, the project's main tool is STEPS.

STEPS stands for Skills Through English for Public Servants, a suite of courses from post-elementary to lower advanced that GIZ has designed and contracted the British Council to deliver. As a Content and Language Integrated Learning programme, it combines good governance and development topics with skills in critical thinking, cross-cultural communication, conflict resolution and English. Staff of government bodies and non-government organisations (NGOs) gain confidence in problem solving, distinguishing factual information from media hype, finding ways of achieving equity and diversity in a deeply divided society and understanding the value of dissent. STEPS works towards removing traditional barriers within a largely hierarchical, seniority-based management system.

A placement test is used to group participants according to their English language needs alone. This throws together people from diverse backgrounds – from Sinhala, Tamil and Muslim communities, rural and urban districts, central and devolved government structures – and from different age groups and management positions. English works here as a connector, encouraging people who would never normally meet to sit down together and share ideas in an environment that inspires them to work together towards a more tolerant and diverse society.

By the middle of 2010, over 2,000 public servants and NGO staff working to support vulnerable, conflict-affected communities in the North and East of Sri Lanka had successfully completed at least one of the four-week intensive courses in the STEPS suite. GIZ's target is to double that number by 2013.

In the North, 40 per cent of places on STEPS courses are now being filled with English language and English medium Mathematics and Science teachers in a bid to support public service teachers who work with English in schools as well as public service managers who work with English in governance. STEPS participants can then reach out to children and citizens alike.

The need for conflict transformation

Conflict transformation to ensure social cohesion and lay the ground work for socio-economic development is beyond the remit of most English language educators working in development, but teaching conflict resolution in the classroom is relevant to all. Addressing domestic violence, community conflict and conflict in the workplace is appropriate in any capacity development project. So is promoting civic alternatives to violent conflict and teaching critical thinking and the value of dissent.

Interestingly, the same tools for conflict transformation at macro level, outlined in Wallensteen (2002) and Miall et al. (2005), also apply at micro level:

- *Shifting power relations* in order to de-militarise, de-marginalise and democratise society is not just a job for UN peacekeepers or heads of state. These things can be done in the classroom too.

- *Working towards social equality and empowering minorities* can also begin with the way participants are selected and grouped on a training programme.

- *Creating governable spaces* (Watts and Bohle 1993) – space for dialogue, empathy and grievance redress – can be done for the office as well as for the truth commission.

- *Resolving incompatibility and distrust* may take years, but getting divided groups to work together as participants on the same course is a good place to start.

- *Establishing new social networks and inclusive support structures* can start with the formation of informal networks during the course and continues after the course is over.

- *Changing social relationships, interests and public discourse* at a national level may take years, but it can begin with the way participants learn to listen to and address each other. Just as we can choose to talk about 'civilians' and 'ex-combatants', instead of 'collaborators' and 'terrorists', we can learn to say 'us' instead of 'them'.

When viewed in this way, many teachers might find that they are already working on conflict transformation in the classroom. The point is to make it an explicit process in lesson and programme planning and to consciously utilise content and task types that accentuate 'connectors' not 'dividers' (Anderson, 1999).

English as a link language

English has been used as a tool for conflict transformation, as a link language, a connector, for conflict-prone societies where national languages have traditionally become social or ethnic dividers. In Rwanda, English has replaced French as the official language for policy and secondary education, although KinyaRwanda is still the first language. Some argue that this benefits those who do not speak French, but latent conflict with France – and the fact that English is the language of the country's youth – makes French a greater 'divider' (Samuelson and Freedman 2010).

In Sri Lanka English was used in the past to divide and rule but it is now the one language that all three ethnic groups – Sinhalese, Tamils and Muslims – are willing to learn. In principle it would be better to strengthen Tamil-Sinhala bilingualism and treat them as equal first languages for commerce, media and public life. But this is not possible in a country where Sinhala is associated with communal dominance and where subsequent amendments to the constitution have failed, in practice, to put the two languages on an equal footing. English remains for some, returns for others, as the language of business, management, law, higher education and public service above a certain level. As such, it links communities at several levels. Internationally it links the country to the outside world. At the end of a protracted and impoverishing civil war, all groups have a strong need to communicate with foreign governments and to be heard in the international arena. At the provincial level English links the civil service, local government, NGOs, bank-funded projects and other development actors working in the conflict-affected and mainly Tamil-speaking areas of the North and East with the Sinhala-speaking central government. At classroom level it links individuals from different walks of life who would not normally sit and study together. Here it becomes a common denominator that connects people by ability and need, not a subject that divides people by seniority or gender or ethnicity or religion.

In addition, the English language classroom can provide a neutral space where participants have the freedom to express new ideas in the safety of a foreign language. The connotations of nationalism or racism through one or the other national language are absent. If the teacher is also a foreigner, an 'outsider' and a good facilitator, then the 'space' for developing conflict sensitivity in a secure, non-judgmental environment is expanded. For this reason the Performance Improvement Project uses British Council teachers to deliver the STEPS suite, not only for their methodology and native English language skills but also because not being Sri Lankan allows them to create this neutral space in the classroom. People need to feel safe if they are going to discuss (and begin to resolve) conflict and the teacher needs to be a skilled facilitator to ensure that the participants' beliefs and experience are heard and respected.

This approach has resulted in the growth of informal networks between participants who have followed the course. A 2008 impact study showed that 36 per cent were still using their network contacts and their English, more than a year after their courses had finished, to solve problems between departments and to communicate between Sinhalese and Tamil-speaking organisations. In addition:

- 60 per cent reported increased knowledge in good governance and conflict transformation

- 55 per cent felt more empowered to deal with conflicts resulting from rank, ethnicity or gender

- 35 per cent reported using new conflict resolution strategies in the workplace

- 20 per cent reported maintaining cross-ethnic contacts once back at work and

- 85 per cent of senior managers clearly agreed that STEPS met the good governance capacity development needs of the Provincial Councils.

Impact studies from 2010 show that, in addition to the above, 85 per cent of participants show an increase of ten per cent in English language ability pre- and post-test scores and 50 per cent show an increase of more than 20 per cent.

Critical thinking and conflict transformation

The teaching and learning of English as a link language provides a platform for conflict transformation, particularly when critical thinking is taught as a sub-skill of reading, writing, listening and speaking. In many countries, critical thinking is taught in schools through mother tongue literacy. Students learn to deconstruct texts, express opinions, rationalise arguments, question the media and indeed question everything they read. They learn the value of dissent and how to use strategies to create their own factual, discursive or persuasive discourse. But in the Sri Lankan school system critical thinking is not taught as such. Rote learning and behaviourism based on outdated models leave little space in the textbooks for instilling the skills of cognitive hypothesising, inferring, problem solving, distinguishing fact from belief and expressing opinions. Worse than this, distortion of facts, myth masquerading as scientific reality and ethnically offensive materials are complaints levelled against the curriculum, particularly by the Tamil Teachers' Union (Wickrema and Colenso 2007). Outside school, freedom of speech is even more problematic: 24 journalists were killed in Sri Lanka between 1992 and 2010, according to the Committee to Protect Journalists (2010), while the state-controlled media are left unchecked to reinforce existing hierarchies and stereotypes.

But if one of the aims of conflict transformation is to redefine social relationships, power structures and vested interests then critical thinking is a must. Teaching English to adults – and in particular to adults who are change agents within government service – is one way of reactivating critical thinking in a society where school has failed its citizens in this regard. This is one of the main strategies that informs the design of the STEPS programme.

Importantly, English language teaching methodology is task based; the task types it uses constitute the sub-skills of critical thinking. These include accessing information, deconstructing ideas and processes, categorising, evaluating, prioritising, improving, empathising, problem solving, agreeing and disagreeing, finding consensus. What is important is for educators to build up and recycle these task types in an explicit way so that participants become aware of the fact that they are acquiring not only English but also critical thinking and – by extension – skills for conflict transformation.

Take, for example, the skill of finding consensus. In a divided society where a significant minority are oppressed, learning to be consensus-oriented is a matter of learning not only to agree on what suits the majority of people but also to incorporate what suits the significant minority. On a course that uses a task-based approach to critical thinking, this can be done by setting a task where the group must find consensus, in a limited period of time, on a set of principles or ideas.

For example, participants are given a task to brainstorm as many ways as possible to improve the situation between two groups in conflict. (This could be an international mining corporation and the indigenous people who live in the mining area, internally displaced women trying to join a benefit scheme where vested interest keeps them out, or internally displaced people who speak one language but are controlled by authorities who speak another). Participants compile their ideas for improving the situation between the conflicting parties in a common list – the longer the list the better. Each participant then writes down his or her top three choices from the common list. Then, in a series of limited-time encounters controlled by the trainer, they negotiate and agree on three common ideas. This is done in pairs, then groups of four, then groups of eight and so on until the whole class has arrived at three ideas that everyone agrees on. At each stage, the teacher allows only five minutes to negotiate and agree, after which time the group must arrive at consensus. Participants have to 'give up' one of their own ideas in order to accommodate someone else's so that they can move forward together.

In methodology terms this task type is called a pyramid and is well known for getting a group of people to agree on a limited number of items from a more extensive list. The extensive list constitutes the base of the pyramid and – through a series of negotiations – the group reaches consensus on a final shortlist at the top of the pyramid. In doing so, participants experience in microcosm the difficulty involved in arriving at consensus when many different opinions are held by communities in conflict. By extension, participants can project the strategies and the levels of tolerance and flexibility needed to find consensus in a real conflict situation.

Content and Language Integrated Learning

English becomes a tool for conflict transformation when:

■ English is the motivation and the link that connects different ethnic groups on a training course

■ studying in a safe environment enables participants to explore different ways of thinking and communicating with each other

■ the methodology is task based and critical thinking can be taught through task types

■ the course content includes conflict transformation as its 'non-language' subject matter and uses English as the vehicle for arriving at that subject matter.

This last point reflects an approach known as Content and Language Integrated Learning (CLIL). According to the European Commission (2008):

Content and Language Integrated Learning (CLIL) involves teaching a curricular subject through the medium of a language other than that normally used. The subject can be entirely unrelated to language learning, such as history lessons being taught in English in a school in Spain. CLIL is taking place and has been found to be effective in all sectors of education from primary through to adult and higher education. Its success has been growing over the past ten years and continues to do so.

Teachers working with CLIL are specialists in their own discipline rather than traditional language teachers. They are usually fluent speakers of the target language, bilingual or native speakers. In many institutions language teachers work in partnership with other departments to offer CLIL in various subjects. The key issue is that the learner is gaining new knowledge about the 'non-language' subject while encountering, using and learning the foreign language. The methodologies and approaches used are often linked to the subject area with the content leading the activities.

The CLIL course STEPS follows this model. It is a four-week course that teaches government servants and their civil society counterparts the basics of governance and development through four components: Economy, Conflict, Social Development and Environment. The one-week component on conflict transformation uses the medium of English to sensitise participants to different types of conflict: conflict at home and with neighbours, conflict in the workplace, causes and key issues in armed conflict and some strategies for conflict resolution. Conflict transformation is also integrated as a cross-cutting skill for daily use on the course, and later in the workplace, through the development of interpersonal skills, positive group dynamics, team building, negotiation skills and critical thinking.

One of the challenges of CLIL is how to combine complex concepts in the non-language syllabus with often quite low levels of English. Accuracy in English on CLIL courses often remains a problem, but if the subject matter is relevant and the tasks capture a real need to communicate, then enormous increases can be seen in participants' fluency and confidence as well as their knowledge of the subject matter. The participatory approach allows for 'experts' among the participants to come to the fore and share their experience. At the same time the trainer, as facilitator, can activate the less vocal human resources within the group and provide a positive management model for the workplace.

However, it is important not to make the teaching material too confrontational in the aftermath of war. Addressing conflict transformation through the STEPS programme is a delicate business. During the war years many people were reluctant to talk about the violence and now that the war is over there is pressure to sweep difficult issues under the carpet. Taking advice from GIZ's conflict transformation experts, the course designers used a progression from conflict at home and between men and women, through conflict with neighbours and in the workplace, to armed conflict and the rehabilitation of child soldiers. The emphasis in each case is on using conflict resolution skills. Participants learn how to use active listening to become less judgemental, how to recognise bias in the media, how to be assertive without being aggressive and how to promote discussion on emotionally or politically sensitive topics.

A variety of approaches is needed to motivate and empower learners, to build tolerance and to find ways forward. STEPS uses an ongoing storyline based on conflict in the workplace at a fictional NGO to look at miscommunication between national and international staff. Through this, participants deal with cross-cultural conflict in a dramatised, light-hearted way. A short film, *The Slipper* (Kowthaman 2003), about children who step on mines, is in stark contrast. Produced by the NGO

ScriptNet for a project called Reel Peace, the change in tone gives learners the opportunity to consider the media as a powerful tool for peace and reconciliation. Participants also learn how to deconstruct messages in print and, using similar discursive and persuasive text types, write their own project proposals to international donors in a bid to capture some of the post-conflict rehabilitation funds presently flowing into the war-ravaged Northern Province.

To illustrate these points, two extracts from the STEPS Trainer's Notes (Disken et al. 2008) are shown here.

Box 1 : STEPS Trainers' Notes : Session 2.5

Session 2.5

Conflict in the workplace (2)

Learner objectives

By the end of the session participants will be able to:

• listen for specific information

• get information about past events by asking questions

• differentiate between /p/ and /f/

• predict possible causes of conflict between two colleagues.

Time

90 minutes

Session overview

A Listening	20 minutes
B Language focus	15 minutes
C Pronunciation	25 minutes
D Speaking	30 minutes

Resources

Resource 2.5A	Tapescript 2.5A (parts 1 and 2)
Resource 2.5B	Tapescripts 2.5B and 2.5C

Two sets of different coloured cards (enough for participants to have one of each colour)

Worksheets

Worksheet 2.5A	Patrick and Fernando: their stories
Worksheet 2.5B	Timeline for Patrick (1)
Worksheet 2.5C	Timeline for Patrick (2)
Worksheet 2.5D	Timeline for Fernando (group A)
Worksheet 2.5E	Timeline for Fernando (group B)

Context

This session is the first in the saga of Patrick and Fernando which continues through this unit. The session sets the scene by highlighting their relationship as colleagues in the same office and the differences in approach and knowledge of procedure.

Patrick is a new expatriate manager in a fictional NGO (FLO). He is very procedure-oriented and assumes that everyone else is too. Fernando works in the same department but (as we find out later) is not aware of the procedures. He does his best to do a good job but, as he is unaware of the procedures, doesn't follow them.

There is a pronunciation focus in this session as misunderstanding of spoken instructions is one of Fernando's problems. The distinction between the /p/ and /f/ phonemes is difficult for Tamil speakers and can cause confusion.

The other mistakes that Fernando makes are not testing electrical equipment, buying things from his uncle's shop and failing to get three quotes before making a purchase (a requirement in many organisations' purchasing/procurement procedures in order to find the most competitive price). These mistakes are touched on in this session and are dealt with in Session 2.6.

Initially it looks like Fernando is in the wrong. Ultimately, though, in Session 2.12, we find out that it is Patrick's failure to provide training that is the real problem. Do not give that away in this session as it will be detrimental to Session 2.12.

The main point to come out of this and the following session is that misunderstanding can cause (potentially serious) conflict in the workplace. Clear communication is essential to avoid these misunderstandings.

STEPS : Trainer's Notes : Session 2.5   87

In Session 2.5 participants combine the language skills of listening, pronunciation and the use of the simple past tense with conflict sensitising skills of predicting causes of conflict in the workplace.

In Session 2.10, towards the end of the unit, participants consolidate their ideas about the victims of conflict and discuss ideas for peace building measures in the media while practising their fluency skills in English.

Course management and conflict transformation

One of the biggest successes of the STEPS programme in terms of conflict transformation is the way course content is mirrored in course management. Through the organisation and delivery of the sessions, key governance and conflict transformation concepts are seen in action. Towards the end of the course the 'loop' is made explicit and participants reflect on the way aspects of good governance and conflict transformation have been demonstrated throughout. The aim is to get participants to realise that participation, responsiveness, transparency, inclusion and the establishment of new social networks all happen during the course. This provides them with a model for their own working environment. Participants notice that:

- the classes are managed in a participatory and consensus oriented way

- the teachers demonstrate empathy and responsiveness through the use of learner-centred approaches and a syllabus which demonstrates an objective, needs-based approach

- everyone is treated as an equal in a democratic environment; different voices are heard through different pairings and groupings

- the use of objectively marked placement tests provides a platform for transparency, inclusion and diversity; participants are selected and grouped by ability, not seniority, gender or race.

The possibility of inclusiveness and the opportunity to work in harmony for a protracted period of time is perhaps the most empowering part of this 'loop'. The classes include a mixture of Tamils, Sinhalese and Muslims with English as the leveller. Senior managers and support staff, men and women, old and young sit side by side. Staff from urban and rural contexts, central and devolved government structures, civil society and NGOs work together as equals to exchange views and experience. What is more, the intensive, long-term, residential courses help foster informal networks and support systems among participants. Cross-ethnic communication continues once they return to the workplace.

Box 2 : STEPS Trainers' Notes : Session 2.10

Session 2.10 Consolidation: effects of conflict

Learner objectives

By the end of the session participants will be able to:

• consolidate their ideas about the effects of armed conflict

• express opinions and speak at length on a topic

• use visual media – films and posters – for conflict sensitivity.

Time

90 minutes

Session overview

A Designing an anti-war film	35 minutes
B Film: The Slipper	55 minutes

Resources

Resource 2.10	Pairwork cards (cut-ups, 1 card per participant)
DVD	The Slipper

Worksheets

Worksheet 2.10A	Film outline
Worksheet 2.10B	The Slipper Points for discussion

Context

This session draws together ideas about victims of conflict and extends the concept of victims to cover 'truth', 'democracy', 'values' and 'communities' which are also destroyed by militarisation and armed conflict. Instead of getting participants to respond in terms of what they can do through their work as public servants, the session asks participants to respond on a more emotional level, and to view films and posters as vehicles for conflict sensitivity in terms of campaigning for empathy and understanding, as a pre-cursor to action.

The Slipper is a 10-minute film produced in 2003 by ScriptNetSL as part of a series of films which visualise the effects of conflict in Sri Lanka with the specific intention of generating discussion for conflict transformation. It is in Tamil with English subtitles, making it suitable for a mixed-language audience. It is not important that English is not spoken. The film serves as a vehicle to stimulate discussion in English, not to teach English-listening comprehension. (The English subtitles work as reading comprehension for Sinhala-speaking participants.) Viewers, especially those who have not lived in conflict affected areas of Sri Lanka, may find the content disturbing, so it is important for the trainer to anticipate emotional responses and to facilitate participants' reaction to the film with sensitivity and in an unbiased way. Immediately after the film is played, trainers should not expect participants to start speaking. Instead, quiet time should be provided, so that participants have a chance to reflect and digest the images before 'returning to the classroom'.

In terms of language focus, the session is designed to get participants to talk at length– consolidating their ideas and what they have learned in Sessions 2.7, 2.8 and 2.9. As such, the trainer should focus on participants' ability to put together structures already taught on the course, as in a production, or free practice, stage. Anticipated language items are *should, could* and *why don't we ...* for making suggestions and the language of expressing opinions. In addition, participants get the opportunity to use the criteria for designing posters with good visual impact, as introduced in Session 2.9.

A critical mass of change agents

A CLIL approach to conflict transformation as described above will only make an impact in peace building terms if large numbers of people from government and civil society successfully complete longer and more intensive training like that which is provided by STEPS. Large numbers are needed because in conflict-affected areas there is a constant flux of personnel. Frequently, people move away and are replaced. Longer, more intensive courses are needed because attitudes and behaviours will not change after a short workshop or day-release training. Experience shows that 120 hours delivered in one block is the 'unit of change' in these situations.

The aim of such a strategy is to create a critical mass of change agents – a sustainable group of like-minded middle and senior managers in government and civil society – who are both willing and able to instigate conflict-sensitive change. With roughly 15,000 decision makers (public servants and community leaders) in the North and East of Sri Lanka, the Performance Improvement Project has targeted over 90 departments and organisations and defined its critical mass as one third of those decision makers. At the same time, the project endeavours to train a minimum of three staff from each organisation as a way of avoiding the challenge presented when an isolated 'changed' individual returns to an 'unchanged' environment.

But to make this critical mass happen, managers have to buy into releasing their key staff for periods of a month at a time. This often proves difficult at the start. STEPS tackled this problem by including senior management in publicity and training, by building a strong reputation for the course and by implementing a system that gave line managers choices on when and where they could send their staff for training. It is therefore important to note that a large pool of client organisations is needed not only to build a critical mass of change agents and to ensure an ethnic and social mix of participants but also to reduce pressure on human resource management and to keep managers supportive.

'STEPS stories' – qualitative impacts that are recorded and disseminated to project partners and donors – are key to ensuring the release of decision makers from their full-time jobs so that they can attend the courses. An example of a STEPS story is that of the probation officer who in March 2009 – after studying the unit on child soldiers – was put in charge of 600 children accused of being child soldiers. The probation officer's understanding (gained through her participation in STEPS) of the complex social issues that lead to child soldier recruitment and decommissioning helped to sensitise the judge and other colleagues who were handling the case.

Another STEPS story is that of the senior manager who, after learning about disaster management on STEPS, made sure that all his staff received adequate training in land mines awareness before being relocated to war-affected areas. Yet another example concerns the entire staff of the office of the Assistant Commissioner of Local Government, Vavuniya, who were in charge of water and sanitation for more than a quarter of a million internally placed people in Menik Farm at the end of the war in 2009. Undeterred by senior military officials who used English as a means of asserting their authority, the staff responded with their newly improved confidence and English skills (gained through STEPS), and, refusing to be intimidated, turned the situation into one of liaison and collaboration rather than one of division and conflict.

Sustainability

Using English as a tool for conflict transformation and development through CLIL programmes like STEPS will only begin to have an impact if sufficient numbers are involved, as described above. In addition, the course itself must be sustainable, in terms of teachers as well as learners. It is not easy to find teachers with the right balance of English language and conflict transformation skills willing to work in a conflict-affected environment where displacement and transfers create a constant depletion of human capital. Course managers need to create some sense of permanency in an impermanent situation. One such approach is to ignore the traditional training cascade and create permanence through materials and systems instead. High quality, published course books with extensive notes for trainers and comprehensive course administration handbooks, like those for STEPS, will not disappear when the teachers leave or are transferred. Institutional memory and quality assurance can be retained in print or electronically when they cannot be retained in person.

At the same time it is crucial to be able to buy in the services of a quality CLIL provider. In this model, sustainability then depends on access to funding rather than access to a pool of local teachers. Such funding, contrary to common belief, may be more readily available in a conflict-emerging situation than in a more peaceful development context.

The Performance Improvement Project has taken this non-cascade approach to making STEPS sustainable in the Northern Province of Sri Lanka. The Sri Lankan publishing rights of STEPS are owned by the Northern Provincial Council, as are the course administration system, the certification and the participant records. Northern Provincial Council staff are being trained to manage the STEPS placement test and quality assurance systems independently. With assistance from the Performance Improvement Project, the Chief Secretary and the Secretary of the Provincial Ministry of Education, Northern Province, have created the STEPS Institute in Jaffna where STEPS courses run on a regular basis and where the Provincial Ministry of Education pays for the running costs and administration staff.

But beyond the elementary level of the STEPS suite, which are now delivered by Sri Lankan teachers, the Performance Improvement Project has not worked with the Northern Provincial Council to train government teachers to take over the delivery of the higher level courses of STEPS. Several reasons inform this decision. In the conflict-affected Northern Province there are very few teachers or university staff able to deliver STEPS. Training them to have the right skills would be hard; getting them released to work full time, as STEPS would require, would be even harder; retaining them in the system would be almost impossible. Instead, the Performance Improvement Project has taken the perhaps unusual step of encouraging the Northern Provincial Council to continue to buy in the services of the British Council for course delivery and to pursue a realistic approach to sustainability in this way. Such an approach banks on the fact that money is available for the rehabilitation of the North now that the fighting has ceased, through new donors, and will continue to be available for years to come.

It is crucial for this type of sustainability that partners and stakeholders are trained in how to access donor funds to back existing products like STEPS. To do this, they need to be able to persuade donors not to reinvent the wheel but to pay for something that is already proven in the field. For example, instead of accepting USAID's offer to provide English language teaching in the Eastern Province in 2007 when STEPS had already been running there for three years, the Chief Secretary would have achieved better impact by persuading USAID to put their money into STEPS. Although this did not work in 2008, in 2010 AusAID were convinced of the value of STEPS and signed up to back it through the Australian Communities Rehabilitation Project 3 (ACRP3) until 2013.

For partners and stakeholders to negotiate in this way with donors, they need to be able to argue that bought-in native speaker English language teachers, as outsiders, will ensure a neutral, conflict transforming space for learning and a level of expertise which is not readily available among local teachers. Thereafter the local stakeholders will also need some background in the business side of English Language Teaching (ELT) so that they can select the most appropriate service provider in terms of quality and qualifications as well as affordability. The local stakeholders will also need to be able to keep the placement testing and certification processes transparent and equitable and they will need to know how to sustain the right ethnic mix in the groups of participants who take part in the STEPS training.

In short, the future of STEPS depends on it being locally managed and internationally delivered by a team of like-minded change agents who understand the interface between language and development and who espouse the tenets of good governance and conflict transformation which are embedded in the course itself. Given the important impact that the STEPS programme has had on public service in the North and East since 2006, the extension of funding by the Australian and German governments until 2013 and the project's ability to operate successfully outside the national school system (where previous projects promoting English as a link language may have been less successful), the future of using English as a tool for conflict transformation in Sri Lanka looks positive.

Note

1. An earlier version of this chapter was presented at the 8th Language and Development Conference, Dhaka, 23–25 June 2009.

References

Anderson, M. 1999. *Do No Harm: How Aid Can Support Peace – or War. London: Lynne Rienner.*

Committee to Protect Journalists. 2010. *18 Journalists Killed in Sri Lanka Since 1992/Motive Confirmed. New York: Committee to Protect Journalists.* Available online at *www.cpj.org/killed/asia/sri-lanka*

Disken, F., Edworthy, J., Horn, G. and Subhan-Brewer, Z. 2008. *Skills Through English for Public Servants, Trainer's Notes. Trincomalee: GTZ.*

European Commission. 2008. *Multilingualism: Content and Language Integrated Learning. Brussels: European Commission.* Available online at *http://ec.europa. eu/education/languages/language-teaching/doc236_en.htm*

Holleman, C. 2008. *Conflict, economic crisis and drought: A humanitarian emergency out of control. Humanitarian Exchange Magazine* Issue 40. *London: Humanitarian Policy Group, Overseas Development Institute.* Available online at *www.odihpn.org/report.asp?id=2944*

Kowthaman, K. 2003. *Seruppu (The Slipper). Reel Peace 6 Short Films. ScriptNet.* Available online at *www.youtube.com/watch?v=6GiljXULrjQ* (Reproduced in Disken et al. 2008.)

Miall, H., Ramsbotham, O. and Woodhouse T. 2005. *Contemporary Conflict Resolution: The Prevention, Management and Transformation of Deadly Conflict. Cambridge: Polity.*

OECD (Organisation for Economic Cooperation and Development). 2005. *Water and Violent Conflict.* (Issues Brief.) *Paris: Development Assistance Committee, OECD.*

Robinson, B.A. 2006. *Religiously-Based Civil Unrest and Warfare. Ontario: Ontario Consultants on Religious Tolerance.* Available online at *www.religioustolerance.org/curr_war.htm*

Samuelson, B.L. and Freedman, S.W. 2010. *Language policy, multilingual education and power in Rwanda. Language Policy* 9(3), 191-215.

UNHCR (United Nations High Commissioner for Refugees). 2009. *2008 Global Trends: Refugees, Asylum Seekers, Returnees, Internally Displaced and Stateless Persons.* Geneva: UNHCR. Available online at *www.unhcr.org/4a375c426.html*

Wallensteen, P. 2002. *Understanding Conflict Resolution: War, Peace and the Global System. London: Sage.*

Watts, M. and Bohle, H.G. 1993. *The space of vulnerability: The causal structure of hunger and famine. Progress in Human Geography* 17(1), 43-67.

Wickrema, A. and Colenso, P. 2007. *Respect for Diversity in Educational Publications: The Sri Lankan Experience. Washington DC: World Bank.* Available online at *http://siteresources.worldbank.org/EDUCATION/ Resources/278200-1121703274255/1439264-1126807073059/Paper_Final.pdf*

16

English language teaching in fragile states: Justifying action, promoting success and combating hegemony[1]

Danny Whitehead

Introduction

These are challenging times for conscientious English language teaching (ELT) professionals working in fragile states.[2] Large cuts in funding have affected projects across the globe as donor priorities have been reorganised in light of changing geopolitical realities. From the left of the political spectrum have come louder accusations of covert linguistic imperialism (Horvath 1998, Phillipson 1992, 2009), or linguistic genocide (Skutnabb-Kangas 2000); from the right has come increased pressure to pursue these very policies that the left decry (Pascoe-Watson 2008, Sharlet 2010: 78[3]).

In her introduction to the *TESOL Quarterly* special topic issue on language and identity, Norton (1997:425) reiterates a question that has been debated at length by educational researchers: 'Are TESOL[4] educators perpetuating Western imperialism in different parts of the world?' (See also Edge 2003, 2006, Kachru 1990, Ngũgî 1986, Pennycook 1994 and Phillipson 1992.) This concern is particularly relevant in the context of a fragile state, where sensitivity to direct or indirect hegemonic[5] influence is magnified due to the vulnerability of the state and its citizens.

The criticisms levelled by the academics above have particular relevance to the Peacekeeping English Project (PEP), which entails the teaching of English in the Democratic Republic of Congo (DRC), a fragile state vulnerable to external influence. DRC also has French as an existing official state language as a relic of its colonial history, which has its own hegemonic influence on the thought and behaviour of the subaltern[6] in their relations with local elites or with Europe.

The Peacekeeping English Project – a military English[7] project managed by the British Council on behalf of the UK's Foreign and Commonwealth Office (FCO), Department for International Development (DfID) and Ministry of Defence (MoD) –

commenced in DRC in March 2007. The project operates in support of the Institut Militaire des Langues Appliquées (IMLA) of the Forces Armées de la République Démocratique du Congo (FARDC). The project has five goals, which are summarised in Box 1.

Box 1: Goals of Peacekeeping English Project in DRC

1. To facilitate the short-term rapid build up of a specific number/target of English language users to meet the country's regional and multinational obligations, or facilitate international contact for senior personnel.

2. To promote the development of a long-term sustainable host nation language-teaching infrastructure to eventually enable a self-sufficient strategy to meet that country's needs.

3. To assist with the provision of short- and long-term functional ELT for specific purposes e.g. conference participation, preparation for international assignments or work requirements, preparation for international exchanges and training courses, career development and promotion.

4. To promote greater co-operation, understanding, interoperability and dialogue between armed forces in the region.

5. To contribute, through exposure to UK values and ethos, to the improvement of the professionalism, standards and capabilities of the Armed Forces and public security agencies, particularly with regard to their respect for human rights, the rule of law and the primacy of a democratically elected executive. *(British Council 2008)*

PEP DRC has training sites in Kinshasa, Mbanza-Ngungu and Kananga. IMLA trains over 250 full-time learners every year and a further 120 part-time learners.

Of particular concern is whether the PEP project is what Althusser (1994) might describe as an 'ideological state apparatus', imposing (or infiltrating) culture and beliefs through coercive education. A Gramscian analysis would certainly suggest so, as Ives (2004) explains:

> Language [in Gramsci's analysis] is spread predominantly not by government or state coercion, military or police action, but by speakers accepting the prestige and utility of new languages, phrases, or terms. *(Ives 2004:7)*

If the project has the potential to perpetuate post-colonial hegemony (and, in a Marxist analysis, if this is unavoidable[8]), efforts need to be made to minimise the hegemonic aspect, or even to act as a counter-hegemonic influence, taking into account the very specific local context of the English language in DRC.

Through a case study of PEP DRC, I will examine arguments over the justification for ELT projects in fragile states. In the next section of the chapter, I look at the language of justification in project planning and how, in the initial stages of project planning, this language steers a project towards being a tool of external hegemony. The following section then reports on a longitudinal study conducted with teachers and learners from IMLA (working with PEP DRC) in 2009. The study investigates whether it is possible to support the development of complex learner identities and foster counter-hegemonic discourses and complex language identities through critical praxis[9] in ELT. The study is informed by Gramsci's theories of language and hegemony and by post-colonial considerations of implementing ELT projects in fragile states.

The final section of the chapter draws conclusions, summarises recommendations for ELT practice in fragile states and indicates areas for further research.

English language teaching in fragile states

Let me start by exploring the justification (or, perhaps more accurately, by addressing the criticisms) of ELT projects in fragile states. I will try to address the fundamental objections to such projects and make recommendations for projects in similar contexts. I will also look briefly at operational aspects of PEP DRC, and, drawing on my experience as manager of the project[10], I will make further suggestions for the successful management and implementation of an ELT project in a fragile state.

Beyond 'linguistic imperialism'

Several voices have described ELT and the global spread of English as integral components of Western imperialism in colonial and post-colonial times: Phillipson (1992) and Pennycook (1994) have detailed the British Council's formation in the 1930s as a disseminator of British propaganda and argued that its capacity in that respect has not diminished or changed with time. In 2007, the Russian FSB (the successor to the KGB) described the British Council as a 'nest of spies' (Harding 2008) and commentators such as Horvath (1998) still see the British Council (and the United States Information Service) as 'the vehicles whereby the British and American governments respectively exert pressure on foreign governments ... while at the same time providing a convenient front for MI5/CIA activities.' It is unfortunate that these views, grounded in the theory of linguistic imperialism (Phillipson 1992), have become so widely and unquestioningly accepted that at a recent conference on applied linguistics a colleague was 'accused of being complicit in the bombing of Basra' for daring to support the role of English in development.[11] As linguistic imperialism has become part of the ELT profession's 'received wisdom', it has concurrently become more difficult to engage in balanced debate in support of English projects in fragile states.

Robert Phillipson's seminal text (1992) has provided (and continues to provide) a stimulating point of departure for the consideration of the role of ELT and the role of ELT projects in imposing or perpetuating Western capitalist hegemony. However, the theory sometimes understates the agency of speakers of other languages, who are not always passive recipients of imposed hegemony directed by the decision makers in the centre and their puppet elites in the periphery. This does a disservice to speakers of other languages and is not consistent with the complex realities of hybrid multilingualism evident in DRC and in other states, particularly states in which English does not exist as a former colonial language where the residues of colonialism have greater potential for hegemonic influence. In many multilingual societies, English can be seen as adding to (or at least having the potential to add to) an already rich and complex linguistic mix and in which multilingual speakers create their own linguistically hybridised discourses[12]. English is not a static, finished object; I would like to frame the current discussion within a conception of English as a fluid, living construct which is constantly being (re)invented by speakers and speech communities (Brutt-Griffler 2002).

I do not argue that ELT is always benign, or that there is no potential for hegemonic influence; I argue, rather, that any negative influences are not always the result of intentional imperialist policies from the centre (as the theory of linguistic imperialism posits). Care certainly needs to be given in planning and delivery of ELT projects in fragile states (see the next section in this chapter), and Phillipson's work has been (and continues to be) thought provoking and important in continuing to draw attention to inequality and hegemony in ELT.

Therefore, it is fair to ask why the theory of linguistic imperialism has been adopted by ELT practitioners, often without close enough analysis of its relevance to their situation, in contexts where its central tenets are less relevant. To answer that question, we might first look at ELT professionals operating in the field of development.

I sense that there is a general lack of pride in the ELT profession, especially within ELT in development and often for good reason. The abundance of unqualified native-speaker teachers (particularly in developing countries and fragile states, where the lack of competition from other qualified and experienced expatriate teachers lowers standards for recruitment[13]), the explosion of profit-focused private language academies which perpetuate the myth of the inherently superior native-speaker teacher and the profusion of 'back-packer' teachers devalues the profession in the eyes of the internal and external observer, leading to a sense of shame or embarrassment in admitting that one is an ELT professional. As Kennett (2002:235) says, ELT professionals 'avoid the "E" word, anything to avoid the condescension, when [they admit to being] English language teachers, to be told, "Oh, I did that once".' As a result, ELT professionals are more likely to accept criticism of their own industry; it confirms their worst fears and plays to their sense of embarrassment.

Added to this is the false correlation of the legally questionable foreign policies of the UK and the USA in recent history (reaching a peak under Tony Blair and George W. Bush, but not limited to that period) with the global spread of English. While the USA and UK are English-speaking nations, the concept of their owning the language, or of the language being inherently tied to British or American cultural values (if there are even such definable terms) is no longer valid. Criticism of UK and USA foreign policy (particularly in fragile states) should not be conflated with the issue of the spread of English. The result of this false association is that liberally minded ELT professionals, already lacking confidence in their industry, have been all too apt to adopt the incomplete – but forcefully argued – critical theory of linguistic imperialism.

In multilingual contexts that do not have English as a colonial language, such as DRC, a more relevant theoretical framework for analysing the role of English is Higgins' (2009) theory of multivocality. Drawing on Bakhtin, Higgins describes a complex multiplicity of language identity in multilingual societies in East Africa. Here, English is no longer a foreign or alien language, it is also a local language. It is not used simply as a tool of Western political, economic and cultural imperialism, but also – and concurrently – as a creative tool which has been appropriated locally to create new discourses (cf. Kachru 1990). Higgins' theory accepts the potential for negative hegemony when considered in the context of a fragile state, while acknowledging the latent power for the creation of new (and possibly counter-hegemonic) discourse through hybridisation; in its duality, it is richer and more realistically complex than other dichotomous narratives.

Afrocentricity and potential of English in DRC

Recent currents in Afrocentric thought provide encouragement for the use of English in Africa to counter hegemonic influence. Afrocentricity can be defined as:

> ... a view of the world that puts Africa at the centre of global concerns and idealises its role in human affairs ... to restore pride and confidence to black people in their own African heritage. *(Mazrui 2004:95)*

Mazrui acknowledges that Eurocentric hegemony makes it difficult for Africans to use the English language to create their own counter-hegemonic discourses. He continues:

> The linguistic challenge and dilemma confronting the Afrocentrist, then, has been how to articulate a counter-hegemonic and anti-Eurocentric discourses [sic] in a language of 'internal' imperialism. *(Mazrui 2004:99, emphasis added)*

This accords with Gramscian analysis. Africans remain in a state of conditioned subalternity as their language identity is coerced by the power structures and latent imagery inherent in the post-colonial languages.

Mazrui and Gramsci acknowledge that there are possible options open to the subaltern to create counter-hegemonic discourse through the development of a counter-hegemonic foreign/additional language identity, which can be through English. As Mazrui states above, this is a 'linguistic challenge', not an impossibility and he describes a 'revolutionary potential' in English (Mazrui 2004:102). Gramsci also argues strongly that language allows the development of identity and that the subaltern is capable of creating his/her own language identity (or 'spontaneous grammar', see below) to create counter-hegemonic discourse. Mazrui (2004:104–107) further suggests that English could provide a bridge between Islamophobia and Swahiliphilia, leading to a more 'democratised Afrocentrism'.

Afrocentrism therefore provides a suitable theoretical and ideological grounding for further exploring the possibility of English being coerced by the subaltern for their own purposes to create counter-hegemonic discourse in fragile states. This needs to be further considered with regard to the linguistic milieu of DRC.

DRC has an existing triglossic linguistic structure. However, recent changes in language policy in Rwanda and the increasing importance of the Anglophone international minerals market are moving DRC swiftly towards a quadriglossic structure, in line with Batibo's (2006) model: the market for English language teaching products is booming, the demand for English teaching far outstripping supply and concurrently there is a decrease in the stature of French. It is worth reproducing Batibo's quadriglossic structure in tabulated form, which I have adapted for the DRC context ('H' and 'L' refer to high and low status):

Table 1: Quadriglossic language structure in DRC (adapted from Batibo 2006:137)	
Status	**Type of language**
H1	Super-international language English
L1 / H2	Ex-colonial language French
H3 / L2	Indigenous lingua franca Lingala
L3	Indigenous languages Kicongo, Tshiluba, Ngbala, etc.

English is described here as a 'super-international language', used for global business and regional and international communication. French is seen as of lesser status, but still as a locally 'higher' language of official national institutions. The indigenous lingua franca is used for inter-ethnic linguistic group communication whilst the other indigenous languages are used within ethnic linguistic groups.

An important point to note here is that English (H1) is superior to French (H2) and Lingala (H3) but is not in the same power structure as the indigenous languages (L3). This indicates a clear potential for English to be used in conjunction with indigenous languages to overcome the hegemony of the ex-colonial language and the indigenous lingua-franca (Lingala) which was imposed by physical force, coordinated language policy and overt coercion under the Mobutu regime (1965-1996). English as a 'super-international language' can create counter-hegemonic discourses for indigenous speakers against the historically imposed Lingala and French language identities: it allows for the bypassing of traditional hegemonic languages and can work alongside – rather than against – these languages as they are not in competition for usage.

Theoretical underpinnings are an essential starting point in the design of ELT projects in fragile states. But they must also be supported by the right intent and by careful statements of purpose.

Intent and purpose

As noted above, Marx (1867) did not paint capitalists 'in a rosy light', but he also did not believe that individual capitalists were in themselves evil. It was more that under the capitalist economic system, inequality was (is) unavoidable. In the same way, we must acknowledge that in the current global political and economic system, an ELT project funded by the UK government and implemented by the British Council in a fragile state cannot avoid the potential for hegemony or cultural 'depositing' (Freire

1970). This hegemonic influence is not necessarily through coercion or design (as implied by linguistic imperialism) but through perceived prestige and attraction to English (as described by Tembe and Norton 2011, Chapter 6 this volume) which generates consent. Consent and coercion are not diametrically opposed concepts; promotion of English, whether with good intent or without, feeds the perceived value of English as a commodity.

In the next section I report on the principles which were developed to minimise that hegemonic influence and indeed to attempt to create counter-hegemonic discourses by encouraging complex multilingual identities with English through the implementation of PEP DRC. However, it is interesting at this point to address the issue of intent and goal in ELT projects in fragile states more closely.

Goals one to three of PEP DRC listed in Box 1 are neutral and perhaps consistent with what would be expected from any capacity-building project for ELT or ESP teachers in a government institution. Goal four, while rooted in the security context, is representative of the British Council's primary role as a cultural relations organisation – an organisation committed to 'the building of engagement and trust between people of different cultures through the exchange of knowledge and ideas' (Knagg 2010). Goal five is more interesting and warrants further attention:

5. *To contribute, through exposure to UK values and ethos, to the improvement of the professionalism, standards and capabilities of the Armed Forces and public security agencies, particularly with regard to their respect for human rights, the rule of law and the primacy of a democratically elected executive.*
   (British Council 2008)

This raises three immediate questions. What are 'UK values and ethos'? Is this a sound goal for an ELT project in a fragile state? And, more generally, why does the UK government support PEP DRC?

A short questionnaire was sent to project stakeholders to investigate these issues. Two questions were asked:

1. In your opinion, why does the UK finance and support the Peacekeeping English Project in DRC?

2. According to project goals, the Peacekeeping English Project exposes its stakeholders/participants/partners to 'UK values' and 'UK ethos'. What do you understand by the terms 'UK values' and UK 'ethos'?

In August 2010, the questionnaire was sent to nine UK-based senior stakeholders from the British Council, FCO, DfID and UK Ministry of Defence and to 40 trainees currently undertaking courses supported by PEP DRC.[14] (Questionnaires were sent in French to trainees and answers were collated in French.[15]) Seven responses were received from the UK-based stakeholders with a further 32 from project trainees.

With regard to Question two, answers from UK-based stakeholders were very similar. All seven respondents associated 'UK values and ethos' with human rights, mentioning 'tolerance and diversity', 'respect for universal human rights', 'human rights and the rule of law' and 'human rights and freedom of speech, thought and movement'. Three respondents linked the concepts of 'UK values and ethos' with 'civilian management of uniformed services', 'subordination of military to the civilian' and 'the principle that the army is under civilian control'. The concept of democracy was also noted by a number of respondents: 'the embedding of democracy in [Congolese] training structures', 'democracy and the right to free and fair elections'.

However, Congolese training participants had very differing views of what UK ethos and values are. Responses included 'love', 'sharing' and 'peace'. Over 30 per cent of respondents saw 'political stability' (or a variant term relating to the stability of the state) as a symbol of the UK's values or ethos. Only one of the respondents mentioned 'democratic values', while – markedly – none of the respondents mentioned human rights as being a particular 'UK value or ethos'.

One cannot criticise the UK-based respondents for their focus on integrating issues such as human rights and the subordination of the military to civilian control, particularly in the context of continuing atrocities committed by the security forces in DRC. (For a defence of including such topics in English language training or other educational programmes, see Harwood and Hahn 1990, Snow et al. 1989 and Whitehead 2009.) However, what is interesting is that this is defined in the project goals as 'UK values and ethos' rather than universal values or rights – quite what makes these values specific to the UK is unclear. This is reflected in the trainees' responses which make not one association of universal human rights as a specifically UK concept, arguably because they too shared those values as a universal concept. In the project goals, the equating of human rights and specifically 'UK values and ethos' can be seen as paternalist, or indeed somewhat patronising, in the related assumption that because abuses are being committed in DRC, this means that respect for universal human rights is not a Congolese value. The inferred inferiority of the Congolese (and their lack of humanity or respect for basic human rights) in this assumption is also reflected in one response from a UK-based stakeholder, who stated that; 'Basically the project is there to improve the Congolese capability to govern themselves without murdering people [sic]'.

I am not suggesting that – perhaps with the exception of the last example above – the UK-based stakeholders believe that the citizens of DRC do not value universal human rights. However, the language usage in the project goals certainly implies this, which opens projects such as this to accusations of colonial paternalism and linguistic imperialism.

On the wider question of why the UK supports the PEP project in DRC (Question one), there was a great deal more agreement between UK-based respondents and Congolese project trainees. All of the UK-based stakeholders and over 90 per cent of the project participants stated that it was to enable the DRC to participate more effectively in peace support or peacekeeping operations, or to improve regional stability. Some critics might argue that the UK's aim here is to use African soldiers as proxies in international conflicts so as to avoid UK soldiers facing danger, but this ignores the realities of the situation. In DRC, this is not the case[16]. The conflict in the East of DRC is an African regional conflict; while it has its roots in colonialism and colonial mismanagement, it must be solved locally, by locals. The desire to take ownership of the situation is reflected in DRC President Kabila's recent push for the withdrawal of international UN forces (under their acronym MONUC, or since July 2010 under the new mandate, MONUSCO) under a clear timetable. Functionally, English is a tool which supports peacekeeping and peace support operations; as the UK-based Ministry of Defence respondent confirms: 'On several occasions locals have lost their lives due to the inability to communicate with the United Nations Troops and also the FARDC have misunderstood joint orders with their UN partners.' English, as the language of the SADC (Southern African Development Community) peacekeeping forces and of international peacekeeping forces under the auspices of the UN, plays an integral role in improving the effectiveness of peacekeeping and peace support operations.

Some UK-based respondents also admitted that the project goals went beyond the stated ones related to improving the English language capacity of the FARDC. One UK-based stakeholder said that the UK has a number of goals, 'some direct and some non-direct'. These were described by another UK-based respondent as a need to better position the UK for influence, 'in contrast to France, which has been marketed better.' Another admitted that '[t]he DRC is of significant strategic importance to the UK as a source of minerals ... hence its stability is important to the UK's economy.' These responses indicate that UK interest plays a role in projects such as these; while they were more than outweighed by UK-based responses centring on encouraging regional stability to bring peace and alleviate poverty and suffering, this UK interest cannot be ignored. It is perhaps naïve to expect projects in fragile states to be motivated purely by altruism, or internationalism (and I am certain that stakeholders in fragile states are fully aware of the unspoken reasons underpinning certain projects), but broader intent related to strategic or commercial interest should be acknowledged, otherwise accusations of covert imperialist influence are justified. I would argue that these could be acknowledged clearly in project documents (under 'benefits to the partner' and 'benefits to the UK') without damaging relationships or undermining the projects themselves; codifying intent and objectives leads to greater openness between partners and lessens potential for covert hegemony and for donor competition (and, therefore, a greater chance of project success[17]).

Of final note is that a number of Congolese respondents also acknowledged the inherent hegemonic power of the project and identified hegemonic project outcomes which are unstated in the project goals. One Congolese respondent wrote 'the United Kingdom presents its culture and mentality as a just virtue and a model reference to follow for the rest of the world. All the powerful countries have done this to maintain authority for a long time'. Another respondent suggested that a goal of the project is 'so that our country can speak English even though it wasn't colonised by the English'. A further respondent stated that 'the UK supports the primacy of the English language across the world', while another pointedly noted that '[t]o study a language without knowing its culture is nonsense'. This awareness of the potential hegemony supports my contention that the theory of linguistic imperialism does not acknowledge the agency of speakers of other languages. These responses show full awareness of the potential hegemonic role of English, but demonstrate a willingness to engage with it on their own terms.

Structural problems: Measuring achievement and securing continued support

One of the primary weaknesses of PEP DRC was the structural agreement on funding. While the project was planned and agreed as a three-year project, funding for each consecutive year was only approved on a yearly basis. The approval for project continuation at best arrived in the last month of the financial year and on two occasions actually after the end of the financial year. This seriously constrained project activities, as the project had to operate in effect as three one-year projects rather than one three-year project, with little or no opportunity for long-term planning and with uncertainty every March as to whether the project would still be there in April.[18] While PEP DRC was successful in securing annual funding to complete the project cycle (and to develop into a second three-year project 2010–2013), PEP projects in other countries were arbitrarily terminated early (in one case after just one year), with great damage to the relationship between the host country and the UK and to the local stakeholders (including learners and teachers).

I am of course aware that this is not a problem specific to ELT projects in development, but more a general reflection of the fact that development funding from governments is subject to swift-changing geo-political priorities. However, I strongly believe that ELT projects in development are easy targets and suffer disproportionally from funding cuts and early closure due to the following factors.

Firstly, the ELT in development sector is years behind other development sectors in terms of monitoring, evaluation and measuring impact. Coleman (2002) provides a detailed discussion of this problem and little has changed in the years since Coleman's study. PEP DRC was no different in this respect: no impact assessment was written into the project plan and no funds were allocated for this purpose. It is unfeasible to think that a development project in a fragile state outside the field of ELT would not have a dedicated period, of post-project impact assessment and have dedicated funds and human resources for this purpose. PEP DRC measured numbers – of trainees, of deployments on Peace support activities, of teacher training sessions, workshops, etc. – but numbers do not tell the story of impact.[19] While it is much easier to count the number of teachers at a seminar than it is to measure behaviour change as a result of project activity, this is no excuse for not attempting the latter. The rest of the development sector is doing this and so should ELT professionals.

This perhaps explains a related problem, that of the relationship between ELT organisations, international organisations (such as the UN) and donors operating in fragile states (such as DfID). Despite DfID being a co-owner of PEP DRC, DfID staff failed to visit the project on any occasion during the project lifespan. This is indicative of a more general problem, that international organisations are paying little attention to ELT: for example, the international conference on Language, Education and the Millennium Development Goals, organised by UNESCO, UNICEF and SEAMEO in November 2010, had only one session concerned with ELT in development. Kennett (2002) has argued that the DfID 1997 White Paper signalled an end to support for English language training projects in fragile states, and, other than a few isolated exceptions[20], little has changed since then. This lack of interest from international organisations and donors is unsurprising given the lack of focus on measuring impact, monitoring and evaluation and the lack of research into ELT in development (Coleman 2010) which might justify further engagement.

I acknowledge above (as did the Congolese project participants in their responses to the questionnaire) the unavoidable potential for negative hegemonic impact of an ELT project in a fragile state. To address this, a longitudinal study was conducted as part of PEP DRC in 2009, which investigated whether critical praxis could encourage the development of complex language identities leading to learner-generated counter-hegemonic discourses. The following section reports on this study.

Towards critical praxis and counter-hegemonic discourses in post-colonial English language teaching

There is a growing recognition within ELT, catalysed by projects such as PEP DRC operating in fragile states, that greater sensitivity is needed to the potential of hegemonic influence through ELT projects. This has certainly been recognised by the British Council (Knagg 2010) and this recognition was the stimulus for the study outlined here.

Hegemony, language and identity in fragile states

Identity crisis catalysed by globalisation and the encroachment of powerful hegemonic alien cultures affects fragile states disproportionately. As a result, there is strong potential for the hegemonic depositing of alien beliefs through the teaching of English as an additional language. However, there is also the possibility for English to produce counter-hegemonic discourses in the quadriglossic linguistic structure of DRC. If spontaneous grammars (see below) can be encouraged in the classroom, through the medium of English as an additional language and the encouragement of immediate learner-ownership of the language through subversion, learners can create identities (and even their own 'language') counter-hegemonic to the colonial language identity and separate from an English language identity. This provides the theoretical underpinning to the design of the research study, which was conducted as a component of PEP DRC in 2009.

Language change, or a significant challenge to the language identity of its citizens, constitutes a significant external and internal challenge to the fragile state. This problem has become more pronounced with technological and socio-economic developments since the end of the colonial era:

> identity has become an issue because the reference points for the self have become unstuck ... The contemporary understanding of the self is that of a social self framed in relations of difference rather than unity and coherence. Identity becomes a problem when the self is constituted in the recognition of difference rather than sameness. **(Delanty 2003:135)**

These themes are also taken up by Bendle (2002), who argues that, since the start of the 20th century, there has been increasing secularisation and a growing focus on self-fulfilment. He also argues that there have been advances in human rights and an eroding of national institutions of state and power. Globalisation has led to a loss of local and national economic controls and a growing cynicism in culture, encouraged by increasing flows of information and increasing public access to that information.

Bendle and Delanty are describing Western society, but their critique is also true of current happenings in fragile states in Africa and elsewhere. The hegemonic influence of Western culture and the economic and political norms forced on African societies by international organisations such as the UN, the IMF and the World Bank (or through conditionality in bilateral aid, see Moyo 2009) have led to a crisis of identity. The individual (as opposed to the group) has replaced traditional societal structures and this replacement of community by difference (dichotomous differences) has led to conflict within African identity (Malaba 2006, Ibhawaegbele 2006). It is for this reason that consideration of language identity is critical in the implementation of ELT projects in fragile states.

Gramsci on language and hegemony

Gramsci's theories of language and hegemony provided a framework for developing the study. Gramsci described two grammars[21] of hegemony: 'normative' grammar and 'spontaneous' grammar'.[22] Normative grammar, Gramsci said, is 'the reciprocal monitoring, reciprocal teaching, reciprocal "censorship" ... to create a grammatical conformism, [and] to establish "norms" of correctness and incorrectness' (Gramsci 1985:180). Normative grammars are coerced by fear, or coerced subconsciously by hegemonic forces in society; they are often described as the way people 'should' talk. Spontaneous grammar, by comparison, is that which utilises maximum individualism and free-will in its construction. It is not dictated to by persuasion, coercion, historical pressure, nor is it limited by external structures.

Gramsci acknowledges that spontaneous grammars can (and perhaps ideally will) become normative given time as they will unify into one language. Ives (2004) explains Gramsci's ideal:

> The goal is to achieve a common language, not a singular, dominant interpretation of everything ... this hegemonic (or counter-hegemonic) language must be unified enough, coherent enough, to yield effective resistance to capitalist hegemony (and its language). **(Ives 2004:114)**

It is important that Gramsci's support for the development of a revolutionary language is understood as organic and bottom-up. Gramsci is highly critical of the artificial imposition of a universal single language (as some argue ELT embodies) in his criticism of Esperanto.[23] As a language imposed for the benefit of commerce or leisure travel, Esperanto is described as a tool of bourgeois cosmopolitanism (Ives 2004:56), an attempt to impose a false consciousness on the subaltern. If English wishes to avoid the same drawbacks, it has to be accepted and appropriated organically, with the respect of the individual and the support of the fragile state's citizens.

Overview of the study

The goal of the study, which was approved prior to engagement by all local stakeholders, was to identify the development of textual identities and/or counter-hegemonic discourses in learner-produced texts; as such, this necessitated a qualitative approach to data collection. Following Appleby (2002), Belz (2002), Kramsch (1998, 2000, 2003) and Kramsch and Lam (1999), I decided to design a weekly instrument for encouraging written textual identity which could then be examined through discourse analysis.

'Class Y'[24] was chosen for the study. It comprised 14 learners (13 male, one female). On commencing this tranche of training, the learners had an average proficiency level of 2 on the STANAG 6001 proficiency scale.[25] The learners were all FARDC officers between the ranks of Second Lieutenant and full Colonel and had already completed 420 hours' language training through PEP during the period January to July 2009. Among the 14 learners, there were 11 different mother tongues: Buza, Kibembe, Kicongo, Kimongo, Kinande, Kingombe, Kiswahili, Lingala, Lokele, Mashi and Tshiluba. The programme commenced in August 2009 and lasted for seven weeks.

Principles for the learning environment

Brutt-Griffler and Samimy's research (1999) highlights the importance of the local non-native English-speaking teacher in developing counter-hegemonic discourses. Class Y would be taught by a Congolese teacher at IMLA, Major G. While the focused materials would be used just once per week, a series of principles was agreed for the other classroom sessions to ensure that the methodology and approach were complementary (Box 2). A workshop was held with Major G and other teachers from IMLA where the principles were agreed for Class Y's upcoming course; these were designed with reference to the theoretical principles outlined above.

Box 2: Classroom principles for the research period

1. **Humanist methods**
   To minimise anxiety caused during struggles of identity, humanist methods would be used. These would include soothing music in class, a minimising of criticism or negative feedback, integration of creative right- and left-brain activities, poetry and art as texts and an increase in the amount of tasks which encouraged personal and emotional responses rather than closed, text-specific comprehension questions.

2. **Acceptability of mother tongue in class**
   To stimulate multilingual hybridity, learners should be encouraged to view positively the facets of their existing indigenous language identity and not to see English as 'better', 'more powerful' or a threat. It was agreed to encourage the use of mother tongue in class (if learners thought that concepts could be better expressed in that way) and to encourage mother tongue usage to foster language mixing skills when communicating with learners with the same mother tongue, thereby creating a realistic communication act.

> Box 2: Classroom principles for the research period (continued)

3. Mother tongue and L2 source texts

In order not to encourage the choice of one identity or another, but to encourage a complex interplay of intermingling identities (thereby working outside the English grammatical hegemonic framework and delegitimising it), it was agreed to use an equal mixture of authentic mother tongue and L2 texts (oral and written) as source materials for activities.

4. Afrocentrism

When the coursebook presented non-African role models, or non-African case studies, it was agreed that these would be supplemented with equivalent activities centred on Africans and African experiences. It is important to note that the Afrocentric materials would supplement, not replace, the other materials, thereby avoiding the creation of a binary, dichotomous, zero sum model.

Principles for the design of materials

Following the work of Kramsch (Kramsch 1998, 2000, 2003, Kramsch and Lam 1999) and Appleby (2002), it was indicated that the development of textual identities was a promising method of identity generation and a possible point of departure for learners in beginning to create spontaneous grammars and subvert English for counter-hegemonic discourses. The materials were designed specifically with the goal of stimulating written textual identities where possible. Harwood and Hahn's (1990) recommendations for handling sensitive issues were useful; these advocate that learner consent is necessary for challenging materials and that an open climate in the classroom is necessary. As many of the issues themselves provoke an emotional response, effort was made to include more right-brain activities and reflective tasks, following Tomlinson's (1998) development of 'access-self' materials. These more humanistic 'access-self' activities encourage reflection and reduce anxiety. The particular features of Tomlinson's guide which were followed in the creation of the materials were that tasks should be open ended, should engage the learners personally as human beings and should stimulate both left- and right-brain activities. In addition, it was intended that post-reading activities should first elicit holistic responses, that feedback should be provided through commentaries and suggested answers rather than an answer sheet, and that follow-up activities (possibly involving other learners) should be encouraged (Tomlinson 1998:322-323).

Overview of materials

Box 3 provides a brief explanation of the design and construction of the materials. The materials were delivered as part of a series of weekly sessions.

Data was gathered in the form of the learners' written responses to the materials in Weeks one to seven. An analysis of the texts revealed a number of major themes, which I describe below with illustrative extracts.

Box 3: Overview and rationale of materials (by week)

Week one

The materials in week one were designed to facilitate the development of identity and to aid motivation and hence learning, following Dörnyei's L2 motivational self system (Dörnyei 2005, 2009). Sheldon and Lyubomirsky's (2006) 'Best Possible Self' extensive writing project was the model for these materials: to encourage learners to begin visualisation and imaging of an ideal future self while also engaging the textual identity.

In addition, to activate learners' ideal selves, they were asked to describe a role model and then discuss the values and successes of these models. It was hoped that these role models would be local (or African) and therefore hold less hegemonic baggage than native speaker role models representing the existing hegemony. In this way, the materials also provided a certain diagnostic of existing external hegemonic influence.

Week two

The materials in week two were designed to allow learners to explore pathways to their ideal future self and to look at the role of English in achieving that goal. This was intended to support strong self-criticism so that learners could get a realistic sense of where they and their identity are now, identify how they might develop and encourage self-assessment exercises. Learners were encouraged to make a realistic, critical assessment of the positive and negative factors in their life at present.

Following the delivery of the week two session, frequent visualisation activities (warmers eliciting positive lexis for success, extensive writing about goals and aspirations, metaphor and poetry creation for positivity, etc.) were integrated into lesson plans.

Week three

Week three's focus was on learners' mother tongues and English. Using a number of Lingala proverbs as examples[26], learners were encouraged to explore issues of translation and grammar and to consider how grammar and language affects thought. This was intended to stimulate a recognition of the strength and power of their respective mother tongues and to challenge ideas of the dominance or inherent superiority of English or other colonial or alien languages, or languages of wider communication (such as Lingala or Kiswahili).

Week four

In considering subjectivity and discourse, it was recommended that teachers raise awareness of the embedded cultural hegemony of English to create counter-hegemonic discourse. Benesch (2006) provides an excellent example of raising critical awareness of hegemonic cultural deposits with media analysis activities. In developing classroom activities, she argues that the goal should be to encourage learner exploration for self-awareness through guided discovery, not instruction. The materials for week four therefore covered an analysis of the representation of Africa and Africans in UK newspapers and magazines and a

Box 3: Overview and rationale of materials (by week) (continued)

comparison with the representation of Africa and Africans in Congolese
newspapers and magazines.

Week five

Week five materials were designed as an introduction to language mixing.
Local, well known slogans for commercial products were used as examples of
mixing English and Lingala or French and Lingala. A study of language mixing in
popular music was made.[27] This was intended to open learners to the concept
of language mixing and prepare them for their own generation of spontaneous
grammars through language mixing.

Weeks six and seven

The materials for weeks six and seven recycled issues of representations in the
media and in common culture, through the use of the text *The Complete MAUS* by Art
Spiegelman (2003).[28] Learners were encouraged to investigate anthropomorphism
and to create written and visual representations of groups of people relevant to
themselves. Learners were also asked to engage in an open writing exercise on a
challenging issue and to engage, if they wished, in free language mixing.

Self and Other and the relationship with the developed world

Pervading the learners' texts was a distinct sense of otherness when describing
the developed world. This manifested itself in descriptions of Self closely identified
with local or national community in opposition to the Other represented by the
developed world. One learner described a strong desire 'to communicate with the
other world' (week one, emphasis added).[29] Other learners stated:

> *Other people [non-Africans] aren't have the right news.* **(week four)**

> *I would like them [non-Africans] to descend on terrain to touch the reality, to know
> how to behave of African.* **(week four)**

The imagery in the second quote above is telling. The learner has appropriated a
biblical motif, with non-Africans 'descending' – in effect coming down to the level of
Africans from their heavenly place of abode. A different learner, marking Other with the
clear reference to 'white man', equates the dominance of the Other (with greater travel
opportunities and successful multinational corporations) with a superior intellect:

> *White men walk more and build many firm because of his good mind.* **(week four)**

The idea that personal betterment can only come through experience overseas
(in the terrain of the Other) is repeated in the majority of texts from weeks one and
two, for example:

> *My feeling is to be abroad for working. The Job will allow me to have a living fair
> and permited me to be a best officer.*

> *I'd like to be a big chief in our army ... I need to go abroad for continuing that.*

However, while the developed world was idealised as a place of escape and as a necessary place of transit for future success, there was also a recognition of the natural wealth of Africa and somewhat idealised pastoral ideals:

> In Sub-Saharan there are a lot of wealth like for me, wildlife and mineral wealth. Africa is the ecological lung. The world to day have The problem with the ozone layer. Sub-Saharan Africa have one of the big party of the forest in the world and this forest could help the world fight against the climate matter. **(week four)**

> After my military career, I will choose to live in the countryside, because I like farming and animal raising. **(week one)**

> I will work in UN ... [then] I could organise society of fishery in Congo river. **(week two)**

In the texts, there is some recognition of globalisation and materialism and perhaps a recognition of the threat they pose for the natural environment in DRC.

Self, Community and Supercommunity[30]
While learners' texts exhibited representations of self identity, this was grounded in a continuum of Self, Community and Supercommunity. Individual actions and aspirations were related directly to Community and to Supercommunity rather than being focused solely on individual progress or benefit; the actions of the Self were related to and interdependent upon the actions or future of all. This learner describes an ideal future self, but then related this immediately to Community and then to Supercommunity:

> I will do many things in my country like to teach the children to become the best men and women to show them how to protect people and I will help my country to solve some problem when I will be sent somewhere as a risponsible. **(week two)**

The next learner directly coalesces the future individual Self and the future Supercommunity:

> My ideal future self is that my country DR Congo will participate effectively in the peacekeeping mission. **(week one)**

English as a means of accessing opportunities
There was a recognition in the learners' texts that English was a powerful global force and that developing a capacity in English would provide access to certain opportunities:

> English is a International language and all transactions are used. **(week three)**

> Using English is very interesting and can help us. **(week three)**

For many, this opportunity was the opportunity to travel and therefore to achieve the learning (and perceived success) that time overseas brings. One learner noted that the sole goal of language learning was to learn 'until to be able to use this language for to communicate with the other world' (week three), while, for others, travel was an important factor:

I think that through English I will have an opportunity to travel around the world. **(week three)**

Through English I will have an opportinity to travel around the world. **(week three)**

A number of learners linked English ability to access to the fruits of globalisation and to success in business. There was an awareness that a knowledge of English would play a role in granting or preventing access to other specific fields:

Now with the problem of globalisation it is mandatory to learn English for to integrate the concert of nations. **(week three)**

Actually the use of the computer need the knowledge of English, too. A lot of bussiness in the today world need a good comprehension of the English. **(week three)**

English is one of the language that many people in world use now for communication and business. So, is very important for me to make effort to learn and use it carefully. **(week three)**

In a small number of learners' texts, there could be sensed a degree of perceived threat from English:

English is dominant in the field of education. **(week three)**

All over the world people are now speaking English even in french countries. **(week three)**

The use of the word 'dominant' may suggest a certain menace while the second quote's phrasing of 'even in french countries' indicates that the writer perhaps finds this a little unbelievable, maybe even shocking, for one living in a former Belgian colony where French, the colonially imposed language of wider communication, has previously been so important. In week five, one learner described a personal response to translating proverbs from their mother tongue into English, expressing a personal loss of integral worth:

My feeling was the risk of losing the proverb value.

In these data extracts, it is possible to detect some sense of threat (most clearly in the last example in the use of the word 'risk'). While it is impossible to extrapolate the reasons for this given the limited data set and scale of the research, it may be valid to suggest that one possible reason could be that the learner felt threatened through the negative impact on mother tongue semantic meaning (and, by extrapolation, on their own identity) that the translation into English caused.

Mother tongue and English
Learner responses indicated a developing awareness of linguistic difference and a nascent understanding of the interplay of language and thought. Learners stated:

The grammar and structure of English and my first language are very different. **(week three)**

These [different grammars] result in different ways of thinking because the
structure of African languages is different with European or American.
(week three)

I think these result in different of thinking. **(week three)**

Learners demonstrated an awareness of the difficulty of semantic translation and
a growing awareness of the richness of their own mother tongue. They described a
tangible sense of acknowledging a changing reality when changing languages:

When we translate literally, the meaning of the sentence or expression changes
automaticaly. The translation don't keep the sens the same sens of the local
language. (week three)

It was difficult to translate ... when I was translating the meaning now I was
thinking about the reality and idea. (week three)

There was also evidence of learners linking language and identity. For one learner,
translating from mother tongue into English stimulated feelings of a self displaced
from a native speech community:

I know this at my language and the signification of them ... I feel nostalgic, I think
about my village. **(week three)**

The translation exercise brought the conflict within identity (or between identities)
to consciousness; the learner was able to identify competing language identities
and relate them to past and present life paths.

Political consciousness and response to globalisation
In a number of texts, the learners displayed a strong political consciousness. One
learner stated that:

other parts of the world see that the government can have many problems. And
they [the government] prefer to hide some realities. **(week four)**

The texts also gave evidence of a developing political consciousness in a
recognition of false perceptions of Africa from outside the continent and the role of
the media in perpetuating these perceptions. This is highlighted in this excerpt:

The Sub-Saharan Africa is not only where the people are suffering. The are some
people who are in the best life like in the Europe. **(week four)**

They [non-African media] usually shown Sub-African countries as part of world
that is under-developed or a part of world that is very potentially rich but in which
people live poorly. This way of seeing Sub-Africa, let people who live in developed
countries to qualify Sub-Africans non intelligent, lazy people and people who can't
be developed without be assisted by developed countries. **(week four)**

Learners also identified the force of the media and its effects on their life in
DRC as well as advertisers' usage of the perceived value or superiority of English
in marketing:

The media influence many things in the life for the people. **(week five)**

The company used this mixture of English and Lingala for marking on attention on this. **(week five)**

One learner also identified a potential feeling of threat felt by the Other – the developed world – when faced with the media-fed and selective images of Africa; after analysing the content of several editions of the UK *Sunday Times* newspaper, the learner stated:

They [the readers] may also be threatened [by] the witchcraft oaths. **(week five)**

Learners showed a consciousness of the effects of globalisation and the demands that it placed upon them as members of a Community and Supercommunity. In addition to the examples above, a theme that was present in many learner texts was that of a resistance to globalisation, highlighted in one learner's description of 'the problem of globalisation' (week three, emphasis added). While bringing possibilities for personal, Community and Supercommunity development, globalisation was not seen as a benevolent and inherently positive force: it was a problem which must be tamed. In a striking metaphor, one learner described the 'problem' of 'integrat(ing) the concert of nations' (week three). Here, globalisation is seen as a difficult process of co-ordinating competing and disparate melodies and notes to achieve a musical harmony.

Silence in the political consciousness

In contrast to the political consciousness in learners' texts detailed above, there was a distinct silence on military and political issues surrounding the then ongoing conflicts in the East and Northeast of DRC. This was manifested in an inaccurate scaling of lesser conflicts within the continent against conflicts in DRC and – in a number of learners' texts – as an expressed (but incorrect) conviction that the conflict in DRC had already ended, that it was a past event:

South Africa was one of the country where were the worst situations as act of killing and so on. **(week one)**

my native country is in the East of DRC where were many troubles some years ago. **(week one)**

when we were during the bad situation of war. **(week four)**

This is particularly interesting given the period during which the texts were created, which was a period of escalated conflict: joint military operations by DRC and Rwanda, supported by MONUC, in Eastern DRC against the FDLR[31] peaked in the period of research; Laurent Nkunda was deposed as head of the CNDP[32] and arrested by Rwandan authorities; and new and bloody conflicts erupted along the DRC's borders with Uganda and Central African Republic (respectively due to incursions by the LRA[33] and inter-tribal conflict).

This silence – or, perhaps, more than silence, an unwillingness to admit to the past and current state of one's Community and Supercommunity – indicates a defence mechanism in the self. Hopkins et al. (1990:312) describe respondent self-deception in research as an attempt to 'maintain a sense of personal worth' and this could be an example of such an action in progress.

Christian faith and anti-Semitism

A number of learners' texts expressed a strong Christian faith in the responses to the materials.[34] One learner appropriated the biblical story of the Good Samaritan when describing his/her role model; another, when describing the pathway to the ideal self, stated simply; 'I'll pray God and ask him to protect me' (Week 2). Other examples in the learners' texts were:

> *First of all, if I see my Vision I think depend on the God.* **(week one)**

> *The best role model in life is first of all following the Christ language.* **(week one)**

In certain cases this prevented the learner from engaging with the materials or from completing the activity:

> *I'm the one who has been created by God. I don't know what I can write in this question [asked to describe an ideal future self]: there is only the God who knows what he'll do for me.* **(week one)**

> *It's very tough for me to watch this video according to my position as a 'God man'.* **(week five)**

> *My religion don't permit me to listen for this music.* **(week five)**

This strong expression of Christian faith was matched with an equally strong voicing of anti-Semitic feelings when responding to the materials in week six (stimulated by Spiegelman 2003):

> *mice represent jewish people because they work like mice. Jewish people never show their real face. They can be doing something but showing other thing different. You'll think they're friendly but enemies.* **(week six)**

> *they [Jewish people] want to kill you, you don't know because they look for to be your friend after that they accomplish his mission for killing you.* **(week six)**

> *Mice is hypocritical animal like Jewish people.* **(week six)**

This anti-Semitic sentiment was most surprising. There is no real Jewish community of note in DRC. While DRC was a known place for European Jews to reside before the creation of Israel in 1948, there was little or no attempt to convert the local population and the Jewish population of DRC is now estimated at less than one thousand (Rorison 2008). There is only one remaining synagogue in DRC, in Lubumbashi, in the far Southeast of the country. It can only be assumed, therefore that these sentiments have been appropriated from the numerous expatriate Christian preachers and missionaries who regularly visit DRC (or have missions in the provinces) as it is difficult to believe that any anti-Semitism which may have existed pre-1948 (of which there is no evidence) would have fossilised in local identities to the extent that it was still a strong aspect of religious identity in 2009–2010.

Anthropomorphic representations

The materials in week six asked learners to consider a grouping of people which was important to the learner and to draw an appropriate animal representation of that group considering the certain characteristics of different animals (following Spiegelman 2003). Table 2 summarises the learners' responses.

Group	Animal	Explanation
Table 2: Learners' responses to week six materials		
Congolese people	Snake	'Snake will better represents Congolese people. Although they are very kind and express hospitality to anyone, they become very hostile and angry when attacked or provoked. They keep calm only when their enemies or perpetrators are killed or kick out.'
FARDC	Leopard	'because they are very strong'
	Cat	'very clever and wicked like a lion'
MONUC	Mice	'you can live with them and you never know what they're doing'
	Cat	'protect ... peace'
	Cat	'protect ... peace'
	Cat	No explanation provided

Several of these representations deserve comment. In describing Congolese people as snakes, the learner's comment indicates a perceived threat. It is interesting to note that this learner has thus already considered responses to (an anticipated, perhaps expected) future threat.

The descriptions of the FARDC are also of note. The leopard became the national symbol of DRC after Mobutu proclaimed 'The Leopard' to be his own nickname, printed the image of the animal on national symbols (including all banknotes) and nicknamed the ever-popular Congolese national football team 'Les Leopards'. It remains a frequent symbol for the armed forces, appearing on many regimental crests.

Even more interesting is the choice of the cat for the FARDC, with the comment that the cat is 'wicked like a lion'. The FARDC have a very poor reputation; indeed, many believe that they are equally as responsible for the rape and murder of Congolese civilians as other negative forces (International Alert 2005, IRIN 2007, Kristof 2008). A FARDC officer openly calling the FARDC 'wicked' is quite a criticism, even more so when considered in relation to the possible horizontal intertextuality (q.v. Kristeva 1986) of the learners' immediately preceding lesson studying Spiegelman (2003) in which cats represent German Nazis.

Finally, the explanation for representing MONUC as mice also warrants comment. Relations between MONUC and the government of DRC – in particular between MONUC and the FARDC – were constantly strained. There is a general perception among the Congolese that MONUC failed to adequately support the FARDC in operations against negative forces in the East, while from MONUC came criticism that the FARDC continued (and continues) to conduct operations under unit commanders who face extant warrants to appear before the International Criminal

Court on charges of crimes against humanity. A statement from a FARDC officer that 'you never know what they [MONUC] are doing' highlights the mutual mistrust and lack of respect. These feelings are rarely expressed openly. FARDC officers are discouraged from making open criticism as there is a general (if grudging) understanding that in many areas MONUC was the sole provider of security for civilians. However, the learner's statement here indicates that he or she was comfortable to express these sentiments through anthropomorphic metaphor, albeit through English rather than their mother tongue. This can be seen as a seed of counter-hegemonic discourse.

Language mixing and emerging spontaneous grammars

The written responses to week six materials provided evidence, through learners' language mixing, of the development of complex language identities and emergent spontaneous grammars. Box 4 is an example of this; the learner's original text is provided, together with accompanying translation of the French and Lingala phrases. Here Captain A describes the difficulties of living in Kinshasa, explaining the problem of getting goods from the villages into the cities with poor roads; a lack of food getting to Kinshasa results in fewer farmers growing crops for sale, which results in high prices. These high prices for staple foods push people towards theft or, in some cases, prostitution. Captain A calls for employment, better salaries and better infrastructure.

Box 4: Captain A's written response (week six)

Translation key

Standard text: originally written in English
Underlined text: originally written in Lingala
Italic text: originally written in French

Original text	Text with English translation
Living in Kinshasa as in my language says okemaka, okemaka, do your best, soki te! O kokufa. *Tellement vie* ezali pasi, *vie* eva mbazi na plan eco [?], *vie* eyali mbazi *dans tout les plans, politique, economique* and *social*.	Living in Kinshasa as in my language says do your best, do your best, do your best! Otherwise you die. Because *life* is tough, *life* is hard in plan eco [?³⁵], *life* is hard in all aspects, politics economics and social.
A country needs *de ces petits points mais caustaud pour que* ezala *developpe*, ba nzela ya *bien* and transportations if not pasi nde eko envahir mboka. If the difficulties are in Kinshasa it is about those points, *interieur* nde ezali ko provide *ville* ya Kinshasa with food, na *interieur* the roads ekufa, no cars, they are *diminue productions* ya bilanga, ndenge nini *difficulte* ndengo yala na mboka?	A country needs *those small points but rough for that* to be *developed*, the roads of good and transportations if not hard will invade country. If the difficulties are in Kinshasa it is about those points, *village* is be to provide *town* of Kinshasa with food, at *village* the roads died, no cars, they are *less productions* of plantation, how come difficulty be in the country?
In Kinshasa, the transportations kwanga, likemba if you aren't makasi you will stay at *arret* longtime, no money to pay car, misala ezali kasi *maigre salary*, nde origine ya moyibi na misala that's why they say 'mbongo muke, small job'.	In Kinshasa, the transportations cassava leaves, plantain if you aren't strong you will stay at *stop* longtime, no money to pay car, work is yes *little salary*, then origin of theft at work that's why they say 'little money, small job'.

Bana ebele they don't study, minerval pasi, baboti baza maniolo, at home if the mother cooks food, they talk with her daughters biloko yango wana somba kwanga, that girl where she can get l'argent d'acheter duma? A partir de ca, muana mwasi goes out ask mbongo a paye guys and men ask her sex.	Children lots they don't study, school fee hard, family is problem, at home if the mother cooks food, they talk with her daughters food over there buy cassava leaves, that girl where she can get money to buy food? From that, child girl goes out ask money to pay guys and men ask her sex.
That's the difficulties regnant ici à Kinshasa. Oyo biso demandons na ours chiefs, misala and good salaries. Et puis naba interieur they build good roads, pour permettre ba evacuations ya ba produits vivieres.	That's the difficulties rule here in Kinshasa. This us demands of ours chiefs, work and good salaries. And then at villages they build roads, to allow the shipping of products for life.

There is a pattern to Captain A's language mixing which appears to go beyond simple language fragile games. Lingala is used when describing nature, food and ideas related to home and belonging, in words such as 'plantation', 'cassava leaves', 'plantain', 'children', 'food' and 'country'. Lingala is also used for shared life problems experienced by all in the learner's community: 'school fee is hard', 'family is problem', 'do your best. Otherwise you die'.

English, however, is used when describing problems associated with modernity and more contemporary individual woes: 'no money to pay car', 'men ask her [for] sex'. French appears to be used for concepts of officialdom and for political or administrational strata: 'village', 'town', 'money to pay guys', 'shipping', 'all aspects, politics economics and social'.

The mixing of languages was subconscious as the choice of language was spontaneous, without conscious prior planning. I would argue that the choice of language for the different sections is subconscious, but that it is not random; the learner is demonstrating through this text a microcosm or a cross-section of the complex intermingling of their language identities, demonstrating a rich linguistic resource and a skilful deployment of this resource. Encouraging the learner to explore this openly has led to the creation of an individual spontaneous grammar rooted in the learner's individual associations and emotions towards each language.[36]

The study raised a number of interesting points, which I discuss below.

Complex textual identities
The critical praxis employed during the research period through humanist teaching principles and the design of materials based on critical pedagogy allowed learners to develop complex textual identities which were reflected in the texts created in response to classroom materials.

The learners' sense of Self and Other, brought about through an Afrocentric consciousness, seemed to be demonstrated, as was a complex, multidimensional conception of the individual as a key agent in Community and Supercommunity. The use of repeated extensive writing exercises to nurture these facets of learner identity proved successful (albeit on a limited scale): open and personal writing opportunities acted as a mirror for learners to engage in self-reflection and to further enrich the interplay of their language identities.

Of particular value was Dörnyei's L2 Motivational Self System (Dörnyei 2009), which provided a foundation for the learners' exploration of identity and catalysed the development of textual identities. This was also fully in tune with Gramsci's claim that 'the starting point of critical elaboration is the consciousness of what one really is' (Gramsci 1971:323).

Learners' texts in week six demonstrated a noticeably greater complexity in spontaneous grammar. The value of writing for this process would seem to fit with an Expressivist view of writing, as theorised by Elbow (1998) and Murray (1985). While the Expressivist approach to writing has been much criticised (Faigley 1986, North 1987, Hyland 2002:23-24) for a romanticised view of the writing process and for lacking a clear quality assessment mechanism, when situated within Gramscian theory and critical praxis, these criticisms become obsolete: the writing process is an expression of self-exploration. Furthermore, questions of quality or 'good' writing are here based on the degree of self-reflection or identity development. They are therefore self-ascribed by the learner as author and assessor, rather than enforced by external validating bodies in comparison to alien standards in textual models or in standards of accuracy.

Politicised learners and counter-hegemonic discourses

The learners demonstrated a political consciousness in their responses. This was manifest in their reactions to globalisation (and slight aversion in some learner responses to Western values surrounding the pursuit of wealth). These were quite critical, rooted in Community values and a clear Afrocentrism and recognised the dominant power and role of English in the learners' own development and in the wider world. It should be noted that learners did not fully reject Western or European concepts; learners showed a complex hybridity of thought in their acceptance and critique of alien values (cf. Higgins 2009). This highlights the importance for teachers, particularly in fragile states (but not excluding those operating in developed countries), to use critical praxis and to encourage critical engagement in order to help learners protect their own Selves in the face of globalisation's erosion (or assimilation) of subaltern identity.

The research period was just seven weeks. For more developed counter-hegemonic discourses to emerge one would need a much longer period with the learners. However, even during this short period, there was evidence of some counter-hegemonic discourse in learners' negative reactions to globalisation, their critical appraisals of the local and international media and their criticisms of authority and accepted hegemonic forces in their lives (FARDC, MONUC, etc.). That a large part of these counter-hegemonic discourses were stimulated through metaphor (anthropomorphism) and humanist 'right-brain' activities such as art, is indicative of the relevance of Gramsci's calls for the use of imagery and metaphor in identity development.

The spontaneous grammars exhibited in the learners' written responses in week six are themselves strong evidence of emergent counter-hegemonic discourse. The learners subverted not just English but also their own local languages, to take ownership of their expression, thereby resisting the hegemony of thought inherent in the imported colonial (and post-colonial) languages. Eleven of the 14 learners elected to write critical assessments of DRC, Kinshasa, or the FARDC in their texts, suggesting that the use of spontaneous grammar encouraged learners to challenge the hegemony of the status quo. This would support Brutt-Griffler and Samimy's findings (1999), which demonstrated greater learner comfort in addressing issues which threaten the Self in a second language rather than in the mother tongue. This comfort was due to distancing and to differing concepts of Other when taking on a different language identity.

Conclusions, recommendations and further research

I believe that there is a strong case for the teaching and learning of English in fragile states as a valuable component of mother tongue-based multilingual education.[37] As set out in the section on ELT in fragile states, there are well-grounded theoretical underpinnings for this; if these are followed, there is the potential for learners to create powerful counter-hegemonic dialogues.

However, ELT professionals need to take greater steps to ensure professionalism in the ELT industry particularly in (but not limited to) fragile states. This should include the recognition of English in Development as a specific branch of ELT, focusing on developing local Englishes and encouraging appropriation over acculturation, with the corresponding pursuit of a body of research in the field. International ELT bodies (such as the British Council, TESOL and multinational private sector language teaching centres) together with language teaching institutions in fragile states should insist on professional qualifications and experience when recruiting teachers, so that standards can be maintained and they should lobby governments to make such qualifications prerequisites for visas for expatriate teachers.

To further contribute towards this focus on professionalism, ELT projects and operations in fragile states must make monitoring and evaluation a key component of planning and implementation (as does the rest of the development sector), or remain on the sidelines of development efforts and be most vulnerable to cuts when funding decisions are reassessed. This will require a shift towards qualitative assessment of impact, and a recognition that quantitative measurement of participant numbers, numbers of trainings conducted, etc., is not a real measurement of impact at all. In addition, more research needs to be undertaken to examine the role of ELT in development, its risks and benefits. If ELT is to be recognised as a valuable component in the development of fragile states, practitioners need to start gathering data to measure its impact.

With greater professionalism and a more explicit regard to theory, ELT professionals operating in fragile states will be better placed to counter accusations of linguistic imperialism on theoretical and practical grounds. This has the potential to lead to a cycle of improvement, with professionalism leading to confidence, acceptance and research, feeding back into professionalism and so on. At the moment, research and progress are being hindered by the lack of professionalism and the widespread negativity towards English in fragile states based upon the critique of linguistic imperialism.

The same section above also indicates that ELT project designers and managers must be more sensitive to the language in which their goals are expressed.

They must avoid arrogant or presumptive paternalist assumptions of superiority through the association of UK (or Western) values with universal human rights (and the corollary disassociation of these universal rights with non-Western project recipients), or any assumptions of the superiority of English (or the superiority of capitalism and the developed world over the subaltern in fragile states), or of English being some kind of magic salve for poverty, under-development or other related problems. Furthermore, goals must be defined clearly and completely; project participants and other local stakeholders are not so naïve as not to realise that donor and lender organisations have over-arching strategic goals (and not so passive as to simply accept the hegemonic influences). Not codifying these goals in project documents opens projects to accusations of covert imperialism.

While the scale of research in this study has been limited, there is great potential for further research into the development of spontaneous grammars for counter-hegemonic discourse through the methods and approaches described.

The research study reported in the section 'Towards critical praxis ...' suggests that critical praxis in ELT, informed by Gramsci's theories of language and hegemony, can lead to the emergence of counter-hegemonic discourses. It also makes reference to the particular potential of these discourses in a fragile state. A number of recommendations for ELT in fragile states relating to classroom practice can be drawn from the study.[38]

Firstly, ELT practitioners should make critical praxis an integral part of the delivery of language education. In shifting the focus to appropriation and subversion of the language, English can be made to act as an empowering tool for learners – not as a replacement for their mother tongue, but in tandem with their mother tongue and other languages as a component of complex multivocality.

Secondly, ownership of the teaching and learning process should rest with local stakeholders rather than with foreign 'experts'. One corollary of this is that local teachers should be the default choice for project delivery rather than expatriate teachers. Another corollary is that materials should be locally designed and piloted; alien imported materials are likely to reflect inappropriate cultural biases.

In the delivery of ELT courses, it can be recognised that extensive writing activities which develop textual identity are a useful tool in learner development, particularly in language identity development. Such activities should not be seen as less useful than extensive speaking activities, as is often the case; the 'communicative' approach has led in many cases to a revaluing of the spoken over the written and an imbalanced focus on speaking and spoken fluency over writing.

The study also indicates that language mixing activities have a strong potential for creating spontaneous grammars and counter-hegemonic discourses, particularly following critical experiences, or in response to challenging issues. These activities should be integrated into existing syllabi, with a concurrent focus on the importance of code-switching.

The same section also highlights the idea that learners' political consciousnesses are an integral part of their identity and should be respected and explored during the delivery of a language teaching programme. Learners are political beings, just as classrooms are political spaces. Choosing to ignore the political, or to try to shut the political out of the classroom is not only impossible, but is itself a political choice which perpetuates the problem. Sensitive, well-planned activities which allow learners to explore the political through the additional language identity assist the development of empowering counter-hegemonic dialogues.

Finally, learners' mother tongues should be recognised as a rich source of material for exploration in the classroom and should not be treated as a hindrance or interference to the learning of second languages. As noted above, English should be seen as a valuable part of mother tongue-based multilingual education and a recognition and exploration of the mother tongue in the English language classroom addresses the prestige gap between mother tongue and English and aids the development of pride in the mother tongue.

The scale of the research study was limited both in its duration (seven weeks) and in the size of its sample. The positive results achieved in this study indicate that it would be beneficial to replicate the study over a longer term – perhaps investigating learners' changing identities through a year-long, or multi-year programme. It would also be interesting to replicate the study in an English-speaking environment (perhaps with learners from fragile states who are now living in the UK, USA, Australia, Canada, Ireland, New Zealand, etc.) to compare the effects on learners.

In addition, I feel that there is great potential for further investigating Gramscian theory with relation to ELT, particularly in fragile states or in the field of ELT in development. This study has looked at a number of Gramsci's key concepts, but there remains a wealth of Gramsci's writing on education, consent, hegemony and language policy which it would be fruitful and challenging to investigate in other ELT contexts.

Finally, the evidence of the emergence of spontaneous grammars in learners' writing through language mixing is another area which calls for further research and investigation. This would be particularly interesting in studies which looked at developing and recording examples of spoken spontaneous grammar.

Notes

1. I would like to thank the staff and learners at IMLA, Kinshasa, whose work and whose development catalysed the ideas for this chapter. It was an honour and a pleasure to have joined them on their journeys of development and to have spent a rich and rewarding two years learning from them and learning with them. I would like to thank Hywel Coleman for his support and guidance and his encouragement and motivation. Thanks also to Helen Noble and Tania Lundu for their feedback and input into instrument design, for conducting data collection for the section on English language teaching in fragile states and for assistance with translation into/from Congolese languages. Final thanks go to Paul Woods at the British Council, Steve Terry at Sheffield Hallam University and Lt Col Tim Woodman of the UK Army, for their inspiration and encouragement.

2. The Crisis States Research Centre defines a fragile state as 'a state significantly susceptible to crisis in one or more of its sub-systems. It is a state that is particularly vulnerable to internal and external shocks and domestic and international conflicts.' (CSRC 2006)

3. It is worth highlighting the (then) UK Prime Minister Gordon Brown's claim, quoted in Pascoe-Watson's unashamedly triumphalist article *PM Brown's English Invasion (2008)*: 'We will take up with vigour the bold task of making our language the world's common language of choice.' Also of note is Sharlet's (2010: 78) exposure of an English language school in Lebanon funded by US Republican Party congressmen and senators. An alumnus of the school notes that 'The families of Syr are thinking our children are going to the [language school] just to learn the English language ... [b]ut there are a lot of secrets ... [i] t's for changing minds and getting students to study in the US and maybe come back [with] different ideas about Muslims and Jesus. To change our culture and our religion.'

4. TESOL: teaching English to speakers of other languages.

5. Gramsci did much to develop our current understanding of the term 'hegemony', yet nowhere in his writings does he codify succinctly what he took the term to mean; rather, the understanding of hegemony that has become associated with Gramsci is an aggregate of his entire writing on the subject. In this chapter, hegemony is taken to mean the organisation of consent and its relation to coercion in unequal power relationships, whether that consent is in the interests of the subaltern or not.

6. Gramsci used the term 'subaltern' in the military sense of a non-commissioned officer or soldier (perhaps to avoid censorship while writing in prison). In this chapter, I use the term subaltern as expanded by Spivak (1992): the subaltern is not simply the dominated, or the oppressed (e.g. the working classes); the subaltern is wholly disempowered and is positioned outside the power structures and therefore 'inaudible', or without voice to change the system from within (for example, the subjects of colonialism in Africa, Asia and the Americas).

7. The teaching of English to security forces (here described in shorthand as 'military English') is also one of contention. Edge (2003:704), for example, argues that military English teachers (in Iraq and Afghanistan) are 'working to facilitate the policies that the tanks were sent to impose.' However, this chapter takes the view that teaching English to security forces is justified when implemented sensitively and with peace support and mutual security through internationalism as its objectives. See Woods (2006) and Whitehead (2010a) for a more detailed defence of this position.

8. As Marx (1867) argues, capitalism's problems are not caused by the flawed, selfish or somehow 'evil' intentions of individual capitalists per se; rather, regardless of intent, the nature of the relationships inherent in the capitalist structure inevitably and unavoidably lead to inequality, neglect and suffering for the proletariat. In the same way, could the promotion of ELT, funded by the UK government and in the current geo-political climate, not be hegemonic, given

the relationships inherent in the structure of donor–educator–recipient and in the structures of power within the globalised economy? This is discussed in greater detail in the sub-section on 'Intent and purpose'.

9. 'Critical praxis' in this chapter is taken to mean praxis which recognises the power of English, but seeks to subvert it or use it for the creation of new identities and counter hegemonic discourses; this definition draws on Auerbach (1995) and Appleby (2002).

10. I was the Project Manager of PEP DRC from February 2008 to June 2010.

11. Personal email, 14 September 2010.

12. See also Hailemariam et al. (2011, Chapter 11 this volume) and Tembe and Norton (2011, Chapter 6 this volume).

13. An experienced manager working for a highly respected international chain of ELT schools in a fragile state admits that while company policy dictates that expatriate teachers need at minimum a CELTA-equivalent qualification and experience, in reality this policy is routinely ignored: 'Actually [our schools] can recruit who they damn well like, especially if they can use the excuse of operational necessity – we don't tell people this though.' (Personal email, 14 September 2010)

14. I am extremely grateful to my colleagues Helen Noble and Tania Lundu for their feedback and assistance with the design of the instrument and with the data collection.

15. Responses of Congolese participants are provided in English. As I translated these myself, I accept any responsibility for problems in translation.

16. Another interesting question raised is why the FARDC should learn English rather than international forces learning French or Lingala. There are two responses to this: 1) international forces typically work on six-month rotating deployments and it makes more sense in terms of efficiency to train the local forces who remain constant than to retrain international forces every six months with the new deployments. 2) Improving the English language ability of the FARDC is also envisaged to prepare them to be deployed on other peacekeeping operations outside DRC in the future, supporting internationalism.

17. One of the greatest hindrances to success of PEP DRC was the suspicion of another European partner at GESM (the central officer training facility for the Armed Forces) and that partner's attempts to undermine the project. Clearly stated, open goals may have been more successful at addressing this than post-hoc liaison. Interesting suggestions for addressing donor competition in fragile states are Carvalho (2006) and Leader and Colenso (2005).

18. Based on the British financial year running from April to March.

19. There was a call for 'scorecard' reporting of statements from stakeholders, but this falls well short either of effective monitoring and evaluation or of impact assessment.

20. The DfID-funded 'English in Action' project in Bangladesh (Seargeant and Erling 2011, Chapter 12 this volume) is a rare exception to this statement, but projects such as this are far less common than they were in the 1990s.

21. For Gramsci, language was not a fixed, static item. It was a living concept, constantly evolving and changing. Therefore, Gramsci saw grammar (or at least normative grammar) as a 'snapshot' (Helsloot 1989) of the current rules and norms which have been agreed as standard or enforceable by the speech community. Language and grammar retained traces of their evolution and are therefore similar to historical documents showing (and packaging) cultural influences through the language's development.

22. Gramsci also refers to this as 'immanent' grammar. While the implications of the association of immanence are of great interest and broaden the understanding of the term, it is beyond the scope of this chapter to provide a full discussion. (However, see Ives 2004:90-101.) The term 'spontaneous grammar' will be used exclusively in this chapter, as the associations with free will are more relevant to the themes discussed.

23. It could also be argued that, for this reason, Gramsci would be critical of the development of English as an international language (or as a local language, cf. Higgins 2009). It is for this reason that I have attempted to make reference to Gramsci's writing at all stages of the project design.

24. Due to sensitivities regarding the direct reporting of FARDC personnel activity and also to ensure participant anonymity, all class designations, teacher names and learner names have been changed.

25. STANAG 6001 is the six-level language proficiency scale used by NATO. A STANAG 6001 score of two is roughly equivalent to the Threshold Level of the Council of Europe's Common European Framework of Reference for Languages. Threshold Level is the level at which learners '[c]an understand the main points of clear standard input on familiar matters regularly encountered in work, school, leisure, etc. Can deal with most situations likely to arise whilst travelling in an area where the language is spoken. Can produce simple connected text on topics, which are familiar, or of personal interest. Can describe experiences and events, dreams, hopes and ambitions and briefly give reasons and explanations for opinions and plans' (Council of Europe 2010:5). For further information on STANAG 6001, see *www.dlielc.org/bilc*

26. While Lingala was not the mother tongue of all of the participants, all were fluent in it as a language of wider communication.

27. The song used was *Chaise Électrique* by Fally Ipupa and Olivia *(2009, Boss Playa Productions, DR Congo)*.

28. The graphic narrative MAUS by Art Spiegelman, first published in two volumes in 1986 and 1991, is a biography of Spiegelman's father's experience of the Holocaust described in flashback from the present day. It was awarded a Pulitzer Prize Special Award in 1992. In MAUS, Spiegelman uses animals to represent different people: Jews are represented as mice, Nazis are represented as cats, whil other nationalities and groups are represented as other animals. Characters from a single group or nationality are drawn with identical features, highlighting the insanity of identifying people by racial, ethnic religious or other characteristics. The section chosen for classroom activities depicts Spiegelman's father's early experience as a Polish soldier, where he faces combat for the first time, kills for the first time and is captured as a prisoner of war by the Nazis.

29. Rather than create individual aliases for individual learners – and because the texts are being considered as representative of the group as a whole rather than as distinct individuals – extracts are not attributed to individual learners but instead are marked for the week of research in which the text from which they are taken was created.

30. I use the terms Community and Supercommunity to avoid the embedded ideas of hierarchical strata in the local/national/international terms of identification. Here, I use Supercommunity not as an agglomeration of differing individual communities and I use Community not as an agglomeration of individuals. Rather, the terms Supercommunity (which could be represented as a community of Communities) and Community (a community of individuals) themselves represent distinct identities which are not opposed to each other, nor to the individual, but which exist concurrently in a complex interplay to create identity.

31. FDLR (Forces Démocratiques de Liberation du Rwanda): a guerrilla organisation of former genocidaires who fled Rwanda after the 1994 massacres and have since been operating from Congolese territory.

32. CNDP (Congrès National pour la Défense du Peuple): a renegade faction of the FARDC operating in Eastern DRC which refused to recognise the authority of Kinshasa (amalgamated into the FARDC following the arrest of Nkunda).

33. LRA (Lord's Resistance Army): a rebel Ugandan guerrilla group.

34. It is impossible to estimate accurately the spread of Christianity in DRC as many communities (particularly rural communities) blend animism with Christian dogma. However, recent estimates (Rorison 2008) are that over 90 per cent of the population is either Catholic, Protestant or other Christian (including followers of other native Congolese Christian beliefs such as Kimbanguism and the pseudo-anarchist Matsouanism).

35. I have been unable to interpret the words 'plan eco' in the learner's text, as they appear to be French or English, but I cannot determine their meaning.

36. This is just one example taken from the research. See Whitehead (2010a) for the full study with further examples and more detailed analysis.

37. For further discussion of the role of English in multilingual education in fragile states, see Whitehead (2010b).

38. Examples of materials developed for PEP DRC can be found in Whitehead (2010a). More detailed ideas for classroom activities stemming from these principles are in Whitehead (2010b).

References

Althusser, L. 1994. *Ideological state apparatuses.* In S.Zizek (ed.), *Mapping Ideology,* 100–140. *London: Verso.*

Appleby, R. 2002. *English and East Timor.* In J.Lo Bianco (ed.), *Voices from Phnom Penh: Development and Language: Global Influences and Local Effects,* 23–35. *Melbourne: Language Australia.*

Auerbach, E.R. 1995. *The politics of the ESL classroom: Issues of power in pedagogical choices.* In J.W.Tollefson (ed.), *Power and Inequality in Language Education,* 9-33. *Cambridge: Cambridge University Press.*

Batibo, H.M. 2006. *The imposition of English on the triglossic structure of language use in African countries.* In A.E.Arua, M.M.Bagwasi, T.Sebina and B.Seboni (eds.), *The Study and Use of English in Africa,* 133–141. *Newcastle: Cambridge Scholars Press.*

Belz, J.A. 2002. *Second language play as a representation of the multicomponent self in foreign language study. Journal of Language Identity and Education* 1(1), 13 – 39.

Bendle, M. 2002. *The crisis of identity in high-modernity. The British Journal of Sociology* 53(1), 1-18.

Benesch, S. 2006. *Critical media awareness: Teaching resistance to interpellation.* In J.Edge (ed.), *(Re)Locating TESOL in an Age of Empire,* 49-64. *New York: Palgrave.*

British Council. 2008. *Country Plan 2008-2010: PEP DRC.* Unpublished report.

Brutt-Griffler, J. 2002. *World English. Clevedon, UK: Multilingual Matters.*

Brutt-Griffler, J. and Samimy, K.K. 1999. *Revisiting the colonial in the post-colonial: critical praxis for non-native-English-speaking teachers in a TESOL program. TESOL Quarterly* 33(3), 413-431.

Carvalho, S. 2006. *Engaging with Fragile States: An IEG Review of World Bank Support to Low income Countries under Stress. Washington, DC: World Bank.*

Coleman, H. 2002. *Evaluating development programmes: Time to watch our language.* In J.Lo Bianco (ed.), *Voices from Phnom Penh: Development and Language: Global influences and Local Effects,* 103-116. *Melbourne: Language Australia.*

Coleman, H. 2010. *English and Development. London: British Council.* Available online at *www.teachingenglish.org.uk/transform/books/english-language-development*

Council of Europe. 2010. *Common European Framework of Reference for Languages: Learning, Teaching, Assessment.* Available online at *www.coe.int/T/DG4/Portfolio/documents/All per cent20scales per cent20CEFR.DOC*

CSRC (Crisis States Research Centre). 2006. *Crisis, Fragile and Failed States – Definitions Used by the CSRC. London: London School of Economics.* Available online at *www.crisisstates.com/download/drc/FailedState.pdf*

Delanty, G. 2003. *Community. London: Routledge.*

Dörnyei, Z. 2005. *The Psychology of the Language Learner: Individual Differences in Second Language Acquisition.* Mahwah, NJ: Lawrence Erlbaum.

Dörnyei, Z. 2009. *The L2 Motivational Self System.* In Z.Dörnyei and E.Ushioda (eds.), *Motivation, Language Identity and the L2 Self,* 9-42. *Bristol: Multilingual Matters.*

Edge, J. 2003. *Imperial troopers and servants of the Lord. TESOL Quarterly* 37, 701-709.

Edge, J. (ed.). 2006. *(Re)Locating TESOL in an Age of Empire. Basingstoke: Palgrave Macmillan.*

Elbow, P. 1998. *Writing with Power: Techniques for Mastering the Writing Process. New York and Oxford: Oxford University Press.*

Faigley, L. 1986. *Competing theories of process: A critique and a proposal. College English* 48, 527-542.

Freire, P. 1970. *Pedagogy of the Oppressed. New York: Seabury Press.*

Gramsci, A. 1971. *Selections from the Prison Notebooks* (Q.Hoare and G.Nowell Smith, eds and trans.) *New York: International Publishers.*

Gramsci, A. 1985. *Selections from Cultural Writings* (D.Forgacs and G.Nowell Smith, eds. W.Boelhower, trans.). *Cambridge, MA: Harvard University Press.*

Hailemariam, C., Ogbay, S. and White, G. 2011. *English and development in Eritrea.* Chapter 11, this volume.

Harding, L. 2008. *Russia arrests two men in British Council spying row. The Guardian,* 20 March 2008. Available online at *www.guardian.co.uk/world/2008/mar/20/russia.arrests*

Harwood, A.M. and Hahn, C.L. 1990. *Controversial Issues in the Classroom. Bloomington, IN: ERIC Clearinghouse for Social Studies/Social Science Education.*

Helsloot, N. 1989. *Linguists of all countries ...! On Gramsci's premise of coherence. Journal of Pragmatics* 13, 556-558. Available online at *www.nielshelsloot.nl/tekst/1989/50.htm*

Higgins, C. 2009. *English as a Local Language: Post-colonial Identities and Multilingual Practices. Bristol: Multilingual Matters.*

Hopkins, K.D., Stanley, J.S. and Hopkins, B.R. 1990. *Educational and Psychological Measurement and Evaluation.* (7th edition.) *Englewood Cliffs, NJ: Prentice Hall.*

Horvath, J. 1998. *Cutting edge of imperialism. Left Curve 22.* Available online at *www.leftcurve.org/lc22webpages/cutedge.html*

Hyland, K. 2002. *Teaching and Researching Writing. Harlow: Pearson.*

Ibhawaegbele, F.D. 2006. *Culture and language in Achebe's Things Fall Apart and Arrow of God.* In A.E.Arua et al. (eds), *The Study and Use of English in Africa,* 142-150. *Newcastle: Cambridge Scholars Press.*

International Alert. 2005. *Women's Bodies as a Battleground: Sexual Violence against Women and Girls during the War in the DRC. Kinshasa: Réseau des Femmes pour un Développement Associatif et Réseau des Femmes pour la Défense des Droits et la Paix.*

IRIN (Integrated Regional Information Networks). 2007. *The Shame of War: Sexual Violence against Women and Girls in Conflict. Nairobi: UN OCHA/IRIN.*

Ives, P. 2004. *Language and Hegemony in Gramsci. London: Pluto.*

Kachru, B.B. 1990. *World Englishes and applied linguistics. World Englishes* 9, 3-20.

Kennett, P. 2002. *Language, development and political correctness.* In J.Lo Bianco (ed.), *Voices from Phnom Penh: Development and Language: Global Influences and Local Effects,* 235-242. *Melbourne: Language Australia.*

Knagg, J. 2010. *Language and Politics. Presentation given to Sociolinguistics Symposium 18, University of Southampton,* September 2010.

Kramsch, C. 1998. *Culture. Oxford: OUP.*

Kramsch, C. 2000. *Social discursive constructions of self in L2 learning.* In J.P.Lantolf (ed.), *Sociocultural Theory and Second Language Learning,* 133-153. *Oxford: Oxford University Press.*

Kramsch, C. 2003. *Identity, role and voice in cross-cultural (mis)communication.* In J.House et al. (eds), *Misunderstanding in Social Life,* 129-153. *London: Longman.*

Kramsch, C. and Lam, W.S.E. 1999. *Textual identities: The importance of being non-native.* In G.Braine (ed.), *Non-Native Educators in English Language Teaching,* 57-71. *Mahwah, NJ: Erlbaum.*

Kristeva, J. 1986. *The Kristeva Reader.* (T.Moi, ed.) *Oxford: Blackwell.*

Kristof, N.D. 2008. *The weapon of rape. The New York Times,* 15 June 2008. Available online at *www.nytimes.com/2008/06/15/opinion/15kristof.html?_ r=2&oref=slogin&oref=slogin*

Leader, N. and Colenso, P. 2005. *Aid Instruments in Fragile States.* (DfID PRDE Working Paper 5.) *London: DfID.* Available online at *http://ageconsearch.umn.edu/ bitstream/12818/1/pr050005.pdf*

Malaba, M.Z. 2006. *Literature and humanistic values.* In A.E.Arua et al. (eds.), *The Study and Use of English in Africa,* 2-14. *Newcastle: Cambridge Scholars Press.*

Marx, K. 1867. *Capital: A Critique of Political Economy.* (E.Aveling and S.Moore, trans.) *New York: New Modern Library.*

Mazrui, A.M. 2004. *English in Africa After the Cold War. Clevedon: Multilingual Matters.*

Moyo, D. 2009. *Dead Aid. New York: Farrar, Straus and Giroux.*

Murray, D. 1985. *A Writer Teaches Writing. 2nd edition. Boston, MA: Houghton Mifflin.*

North, S. 1987. *The Making of Knowledge in Composition. London: Heinemann.*

Norton, B. 1997. *Language, identity and the ownership of English. TESOL Quarterly* 31(3), 409-429.

Pascoe-Watson, G. 2008. PM Brown's English Invasion. *The Sun,* 18 January 2008. Available online at *www.thesun.co.uk/sol/homepage/news/article701093.ece*

Pennycook, A. 1994. *The Cultural Politics of English as an International Language. London: Longman.*

Phillipson, R. 1992. *Linguistic Imperialism. Oxford: Oxford University Press.*

Phillipson, R. 2009. *Disciplines of English and disciplining by English. Asian EFL Journal* 11(4). Available online at *www.asian-efl-journal.com/ December_2009_rp.php*

Rorison, S. 2008. **Congo: Democratic Republic, Republic**. Guildford, CT: Globe Pequot Press.

Seargeant, P. and Erling, E.J. 2011. *The discourse of 'English as a language for international development': Policy assumptions and practical challenges.* Chapter 12, this volume.

Sharlet, J. 2010. *Junkets for Jesus. Mother Jones* December 2010, 58-79.

Sheldon, K. and Lyubomirsky, S. 2006. *How to increase and sustain positive emotion: The effects of expressing gratitude and visualizing best possible selves. Journal of Positive Psychology* 1(2), 73-82.

Skutnabb-Kangas, T. 2000. *Linguistic Genocide in Education – or Worldwide Diversity and Human Rights?* Mahwah, NJ: Lawrence Erlbaum and Associates.

Snow, M.A., Met, M. and Genesee, F. 1989. *A conceptual framework for the integration of language and content in second/foreign language instruction. TESOL Quarterly* 23(2), 201-217.

Spiegelman, A. 2003. *The Complete MAUS. London: Penguin.*

Spivak, G.C. 1992. Quoted in de Kock, L. 1992. *Interview with Gayatri Chakravorty Spivak: New Nation Writers Conference in South Africa. A Review of International English Literature* 23(3), 45-46.

Tembe, J. and Norton, B. 2011. *English education, local languages and community perspectives in Uganda.* Chapter 6, this volume.

Tomlinson, B. 1998. *Access-self materials.* In B.Tomlinson (ed.), *Materials Development in Language Teaching,* 320-336. *Cambridge: Cambridge University Press.*

Whitehead, D. 2009. *The elephant in the corner: Controversial content in the classroom.* Paper presented at IATEFL conference, April 2009, Cardiff, UK.

Whitehead, D. 2010a. *Gramsci, Language Identity and the L2 Motivational Self-System: Towards Critical Praxis and Counter-Hegemonic Discourses in Post-Colonial TEFL.* Unpublished Master's thesis, Sheffield Hallam University.

Whitehead, D. 2010b. *English bilingual education: Rationales, realities, risks and rewards.* Paper presented at the International Conference on Language, Education and the Millennium Development Goals, November 2010, Bangkok, Thailand.

Woods, P. 2006. *The hedgehog and the fox: Two approaches to teaching English for the military.* In J.Edge (ed.), *(Re)Locating TESOL in an Age of Empire,* 208-226. *Basingstoke: Palgrave Macmillan.*

Appendices

Countries with 'low' and 'medium' human development

The annual Human Development Report of the United Nations Development Programme (UNDP 2010) includes a Human Development Index (HDI). The HDI ranks 169 countries and categorises them as follows:

- Very high human development (42 countries)

- High human development (43 countries)

- Medium human development (42 countries)

- Low human development (42 countries)

A further 25 states and territories cannot be ranked because insufficient data are available.

The United Nations (UN) identifies 23 countries and states which it considers to be 'least developed'. 16 of these fall into UNDP's 'low human development' category and a further 7 are among the unranked states for which data are incomplete.

For the purposes of this book, 'developing countries' are taken to include all 84 states in the 'medium' and 'low' human development categories with the addition of the seven unranked states considered by the UN to be 'least developed'. This brings the total number of 'developing countries' to 91.

In the table that follows, the countries discussed in this book are highlighted.

It should be noted that the HDI is revised in November each year.

Source: UNDP. 2010. **The Real Wealth of Nations: Pathways to Human Development**. (Human Development Report 2010, 20th Anniversary Edition.) Basingstoke and New York: Palgrave Macmillan for UNDP. Available online at *http://hdr.undp.org/en/*.

List of developing countries

HDI rank	Medium human development	HDI rank	Low human development	HDI rank	Unranked
86	Fiji	128	**Kenya**	-	Bhutan*
87	Turkmenistan	129	**Bangladesh**	-	**Eritrea***
88	Dominican Republic	130	Ghana	-	Kiribati*
89	**China**	131	**Cameroon**	-	Samoa*
90	El Salvador	132	Myanmar	-	Somalia*
91	**Sri Lanka**	133	Yemen	-	Tuvalu*
92	Thailand	134	Benin	-	Vanuatu*
93	Gabon	135	Madagascar		
94	Suriname	136	Mauritania		
95	Bolivia	137	Papua New Guinea		
96	Paraguay	138	Nepal		
97	Philippines	139	Togo		
98	Botswana	140	Comorros		
99	Moldova	141	Lesotho		
100	Mongolia	142	Nigeria		
101	Egypt	143	**Uganda**		
102	Uzbekistan	144	Senegal		
103	Micronesia	145	Haiti*		
104	Guyana	146	Angola		
105	Namibia	147	Djibouti		
106	Honduras	148	Tanzania		
107	Maldives	149	Cote d'Ivoire		
108	**Indonesia**	150	**Zambia**		
109	Kyrgyzstan	151	Gambia		
110	South Africa	152	**Rwanda**		
111	Syria	153	**Malawi***		
112	Tajikistan	154	Sudan		
113	Vietnam	155	Afghanistan*		
114	Morocco	156	Guinea*		
115	Nicaragua	157	**Ethiopia***		
116	Guatemala	158	Sierra Leone*		
117	Equatorial Guinea	159	Central African Republic*		
118	Cape Verde	160	Mali*		
119	**India**	161	Burkina Faso*		
120	Timor Leste	162	Liberia*		
121	Swaziland	163	Chad*		
122	Laos	164	Guinea Bissau*		
123	Solomon Islands	165	Mozambique*		
124	Cambodia	166	Burundi*		
125	**Pakistan**	167	Niger*		
126	Congo	168	**Congo, DR***		
127	Sao Tome and Principe	169	Zimbabwe		

The 15 **highlighted** countries in this list are those which are discussed in this book
*23 countries categorised by the UN as 'least developed'

Key development indicators for countries discussed

UNDP's Human Development Index is

a composite index measuring average achievement in three basic dimensions of human development – a long and healthy life, knowledge and a decent standard of living. **(UNDP 2010:224)**

The HDI draws on 169 different indicators which are grouped into 17 categories:

1. HDI and its components
2. HDI trends, 1980–2010
3. Inequality-adjusted HDI
4. Gender inequality index
5. Multidimensional poverty index
6. Empowerment
7. Sustainability and vulnerability
8. Human security
9. Perceptions of individual wellbeing and happiness
10. Civic and community wellbeing
11. Demographic trends
12. Decent work
13. Education
14. Health
15. Enabling environment: financial flows and commitments
16. Enabling environment: economy and infrastructure
17. Access to information and communication technology

The table which follows extracts just 15 key development indicators from the 169 which make up the HDI. Data is provided for each of the 15 principal countries discussed by the contributors to this volume. For comparative purposes, aggregate or average data are also given for the 42 countries with 'very high' human development and the 23 'least developed' countries, where these are available. Aggregate or average results for the whole world are also provided wherever possible.

Source: UNDP. 2010. **The Real Wealth of Nations: Pathways to Human Development**. (Human Development Report 2010, 20th Anniversary Edition.) Basingstoke and New York: Palgrave Macmillan for UNDP. Available online at *http://hdr.undp.org/en/*.

Key development indicators for 15 countries (UNDP 2010)

Indicator	Bangladesh	Cameroon	China	Congo, DR*	Eritrea*	Ethiopia*	India	Indonesia	Kenya	Malawi*	Pakistan	Rwanda	Sri Lanka	Uganda	Zambia	Very high human development (42 countries)	Least developed (23 countries)	World
HDI rank/169	129	131	89	168	n.a.	157	119	108	128	153	125	152	91	143	150	-	-	-
Population (millions)	164.4	20.0	1,354.1	67.8	5.2	85.0	1,214.5	232.5	40.9	15.7	184.8	10.3	20.4	33.8	13.3	1,056.0	854.7	6,908.7
Gross national income per capita per annum (USD)	1,587	2,197	7,258	291	643	992	3,337	3,957	1,628	911	2,678	1,190	4,886	1,224	1,359	37,225	1,393	10,631
Population living on < USD1.25 per day (%)	49.6	32.8	15.9	59.2	n.a.	39.0	41.6	29.4	19.7	73.9	22.6	76.6	14.0	51.5	64.3	-	-	-
Gender inequality rank/137	116	129	38	137	n.a.	n.a.	122	100	117	126	112	83	72	109	124	-	-	-
Maternal mortality rate**	570	1,000	45	1,100	450	720	450	420	560	1,100	320	1,300	58	550	830	8	786	273
Infant mortality rate***	43	82	18	126	41	69	52	31	81	65	72	72	13	85	92	5	82	44
Life expectancy at birth (years)	66.9	51.7	73.5	48.0	60.4	56.1	64.4	71.5	55.6	54.6	67.2	51.1	74.4	54.1	47.3	80.3	57.7	69.3
Doctors per 10,000 people	3	2	14	1	1	<0.5	6	1	1	<0.5	8	<0.5	6	1	1	-	-	-
Mean duration of schooling (years)	4.8	5.9	7.5	3.8	n.a.	1.5	4.4	5.7	7.0	4.3	4.9	3.3	8.2	4.7	6.5	11.3	3.7	7.4
Pupils per teacher (primary school)	43.7	n.a.	18.3	39.0	47.4	59.3	40.7	21.4	46.5	n.a.	40.7	70.2	22.5	49.9	63.4	-	-	-
Public expenditure on education (% GDP)	2.4	2.9	1.9	n.a.	2.0	5.5	3.2	3.5	7.0	4.2	2.9	4.1	n.a.	3.8	1.4	-	-	-
Public expenditure on health (% GDP)	1.1	1.3	1.9	1.2	1.5	2.2	1.1	1.2	2.0	5.9	0.8	4.9	2.0	1.6	3.6	-	-	-
Public expenditure on military (% GDP)	1.0	1.5	2.0	1.4	n.a.	1.4	2.6	1.0	1.9	n.a.	2.6	1.5	3.6	2.3	2.0	-	-	-
Population without electricity (%)	59.3	70.2	0.6	88.7	69.0	85.1	34.2	35.7	84.6	87.6	39.8	n.a.	23.4	91.9	78.4	-	-	-

* Countries categorised by UN as 'least developed'   ** Maternal deaths per 100,000 live births   *** Infant deaths per 1,000 live births

The Millennium Development Goals

These are the eight Millennium Development Goals and their 21 associated Targets, which were agreed by the General Assembly of the United Nations in 2000.

Goal 1: Eradicate extreme poverty and hunger

Target 1.A: Halve, between 1990 and 2015, the proportion of people whose income is less than USD1 (GBP0.65) a day

Target 1.B: Achieve full and productive employment and decent work for all, including women and young people

Target 1.C: Halve, between 1990 and 2015, the proportion of people who suffer from hunger

Goal 2: Achieve universal primary education

Target 2.A: Ensure that, by 2015, children everywhere, boys and girls alike, will be able to complete a full course of primary schooling

Goal 3: Promote gender equality and empower women

Target 3.A: Eliminate gender disparity in primary and secondary education, preferably by 2005, and in all levels of education no later than 2015

Goal 4: Reduce child mortality

Target 4.A: Reduce by two-thirds, between 1990 and 2015, the under-five mortality rate

Goal 5: Improve maternal health

Target 5.A: Reduce by three-quarters the maternal mortality ratio

Target 5.B: Achieve universal access to reproductive health

Goal 6: Combat HIV/AIDS, malaria and other diseases

Target 6.A: Have halted by 2015 and begun to reverse the spread of HIV/AIDS

Target 6.B: Achieve, by 2010, universal access to treatment for HIV/AIDS for all those who need it

Target 6.C: Have halted by 2015 and begun to reverse the incidence of malaria and other major diseases

Goal 7: Ensure environmental sustainability

Target 7.A: Integrate the principles of sustainable development into country policies and programmes and reverse the loss of environmental resources

Target 7.B: Reduce biodiversity loss, achieving, by 2010, a significant reduction in the rate of loss

Target 7.C: Halve, by 2015, the proportion of the population without sustainable access to safe drinking water and basic sanitation

Target 7.D: By 2020, to have achieved a significant improvement in the lives of at least 100 million slum dwellers

Goal 8: Develop a global partnership for development

Target 8.A: Develop further an open, rule-based, predictable, non-discriminatory trading and financial system

Target 8.B: Address the special needs of least developed countries

Target 8.C: Address the special needs of landlocked developing countries and small island developing states

Target 8.D: Deal comprehensively with the debt problems of developing countries

Target 8.E: In co-operation with pharmaceutical companies, provide access to affordable essential drugs in developing countries

Target 8.F: In co-operation with the private sector, make available benefits of new technologies, especially information and communications

Source: United Nations. 2010. **We Can End Poverty 2015: Millennium Development Goals**. New York: United Nations. Available online at *www.un.org/millenniumgoals/bkgd.shtml*

Abbreviations

ACRP 3	Australian Communities Rehabilitation Project 3
AD	Anno Domini, year of the Christian Era
ADEA	Association for the Development of Education in Africa
AIDS	Acquired immune deficiency syndrome
AILA	Association Internationale de Linguistique Appliquée, International Association of Applied Linguistics
AJK	Azad Jammu and Kashmir
ASEAN	Association of Southeast Asian Nations
AU	African Union
AusAID	Australian Government Overseas Aid Program
BA	Bachelor of Arts
BBC	British Broadcasting Corporation
BMZ	Bundesministerium für wirtschaftliche Zusammenarbeit und Entwicklung, Federal Ministry for Economic Cooperation and Development (Germany)
BOS	Bantuan Operasional Sekolah, school operational support grant (Indonesia)
BPS	Badan Pusat Statistik, Central Statistics Board (Indonesia)
BSc	Bachelor of Science
BRPS	Bugagga Rural Primary School (Uganda)
CABE	Central Advisory Board on Education (India)
CAD	Canadian dollar
CCP	child centred pedagogy
CDP	CREAM [see below] Discussion Paper
CELTA	Certificate in English Language Teaching to Adults
CERDOTOLA	Centre régional de recherche et de documentation sur les traditions orales et pour le développement des langues africaines, Regional Centre for Research and Documentation of Oral Traditions and for Development of African Languages (Cameroon)
CfBT	Centre for British Teachers
CIA	Central Intelligence Agency (USA)
CIES	Comparative and International Education Society
CILT	Centre for Information on Language Teaching (now National Centre for Languages) (UK)
CJGTC	Commission on Japan's Goals in the Twenty-First Century
CLIL	content and language integrated learning
CLT	communicative language teaching
CNDP	Congrès National pour la Défense du Peuple, National Congress for the Defence of the People (DRC)
CNN	Cable News Network
COMESA	Common Market for Eastern and Southern Africa
CPDS	Centre for Political and Diplomatic Studies
CPI	Consumer Price Index
CREAM	Centre for Research and Analysis of Migration (UK)
CSO	Central Statistical Office (Zambia)
CSRC	Crisis States Research Centre
DBIS	Department for Business, Innovation and Skills (UK)
Depdiknas	Departemen Pendidikan Nasional, Department of National Education (later Kemdiknas) (Indonesia)
DfID	Department for International Development (UK)
DIUS	Department for Innovation, Universities and Skills (UK)
DR	Democratic Republic
DRC	Democratic Republic of Congo
EADI	European Association of Development Research and Training Institutes
EAP	English for academic purposes
ECOWAS	Economic Community of West African States
EE	English language environment
EEA	European Economic Area
EFL	English as a foreign language
EIA	English in Action (Bangladesh)
ELF	English as a lingua franca
ELfID	English language for international development

ELT	English language teaching
ELTIP	English Language Teaching Improvement Project (Bangladesh)
ELTR	English Language Teaching Reforms (Pakistan)
ENL	English as a native language
ERIC	Education Resources Information Center
ESL	English as a second language
ESOL	English for speakers of other languages
ESP	English for specific purposes
ETB	Ethiopian birr
ETC	English Teachers' Club (India)
EU	European Union
FARDC	Forces Armées de la République Démocratique du Congo, Armed Forces of the Democratic Republic of Congo
FCO	Foreign and Commonwealth Office (UK)
FDLR	Forces Démocratiques de Liberation du Rwanda, Democratic Forces for the Liberation of Rwanda
FDRE	Federal Democratic Republic of Eritrea
FGD	focus group discussion
FM	frequency modulation (broadcasting)
FSB	Federal'naya sluzhba bezopasnosti Rossiyskoy Federatsii, Federal Security Service of the Russian Federation (previously KGB)
GBP	Great Britain pounds (£)
GDP	gross domestic product
GE	great extent
GESM	Groupement des écoles supérieures militaires, Central facility for military officer training (DRC)
GIZ	Deutsche Gesellschaft für Internationale Zusammenarbeit, German International Co-operation (formerly GTZ)
GOI	Government of India
GTZ	Deutsche Gesellschaft für Technische Zusammenarbeit, German Technical Co-operation (now GIZ)
GWP	Government White Paper (Uganda)
H	Hijrah, year of the Islamic era
H1, H2, H3	high status languages

HDI	Human Development Index
HIV	human immunodeficiency virus
IATEFL	International Association of Teachers of English as a Foreign Language
ICG	International Crisis Group
ICT	information and communication technology
IDR	Indonesian rupiah (Rp)
IEG	Independent Evaluation Group (World Bank)
IELTS	International English Language Testing System
IFAD	International Fund for Agricultural Development
IGAD	Intergovernmental Authority on Development
IGPBIL	Inspectorate General of Pedagogy for Bilingualism (Cameroon)
IHK	Indeks Harga Konsumen, Consumer Price Index (Indonesia)
ILEA	Inner London Education Authority
ILO	International Labour Organisation
IMF	International Monetary Fund
IMLA	Institut Militaire des Langues Appliquées, Military Institute of Applied Languages (DRC)
IOM	International Organisation for Migration
IPPR	Institute for Public Policy Research (UK)
IRIN	Integrated Regional Information Networks
ISCED	International Standard Classification of Education
ISS	International Standard School (Indonesia)
IT	information technology
Kemdiknas	Kementerian Pendidikan Nasional, Ministry of National Education (previously Depdiknas) (Indonesia)
KGB	Komitet Gosudarstvennoy Bezopasnosti, Committee for State Security (later FSB) (Soviet Union)
KIE	Kenya Institute of Education
L1, L2	first language, second language
L1, L2, L3	low status languages
LandD	language and development
LCD	liquid crystal display (projector)
LE	little extent

LIA	Lembaga Indonesia-Amerika, Indonesian-American Institute	OECD	Organisation for Economic Co-operation and Development
LP	language planning or language policy	P1, P2	Primary School Year 1, Year 2
		PELP	Primary English Language Project (Sri Lanks)
LLA	Lunyole Language Association (Uganda)	PEP	Peacekeeping English Project
LRA	Lord's Resistance Army	PERURI	Perusahaan Umum Percetakan Uang Republik Indonesia, National Mint (Indonesia)
LWC	language of wider communication	
MA	Master of Arts	PETT	Primary English Trainer Training Programme (China)
MDGs	Millennium Development Goals	
MEd	Master of Education	PHC	Population and Housing Census (Uganda)
MI5	Military Intelligence, Section 5 (UK)	
		PhD	Doctor of Philosophy
MIL	Modern Indian language	PISA	Programme for International Student Assessment
MoD	Ministry of Defence (UK)	
MOE	Ministry of Education (India, Pakistan)	PKR	Pakistan rupees (Rs)
		PM	Prime Minister
MONUC	United Nations Organisation Mission in the Democratic Republic of the Congo (later MONUSCO)	POA	Programme of Action (India)
		PRDE	Poverty Reduction in Difficult Environments Team (DfID)
		Pre-STEP	Pre-Service Teacher Education Programme (Pakistan)
MONUSCO	United Nations Organisation Stabilisation Mission in the Democratic Republic of Congo (previously MONUC)	
		PTA	Parent Teacher Association (Uganda)
		RELC	Regional English Language Centre (Singapore)
MTV	Music Television	
n.a.	not available	RENSTRA	Rencana Strategis, Strategic Plan (= 5 Year Development Plan) (Indonesia)
NATO	North Atlantic Treaty Organisation	
NCDC	National Curriculum Development Centre (Uganda)	RI	Republik Indonesia, Republic of Indonesia
NCERT	National Centre for Educational Research and Training (India)	RLS	reversing language shift
		RPF	Rwandan Patriotic Front
NCTB	National Curriculum and Textbook Board (Bangladesh)	RSBI	Rintisan Sekolah Bertaraf Internasional. Fledgling International Standard School (Indonesia)
n.d.	no date [of publication]	
NEPAD	New Partnership for Africa's Development	
		SACMEQ	Southern Africa Consortium for Monitoring of Educational Quality
NFER	National Foundation for Educational Research	
NGO	non-governmental organisation	SADC	Southern African Development Community
NIACE	National Institute of Adult Continuing Education (UK)	
		SBI	Sekolah Bertaraf Internasional, International Standard School (Indonesia)
NKC	National Knowledge Commission (India)	
NORRAG	Network for Policy Research, Review and Advice on Education and Training	SD	Sekolah Dasar, Primary School (Indonesia)
		SDS	Sekolah Dasar Swasta, Private Primary School (Indonesia)
NPE	National Policy on Education (India)	
		SEAMEO	South East Asia Ministers of Education Organisation
NTB	Nusa Tenggara Barat, West Nusa Tenggara (Indonesia)	
		SIDA	Swedish International Development Co-operation Agency
OCHA	United Nations Office for the Coordination of Humanitarian Affairs	
		SIL	Summer Institute of Linguistics

Sisdiknas	Sistem pendidikan nasional, National education system (Indonesia)
SMA	Sekolah Menengah Atas, Senior Secondary School (Indonesia)
SMC	School Management Committee (Uganda)
SMK	Sekolah Menengah Kejuruan, Vocational Secondary School (Indonesia)
SMP	Sekolah Menengah Pertama, Junior Secondary School (Indonesia)
SPELT	Society of Pakistan English Language Teachers
STANAG	Standardisation Agreement
STEPS	Skills through English for Public Servants (Sri Lanka)
TBLT	task-based language teaching
TESOL	teaching English to speakers of other languages
TEYL	teaching English to young learners
TKI	Tenaga Kerja Indonesia, Indonesian migrant worker
TOEFL	Test of English as a Foreign Language
TOEIC	Test of English for International Communication
TP	teachers' English language proficiency
Triw	Triwulan, quarter (3 months) (Indonesia)
TUPS	Tiriri Urban Primary School (Uganda)
TV	Television
UAE	United Arab Emirates
UBOS	Uganda Bureau of Statistics
UIS	UNESCO Institute for Statistics
UK	United Kingdom of Great Britain and Northern Ireland
UKBA	United Kingdom Border Agency
UN	United Nations
UNDP	United Nations Development Programme
UNESCO	United Nations Educational, Scientific and Cultural Organisation
UNHCR	United Nations High Commissioner for Refugees
UNICEF	United Nations Children's Fund
UNMEE	United Nations Mission to Ethiopia and Eritrea
UNRISD	United Nations Research Institute for Social Development
US/USA	United States of America

USAID	United States Agency for International Development
USD	United States dollar ($)
UT	Union Territory (India)
UU	Undang-Undang, Law (Indonesia)
VGE	very great extent
VLE	very little extent
VSO	Voluntary Service Overseas
WE	World Englishes
WST	World Service Trust
WTO	World Trade Organisation

Note on currency exchange rates

All sums of money are expressed in both British pounds (GBP, £) and United States dollars (USD, $). Where appropriate, local currency equivalents are also given.

Except where otherwise indicated, the exchange rates used are those which applied on 29 December 2010, as follows:

GBP1.00 = *USD1.54*
CAD1.55   *(Canadian dollars)*
ETB25.36   *(Ethiopian birr)*
IDR14,084 *(Indonesian rupiah)*
PKR130.82 *(Pakistani rupees)*

USD1.00 = *GBP0.65*
CAD1.003
ETB16.43
IDR8,921
PKR84.77

Contributors

Tony Capstick is currently English Language Adviser at British Council Pakistan where he leads the language in education and teacher development work across the country. After teaching English in Greece and Italy, Tony worked on teacher education projects in Cambodia and as a teacher developer in Indonesia and North Korea. Before moving to Pakistan, Tony taught at Lancaster and Manchester universities. His PhD investigates the multilingual literacy practices of migrant families in Pakistan and the UK.

Hywel Coleman is Honorary Senior Research Fellow in the School of Education, University of Leeds, UK. He is a Trustee of the Language and Development (LandD) Conferences and has edited the proceedings of the 6th and 7th LandD Conferences (Tashkent 2003, Addis Ababa 2005 respectively). Recent consultancies have been concerned with language in education policy (Pakistan) and education management for madrasahs (Indonesia). See *www.langdevconferences.org* and *www.hywelcoleman.com*.

Elizabeth J. Erling is a lecturer in English Language Teaching at the Open University, UK, and works on the project 'English in Action', an English language learning and teacher education project in Bangladesh which is funded by DfID. She is co-editing with Philip Seargeant a forthcoming collection on English and international development and has published papers in journals such as *World Englishes, Language Policy* and *Innovations in Language Learning and Teaching*.

Gladys Ngwi Focho is a regional pedagogic inspector for the promotion of bilingualism in the West Region of Cameroon. She has been a teacher of English as a Foreign Language (EFL) to Francophone secondary and high school students for over 20 years. She holds a doctorate in Educational Administration and Planning from the University of Nigeria, Nsukka. Her research interests include teacher development, global issues, EFL, bilingualism and English and development.

Chefena Hailemariam obtained his PhD from Tilburg University in the Netherlands. Currently, he is a visiting researcher at Liverpool Hope University and an associate tutor at Edge Hill University in Ormskirk, both in the UK. He is a sociolinguist by training and he has taught courses in applied linguistics (mainly academic English and language and education). His research interests include language and nation-building, sociolinguistics of globalisation, discourse in educational and social locations, social identity and teacher education.

Chris Kennedy has worked as teacher, trainer, adviser, manager and academic in Africa, Europe, the Middle East, Southeast Asia and South America. His research publications focus on language policy, innovation, English as a global language and project evaluation. He is a past-President of IATEFL and was Chair of the British Council English Teaching Advisory Committee for many years. He is Professor and Director of the Centre for English Language Studies at the University of Birmingham, UK.

Psyche Kennett is Team Leader of the Performance Improvement Project implemented by German International Cooperation (GIZ) on behalf of the German Federal Ministry for Economic Cooperation and Development (BMZ) and the Australian Government (AusAID) in the North and East of Sri Lanka. She specialises in English, education, good governance and change management at national and sub-national levels in developing countries in South and Southeast Asia. She is a Trustee of the Language and Development Conferences.

Martin Lamb served for two years as a VSO English teacher at Hasanuddin University in Ujung Pandang (now Makassar), Indonesia, overlapping briefly with the editor of this volume. He spent many subsequent years as a teacher and teacher trainer on British Council contracts in Indonesia, with an intervening five-year spell in Bulgaria. He is now Senior Lecturer in TESOL at the University of Leeds, UK, teaching BA and MA courses and researching aspects of language learning motivation.

Ramanujam Meganathan is Associate Professor in Language Education in the Department of Languages, National Council of Educational Research and Training (NCERT), India. He has worked as a schoolteacher, a curriculum designer and a textbook developer. He has authored articles and research papers on English language teaching, classroom teaching, language policy and school management. He has also published *Sounds of Silence*, a poetry collection. He was a Hornby Scholar during 2009–2010 (Hornby Trust, UK).

Nigussie Negash is Associate Professor of ELT/Education at the Ethiopian Civil Service College, Ethiopia. He is a consultant and teacher trainer for the British Council Hornby School in Africa, has published articles in journals and books, and co-authored British Council published books for teachers and teacher trainers in difficult circumstances. He is a member of an international research committee on teaching English in difficult circumstances. He has presented papers at the IATEFL and Language and Development Conferences.

Bonny Norton is Professor and Distinguished University Scholar in the Department of Language and Literacy Education at the University of British Columbia, Canada. Her research addresses identity, language learning, and international development. Further details can be found on her website at *http://lerc.educ.ubc.ca/fac/norton/*.

Sarah Ogbay completed her doctorial degree in Applied Linguistics at Lancaster University, UK. After graduating in Teaching English as a Foreign Language from Addis Ababa University, Ethiopia, she began to teach at the University of Asmara, Eritrea. She has been teaching there for 26 years so far. Her main research interests include language, gender and linguistic social identity construction.

Philip Seargeant is Lecturer in Applied Linguistics in the Centre for Language and Communication at the Open University, UK. He is author of *The Idea of English in Japan: Ideology and the Evolution of a Global Language* (2009), and co-editor with Elizabeth J. Erling of *English and International Development* (forthcoming). He has also published in journals such as *Language Policy, World Englishes, Language Sciences* and *Language and Communication*.

Fauzia Shamim is a Professor of Applied Linguistics and presently Chairperson in the Department of English, University of Karachi, Pakistan. She holds a PhD in TESOL from the University of Leeds, UK. She is a founder member of the Society of Pakistan English Language Teachers (SPELT) and founding co-ordinator of its Research Special Interest Group. Her current research interests include the development of non-native speaker teachers of English and teaching-learning English in large classes.

Juliet Tembe completed her doctoral programme in TESOL in the Department of Language and Literacy Education at the University of British Columbia. Since graduating from Makerere University she has taught English at secondary and university levels in Uganda. Currently she is a senior lecturer in the Department of Languages, Literature and Linguistics at Islamic University in Uganda. Her research interests include second language teaching, language policy and planning, bi-/multi-lingual literacy and international development.

Martin Wedell is Head of International Education at the School of Education, University of Leeds. From 1977 to 1998 he worked on state and private English language teaching programmes and on 'aid' projects in Kenya, Saudi Arabia, China and Hungary. He continues to travel widely. His interest lies in the leadership/management of English provision in the state education systems within which most English teaching worldwide occurs and he questions whether English for Everyone really supports individual or national development.

Goodith White is a Senior Lecturer in Language Studies at Canterbury Christ Church University, UK. Her research interests include the relationship between language and identity, the global role of English and attitudes to lesser known languages. She was introduced to Eritrea by her late colleague Dr John Holmes and has visited the country a number of times over the last nine years.

Danny Whitehead is the British Council's Head of English Language Development in Indonesia. He has worked for 12 years in English language teaching in fragile states, primarily in Cambodia and Democratic Republic of Congo.

Eddie Williams is Professor in the School of Linguistics and English Language at Bangor University, Wales. His areas of research and publication include development in Africa, the linguistic practices of minorities, and the teaching of English. His first degree is from the University of Oxford and he did postgraduate work at Edinburgh and Reading. He has worked at the University of Reading, the University of Malta and the Government Foreign Language Institute in Cyprus.